D1192594

The Irish and British Wars, 1637–1654

The Irish and British Wars, 1637–1654 is an accessible and well-documented study of the wars of Britain and Ireland in the mid-seventeenth century. After a period of stability and peace during the early years of the century, Charles I set about carrying out administrative and religious reform in England, Scotland and Wales. The revolution that this prompted in Scotland was to repeat itself in Ireland, and four years later lead to civil war in England.

Connecting the strategic and tactical levels of war with political actions and reactions, Wheeler discusses how Britain and Ireland became battlegrounds in the 'war of three kingdoms'. With numerous maps and illustrations, the various stages of this period of turmoil are clearly demonstrated, right through to the execution of Charles I, the conquest of Catholic Ireland, and the eventual death of the English Republic.

James Scott Wheeler is Professor of European History at the United States Military Academy, West Point. His other publications include *Cromwell in Ireland* (1999) and *The Making of a World Power* (1999).

WARFARE AND HISTORY

General Editor: Jeremy Black

Professor of History, University of Exeter

DA
941.5
W48
2002
UAN

The Irish and British Wars, 1637–1654

Triumph, Tragedy, and Failure

James Scott Wheeler

London and New York

First published in 2002
by Routledge
11 New Fetter Lane, London EC4P 4EE

Simultaneously published in the USA and Canada
by Routledge
29 West 35th Street, New York, NY 10001

Routledge is an imprint of the Taylor & Francis Group

© 2002 James Scott Wheeler

Typeset in Bembo by
HWA Text and Data Management, Tunbridge Wells
Printed and bound in Great Britain by
TJ International Ltd, Padstow, Cornwall

All rights reserved. No part of this book may be reprinted or reproduced or utilised in any
form or by any electronic, mechanical, or other means, now known or hereafter invented,
including photocopying and recording, or in any information storage or retrieval system,
without permission in writing from the publishers.

British Library Cataloguing in Publication Data
A catalogue record for this book is available from the British Library

Library of Congress Cataloging in Publication Data
A catalog record for this book has been requested

ISBN 0-415-22131-5 (hbk)
ISBN 0-415-22132-3 (pbk)

Contents

Maps

Plates

(between pages 144 and 145)

Preface and acknowledgments

Warfare and the need of participants to support their war machines drove the political and institutional changes that took place in Britain and Ireland in the period 1637–54. That is, military considerations drove political developments after 1638, not vice versa. Religious and political controversies between Charles I and his Scottish subjects precipitated an armed insurrection in Scotland. The ways in which the King and his subjects reacted to Scottish resistance led to wars and revolutions in all three Stuart kingdoms. Once hostilities commenced, military considerations and needs confined political options to a narrow range. The need to sustain armies and navies forced the English to create new military and political institutions and practices that fundamentally changed the nature of the British and Irish states.

This narrative history of the tumultuous events in Britain and Ireland from 1637 to 1654 shows how and why the controversies between Charles I and the Scots led to the Scottish and Irish revolutions, the English civil wars, and the English conquests of Ireland and Scotland. This narrative demonstrates that, given the intransigence of the king, his opponents had little choice between abject surrender or total commitment to his defeat and execution. In the process of defeating Charles I, the English parliamentarians harnessed the economic resources of England to military forces that proved invincible on land and sea by 1653.

England triumphed in the wars fought in Britain, Ireland and the surrounding waters in the mid-seventeenth century. Albion's victories, and England's efforts to sustain her military forces, laid the foundation for her future greatness as a world power. In the process, the English transformed their constitution and state institutions to meet the demands of continuous warfare. Following the triumph of the parliamentarians in 1648, the English used their military power to conquer and incorporate Ireland and Scotland into the English state. This was a tragedy for Scotland and especially so for Ireland, where the seeds of future troubles were sown. As civil wars and foreign conquests consumed men and resources, they prevented the reforming impulses that were evident in the parliamentarian cause from transforming English political culture into one characterized by democracy and religious tolerance. The English republicans' failure to carry out the program outlined in the *Agreement of the People*, in 1649, was a direct result of the Commonwealth's need to focus its efforts and energy on its wars in Ireland and Scotland. Cromwell struck the final blow against English republicanism with his usurpation of power in 1653–54.

I owe thanks to so many people for help in this project. First and foremost, my wife Jane has been tremendously supportive of my work, to include many days as a research assistant in English and Irish archives. Victoria Peters, senior commissioning editor of Routledge, provided me with wonderful encouragement and guidance. Professors Jeremy Black and Mark Fissel gave me sound editorial advice, helping to clarify my thinking and writing. Frank Martini, cartographer of the History Department of the US Military Academy, developed the maps that are so essential for a military history. And my dear friend Edith Loe graciously proofread the entire book and asked the questions of the non-professional historian that hopefully make this narrative understandable to all readers. In spite of all of this help, all mistakes are my own, although I hope few.

Map 1 The British Isles, 1638–60

Introduction

During the first third of the seventeenth century, as most of Western Europe suffered the ravages of war, England, Scotland, and Ireland experienced one of the most peaceful and prosperous periods in their histories. The Stuarts had successfully ruled these three kingdoms and Wales since 1603. For the first time in history, Britain had no internal hostile borders, and the coasts of the Irish Sea were controlled by a common power. This peace and tranquility was disturbed in the 1620s as England fought briefly in the Thirty Years War and engaged in largely maritime wars against Spain and France. While these military endeavors failed, Ireland and Britain were spared the direct impact of war because of their insularity. Charles I restored peace to his domains by 1630 and then attempted to carry out programs of administrative and religious reform that came to be called 'thorough'.

Many of the ecclesiastical and administrative innovations that Charles made in his domains, and the manner in which he and his servants carried out those changes, brought on an Anglo-Scottish war known as the First Bishops' War. Once the king and the Scots engaged militarily, political considerations took a back seat to the armed violence and military policies that became the primary instigators and agents of change.

Caroline political and religious reforms did not directly cause the revolutions or wars that broke out in Britain and Ireland. Rather, they set the stage in which Charles's maladroit leadership and poor decisions incited violence. The violent confrontations that commenced in 1637–8 in fact caught most contemporaries off guard.

Charles I achieved significant results in his reforms, strengthening royal authority while buttressing crown finances in his three kingdoms. Samuel R. Gardiner, the masterful late Victorian historian, correctly assessed the results of the king's reforms.

> To all outward appearance Charles's authority had never been stronger than in the summer of 1636. Ship-money was paid with reluctance, but reluctance had not yet ripened into defiance. The judges, the sheriffs, and the justices of the peace were ready instruments of the King. The bishops, with a large and increasing number of the clergy, were his enthusiastic supporters. Everything was on his side, except the people of England.[1]

By 1638, in spite of his enviable position of strength two years earlier, Charles I faced a revolution in Scotland that was soon to be emulated in Ireland and to lead to a civil war in England four years later. Charles had himself to blame for such a disastrous disintegration of the situations in his three kingdoms from 1637 to 1642. His decision to resort to armed force to make his Scottish subjects submit to his religious and political reforms in 1638–9 solidified Scottish resistance around their church and representative institutions. Once Charles unleashed the dogs of war there was nothing he could do short of a military victory to restore his rule in Scotland. Conversely, once the Scottish Covenanters resorted to arms and aroused nationalist and religious sentiment against the seemingly popish and unconstitutional claims of the king they had little choice but to pursue military victory or face the scaffold. Thus, the manner in which Charles attempted to impose his authority on the Scots precipitated the first of three revolutions in his domains.

Events in Scotland directly affected the political and military developments in Ireland and England, ultimately destroying the Stuart monarchy. Once war was joined in Scotland, resorting to a military solution for the difficult problems facing Charles's other two kingdoms became an attractive option to all sides. By 1642, Britain and Ireland were battlegrounds in the 'war of the three kingdoms'. This train of events was not inevitable, nor could someone in 1637 have predicted such outcomes. In fact, Charles I's three kingdoms were well governed and remarkably calm in the mid 1630s, and the king's ability to rule and defend his kingdoms without resort to English parliaments seemed assured. From 1631 to 1638 the crown's income ran ahead of expenditures for the first time in over half a century.[2] As long as Charles's realms remained at peace, his 'personal rule' was secure.

How and why did the king's political circumstances deteriorate so rapidly and how did wars in Scotland and Ireland drive political developments in England? The short answer to these questions is that Charles I chose to use force to bend his peoples to his will and they refused to submit without a fight. A vicious cycle of revolution and war spread to all of the Stuart domains, eventually destroying the monarch and his political aspirations and changing the English state forever.

The background

Charles I inherited a kingdom at war with Spain in 1625, a war he had done much to promote. During the next five years English military leadership proved disastrous for the poorly trained and badly supported English forces. The humiliation of English arms was due to England's lack of competent military forces and inadequate financial resources. Yet, in spite of his lack of funds, Charles expanded the war to include France as an enemy by 1627, further straining English resources and institutions.

England's abysmal showing against the French and Spaniards weakened the respect of many Englishmen for a king whom they had greeted with such hope in 1625. Charles had seemed to be a prince who would revive the glories of Elizabethan England. James I's last parliament and Charles's first parliament had supported the decision to go to war against Spain enthusiastically. The 1624 parliament provided three subsidies of roughly £60,000 each for the war effort, while the 1625 parliament provided two subsidies totaling perhaps £120,000. These sums, however, were well below the costs of raising and shipping an army to the continent even though, by Elizabethan standards, these parliamentary grants seemed generous.[3]

As military disasters unfolded, many Englishmen became disgruntled with their government's poor performance. The king's chief advisor, George Villiers, Duke of Buckingham and Lord High Admiral, served as a lightning rod for much of this discontent. English parliaments became unwilling to provide more money for the war before changes were made in the king's council. Charles refused to allow parliamentary interference in his choice of advisors or his conduct of foreign and military policy. Consequently, parliament provided only two subsidies in the period from 1626 to 1628. This parliamentary parsimony plunged Charles's government into a severe financial crisis, as military costs outstripped the king's revenues.

The military results were predictable. Expeditions to Spain and France failed. When the fleets limped back from overseas debacles the ports of southern England became crowded with soldiers and sailors who had not received their pay in months. These poor unfortunates strained the resources of the southern counties and sorely tried the patience of local officials. Charles, desperate for cash, resorted to a forced loan in 1626–7 and continued to collect the customs without parliamentary approval.[4] Although he raised over £400,000 from these two sources his government fell deeply into debt, owing as much as £1.1 million by 1630, with an annual average revenue of less than £700,000.[5] The crown derived a significant portion of this revenue from the sale of property, further undermining the king's long-term financial position. Charles's resort to non-parliamentary taxation widened the breach between him and his people. War was too expensive for an English monarch to conduct using traditional financial methods, especially given parliament's unwillingness to provide sufficient funds for a war it had sanctioned.

The political results of the fiscal and military crises were equally predictable. Charles's relations with his parliaments deteriorated, preventing him and his subjects from agreeing on solutions. Charles was forced to make peace with France (1629) and Spain (1630) because he could not convince his parliaments to grant the taxes essential to the conduct of war. Trust between monarch and subject was undermined. Parliament refused to grant the crown further revenues until Charles addressed its grievances about his advisors and the methods he had used to raise money. The king refused to do so and dismissed the parliament. Only the return of peace allowed Charles to stave off his critics and creditors.

For the following eight years Britain and Ireland enjoyed the fruits of peace. Remembering the humiliating failures of English armies and fleets in the 1620s, the king determined to rectify England's martial weaknesses. He attributed these failings to the inadequacy of English military institutions and practices and to the parsimony and meddling of parliament. Therefore, his government attempted to reform England's military forces without having to call a parliament. This period of 'personal rule' included significant reforms made by Charles in English military, political, and religious practices, at least before 1637.[6]

To improve English land forces Charles continued the Jacobean system of military reform called 'the exact militia'. Under this scheme, the lord lieutenants and their deputies were to ensure that the militia bought modern weapons and mustered regularly. While many county leaders ignored their defense responsibilities, a number of lord lieutenants arranged for professional drillmasters to provide the best armed of the militia units, known as the trained bands, with monthly training. This program continued through the 1630s.[7] These mustered regularly, and well-armed trained bands were to play important roles in the early days of the British wars that lay ahead.

Local taxes paid for the reform of the militia. This allowed the Caroline government to improve its land forces at little cost to the exchequer in Westminster. The same financial method could not be replicated for the navy, however, since there were no naval reserves maintained by the counties. The king's 'ordinary' revenues traditionally had supported the Royal Navy in peacetime. During the reign of James I, from 1603 to 1625, the fleet had decayed due to shortages of money and incompetent management. When the Spanish war began, only ten per cent of the ships in the fleet sent to Cadiz were royal warships. Merchant ships provided most of the vessels needed for the expedition. This system had been used regularly during the Elizabethan wars and was an effective way to raise a navy for the defense of the home islands and for raids against a vulnerable Spanish Empire.[8]

By 1625, however, a revolution was underway in military affairs in Western Europe, and the requirements of naval warfare were changing rapidly.[9] New purpose-built ships, such as the frigate, were developed and the number and size of cannon on warships rapidly increased. Merchant vessels were no longer an efficient substitute for a regular warship. During the Cadiz raid, the Lord Admiral found it difficult to control captains of the hired merchant vessels when the mission did not appear to be financially lucrative, and merchant captains were reluctant to risk their ships in battle.

Naval operations changed as well, as a new kind of navy was needed to fight wars far from home. The early Caroline war fleets could not sustain the long-term deployments needed to win these long-range wars. English naval administration was poorly organized and badly under-funded. The logistical organizations and administrative procedures required to provide distant fleets with victuals and munitions on a regular basis had not been developed. Even the energetic leadership of the Duke of Buckingham could not redeem England's naval honor or the military situation. English failures at Cadiz in 1625 and at La Rochelle in 1627 were symptomatic of the operational, organizational, and financial problems faced by the English navy and government.[10] In the judgment of most Englishmen, including the king, the Spanish and French wars were disastrous.

The impotence of the Royal Navy meant that English diplomatic influence was minimal. Charles was unable to aid his brother-in-law, Frederick I of the Palatinate, to recover his patrimony because he could not affect Habsburg or Bourbon policy in Western Europe. Charles soon concluded that the possession of an effective navy would give him the diplomatic leverage needed to convince either France or Spain to restore the Palatinate to Frederick. To do this, he would offer to use his fleet to prevent one of these Catholic powers from using the Channel and the North Sea to support military operations in the Netherlands.[11] However, to convince either nation that England could affect maritime affairs, Charles needed to revitalize his navy.

Charles was unable to resolve many of the problems of naval administration and operations in the early 1630s because he lacked the money needed to do so. However, he did much to improve the shore establishment and shipbuilding by replacing the Lord Admiral with a commission. Administrative positions in the navy dockyards and on the Admiralty Board were no longer considered the personal possession of the incumbent, although the shift to impersonal bureaucratic principles was to be a long process. Men such as Phineas Pett, a full time naval administrator and warship designer, developed more efficient bronze cannon, while the Ordnance Board's Master Gunfounder, William Brown, 'claimed to be able to cast iron guns lighter than bronze'.[12] The king's shipwrights built new warships, such as the famous *Sovereign of the Seas*. Such battleships, mounting 80 to 100 cannon, promised to give the Royal Navy the power needed to defend Britain from the growing French and Dutch fleets. To exploit these advances in naval administration and design, Charles had to provide a great deal more money to his navy than had ever been provided before in peacetime. Further, he needed to maintain naval operations year round, again increasing the maintenance and operating costs.

To play the maritime role of a major power, the Royal Navy needed to become a professional force of ships and crews continuously maintained on active duty. In the past, most of the navy had been demobilized when not needed for active service. This system made it impossible for the commanders to learn how to maneuver and fight their ships in modern naval operations. Since money was the root of Charles's military problems, he decided, in late 1634, to raise funds to sustain the navy by levying ship-money on the maritime counties. Elizabeth I had used ship-money taxes to help finance her fleets during the Spanish war of the 1590s. Now Charles used his prerogative powers to declare that ship-money was needed to enable the navy to set out a fleet to face imminent threats to English security. Such a fleet also would allow the navy to rid British waters of pirates. The ship-money levied on the maritime counties in 1635 produced £79,586 of the £80,069 assessed, a remarkable rate of return for a government that had been plagued by a steady deterioration of parliamentary subsidies.[13] This success encouraged the king to extend the levy to the inland counties.

Charles took the logical step of asking all Englishmen to support a navy that he intended to use to face the threats posed to the well being of the entire nation. Although there was scattered resistance to the innovative extension of the levy, county sheriffs collected the vast majority of the money assessed during the next three years.[14] While ship-money was a financial success, and Charles used its entire proceeds for its intended purposes, the political costs were high. Many Englishmen saw the way this tax was levied as another example of Charles's unconstitutional rule. This political discontent did not lead to widespread resistance, but it was part of the tinder from which the fires of revolution would ignite.

By 1635, Charles's government was on its way to financial solvency, with ordinary revenue running ahead of expenditures and ship-money paying for the reform and expansion of the navy. During this same period, the king's Lord Deputy of Ireland, Thomas Wentworth, was achieving similar results in his administrative and financial reforms in Ireland. Through a clever but unscrupulous manipulation of the major groups in Ireland, Wentworth got the Irish parliament to grant sufficient revenues for the king's Irish government to remain solvent. Further, commercial growth made possible by peace allowed the king to tap increasing customs revenues, further solidifying the crown's financial situation.

Wentworth's administrative policies in Ireland, characterized as 'thorough', were mirrored by the reforming efforts of William Laud. Laud, Archbishop of Canterbury from 1633 on, was attempting to reform the Church of England. His reforms included the provision of adequate funding for the clergy to end the abuse of pluralism and efforts to ensure that the clergy were well educated. He worked to force English parishioners to pay appropriate respect to their clergy and to the ceremonies symbolizing the saving grace of the Christian faith. Finally, he did all he could to roll back what he saw as the doctrinal errors of the puritan clergy within the church. Laud was impeccably honest and sincere in his desires to rid the English church of abuses inherited from the Erastian reformation of the past century. In the process he alienated many who believed that his reforms were popish.

Charles I warmly approved of Laud's reforms, imposing many of them by royal order on the Protestant Church of Ireland as well. From the king's perspective, uniformity in religion and the increase in respect by parishioners for their clergy and liturgy would do much to ensure his peoples' respect for God's anointed monarch. To enforce reforms in church and state, Laud and the king's other councillors used the quasi-judicial bodies of Star Chamber and the church's Court of High Commission to exact obedience.

Laud's correction of what he saw as abuses met fierce resistance from a number of puritans. Perhaps the most famous of the resisters were William Prynne, Henry Burton, and John Bastwick. Prynne had attacked Laud's reforms since the early 1630s, and had lost his ears to the executioner's knife in 1634 as a reward for his efforts. In 1636 he published *A Divine Tragedy Lately Acted*, condemning Laud's work as popish. Burton delivered a series of sermons in 1636–7 with the same theme. Bastwick attacked Laud for moving the communion table from the center of the church to the east end, an alteration that Bastwick believed treated the table like the altar of a Roman Catholic church.[15]

These protesters were hailed before the Star Chamber for trial. Laud and the other members of the Star Chamber concluded that these men's attacks warranted punishment and ordered horrific punishments to be imposed. They were pilloried, had their ears cropped, and since Prynne had already lost his ears, he had S. L. burned into his cheek to label him as a 'seditious libeller'. They then were imprisoned for life.[16]

Such savage punishments did not incite widespread resistance, although they certainly did not win the hearts and minds of many Englishmen to Laud's reforms.

None the less, Laud seemed to move from success to success with his efforts to bring conformity to church affairs. His work faithfully served a king 'who was obsessed with order and decorum … and who was a vigorous reformer' of church and state.[17] In most of England, the reform of the church was accepted quietly, if not actively welcomed. This became evident when many members of the Church of England rallied in the 1640s to defend the Caroline church. There were religious problems and protests in 1637, but no signs of revolution.

Charles's administrative and fiscal reforms similarly provoked protest and legal challenges. In 1635, understanding that the extension of ship-money to the inland counties was innovative, the king asked his leading twelve judges to determine if his imposition of ship-money was legal. The judges declared unanimously that it was within the royal prerogative to extend the levy to all of England. Ten of them also ruled that the king was the sole judge as to when the nation faced a security risk that warranted the levy of the tax. In early 1637, the judges again unanimously ruled in favor of the royal prerogative when Charles asked them to determine if his third levy of ship-money was legal.[18]

Resistance to these levies did not cease with these rulings. In late 1637, the most famous 'ship-money case' was argued on behalf of John Hampden. Hampden's lawyer, Oliver St John, accepted the decision that the king could order the levy of ship-money throughout the realm and that the monarch was the sole judge of when the nation's security was threatened. But he argued that the rates and apportionment of the levy must be set by a parliament since ship-money was a tax and, constitutionally, only a parliament could approve tax rates. This line of argument influenced the judges. Five of the twelve broke ranks and ruled partially in favor of St John's argument. But the king still won the case, leaving him free to continue the imposition of ship-money on the entire nation.

The decisions in the ship-money cases, and the cry by many that the king was collecting the customs illegally, did not lead to revolution. The customs was collected with little difficulty and, from 1635 through 1638, over ninety per cent of the ship-money assessed was paid, both with little open protest. There was a growing opposition to the crown's religious and political programs led by men such as John Pym and Lord Brooke. This opposition, however, lacked a national platform from which to attack the king's innovations.

Charles's efforts to improve the navy and to use it as an instrument of English foreign policy were successful. In 1637, a squadron led by Captain William Rains-borough freed English sailors from the Barbary pirates after a five-month blockade of their base at Sallee, in North Africa.[19] In the same year Cardinal Richelieu of France offered to sign an 'auxiliary alliance' with England. Richelieu promised French aid for the recovery of the king's nephew's Palatine patrimony without requiring English participation in the war against the Habsburgs. In this proposed treaty, the English navy would protect French and English interests at sea, while the French did the fighting in the Rhineland. The English could operate against Spanish ships carrying gold and military materials between Spain and the Netherlands.[20] Although England and France did not sign this treaty, its proposal by the French showed that

Charles's efforts to strengthen the navy increased English diplomatic clout. As long as Charles I kept England out of war, or if he could make war pay for itself by limiting it to the maritime arena where England could prey on enemy commerce, there appeared to be little threat to his continued personal rule.

The situation in mid-1637

After seven years of peace, Caroline England was prosperous and Charles I secure in his kingdoms. Local elites carried out royal military and fiscal policies. Sheriffs and justices of the peace assessed and collected ship-money along with the rates for poor relief and the militia. The legal system continued to function throughout the land. At the highest level, the judges had reinforced royal authority. The Star Chamber and the Court of High Commission in England, and the Castle Chamber in Ireland, enforced the religious and administrative reforms carried out by Laud and Wentworth. To Edward Hyde, later Earl of Clarendon, it seemed that England experienced 'so excellent a composure throughout the whole kingdom, that the like peace and plenty, and universal tranquility for ten years was never enjoyed by any [other] nation.' He further noted, in spite of the reforms and protests of the period 1629–37,

> that during the whole time that these pressures were exercised and those new and extraordinary ways were run, ... this kingdom, and all his majesty's dominions (of the interruption in Scotland somewhat shall be said in its due time and place) enjoyed the greatest calm, and the fullest measure of felicity, that any people in any age, for so long time together, have been blessed with; to the wonder and envy of all the other parts of Christendom.[21]

How and why did this period of peace end, when it is evident that rebellion or civil war was not to be expected? How and why was the 'thorough' reforming work by Laud, Wentworth, and Charles I so quickly undone? The answer is not found in an interpretation that sees the reign of Charles I as part of a process that was logically flowing toward the triumph of parliamentary government in the English civil wars and revolution – the 'Whig View' of history. Instead, the answer is found in the decisions and actions of the king and thousands of his subjects, beginning in 1637. These actions and decisions, which led to revolutions and wars, were taken in a situation in which Charles's religious and fiscal policies had alienated significant portions of the Scottish, Irish, and English ruling classes. When these men were presented with an opportunity to undo what they saw as unconstitutional changes in their nations, and popish reforms in their churches, they acted to redress the balance.

What, then, caused the undoing of Charles I? We need to look no farther than the way in which he attempted to crush Scottish opposition to his ecclesiastical policies to find the proximate cause of the revolutions against him. His decision to impose a Scottish Book of Common Prayer upon the Scots led them to resist and then to revolt. Charles's decision to brook no resistance to his prerogative, coupled with his unbelievable ignorance of the character of his subjects, led to the rise of political movements in his kingdoms that organized and galvanized opposition to his rule.

Scottish resistance in 1637–9 led Charles to mobilize the resources of his other kingdoms to wage war against Scotland. The king's wars against his Scottish subjects, known as the Bishops' Wars, brought on fiscal and political crises in England that forced Charles to call two English parliaments in 1640. The first of these is known as the Short Parliament, since he dissolved it shortly after it convened. The second is known as the Long Parliament because it legally remained in session for nearly twenty years. The Long Parliament carried out a political revolution that fundamentally changed the English constitution. Charles's attempts, through parliament, to undo this constitutional settlement by force of arms led to two English civil wars and two more Scottish invasions of England. The ascendancy of militant puritanism in the Long Parliament, coupled with the evident weakness of Caroline government in Ireland, led Irish Catholics to rebel in 1641, making the revolutions against Charles also the war of the three kingdoms.

The Long Parliament created the military forces on land and sea that it needed to defeat its enemies. In the process, it united Ireland and Britain in their most complete political union until 1801. The English Commonwealth then challenged Europe's strongest western nations to naval wars, soundly defeating them. To pay for and administer these military operations, the parliamentary government reorganized England's fiscal and administrative systems. Charles paid dearly for his poor leadership and his ignorance of his peoples. His subjects suffered terribly, even while they transformed the English state into a formidable European power and laid the foundations for later British imperial grandeur.

Notes

1 S. Gardiner, *The History of England, 1603–1642* (London, 1883–4), viii: 199.

2 J. Wheeler, *Making of a World Power* (Stroud, 1999), 97.

3 K. Sharpe, *The Personal Rule of Charles I* (Yale, 1992), 3–9; C. Russell, *The Crisis of Parliaments* (Oxford, 1971, 1992 edn), 298–302.

4 R. Cust, *The Forced Loan and English Politics, 1626–28* (Oxford, 1987).

5 F. C. Dietz, *English Public Finance, 1558–1641* (New York, 1932), 270.

6 K. Sharpe, *Charles I*, chapters 5–7; A. Fletcher, *Reform in the Provinces: The Government of Stuart England* (Yale, 1986); J. Barratt, *Cavaliers: The Royalist Army at War, 1642–1646* (Stroud, 2000), 16.

7 Fletcher, *Reform in the Provinces*, chapter 9; L. Boynton, *The Elizabethan Militia, 1558–1638* (London, 1976), 126–206.

8 N. Rodger, *The Safeguard of the Seas: A Naval History of Britain, 660–1649* (New York, 1998), chapters 24–5.

9 G. Parker, *The Military Revolution: Military Innovation and the Rise of the West* (Cambridge, 1996 edn), 82–114; J. Glete, *Navies and Nations: Warships, Navies, and State Building in Europe and America* (Stockholm, 1993).

10 Rodger, *Safeguard of the Seas*, 353–78.

11 Sharpe, *Charles I*, chapter 2.

12 Rodger, *Safeguard of the Seas*, 388–90.

13 Ibid., 381–3.

14 Wheeler, *Making of a World Power*, 35.
15 Gardiner, *History of England*, viii: 224–32.
16 Ibid., 229–31.
17 Sharpe, *Charles I*, 209.
18 Gardiner, *History of England*, viii: 94–6, 107–8.
19 Rodger, *Safeguard of the Seas*, 385.
20 Sharpe, *Charles I*, 526–35.
21 E. Clarendon, Earl of, *A History of the Rebellion and Civil Wars in England* (Oxford, 1732), vol. 1, 74.

CHAPTER ONE

The Scottish Revolution and the two Bishops' Wars

With the rioting in Edinburgh, Scotland shattered the apparent calm of Britain in the summer of 1637. The tumultuous protest against the Dean of St Giles Cathedral, when he attempted to read the king's new Scottish Book of Common Prayer, took Charles and his council in London by surprise. Until reports reached London from Scotland, 'there were very few in England who had heard of any disorders there, or of any thing done there which might produce any.'[1] Probably even fewer Englishmen cared about Charles's northern kingdom. The English soon would care deeply about what transpired across their northern border, as the revolt in Scotland provoked a series of decisions by Charles that eventually led to the outbreak of the English Revolution.

Caroline Reform in Scotland, 1625–37

Upon his inheritance of the Scottish throne in 1625, Charles I initiated reforms in Scottish government, church affairs, and land-holding that previewed his policy of 'thorough' in England and Ireland in the 1630s. Charles's first step in this burst of royal reform was to revoke many titles to Scottish crown and church lands that Scottish nobles had acquired since 1540. This revocation of land titles was precedented. Traditionally, Scottish monarchs had the right to do so after their accession, as long as they did so between their twenty-first and twenty-fifth birthdays. Charles had to act fast in 1625, since his twenty-fifth birthday was approaching shortly.[2]

While there was precedent for the revocation, the scale on which Charles revoked titles to land was new. Normally, a monarch revoked titles to royal and church land that had been obtained while that monarch was a minor. Such a policy protected a monarchy that often had suffered the ill-effects of having kings succeed to the throne as children. However, in going back to 1540 in his revocation, Charles expanded his claim to dispose of the property of his subjects. While he intended to regrant most of the titles to the current owners, this startling display of the royal prerogative frightened many Scottish nobles, lairds, and clergymen.[3]

Charles planned to pay compensation for any property rights that he kept and to use the income from tithes that he acquired to improve the support for the clergy of the Church of Scotland. Unfortunately for his reputation, the king failed to make his plans clear to his Scottish council or his leading nobles. The revocation and regrant seemed to be a demonstration of raw power at the start of his reign, and a warning to those who opposed him. Charles reinforced his Scottish subjects' distrust in him by also changing the terms upon which land was held. These actions brought the king 'the lasting distrust of most of his Scots tenants in chief.'[4]

In the revocation process, Charles reformed the way in which teinds, or tithes, were raised for the support of the clergy. Tithes that had been paid in kind were commuted to a monetary rent. Tenants who wanted to buy out their tithes could do so by paying nine years' purchase in cash. Otherwise, the tithe payers paid a small annual amount to the landowners, who in turn paid much of this revenue to the parish minister.[5] With the king's reform of tithes, nobles and lairds lost some of their influence over their tenants and the clergy, which they resented even though they were compensated for their financial losses. The uproar over the revocation and the turmoil it caused lasted for four years, until the final terms were agreed upon in 1629. The massive revocation failed to improve the financial position of the king in Scotland. The annual income of the Scottish crown averaged only about £16,500 sterling in the 1630s. Consequently, royal finances continued to rely upon Scottish parliamentary grants.

Charles also revoked hereditary possession of crown offices in 1625, although again he offered compensation for the losses incurred by the incumbents. This move offended nobles who considered it part of their patrimony to play a role in the government. During the following twelve years, Charles relied on a small group of advisors in London and a council in Edinburgh to carry out his decisions in his northern kingdom. Most prominent amongst these men were James, Marquis of Hamilton, in London and John Stewart, Earl of Traquair, in Edinburgh. Hamilton was a man who often bent with the strongest wind during the coming hurricanes of civil war and revolution. He also had a marked tendency to play both sides of the fence in disputes between Charles I and his subjects.

Traquair was a hard-working royal servant who often disagreed with the policies he was called upon to implement, but who seldom stood up openly and forcefully to the king. He played a crucial role in the royal reforms of the Scottish administration. With Traquair's help, Charles established the first permanent Scottish Exchequer, providing central accounting for crown revenues. He had his Scottish treasurer provide him with annual financial reports and he consolidated sinecures and offices that had sapped royal income for generations. Traquair became one of two treasurers of the exchequer in 1630, and by 1636 had consolidated that office in his firm grip. During the 1630s he improved the king's revenues and was instrumental in obtaining additional grants of taxes from Scottish parliaments. In the process of improving the financial position and power of the crown, Traquair alienated many of the leading nobles and burghers of Scotland.[6]

As the king narrowed access to power in Scottish affairs to fewer nobles, he increased the number of Scottish bishops in his council and the offices of state in Edinburgh. The long-term consequence of this trend was the further alienation of many Scottish nobles, removing them as a potential prop for royal authority if a major crisis developed.[7]

The crisis created by the revocation of 1625 and the narrowing of his advisors in Scottish affairs subsided with Charles's commitment to compensate owners for any financial losses. His reform of tithes had positive effects on the living conditions of the clergy and weakened the nobles' control over their tenants. As the historian S. R. Gardiner noted, the settlement of tithes achieved in 1629 'is worthy of memory as the one successful action of Charles's reign.'[8] These changes were facilitated by the king's willingness to suspend the controversial religious terms of the Articles of Perth (1618) for those Scottish ministers who had been in office before 1618. This was a major concession to the Calvinist feelings of the Scottish clergy and people, as the Perth Articles seemed popish in their requirement for the kneeling by communicants at communion and for the placing of the communion table at the east end of the church.

By the time Charles finally traveled to Scotland for his coronation in 1633, the furor over his land policies had subsided. As he progressed to Edinburgh the Scots received him enthusiastically and nobles fell all over themselves to entertain their king. Nevertheless, Charles again displayed his immense capacity for insensitivity to the beliefs and feelings of his subjects when he had himself crowned in Holyrood chapel with English religious ritual that was alien to Scotland and smacked of popery. He further insisted that services conducted in his presence in St Giles church in Edinburgh be done according to the rites of the Church of England. Remarkably, the Scots still cheered him as Charles progressed through the country after his coronation, and the Scottish parliament proved far more willing than his English parliaments had been to pass royal legislation.[9]

The favorable Scottish responses to Charles in 1633 contradict the view that revolution was on the horizon in Scotland at that time. Even his ecclesiastical ideas did not seem to be leading the nation to revolt. Nonetheless, Charles's actions in his first nine years as King of Scotland badly eroded the trust between the monarch and the Scottish nobility. Such trust had been an important political tool for his father, who used the nobles to rein in the power of the clergy. Charles I eventually drove the nobles and lairds to make common cause with the strongly Calvinist ministers of the Scottish Kirk because they saw Charles's political and religious policies as two sides of a single strategy to increase the power of the crown at the expense of the traditional elites.

Further church reform, 1634–37

From the beginning of his reign, Charles had planned to continue the reform of the Church of Scotland that his father had started. James I's method of moving gradually toward an episcopal system had born fruit, culminating with the Articles of Perth (1618). By 1634, Charles was ready to push the process of reform toward greater religious conformity among his three kingdoms by providing the Church of Scotland with new canons and liturgy. To do this, Charles commissioned three Scottish bishops to prepare new canons and a Scottish Book of Common Prayer. These documents were drafted and sent to Charles for his approval.

In this process, Charles consulted regularly with the Archbishop of Canterbury. The bishops finished the Scottish canons in January 1636 and Charles quickly approved them. The publication of the new canons was met with surprise and resentment in Scotland. Based on the English canons of 1604, they affirmed the Articles of Perth that many of the Scottish clergy abhorred. They failed to mention the general assemblies, presbyteries, or Kirk sessions that had been traditional institutions in the Scottish Kirk for eighty years.[10] In October 1636, as the furor over the canons continued, Charles approved the Scottish Book of Common Prayer, providing a uniform liturgy for his Scottish church. And in November he sent a draft of the prayer book to the council in Edinburgh, ordering the council to require all ministers to purchase two copies by Easter, 1637.

The problem with these royal actions was fundamental. The Scots did not see the Scottish church as belonging to Charles, nor did they subscribe to the concept of royal supremacy in ecclesiastical affairs. The ritualistic trappings of the new liturgy and the elevation of bishops to positions of religious and political power seemed to confirm that Charles and Laud were moving the church steadily away from Presbyterianism and back to Rome. The notion that an English archbishop had played a prominent role in the development of the Scottish canons and liturgy affronted Scottish national sentiment. As a result, resistance groups among the ministers and the laity of the Kirk came together as word reached Scotland of the progress of the king's new prayer book.

The Scottish council was aware of the rising tide of popular feeling against the Caroline religious innovations. Through the fall and winter of 1636–7, the councillors received petitions against the imposition of the prayer book. Even the Scottish bishops were apprehensive about what would happen when the king forced them to begin using the new liturgy. However, the council in Edinburgh gave Charles little intimation about the depth and breadth of the opposition brewing against his religious reforms. Quite likely he would have done nothing different had he known, but the council left him uninformed at a critical juncture in British and Irish history. The king also kept his English council ignorant of his Scottish affairs and policies, preventing his advisors from perhaps reining in the king when he set out recklessly on a very dangerous course.[11]

The fact that the Scottish council did not warn him of the danger shows how little trust his servants had in his willingness to deal appropriately with the crisis. Charles's inability to inspire trust and confidence in his councillors, coupled with the history of his overweening actions toward the Scots since 1625, set him on a collision course with the increasingly well-organized resistance of nobles, lairds, burghers, and ministers.[12] Once informed of resistance to his innovations, Charles rashly ordered his councillors to support the bishops' use of the new liturgy.

The religious controversy came to a head on 23 July 1637 when the Dean of St Giles attempted to read from the new prayer book. As he did so, all hell broke loose, and only the greatest tact and leadership by Charles and his Scottish councillors could have prevented a general revolt in Scotland. But tact and skillful leadership were lacking in Westminster and Edinburgh. The planned first reading of the Scottish

Book of Common Prayer had been advertised in advance, allowing those who opposed it to organize a response. Women led the riot in St Giles, but the burghers of Edinburgh supported them. The king's Scottish council met hastily and ordered the magistrates to protect the bishop as he read the book at the afternoon services. However, the magistrates found the opposition too dangerous to face head on, and only with difficulty were the bishops in attendance able to escape the mob.

Although the magistrates arrested a handful of rioters, the council suspended the use of the canons and liturgy while awaiting a response from the king to their report of the disturbances. Had Charles taken this opportunity to conciliate the united Scottish clergy and laity, his Edinburgh government probably would have weathered the storm and retained a grip on the country. It was even likely that he could have retained episcopal government in the Scottish church. However, such was not to be the case. The king stiffened his neck to compromise, a trait evident throughout the political, religious, and military conflicts that characterized his reign after 1637.

Charles's initial response to the news of the riots in Edinburgh was to order Traquair and the Scottish council to force the magistrates throughout Scotland to support the bishops in their efforts to achieve liturgical uniformity. This response aroused the Scots against English intrusions into their affairs and united the Scottish people. Petitions flowed into the council in Edinburgh opposing the royal policies. The councillors sent dozens of these on to London, hoping Charles would grasp the magnitude of the opposition.[13] Finally, on 25 August, the council warned the king that the situation was extremely dangerous, insinuating that they were helpless to stem the tide unless he dropped the prayer book.

> We found ourselves far beyond our expectations surprised with the clamours and fears of your Majesty's subjects from almost all parts and corners of the kingdom … and thus we find it so to increase that we conceive it to be a matter of high consequence in respect of the general murmur and grudge in all sorts of people for urging of the practice of the Service Book, as like hath not been heard in this kingdom.[14]

Although infuriated by the situation, Charles procrastinated rather than acting quickly to defuse or crush the resistance. This gave those nobles, ministers, and burghers leading the resistance additional time to organize support throughout Scotland. At this critical point a number of leaders stepped forward to guide the resistance to the king. Among the nobility John Leslie, earl of Rothes, and James Graham, Earl of Montrose, were prominent. Rothes, a natural leader with lands scattered throughout the Scottish lowlands, had widespread connections and influence. Montrose was a handsome and charismatic leader who had traveled widely for a man only twenty-five years old. These men were committed Calvinists and patriotic Scots.

Among the lairds, the Scottish equivalent of the English gentry, Archibald Johnston of Warriston was the most prominent leader. Articulate, wealthy, and fanatically devoted to the Calvinist traditions of the Kirk, Johnston was probably the leading architect of the idea of a national covenant. The clergyman Alexander Henderson, minister of Leuchers in Fifeshire, ably aided him in his political thinking. Henderson played a central role in organizing the initial resistance to the prayer book in July 1637.[15] The coming together of such leading aristocrats, ministers, and commoners was due to the fact that Charles's actions had united Scotland against his religious policies. Brought together to resist religious change, this coalition soon began to resist royal political authority.

By October Edinburgh was thronged with people waiting to hear the king's response to petitions that had been sent to London. On 17 October, the royal councillors opened a letter from the king that ordered them to enforce the canons and liturgy and to punish the citizens of Edinburgh for their resistance by moving the council and the royal courts from Edinburgh to Linlithgow and Dundee. Such a move would economically harm the city's merchants. These instructions caused rioting in the capital on 18 October, encouraging the leaders of the resistance to prepare a new supplication to the king. The council departed Edinburgh as ordered, leaving control of the capital to the men leading the movement against royal policies. The council's abandonment of the capital was a blunder of the first order, making it even harder for the councillors to control events in Scotland.

The Scottish crisis expanded during the next four months. The king refused to concede the substance of the argument to the Scots. His threats to those who petitioned or wrote supplications drove many Scots off the fence and into the camp of the signers of a 'supplication' sent to London in October. After receiving no reasonable response from Charles, the Scots took a major step forward in their resistance to the king when they signed and published the National Covenant. This document reaffirmed the Covenant of the Scottish people and James VI in 1580 to protect the Kirk from Roman Catholicism, innovation, and superstition. It went one step further by binding all signatories to defend one another.[16]

The National Covenant did not openly condemn the new canons, liturgy, or the position of bishops, but the first two were innovations and thus explicitly condemned, while the position of the bishops was threatened indirectly. By the spring of 1638, the Covenanters had elaborated their demands by insisting that parliament be called regularly and that innovations in religion be removed permanently. There was little chance Charles would accept these terms, even though his Scottish council recommended that he back down completely. Charles responded by summoning Traquair to London to explain the situation and his failure to stop the formation of an opposition party.

Traquair's visit to London produced no results, although it convinced the king that the Scottish council could not control events. Therefore, the king sent Hamilton to his native country in hopes that this young nobleman could assess and perhaps control events. Hamilton carried with him two versions of a royal proclamation. Based on the circumstances he found, he was to issue the more appropriate of the two. Neither document conceded anything to the Scots that would conciliate the Covenanters. In Scotland, in June 1638, Hamilton found a united people. Between Leith and Edinburgh he was met by thirty nobles, with hundreds of lairds and ministers, and 20,000 people lining the road. This display of unity convinced him of the precariousness of his mission and the danger to the king's position in Scotland. He decided not to publish either version of the royal proclamation because he sensed that either would incite the Scots to further action.

Hamilton quickly returned to London to consult with Charles and share his impressions. However, before Hamilton arrived, the king decided to impose his will on Scotland by force. Consequently, he ordered Hamilton to return to Edinburgh to issue a royal proclamation. Hamilton complied, publishing the king's missive on 4 July 1638.[17] Charles again had failed to listen to his leading advisors.

As the Covenanters talked with Hamilton, Charles commenced to plan for military operations. He appointed a committee within the English council to deal with Scottish affairs and ordered Berwick and Carlisle to be prepared for defense against Scottish incursions. The Privy Council instructed the Ordnance Office to prepare a train of artillery for operations and to order arms for 14,000 infantrymen and 6,000 cavalrymen. William Juxon, Bishop of London and Lord Treasurer, assured the king that £200,000 in cash could be provided by the exchequer for the mobilization.[18]

Meanwhile, the Covenanters demanded the convening of an assembly of the Kirk and a parliament to settle Scottish affairs. The assembly was to exclude bishops, except in their roles as ministers, and was to be the final authority in doctrinal and organizational matters in the church. Since the king was reluctant to call an assembly, the Covenanters declared that the right to assemblies came directly from God. Scottish religious and national feelings fused over the issue of sovereignty in church and state. The leading Covenanters also established committees of nobles, lairds, burghers, and ministers that were called 'Tables.' The Tables assumed the role of an executive in Edinburgh, giving direction to the resistance to the king.

As Charles and his Privy Council slowly prepared English military resources, the king played for time by accepting the demands that an assembly and parliament should be called in Scotland. He agreed to revoke the new canons, the Scottish Book of Common Prayer, and the High Commission in Scotland. Further, he ordered the suspension of the Articles of Perth. The king's nearly total capitulation to the Covenanters' demands was by no means an indication that he had any intention of giving in peacefully. The slowness of his preparations showed both the weaknesses in his military and financial bureaucracies and his hope that a show of force would be sufficient to convince the Scots to accept his point of view.[19] For the remainder of his life Charles treated all of his subjects duplicitously, hoping to divide and conquer. Sadly for him, his leading opponents in all three of his kingdoms quickly suspected this tactic, helping to undermine his strategic method.

The First Bishops' War

Charles agreed, on 17 September 1638, to allow the summoning of an assembly of the Scottish Kirk to meet in Glasgow in November. He also conceded to the Covenanters' demand for the meeting of a Scottish parliament in the spring, hoping that the Covenanters would fall out amongst themselves by then. Meanwhile, the king continued his efforts to muster English military forces for action against the Scots. An important part of this process of mobilization was the king's development of a military strategy designed to defeat the Covenanters at the lowest cost, with the least risk to English forces.

The king and his advisors developed a campaign plan that included the navy (see map 2). Hamilton was to lead a fleet to the northeast coast of Scotland with an expeditionary force of 5,000 men. Hamilton and this army were to join Lord Huntly and his forces in Aberdeenshire, providing a Scottish royalist force to face the rebellious Covenanters. While this army moved south toward Edinburgh, the navy was to blockade the Scottish coasts, cutting off the Covenanters from trade with the continent and from their major sources of munitions. The navy also was to transport an army led by Randall MacDonnell, Earl of Antrim, from Ulster to western Scotland. Antrim was to attack the Campbell lands, thus drawing Lord Lorne and his troops away from the Covenanters in Edinburgh. Finally, the navy was to transport 500 soldiers from Ireland to northwestern England, where they were to garrison Carlisle, the western buttress of English border defenses.[20]

The main army was to assemble in the north of England, near Newcastle. This force was to be composed of the trained bands from the southern counties, leaving the trained bands of the north free to defend the border as the army assembled. Then, as the other prongs of the royal offensive divided the resources and attention of the Covenanters, Charles could lead this army against Edinburgh, where the castle remained in royalist hands. Many courtiers expected these converging pincers of the king's forces to overawe the Scots, bringing them back to their senses and loyalty without a fight. If that failed, most Englishmen believed that their armies would easily defeat the Scots in battle.[21]

Scottish preparations for war

On 21 November, as the king made plans and his council got preparations underway, the Scottish assembly met in Glasgow. The Covenanters took the initiative, stripping the bishops of all authority and claiming supremacy for the assembly in the Scottish Kirk. The assembly also condemned changes made in the church since 1581. Hamilton, as the king's representative, attempted to dissolve the Glasgow assembly, but the Scots refused to obey his commands. The leading Covenanter nobles and lairds joined the clerical and lay representatives of the presbyteries in the assembly, making it a national representative institution. From this point on the Scottish Covenanters were the effective rulers of Scotland and war was inevitable. As rumors of the king's preparations reached them, the Scots prepared for war. In this effort, Scottish nationalism and religious feelings were united, giving their leaders the ability to tap the nation's full strength.

The Scots created an effective system for raising an army and governing a nation at war. Even before the Glasgow Assembly met, the standing committee of Covenanter leaders in Edinburgh, known as the 'Tables', had ordered two lairds in each parish to compile lists of the men and military equipment available locally and to determine

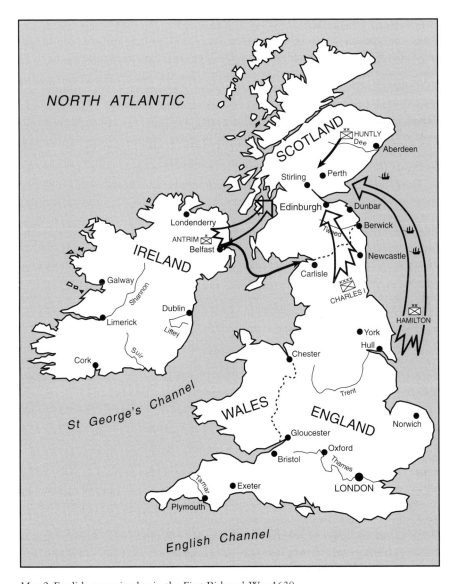

Map 2 English strategic plan in the First Bishops' War, 1638

the names of Scots serving overseas as mercenaries in foreign armies. In January 1639, after Hamilton attempted to dissolve the Glasgow Assembly, the leading Covenanter nobles – Rothes, Montrose, Balmerino, and Argyll – signed and distributed a letter telling the nation that Scotland was menaced by foreign armies that intended to conquer the nation and extinguish its religious and political liberties. Therefore, they went on to say, it was necessary for the Scottish people to prepare to defend themselves.

The January letter from the lords in Edinburgh ordered each shire to appoint three commissioners. Two of these men were to reside in Edinburgh to consult and to pass on instructions to the third commissioner, who was to remain in the shire. The lords ordered each presbytery to appoint a commissioner to transmit orders and news from the shire commissioner down to each parish. The ministers and commissioners in the parishes were to raise men, money, and food for the army.[22] In this way, Scottish society at every level was involved in the war effort. Anyone who resisted the mobilization could be silenced by the leading laird and ministers in his parish. Further, the property of people refusing to support the Covenanter cause was liable for confiscation.

The Covenanters also summoned Scots serving abroad to return home to defend country and Covenant, thus offering them work in their military profession. As the commissioners and nobles in the shires began to raise regiments for an army of 20,000 men, hundreds of Scottish professional soldiers returned home to train the recruits. The Covenanters allowed the nobles who raised regiments to command those units and to appoint the company commanders. However, it was Covenanter policy that the lieutenant colonel and sergeant major of each regiment was to be a professional soldier, as were the lieutenant and sergeants of each company. In this manner professional soldiers served in the key levels of command, facilitating the training and operation of the Scottish army.[23]

The Covenanters' call for the return of the professional soldiers paid off handsomely. Alexander Leslie, a field marshal in the Swedish army, and the most famous Scottish mercenary, returned home in late 1638. The Covenanters made him commander in chief of the army, in spite of his advanced age and physical infirmities. This was a brilliant move. Leslie's selection as commander prevented any noble from gaining primacy, thereby lessening the chances of factionalism among the nobility. Leslie became an ex officio member of the Tables, signing dispatches with the other members. The selection of Leslie to command had the further advantage that the other mercenaries were willing to follow him because of his proven success as a soldier.[24]

While the Covenanters did a tremendous job fielding an army in 1639, they ran into many problems. Money always was in short supply and they had to make special efforts to get the shires to pay their contributions. Merchants like William Dick in Edinburgh eased this situation by providing much of the cash needed to buy munitions in the Netherlands; but shortage of money was always a problem in Scottish military operations. In the January 1639 letter to the shires, the Covenanter leaders ordered the establishment of assessments based on the rents of each parish. Understanding that these assessments would take some time to collect, they borrowed 200,000 Scottish merks[25] from William Dick and began to mint silver and gold coins from bullion borrowed for the cause. In these ways as much as £500,000 (Scots) was raised to pay for the army in the first half of 1639.[26]

The Scots also found it difficult to supply their army with food. With never more than a few days of rations on hand, it would be hard for Leslie to maneuver against the English. During the coming campaign the parish commissioners gathered rations for the men and fodder for the animals in the region from Edinburgh to the English border, but the Covenanters did not have sufficient comestibles on hand to support a long war in 1639. Ultimately, the first Covenanter army was marginally trained, irregularly armed, poorly paid, and badly supplied.[27] Nonetheless, since the English did not know of these weaknesses, the Scots' efforts proved sufficient for their purposes.

English preparations and the war

Charles ran into similar difficulties trying to implement his strategy for the invasion of Scotland. Antrim was incapable of raising an army to lead from Ulster into western Scotland. He had neither money nor men. Thomas Wentworth, the Lord Deputy of Ireland, was unwilling to provide arms and munitions to a Catholic nobleman who planned to arm Irish Catholics. Antrim's tenants did not rush to risk their lives and fortunes in the efforts of the young courtier. Worse, Charles provided no material support and sent conflicting messages to Antrim and Wentworth about this prong of his invasion plan. After ten months of confusion and frustrated efforts the Antrim portion of the grand plan was in shambles.[28] Although Wentworth sent a garrison to Carlisle, the western design against Scotland failed to materialize.

Beginning in January 1639, the English Privy Council's war committee issued orders to the lord lieutenants in the counties to prepare the trained bands for mobilization. Each county was assigned a quota of men to provide for an army to be assembled at York in April. The Privy Council required the counties to pay for the soldiers' coat and conduct money and for their weapons. In this way, the Westminster government was not responsible for the cost of the royal army until its rendezvous in the north. While there were many irregularities in the selection of soldiers, and many members of the trained bands bought their way out of service by hiring a substitute, the English military system performed reasonably well in raising and arming more than 20,000 soldiers in 1639.[29] However, the selection and arming of men was only the first step required to create an effective military force.

Many of the soldiers lacked adequate practice with their weapons and few of their officers had experience with the challenges of training, feeding, and marching soldiers. Consequently, as the troops traveled north to Yorkshire, reports were received by the Privy Council of riots, robberies, and ribaldry committed by the ill-disciplined and often poorly fed soldiers. A fair amount of this aggressive behavior was directed against Catholics, indicating a strong current of anti-Catholicism in the English population. Most of the problems encountered in assembling the army, however, derived from the lack of an experienced officer corps.

By April, Charles had almost 15,000 soldiers near York, while Hamilton commanded another 3,500 in his fleet. Unfortunately for his hopes of victory, the king appointed the Earl of Arundel as commander in chief of the main army because that nobleman was one of the queen's favorites. Arundel had no military experience and, possibly worse, he was a Roman Catholic. His appointment outraged men like the Earl of Essex, who had military experience and was a staunch puritan. Making matters worse, Charles appointed another of Queen Henrietta Maria's favorites, the Earl of Holland, to command the cavalry, a position Essex had expected and for which he was certainly more qualified.[30] Such appointments hindered the efficiency of the army and gave credence to rumors about Charles's secret sympathies for Catholicism.

The king also summoned his nobles to a council in York in April, where he expected them to contribute money or soldiers to his cause, based upon their feudal obligations. When the nobles assembled, Charles was disappointed to find that few of them had armed followers or military experience.[31] This was in contrast to the martial vocation of so many of the Scottish lairds and the greater interest shown in things military by Scottish nobles. Worse, two leading puritan nobles, Lord Saye and Sele and Lord Brooke, refused to take the oath tendered by the king to his nobility.[32] Finding that there was nothing he could do to them legally, Charles let them retire to their homes. This incident encouraged the Scots to think that there were fissures in the English ruling classes.

As these political difficulties swirled around the king, his army came together. By mid April, training of the soldiers was beginning to affect positively their conduct and military aptitude. By using the trained bands, the king at least had a cadre of men familiar with their weapons and tactical formations. Around this core an army took shape. The king's councillors and servants had overcome major obstacles to find the money, men, and material needed for the army. Contrary to the views of some historians, Charles's army in the First Bishops' War was financed adequately, at least for a short war. Compared to the Covenanters' financial situation, the English soldiers were downright well provided for.

During the war the English exchequer provided at least £135,730 in cash for the pay of the army and another £176,000 for the navy, while ship-money revenues provided an additional £70,544 for the fleet. The total cash outlays of the exchequer in 1639 exceeded £600,000, with another £124,408 worth of tallies issued anticipating future revenues.[33] The outcome of the First Bishops' War was not determined by English financial difficulties or institutional breakdown. The armies of both sides suffered the same problem: neither government could sustain a prolonged struggle with their current fiscal practices. The Westminster government found the money needed to raise an army and the county officials raised and equipped the soldiers for the regiments. How the king used his army determined the outcome of the war of 1639.

As the English army assembled at York and the king met with his English nobles, dreadful news came from Scotland. The Covenanters had assumed the offensive in March, capturing the royal castles at Edinburgh, Dumbarton, and Dalkieth. Worse, the Marquis of Huntly had been out-smarted by Leslie and Montrose, who convinced Huntly to disband his 5,000-man royalist army and to surrender Aberdeen and his family to the Covenanters. This transpired before Hamilton could arrive in Aberdeen with his expeditionary force.[34] These developments demolished the king's multi-front strategy, leaving him in the position in which his only hope of bringing the Scots back to obedience was to defeat their main army. Consequently, the king started to march his army north, reaching Newcastle with his advance guard on 6 May.

By 30 May the royal army was concentrated on Birkhill, several miles west of Berwick, where the king awaited the advance of the Covenanters. As he waited he decided to modify his earlier peace terms. Therefore he sent Arundel and a detachment to Duns, Scotland, on 1 June, to spy out the land and to issue another proclamation to the Scots promising clemency if they abandoned their rebellion. Many people north and south of the border interpreted his new proclamation as a sign of vacillation and fear in the face of the approaching Scots army encouraged his foes and disheartened his followers.

Meanwhile, Leslie realized that he could not sustain the Scots army in the field for an extended period of time due to the lack of money and an inadequate logistical system. Therefore he pursued an offensive strategy that would either end in a decisive battle or call the king's bluff, bringing a negotiated settlement that would give the Scots the substance of their demands without bloodshed. Knowing that the English were camped near Berwick, Leslie sent a reconnaissance force to Kelso, twenty miles west. When Charles received word of this movement, on 3 June, he sent Holland with 4,000 men to investigate and possibly to dislodge the Scots from their positions close to the border. Holland set out on a very hot 4 June, marching on the north side of the Tweed toward Kelso. As he marched he failed to keep his cavalry and infantry together, allowing the horse to outrun the foot by miles. When he arrived in the vicinity of the Scottish force, he had only his cavalrymen.

Near Kelso, Holland sighted a small Scottish unit on top of a hill. He ordered his cavalry to advance, as the Scottish detachment withdrew. Holland followed the Scots as they rode toward trenches beyond the hill, but as he did so he perceived that there were thousands of Scottish troops awaiting him in battle array. Although his initial impulse was to attack, discretion soon became the better part of valor. Realizing that without infantry support his cavalry was very vulnerable against a combined force of horse and foot, Holland ordered a withdrawal. Leslie allowed him to do so unmolested.[35]

Some historians have concluded that Leslie did not intend to fight the English at Kelso or later at Duns Law.[36] This conclusion is not supported by the events of June 1639. Leslie understood, as a professional soldier, that when two armies faced off in battle array, as they had at Kelso, it is very likely that a battle will follow. Knowing that he could not sustain his army for long near the border, he understood that a stalemate could have been fatal for the Covenanter army. In such a situation, what course of action should he pursue with his army? If he invaded England he might unite the English against the Scots. To avoid a stalemate he needed to risk a maneuver that could result in a battle in Scotland. If the English took up the challenge and fought, the outcome would be determined by force of arms, a situation in which the Scots had a good chance of success. If the English backed down, the Covenanters might get a favorable political result. Leslie risked battle with the intention of fighting if necessary.

Lord Holland's retreat affected Charles's situation drastically by exposing English weaknesses without casting any light on the problems faced by the Scots. Rumors in the English camp exaggerated the size of the Scottish host, with some estimates reaching London that there were 40,000 armed Scots on the Tweed. Holland claimed that he was outnumbered at least three to one. In reality, he had faced no more than 5,000 Scots. Additionally, the Scots were short of supplies and probably outnumbered by Charles's army, which had recently been reinforced to a strength of about 18,000 foot and 3,000 horse.[37]

On 5 June, as the corrosive psychological affects of Holland's retreat swept the English camp, Leslie moved his army to Duns Law, just five miles northwest of the royal camp. As he did so, Charles fell victim to counsels of fear. Surrounded by nobles who for the most part did not want to fight the Scots on behalf of either their king or the episcopal system, Charles blinked in the face off between the armies. Instead of ordering an attack, he opened negotiations. Consequently the Scots won a bloodless strategic victory.

Leslie's victory came none too soon. In the north the clan of the Gordons, who were adherents of Lord Huntley, had risen against the Covenanters, falling on a small force of them at Turriff on 14 May. In the 'Trot of Turriff', the Gordons routed the Covenanters and occupied Aberdeen. This was the first significant military encounter in Britain and Ireland in what was to become a long series of wars. Although Montrose quickly marched north with a force and joined the Earl Marischal in driving them out of Aberdeen, the Gordons had demonstrated how fragile the situation was in Scotland. The threat from the royalists in Aberdeenshire did not disappear. In mid June, while the negotiations between the Covenanters and the king were in progress, Lord Aboyne, the son of the Marquis of Huntly, again seized Aberdeen, forcing Montrose to fight his way into the city across the Bridge of Dee. It was in the Covenanters' interest to settle with the king quickly, as long as such a settlement confirmed their control of the Scottish church and state.

The Pacification of Berwick, June 1639

Why did the king accept a negotiated settlement after having gone to so much effort to get an army to the border? Why did he negotiate with his rebellious subjects as if they constituted a legitimate government? Basically, he had lost confidence in his army and in his leading councillors, and he had come to accept Wentworth's advice to prepare a much stronger military response to the northern rebellion. He negotiated with the Covenanters with every intention of renewing the armed conflict after he gathered a better English army. He also thought he could use his charm and grace to split the Scottish leadership, making his military tasks easier. He would have been wiser to have forced a battle against the Scots then and there. It is far from certain who would have won, but the correlation of forces was never more in his favor than they were in June 1639.[38]

From 11 to 18 June, six commissioners from each side met to settle the terms of what is known as the Pacification of Berwick. At the first meeting Charles made a dramatic surprise entry, declaring that he would conduct the negotiations. It was one of his better moves because it prevented his English and Scottish subjects from turning the sessions into a discussion of their mutual grievances against his policies. The Scots demanded the king's recognition of the Glasgow assembly and its work in purging the Scottish kirk of prayer book and bishops. They offered to disband their army, but only if the king did the same and agreed to the convening of another assembly and a parliament.

The king countered by demanding that the Scots disband, return the royal castles of Edinburgh and Dumbarton, and end the meetings of the Tables. In return, he promised to demobilize and to agree that ecclesiastical matters should be determined in assemblies of the Kirk and civil matters settled in parliaments and 'inferior judicatories.' These assemblies and parliaments would meet 'yearly or so often as was necessary.'[39] The Scots saw the trap that Charles had set. The agreement for the convening of assemblies and parliaments 'yearly or as often as necessary' would allow the king to determine when it needed to meet. Additionally, Charles refused to ratify the acts of what he termed the 'pretended' assembly of Glasgow.

The Covenanters made most of the concessions, receiving verbal assurances from the king that could be interpreted as accepting the right of the next assembly to renew the decisions of the Glasgow assembly. The Scots were right not to trust the king. As he was negotiating with them, he was renewing Antrim's commission to invade western Scotland. Nonetheless, the Scots determined that the best deal they could get was the mutual disbandment of forces and the acceptance by the king of the roles of their assembly and parliament in religious and civil matters. Their other course of action was to resume hostilities, and this they resolved to do unless the king agreed to their minimum terms. However, on 18 June, the king agreed to call an assembly and a parliament to meet in August, promising to ratify the decisions of these national bodies.

Too much of the Berwick settlement was verbal, and too little written. Each side argued it had achieved its goal, which essentially was de facto sovereignty over Scotland. The Scots believed that their assemblies and parliaments would settle matters of church and state in a manner pleasing to the Scottish nation. Charles believed that he could use his constitutional position to veto their acts that did not please him. Unless he was willing to go to war immediately, the king could only have salvaged his position in the Scottish political structure by accepting a Presbyterian settlement, as the Earl of Montrose and others encouraged him to do. Then, with patience, he might have regained the alliance with the Scottish nobles against the clergy that had served his father so well.[40] Convinced royalists like Montrose and Wentworth, and later Edward Hyde, the Earl of Clarendon, never understood that Charles did not accept the notion of cooperating with his subjects. He saw himself as the Lord's anointed, destined to rule his peoples in the full sense of the word.

The Pacification of Berwick was signed on 18 June, and both sides demobilized. But the treaty soon was a dead letter, as each side held a very different account of the king's verbal assurances. By mid July the Covenanters refused to answer the king's summons of their fourteen key leaders to meet him at Berwick. Instead, six commissioners met with him from 17 to 20 July. Charles ordered them to return to Edinburgh and to bring the remaining eight leaders back to Berwick. Only two returned. This exchange convinced the king that it would be fruitless to attend the assembly and parliament in Edinburgh.

Relations between Charles and the Covenanters deteriorated steadily from this time on. Charles returned to London and, on 11 August, ordered the public burning of a copy of the Scots' account of the treaty. Concurrently, he recalled Thomas Wentworth from Ireland to serve as his chief advisor in London.[41] This decision was a fateful one. Wentworth was the king's most competent servant. He had written to Charles in June, advising him to play for time with the Scots until a more powerful force could be gathered for an assault on Scotland. Charles's recall of the Lord Deputy was a clear sign that he intended to resort to arms again in his struggle with the Covenanters. Wentworth arrived in London in October, just as the king suffered a major international embarrassment.

The assembly of Edinburgh met in August with Traquair presiding. Charles had ordered him to accept the Covenanters' demand that lay elders were to sit with the clergy in the assembly, but he was to avoid any resolution confirming the acts of the Glasgow assembly.[42] The assembly quickly resolved to abolish episcopacy and to reject the royal canons and liturgy. Traquair, amidst a joyous response by the assembly, accepted these resolutions. At this point, many Scots believed that the struggle was resolved favorably. This interpretation was quickly undermined when Traquair announced, at the assembly's last session, 'that the king would not accept the abolition of episcopacy as "unlawful within this Kirk," unless the illegality were defined as arising merely from its being "contrary to the constitution thereof."'[43] From the king's point of view this was essential. If he accepted the idea that bishops were illegal in Scotland, then logically they were illegal in England.

England's international position deteriorates

As Charles dealt with the Scots, England's relations with Holland, France, and Spain deteriorated. Charles's major foreign policy goal had been to help his sister Elizabeth's husband regain the Palatinate. His efforts in the 1620s had failed miserably. By 1639, he thought he could control the English Channel with his revitalized navy and affect the Spaniards' war effort against the Dutch by hindering or helping them send troops and money by sea to the Netherlands.

A test of his ability to play a pivotal role in the Bourbon-Habsburg struggle came in September 1639, when a Spanish fleet carrying troops and money to the Netherlands retreated into the Downs at the mouth of the River Thomas, with a Dutch squadron in pursuit. Charles saw a chance to extort money from either the Spanish or the French, depending on which nation was willing to pay for the support of his navy. After a month of negotiations, the Dutch attacked the Spanish Armada on 11 October, quickly capturing or destroying most of its vessels. The English Admiral Pennington was forced to watch this violation of English territorial waters because his fleet was too weak to intervene against the powerful Dutch squadron. Charles was humiliated. At the same time, his subjects cheered the destruction of the hated Spaniards.[44] Henceforth, Charles was unable to exercise significant influence in continental affairs.

English mobilization, again

The humiliation in the Downs was accompanied by a complete breakdown in relations between the king and the Covenanters. The Scots' parliament had ratified the acts of the assembly of Edinburgh in August. It also forced all Scots to subscribe to the Covenant, although a phrase was added to it that professed loyalty to the crown. The Edinburgh parliament levied a national tax to pay for the last war, while approving the retention of one regiment of the Covenanter army. Charles refused to accept these decisions, and the Scots refused to accept the idea that he could veto their parliamentary acts.

The return of Wentworth, soon to be Earl of Strafford, from Ireland set in motion English preparations for war. After advising the king to reject the decisions of the Scottish parliament, Wentworth and a committee developed a strategy they thought would lead to victory. This strategy again called for converging attacks on Edinburgh. An army of 9,000 men would attack western Scotland from Ireland. Another amphibious force would move into the Firth of Forth, while the main English army of 23,000 men would advance overland from Berwick.[45] The royal garrison in Edinburgh Castle was to threaten the Covenanters' rear, tying them down while the English armies mobilized.

The English made important changes from their previous mobilization. This time a royal army rather than an Irish nobleman's retainers was to be sent to Scotland from Ulster. The council in Dublin was to oversee the preparations of this army. Its rank and file were Roman Catholic, while the officers were Protestant. However, its mobilization was delayed until the spring of 1640 due to a shortage of money. The makeup of the English army also differed from the first war. This army and the amphibious force that was to operate against eastern Scotland were to be raised through conscription, rather than through the mobilization of the trained bands. Most English counties were to provide a quota of pressed men for the regiments. The northern trained bands again were to defend the border, while the army mustered in Newcastle. The council reinforced Berwick and Carlisle as well.

Money was again a crucial determinant of how fast the royal forces could be mobilized. On 10 January 1640, the king's war council established the army at ten infantry and six cavalry regiments. Each foot regiment was to be composed of ten companies of 100 men each, while each horse regiment was to contain 500 troopers. A February report estimated that this force would cost £382,611, while the cost of equipping the artillery train was estimated to be £21,285.[46] Additional large sums were needed for the garrisons in Edinburgh, Berwick, and Carlisle, and for the operating costs of the fleets the king expected to play a large part in his strategy.

How could such sums be raised? The crown had already pledged current and future revenues to repay the costs of the last war. Strafford stepped forward, pledging a loan of £20,000 to the king. His example encouraged other members of the privy council to loan the government another £180,000. The king asked the City of London to loan £100,000, while the council expected the counties to pay for the costs of equipping the soldiers. The privy council also issued ship-money assessments totaling £210,000 for 1640, while the customs farmers were asked to loan the crown £250,000.

Knowing that these sums would only suffice to mobilize the forces needed for a major war, but were insufficient to feed and maintain those forces, Strafford convinced the king to convene an English parliament for the first time in eleven years. Strafford believed that a parliament would be willing to grant subsidies before it was allowed to discuss grievances. These subsidies, spread over three years, would give the crown the collateral it needed to raise cash for the war. Charles accepted Strafford's advice, especially after Strafford suggested that he return to Ireland and convene an Irish parliament, which he was certain would provide subsidies to pay for the Irish army.[47] The news that Charles was going to call a parliament was greeted favorably throughout the country. In the meantime, as writs were sent out for an April meeting, the government went about its business of fielding its armies.

Remarkably, the Westminster government raised enough money to field two armies in 1640 (one in York and the other in Ulster). The exchequer provided Sir William Uvedale, the Treasurer at War, with £352,360 from February to November for the main army and another £50,000 to William Payton, the Treasurer of the Army in Ireland. The Treasurers of the Navy received £121,953 from the exchequer and the sheriffs who were collecting ship-money. Funds were provided to the Ordnance Office to pay for the initial outlays for the artillery train and to the navy's Surveyor of Victuals to buy food for the fleet.[48] Charles I's failure in the Second Bishops' War was not due to shortages of money.[49]

The greatest problems with the English mobilization of 1640 were due to the nature of the forces the crown decided to raise, the slowness with which they were fielded, and the poor way in which the king commanded his army. The decision to use conscripts rather than to mobilize the trained bands meant that the soldiers were untrained and usually the dregs of society. Their officers found the men undisciplined and often mutinous, even before they arrived in the north. Complaints about robberies, murder, and riots flooded into the council from the counties through which the troops marched.[50] None the less, the royal army did assemble in Selby, Yorkshire, and the Ordnance Office shipped the artillery train to Hull.

The Westminster government had learned a lot from the mobilization of the army of 1639. This time the general officers understood the profession of arms. Algernon Percy, Earl of Northumberland, served as Lord General, ably assisted by Lord Edward Conway as cavalry commander. Both of these men had served with the Dutch army, and Northumberland was one of Charles's most dependable administrators. The professional soldier Sir John Conyers commanded the Berwick garrison, ensuring that the English did not lose that critical post before the army assembled at Selby (see map 3, p. 33).

The council successfully fed, armed, and equipped the 1640 armies. It established magazines with two months' rations for the army at Berwick and Newcastle. It purchased 5,550 tents, contracted for the brewing of 145 tuns of beer per week in Berwick, and established ovens there and in Newcastle to bake 23,000 pounds of bread daily to feed the troops. The Ordnance Office ordered 7,000 muskets from

Flanders and 10,000 more from English arms makers. The Lord Lieutenants provided 1,300 horses to haul the artillery and the 100 wagons needed to haul the tents for the army.[51] Efforts were made to reinforce the Edinburgh Castle garrison with English soldiers and food and munitions sufficient to withstand a six months' siege. In this endeavor the English failed.

Scottish mobilization

The Scots were in better shape for war in 1640 than the English. They were united politically and had widespread support for the war. The Scottish parliament met from 2 to 11 June, confirming the decisions of the previous Edinburgh assembly and parliament. The parliament established an executive to replace the Tables, a body known as the committee of the estates. This body had the authority to act when a parliament was not in session. It could levy taxes, maintain and command armies, and direct and organize the entire kingdom. Argyll increasingly dominated the Covenanter cause. The Covenanters crushed royalist opposition before it organized. As the parliament met, Colonel Robert Monro and the Earl Marischal thoroughly cowed potential resistance from the Gordons and other anti-Covenanters in Aberdeenshire, while Argyll led 4,000 Campbells through the territory of the Earl of Atholl, disarming any-one suspected of disloyalty to the Covenant. As a result, the chances of a royalist rising in support of an English invasion diminished dramatically.[52]

As the committee of estates ordered each shire to send one fourth of the eligible fighting men to the rendezvous of the army, the Scots parliament appointed Alexander Leslie, now Earl of Leven, to command the army. It was easier to raise an army in 1640 because of the experiences of 1639. The Scots had kept one regiment of infantry on duty along with many of their officers (on half pay). These officers drilled the militia during the spring, seeing to it that the militiamen knew how to use firearms purchased in the Netherlands. The Scots again used the system of shire and parish committees and commissioners to coordinate the mobilization.[53] By early August, over 20,000 Scots soldiers were assembling near Coldstream, on the border with England.

To provide adequate financial support for its army, the Scottish parliament enacted a national tax known as the tenth, or tenth penny. This tax was more equitable than previous levies because it attempted to tax all kinds of income. Non-Covenanters were fined, encouraging many to remain loyal to the cause while soaking up money that might have funded royalist opposition.[54] To bridge the time from when the taxes were assessed to when they were collected, the Scots borrowed £100,000 (Scots) in Edinburgh, giving Leven money to pay and feed his soldiers. Through such measures the resources were found to raise and arm the Covenanter army. This army was well-officered by a solid core of professional soldiers and, just as important, was composed of men whose commitment to the cause stood in stark contrast to the attitudes of the conscripts of the English army.

The Irish and English parliaments

Once preparations for war were underway in England, Strafford returned to Dublin to preside over the Irish parliament on 16 March. Within a week, he had convinced it to grant the crown four subsidies totaling £180,000 over a period of three years. The following day the Lords Justices ordered the recruitment of 9,000 soldiers to commence. The English exchequer provided cash to defray the costs of initial recruitment until the Irish subsidies began to flow into the treasury.[55] Encouraged by his success, Strafford returned to England to manage the English parliament set to convene on 13 April.

The Lord Keeper had sent out the writs for the election of the parliament in December 1639. For the next four months the political nation selected its represent-atives amidst a great deal of debate about the conduct of government over the past eleven years. The king's decision to convene a parliament had raised hopes that grievances would be aired and corrected, and that the counselors who had advised the king on matters such as ship-money could be confronted.

The elections came when the county leaders were immersed in the work of impressing soldiers, raising coat and conduct money, and collecting the £210,000 of ship-money that had been assessed. The fact that county government continued to function with all of these burdens shows that the Caroline government had not collapsed. But there were increasing signs of strain, protest, and distress throughout England. For example, by April 1640, the sheriffs had collected only eighteen per cent of the ship-money levy of 1639, compared to ninety-one per cent of the 1638 levy.[56] Less that £9,000 of the £210,000 assessed for 1640 had been collected by the time the Short Parliament met, indicating a stiffening of resistance to the tax and a hope that the parliament would find a way to eliminate it altogether. Sheriffs and constables found it exceedingly difficult to raise coat and conduct money for the impressed men, reporting in many instances that these sums exceeded the ship-money they were trying to collect.

A number of English nobles and gentry also were corresponding with the Covenanters and distributing their propaganda in England. These trends were most dangerous because they undermined the crown's position when the king needed the support of the English nobility and gentry most. Pamphlets against the military efforts found wide circulation. By early 1640, domestic protest against the royal efforts to raise money and men had merged with Scottish propaganda about the Catholic elements in Charles's policies and reforms. The king's efforts to suppress or counter Scottish and Puritan propaganda failed, while his dealings with the Spanish increased fears that a Catholic plot to use Spanish troops and money to crush Protestantism was afoot.[57]

Strafford was correct in his judgment that the king needed parliamentary revenue to invade Scotland. The financial measures already undertaken provided enough money to raise and sustain an army for a short while in the north, but not enough to carry on a long war and an invasion of Scotland. Yet the First Bishops' War had convinced the English and the Scots that this war could only be settled on the battlefield. Thus, Strafford hoped to harness English resources for a long war. He felt that, given his experience as a member of the parliaments of the 1620s, and his successes in Ireland, he could manage the English parliament so that it would grant twelve subsidies (roughly £720,000) before it turned to deal with the members' grievances.

Strafford, however, was out of touch with his countrymen due to his seven years in Ireland. He also no longer sat in the Commons since his elevation to the peerage. The management of the House of Commons was left to Sir John Finch, Lord Keeper, and the leading judge who had ruled in favor of ship-money. Clarendon, an active participant in the parliament, described Finch as 'a man exceedingly obnoxious to the people upon the business of ship-money; and not of reputation and authority enough to continence and advance the king's service.'[58]

The Short Parliament met on 13 April, amidst heightened expectations for an amicable settlement of the issues that had aggravated the nation and fears of Catholic machinations by the queen and in the new army. After the king, who suffered from a severe stutter, greeted the opening joint session of the two houses, Finch read a long oration that included a plea for the immediate grant of money to carry out the war that he said had been thrust upon England by the Scots. In return, he promised that parliament would have all the time it needed to discuss grievances. Finch also announced that a bill was being prepared to approve the crown's collection of tonnage and poundage retroactively. This was the only major concession offered by the king. It was important because the collection of the customs had been granted to Charles for just one year upon his accession, and his continued collection of tonnage and poundage since, without parliamentary sanction, was a major grievance. Finch said nothing about ship-money.[59]

Even though the king dramatically produced a letter from the Covenanters to Louis XIII of France, that he interpreted as an act of treason by the Scots, the Commons was not moved to rapid approval of fiscal measures. Instead, after five days of organizational activity, the Commons turned to discuss its grievances. In the midst of these activities a parliamentary leader of immense capability emerged when John Pym gave a two-hour speech detailing the grievances against the eleven years of Charles's 'personal rule'. Pym's moderate tone and calm delivery enhanced his message, which was that the king's and Laud's reforms had violated English traditions. He described the collection of ship-money and of the customs without parliamentary approval as unconstitutional. He also discussed Catholic threats to the church. The Commons responded the next day by constituting itself as a committee of the whole House to discuss royal policies and actions.[60]

On 24 April, in an ill-advised effort to get the financial measures to the top of the agenda, Charles made a speech in the Lords stressing the dangers of delay in the face of a possible Scottish invasion. This speech and Strafford's political skills convinced the Lords that they should send a resolution to the Commons encouraging the lower House to deal with the subsidies before it turned to the discussion of the nation's ills. This resolution caused the Commons to unite against interference in its business. After a joint session on 25 April, the Commons decried the violations of its privileges and resolved to secure redress of grievances before it dealt with requests for money.

Things then steadily got worse for the king. He aggravated the Commons with a message on 29 April reiterating his promise to discuss grievances, but only after the House dealt with financial matters. During the discussion of this message, on 4 May, Secretary of State Henry Vane made things worse by offering to give up ship-money as an act of royal grace in return for the prompt approval of twelve subsidies.[61] Whether or not the king knew of this offer beforehand, it focused the Commons on the issue of unconstitutional taxation. Why, they asked, should parliament trade subsidies to the king in return for his cancellation of a tax that had not been approved by parliament? They should not do so, was the conclusion of a majority of the Commons.[62] With the political tide in the parliament running strongly against him, Charles dissolved the assembly on 5 May. The Second Bishops' War was now solely his to fund and fight.

The Second Bishops' War

With tremendous efforts, the Scots and English fielded armies. The Scots moved faster and more surely than the English, due in large part to their greater political coherence and the availability of a trained officer cadre for their army. Knowing they could not sustain a long war, the Scots determined to invade England. This was an audacious move since Leven and the committee of estates knew that a Scottish invasion of England might unite the English against them. But they understood that the failure of the Short Parliament to provide money to the crown, along with the emergence of an effective opposition to the king, had gravely weakened Charles's situation.

On 20 August, the Scots, led by Leven, crossed the Tweed near Coldstream and marched south toward the Tyne (see map 3). To their northeast was Berwick, held by an English garrison. To the east lord Conway had about 12,000 English troops whom he had marched north from Selby, in Yorkshire. The Earl of Northumberland, the English Lord General, was unable to command due to illness, and Strafford was confined to bed by a painful bout of gout, leaving Conway as the English commander in the north. Charles, hearing that the Scots were moving toward the border, rode to Yorkshire. However, he and Strafford consistently underestimated the speed with which the Scots maneuvered.

By crossing the Tweed at Coldstream, Leven left Conway uncertain as to where he would strike first. He could turn west to seize Carlisle or east to attack Berwick. The Scots could also head to Newcastle, taking at one blow the seaport and region that was the source for much of London's coal supply and the major base for English military operations.

Leven chose to march toward Newcastle, by way of Newburn on the River Tyne. This was a superb move, since possession of Newcastle would make Berwick untenable for the English and would split the English forces in the north. Conway anticipated this maneuver, but he sent troops to fortify the Newburn crossing too late for them to prepare properly to stop the Scots. On the morning of 28 August,

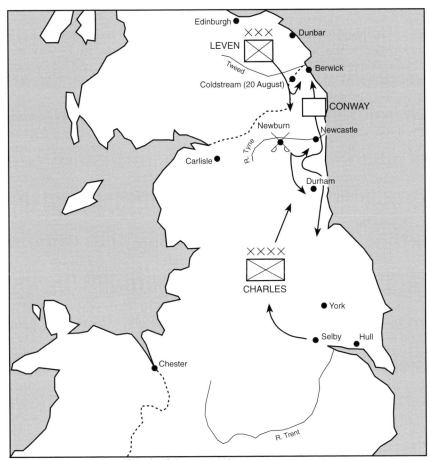

Map 3 Leven's invasion of England, August 1640

Leven sent his advanced guard across the river under the supporting fire of his artillery. Although the English repulsed the first attack, Leven reinforced his assault and placed a cannon in the steeple of the Newburn church from which that gun brought galling fire into the English trenches (see map 3).

After suffering several hundred casualties, the English infantry fled. Conway ordered his cavalry to counterattack, but it proved too little too late to stop the Scots from establishing a bridgehead. Once that was done, Conway ordered a retreat rather than face the much larger Scottish army with his detachment of 4,000 men. During the withdrawal, his cavalry panicked and rode over many of his fleeing infantry. The Battle of Newburn ended the fighting of the Second Bishops' War.

Charles arrived at York too late to affect Conway's handling of the action at Newburn or his feeble defense of Newcastle. As he came north the news got worse. Dumbarton fell to the Covenanters on 29 August, and Edinburgh and Caerlaverock

Castles surrendered during the next two weeks. By 4 September, the Scots had occupied Durham without a fight, as Conway retreated south. The king found himself in a situation in which he could not count on his army in battle, and he could not raise the money needed to fight a war of attrition against the Scots without the help of parliament. As Gardiner noted, 'the army was without heart or discipline. The nation was equally without heart or discipline.'[63]

The Scots exploited their success by enveloping and capturing Newcastle. Conway anticipated this move and retreated south with about 12,000 men. Conway saved his army, but lost Newcastle. Scottish success transformed the strategic situation. The Scots isolated the English garrison in Berwick and established a firm base in northern England. Their capture of Newcastle gave the Covenanters control of London's coal supply as well, providing them with important leverage in their discussions with the English in coming months. By seizing the initiative, the Scots prevented Charles from uniting his army in time to defend the northern counties, highlighting his inability to defend England. This humiliation denied the king the political initiative with the Scots and an increasingly bold English opposition.

Leven's advance unhinged English plans for converging attacks on Scotland. Lacking sufficient forces to drive the Scots out of England, let alone invade Scotland, Charles agreed to another armistice. This time the Scots demanded possession of Newcastle as security for a proper peace. They also demanded that the English pay £850 per day for the maintenance of their army in England until conclusion of a treaty. This last provision made it impossible for Charles to avoid calling another English parliament, since only parliamentary taxation could pay the Covenanters' army. Thus the king was forced by his military defeat to summon the Long Parliament.

Charles recognized that for the time being he could not rectify the military situation. He needed to find enough money to pay his northern army and keep it in existence, and he had to find the resources to pay and ship his army from Ulster to either Scotland or northern England. Consequently he decided to maneuver politically in England so as to gain the support of the English nobility and gentry in his efforts against the Scots.

The repercussions of Charles's resort to arms, 1639–40

During the first ten years of his reign Charles I tried to carry out political and religious reforms in his three kingdoms. He sought uniformity of religious worship with Laud's English reforms and with the canons and liturgy that he imposed on Scotland. He made changes in the Scottish and Irish governments, attempting to improve efficiency and enhance the crown's ability to control those kingdoms. Wentworth accomplished remarkable results in Ireland from 1633 to 1639, enhancing the crown's revenue and power. The king proved that he could rule England without the interference of parliaments, and he won the court cases that gave him the ability to tax Englishmen with non-parliamentary taxes. However, in Scotland, after a series of successful administrative reforms, the king ran into a firestorm of protest over his attempts to reform the church.

The way in which Charles responded to the Scottish protests led to the Bishops' Wars. He consistently refused to give ground gracefully. He alienated his Scottish subjects and then made the fateful decision to use English and Irish forces to crush the Scots. This decision spread discontent and destabilized his other kingdoms because of the ways in which the king raised the resources to field his armies. Once his armies deployed toward the Scottish borders in 1639 and 1640, the king proved militarily inept, frittering away his chances to force a decisive battle. His humiliating defeats further undercut his position in England and Ireland, as did his bungling foreign policy.

Resort to war forced Charles to summon the parliaments that further destabilized his English and Irish governments. He found himself in a position in which he could not win his wars without parliamentary cooperation, but the king was unwilling to pay the political price for such assistance. His unsuccessful Bishops' wars proved even more costly politically than financially, leading directly to the summoning of the Long Parliament and the English Revolution of 1640–41.[64]

Notes

1   Clarendon, *History of the Rebellion*, i: 110.
2   D. Stevenson, *The Scottish Revolution, 1637–44* (New York, 1973), 35–41.
3   Ibid., 35–7; Gardiner, *History of England*, vii: 276–8.
4   Stevenson, *Scottish Revolution*, 36.
5   Gardiner, *History of England*, vii: 278–80.
6   D. Stevenson, 'The King's Scottish Revenues and the Covenanters, 1625–1651', *HJ*, xvii (1974), 20–30.
7   Clarendon, *History of the Rebellion*, i: 87–8.
8   Gardiner, *History of England*, vii: 279.
9   Ibid., 286–90.
10 Stevenson, *Scottish Revolution*, 44–6.
11 Clarendon, *History of the Rebellion*, i: 110.
12 Stevenson, *Scottish Revolution*, 51–61.
13 Gardiner, *History of England*, viii: 315–20.
14 Ibid., 319.
15 C. Wedgwood, *The King's Peace* (New York, 1995 edn.), 184–6.
16 Stevenson, *Scottish Revolution*, 79–87.
17 Ibid., 95–7.
18 Gardiner, *History of England*, viii: 345; M. Fissel, *The Bishops' Wars: Charles I's Campaigns Against Scotland, 1638–1640* (Cambridge, 1994), 112–16.
19 Fissel, *Bishops' Wars*, 34–7; Sharpe, *Charles I*, 795.
20 Fissel, *Bishops' Wars*, 3–16; J. Ohlmeyer, *Civil War and Restoration in the Three Stuart Kingdoms: The Career of Randal MacDonnell, the Marquis of Antrim, 1609–1683* (Cambridge, 1993), 77–80.
21 Fissel, *Bishops Wars*, 37–8.
22 Stevenson, *Scottish Revolution*, 101–30.
23 S. Reid, *Scots Armies of the 17th Century* (Belfast, 1988), 10–12.
24 C. Terry, *Papers Relating to the Army of the Solemn League and Covenant, 1643–1647* (Edinburgh, 1917), i: ix–xviii.
25 D. Stevenson, 'The Financing of the Cause of the Covenanters, 1638–51', *Scottish Historical Review*, li (1972), a merk equaled 13s. 4d. Scots and a Scottish pound equaled 1s. 8d. sterling.
26 Ibid., 89–90.

27 Sharpe, *Charles I*, 805–8; Fissel, *Bishops' Wars*, 30.

28 Ohlmeyer, *Civil War and Restoration*, 86–9.

29 Gardiner, *History of England*, ix: 24.

30 Ibid., viii: 385–86.

31 Sharpe, *Charles I*, 799; L. Stone, *The Causes of the English Revolution* (New York, 1972), 114–17.

32 Gardiner, *History of England*, viii: 11–12; Fissel, *Bishops' Wars*, 19–21.

33 P[ublic] R[ecord] O[ffice], E351/292, 295, 297, and 2282; F. Dietz, *English Public Finance, 1558–1641*, (New York 1932), 285–6.

34 Gardiner, *History of England*, ix: 1–5.

35 Ibid., 23–4; Fissel, *Bishops' Wars*, 22–8.

36 Fissel, *Bishops' Wars*, 30.

37 Gardiner, *History of England*, ix: 20–9.

38 Fissel, *Bishops' Wars*, 30–3.

39 Stevenson, *Scottish Revolution*, 154–5.

40 Gardiner, *History of England*, ix: 52–4.

41 H. Kearney, *Strafford in Ireland, 1633–41* (Cambridge, 1989 edn.), 188.

42 Stevenson, *Scottish Revolution*, 162–4.

43 Gardiner, *History of England*, ix: 50.

44 Ibid., 60–71.

45 Fissel, *Bishops' Wars*, 41–4.

46 C[alendar of] S[tate] P[apers], D[omestic], *1639–04*, (London, 1891), 317–18, 437, 447.

47 B. Whitelocke, *Memorials of English Affairs* (London, 1682), 30.

48 PRO, E351/293–4; AO1/1705/85–6; E351/2444–5.

49 Dietz, *English Public Finance*, 285–6.

50 *CSPD, 1640*, 500–5, 580–3.

51 *CSPD, 1639–40*, 368, 398–9, 413, 451, 586.

52 Stevenson, *Scottish Revolution*, 192–201.

53 Reid, *Scots Armies*, 1–13.

54 Stevenson, ' Financing the Cause of the Covenanters'. 92–5.

55 PRO, E351/294.

56 *CSPD, 1640*, 140.

57 Sharpe, *Charles I*, 795–847.

58 Clarendon, *History of the Rebellion*, i: 131.

59 Sharpe, *Charles I*, 861–3.

60 Clarendon, *History of the Rebellion*, i: 133–34; Sharpe, *Charles I*, 865–7; J. Hexter, *The Reign of King Pym* (Cambridge, 1941).

61 Sharpe, *Charles I*, 869–70.

62 Clarendon, *History of the Rebellion*, i: 135–7.

63 Gardiner, *History of England*, ix: 197.

CHAPTER TWO

The outbreak of the English and Irish Revolutions, 1640–1642

After the Scots' victory at Newburn and their occupation of Newcastle, Charles sought to buy time to rectify his strategic situation. He accepted the Covenanters' offer for a cease-fire and convened a 'Great Council' of his English nobles in York, on 24 September. The armistice prevented the Covenanters from marching further south, giving his army time to prepare for the resumption of hostilities, which was his main goal.[1] By summoning a council of nobles he provided a forum in which they could discuss their concerns and in which he could solicit their ideas about how the Scottish 'invaders' could be driven out of England.

The truce with the Scots took time to negotiate. The king initially insisted on a return to the terms of the Pacification of Berwick, a situation that would have led to the disbandment of the armies and the return of Edinburgh and Dumbarton castles to royal control. The Covenanters rejected those terms, insisting that any basis for an armistice must be the recognition that additional issues had arisen. Meanwhile, the Scots kept their army in England, paid for by the English. Charles was forced to accept the Scots' terms for the cease-fire, especially after most of his nobles at the Great Council insisted that he do so. The Covenanters thus linked their army's status as the dominant military force in Britain with the political situation in London. Only an English parliament could provide the money needed to pay that army, let alone the large sums Charles needed to maintain his army in Yorkshire.

Charles accepted the Scots' terms and summoned an English parliament to meet on 3 November. In the armistice, signed at Ripon on 21 October, the king promised to pay £850 per day for the maintenance of the Scots army until a final settlement was negotiated in London. As Charles was dealing with his English nobles and the Covenanters in Yorkshire, news reached him of rioting in London and of an unfavorable outcome in the mayoral election.[2] The riots were directed at his religious and political policies. This news was accompanied by a petition from Londoners protesting his religious innovations. Making the situation worse, twelve English nobles presented the king with a remonstrance detailing their dissatisfactions with royal policies and actions. These developments indicated the fusion of discontents in the south with the military and political challenges in the north.

The Irish situation deteriorates

The Irish parliament that met in March 1640 had proven pliant to Strafford, granting subsidies to pay for the Irish army that was to have invaded Scotland. By July that army was coming together, although not as swiftly as hoped since the money to pay for its recruitment had been slow in coming. Eventually the English Treasurer at War sent £50,000 to Ireland to pay for the initial costs of the force. A majority of the soldiers were Catholic, while most of the officers were Protestants.[3] This army never got a chance to show its mettle. None the less, the fact that the king was planning to use an Irish army against Scotland was a major propaganda weapon used by the Covenanters to prove that Charles and his agents were involved in a Catholic conspiracy.

Strafford's governance of Ireland had rested on his manipulation of the major political factions in Ireland. These factions were defined by ethnicity, religion, and their antagonism toward each other.[4] The Old Irish were Catholics whose families had resided in Ireland before the English invasions of the twelve century. The English had steadily worked to dispossess these 'native' Irish, a process accelerated by the Elizabethan wars.[5] The second faction, the Old English, were Catholics who traced their ancestry to Englishmen who had arrived in Ireland before the Reformation. Their loyalty generally had been to the crown and they saw their interests as English. The third major faction were the New English, Protestant Englishmen who had come to Ireland since 1540 and who benefited from the confiscation of land made by the Tudors and early Stuarts.[6] The Old Irish and Old English often intermarried, and many Old Irish families saw themselves as Old English, or Anglo-Irish. Finally, thousands of Presbyterian Scots had established themselves in Ulster during the reign of James I, at the expense of the Ulster Irish, who lost much of their property to the newcomers.[7]

The Long Parliament and the breakdown of consensus

The Long Parliament met on 3 November 1640 under the shadows of civil disorder and war. Throughout the summer reports of violence in England had circulated. Apprentices attacked Laud's residence at Lambeth. Men who had been conscripted for military service desecrated churches and destroyed enclosures as they marched north. Officers or magistrates who tried to restore order often found themselves attacked. Taxpayers increasingly refused to pay ship-money or local assessments. These developments throughout England indicated that 'the complex nexus of command, consent, and compliance had fractured, and there were growing suspicions that not all even of the magisterial class would strive to repair it.'[8]

The threat of renewed warfare darkened the horizon. Three armies were on foot in Ireland and Britain, requiring massive amounts of money to sustain until a political settlement could be achieved between Charles I and the Scots. How to provide money for these armies was one of the greatest challenges faced by parliament. The Scottish army was, in a sense, the army of the English parliamentary opposition to

Charles that had emerged under John Pym's leadership. The Covenanters and Pym shared the belief that Charles had tried to subvert the Protestant faith in Britain.[9] Charles's and Strafford's plan to use an Irish army, along with the shift in Stuart foreign policy toward an alliance with the traditional Spanish enemy against the Protestant Dutch, reinforced the belief that such a conspiracy existed.[10]

Strafford was the focal point of the Long Parliament's dissatisfaction with royal policies. Pym and others portrayed him as the evil counselor who had led the king astray. Strafford's enemies in Ireland reinforced the assault against him by accusing him of tolerating Irish Catholics and of recruiting Catholic soldiers.[11] By 7 November, when Sir John Clotworthy spoke in the Commons at length about Strafford's arbitrary and pro-Catholic rule in Ireland, it was clear that parliament was going to punish the king's advisors before it turned to financial matters.

The Covenanters' agenda for the English parliament included the punishment of Strafford and Laud for their roles in the king's efforts to crush Scottish resistance. The history of the Long Parliament makes little sense unless we take into account the triangular relationship between the king, the Covenanters, and the parliamentary opposition in the first year of the Long Parliament. The Scots needed parliament to destroy those royal advisors who had played a prominent role in the Bishops' Wars. They also needed the Long Parliament to remain in session until a peace had been arranged with the king and their army paid for by English taxation. They sought the destruction of Strafford and Laud, the abolition of episcopacy in England and Ireland, and the future restraint on the king's freedom of action.[12]

Charles hoped to convince parliament to grant sufficient taxes so that his government's financial credit could be restored. This was crucial to his plan to resort to arms against the Scots a third time.[13] He had been able to borrow just £50,000 in London in the past three months for his army. Only the London financial community could provide the cash the king needed. But Londoners' purses were closed until parliament secured such loans with future taxation. Charles also believed that Englishmen would rally round his efforts to expel the Scots by force. He made this clear in his initial speech from the throne to parliament when he referred to the Scots as 'rebels', a term he had to explain away as he realized the extent of the support the Covenanters enjoyed.[14] The king could not dissolve parliament until he got the money he needed.

Pym and the parliamentary opposition counted on the Scottish army to prevent the king from dismissing them before they foiled the popish plot and punished the crown's evil advisors. Thus, rather than turning to fiscal matters or local grievances, Pym initiated an attack against Strafford. Following his and Clotworthy's recitations of Strafford's attempts to subvert English religion and liberties, the Commons appointed committees to delve into Strafford's abuses and actions during the Second Bishops' War. These committees were not to meet until 12 November, indicating that Pym planned to move methodically against Strafford and to impeach him only after a case was established.

Strafford threw this process into disarray 10 November by advising Charles to seize the initiative by accusing the opposition leaders of treason. Strafford proposed to launch this campaign in the Lords on 11 November, coincidentally the day on which Charles was going to review his loyal garrison of the Tower of London. Strafford assumed that a coup against the parliamentary leaders would be popular in a nation partially occupied by a foreign army. This assumption was ill founded. Pym got word of the plan on 10 November and convinced the Commons to demand that the Lords order Strafford's arrest. Pym and a Commons delegation marched to the Lords and persuaded them to order Strafford's arrest.[15] Pym then launched Strafford's impeachment without the evidence needed to prove his treason.

For six months the major preoccupation of the Long Parliament was the impeachment, trial, and attainder of Strafford. Throughout these proceedings, Scottish commissioners kept pressure on the English to destroy Strafford, their most dangerous enemy. In the process, the parliamentarians relegated to secondary interest the reform of government finances, while the Scottish army remained in England to protect the parliamentary opposition from violent action by Charles.[16]

After Strafford was committed to the Tower, Scottish and parliamentary commissioners began negotiations to settle the recent war. Charles attempted to insert himself into this process, but the Covenanters and parliamentary commissioners refused to allow the king into the conferences. This startling display of power by parliament was one of many actions during the next six months that indicated a significant growth in parliamentary authority. This power was no longer confined to discussing grievances and passing laws. Parliament now was assuming the tasks of government, using special committees and the committee of the whole House of Commons to carry out judicial and executive functions.[17]

The Long Parliament also made some progress in its efforts to redress the more outstanding grievances of its members. The Commons resolved, on 7 December, that ship-money was illegal unless sanctioned by a parliament, although nothing was done to replace the revenue needed for the navy. On 10 December, it passed an appropriations bill for two subsidies, worth roughly £130,000, to pay the soldiers in the north. Money for the armies remained a major concern during the first six months of the Long Parliament, especially after the Scots requested £785,628, of which they were willing to forgive £271,500.[18]

Most of the energy of the House of Commons, however, continued to be directed toward removing the king's evil counselors. As the case against Strafford was being prepared in November, the Commons summoned Sir Francis Windebank to explain why he had issued seventy-four letters of royal protection for Roman Catholics in the past year. Windebank fled to France rather than face imprisonment. On 21 December the Commons interrogated Lord Keeper Finch about his role in the ship-money cases of the 1630s. Finch soon retreated to Holland aboard a Royal Navy vessel.[19]

As they hounded the king's agents, the parliamentarians also declared that all canons passed by the Church of England's Convocation without parliamentary approval were null and void. At the same time, London presented its first 'Root and Branch' petition, demanding an end to episcopacy. On 18 December 1640, the Commons impeached Archbishop Laud for treason: the Lords committed him to the Tower immediately. These actions showed the resolve of Pym and others to prevent the further success of Arminianism in the English church, a trend that they saw as part of the drift to Rome, because of its rejection of the doctrine of predestination. However, the Root and Branch petition was tabled, on Pym's instigation, because he saw that there was considerable parliamentary resistance to the abolition of episcopacy.[20]

Charles looked for ways to resist his opponents. One way was to seek a marriage between his daughter and the eldest son of the Prince of Orange, hoping the Dutch might assist him against the parliamentarians. Charles also gave offices to leading parliamentarians in the Commons and Privy Council seats to opposition peers. These moves failed because the king was unwilling to allow these men into his inner cabinet council where he discussed most decisions.[21] Consequently, the opposition became convinced that he did not seriously consider making concessions.

Affairs between the king and his opponents took a nastier turn in January 1641, when Sir Walter Erle submitted a report to the Commons about the royal army in Ireland. This 9,000-man force remained ready to strike wherever the king should direct. Charles refused to disband this army until parliament found a way to pay off the armies in northern England. Erle returned to the House of Commons in February with accusations that Strafford had intended to land the Irish army in Wales the previous summer and that the Catholic Earl of Worcester had planned to meet that army in Milford Haven with English Catholic supporters.[22] This revelation came shortly on the heels of another discussion in the House about the Root and Branch petition.

During the discussions about the abolition of episcopacy a new political grouping emerged in the House of Commons. This group included Sir Edward Hyde, Lucius Viscount Falkland, Lord George Digby, and Sir John Culpepper. These men had consistently supported the moves made to punish the king's advisors and to abolish ship-money, but they opposed the elimination of the bishops. Their position was that the bishops should be denied all temporal authority but remain in their ecclesiastical positions. They supported the use of the Book of Common Prayer and rejected the establishment of Presbyterianism in England.[23] Here was a group the king could have worked with, as he was to do in 1642. However, in 1641 he refused to make timely concessions about the roles of the bishops, consequently failing to exploit the potential rift in parliamentary ranks.

Strafford paid for the king's failure to create a parliamentary following. When Charles refused to disband the Irish army, parliament enacted measures that seriously curtailed royal power. On 15 February 1641, the Lords passed a Triennial Bill requiring that parliament be automatically summoned every three years. This was accompanied by a bill for four subsidies for raising the money needed to pay the armies.

Charles, after some vacillation, signed both measures, but his delay in accepting the Triennial Act 'convinced many people that he did not mean to observe it.' Thus, as Conrad Russell has observed, '… he got the worst of both worlds.'[24] Whenever Charles wriggled to free himself of parliamentary reins, he further undermined his credibility. By placing opposition nobles on the Privy Council he seemed to be trying to buy votes in the Lords. When Strafford was finally brought to the Bar of the House of Lords, Charles was present, greatly irritating the Lords. When he withdrew the Lords resolved that all that had been said in the presence of the king was null and void, forcing Strafford to answer the charges again.

When Strafford's trial commenced a new menace or opportunity, depending on one's point of view, emerged. A conspiracy swirled around the court and the Queen that sought to use the English army in the north against parliament. The supporters of this 'army plot' never explained what they would do about the Scots army. None the less, by March, proposals were afoot among officers in Yorkshire to replace Northumberland as commander with the fervently royalist Earl of Newcastle. They also planned to replace Lord Conway with George Goring, then Governor of Portsmouth. Goring was already in correspondence with the Queen since it was vaguely planned by the court to use Portsmouth as a haven if the situation in Westminster deteriorated to the point where the royal family was in danger.[25]

On 20 March the officers of the northern army sent a letter to Northumberland detailing the soldiers' material grievances and complaining that money meant for them had been diverted to pay the Scots.[26] They also intimated to the king their plan to replace the commanders of his army. Charles wisely rejected their offer as too wild to work. Goring, seeing that he was not going to become Lieutenant General, reported the plot of the northern colonels to the Earls of Newport and Bedford, and to Lord Mandeville, who in turn notified Pym.[27]

It was no coincidence that shortly thereafter, on 5 April, the managers of the prosecution accused Strafford of having plotted to bring the Irish army to England. However, even with the evidence found in the notes of Secretary Henry Vane, taken in the Privy Council at which Strafford allegedly suggested this use of the Irish army, the prosecutors failed to convince the Lords of Strafford's guilt. They could not find the second witness required to substantiate a treason charge under the existing statutes.

After some embarrassing defeats in the proceedings, the parliamentarians determined to abandon the impeachment and to attaint Strafford as a traitor. An attainder was a procedure by which a parliamentary vote, requiring no evidence beyond the belief that he was guilty, could condemn a person as a traitor.[28] The knowledge of the army plot and the fear of the Irish army, which the king still would not disband, convinced a majority of the Commons that Strafford had to die. Although Pym initially resisted this resort to attainder, he changed his mind after Charles again refused to disband the Irish army. On 19 April the House of Commons voted 204 to 59 for Strafford's attainder. On 5 May Pym revealed the plot of the northern army to parliament, and on 8 May the House of Lords passed a bill of attainder. In the Lords the final vote was 26 to 19, in a house where there were normally over 60 peers in attendance.[29] This close vote and low attendance reflected fear by a number of nobles of Pym and his Puritan agenda.

Now all rested with the king, whose assent was needed to complete the attainder process. On 9 May, in spite of his promise not to desert his servant, Charles gave way to pressure and assented to the act. Three days later Strafford bravely faced his death.[30]

Significantly, the division in the Commons' vote was publicized by the minority, a sign that a group was solidifying that opposed further radical changes of the constitution. Most of the members of this group opposed the abolition of episcopacy.

The legislative condemnation of Strafford had major repercussions. The king never forgave the parliamentarians who hounded Strafford to his death. Charles transferred his remorse and guilt for abandoning his servant to the men who carried through the attainder bill. Thus, there was little chance of a compromise that would have included the opposition leaders in meaningful offices of state such as Lord Treasurer or Chancellor of the Exchequer. Without such appointments, it was difficult for the parliamentarians to believe that the king would change his ways. A reflection of this belief was evident on 18 May, when Pym pushed through a bill to protect the Long Parliament from royal dissolution. Clarendon correctly characterized this act as one of fatal consequence to the king and kingdom.[31]

The bill against dissolution exemplified the complete lack of trust that the parliamentarians had in the king. The king assented to the act, largely because he realized that the money needed to pay off the Scots would never be forthcoming until the parliamentarians and the Londoners were certain that parliament would be allowed to finish its work.

After Laud's imprisonment and Strafford's execution, parliament attempted to resolve its pressing financial and political problems. Pym devised a £400,000 grant for the payment of the armies that was to be raised as a subsidy with a fixed rate of return. This was a major financial improvement since the traditional parliamentary subsidy had declined steadily in value since the 1590s. Pym applied the Elizabethan subsidy rate of 1593 and ensured that the act eliminated loopholes that had allowed many wealthy people to escape taxes.[32] Parliament passed the tax in May, but its proceeds would not come in until the summer. Therefore Pym arranged a loan of £150,000 from the customs collectors, in exchange for parliamentary protection from prosecution for their earlier collection of the customs without parliamentary approval.[33]

These financial measures were accompanied by important political reforms like the abolition of the Star Chamber and the provision that judges were no longer to serve at the pleasure of the king, but instead were to serve based on good behavior. Parliament also eliminated the Council of the North that Strafford had used as an instrument of royal will in the early 1630s. However, such legislation did not deal with the Scottish treaty, the reform of English finance, or the remodeling of the English church.

The settlement with the Scots: the Treaty of London

Scottish commissioners arrived in London in early November 1640, carrying instructions from the Committee of Estates that included eight major demands. By December, the king had accepted the first, which was to ratify the acts of the Scottish parliament of 1640. Charles also agreed that the royal castles in Scotland be used only for the defense of Scotland and that Scots in England and Ireland could not be forced to take oaths or be censured for signing the Covenant. The commissioners and Charles compromised on the fourth demand that royal servants found guilty of opposing the Covenanters should be punished by the parliaments. Charles conceded that he would never employ such men again, an answer the Scots accepted.[34]

From there the negotiations got harder. The Scots desired things only the English parliament could deliver. Their fifth demand was for the return of all property captured during the war, and that the English should pay for all Scottish expenses in the war. The English parliament agreed to the first part of the demand and approved a 'brotherly assistance' of £300,000 to help defray Scottish expenses. This sum was in addition to the £850 per day that the English had agreed to pay the Scots. Charles also withdrew his condemnation of all Covenanter declarations and proclamations.[35] So after three months of negotiations, seven of the eight Scottish terms had been satisfied. However, the eighth, that the two kingdoms should enjoy perpetual peace and a uniformity of religion, proved much harder to deal with. The Covenanters wanted the English to replace episcopacy with Presbyterianism. This was unacceptable to many English parliamentarians. As a compromise, the two sides agreed that the two churches should be in 'conformity', thus side-stepping the issue of uniformity. With this, both parliaments ratified the treaty in August 1641.[36]

The Treaty of London opened the way for the disbandment of the armies. Pym no longer needed the Covenanter army since the king had assented to the acts that changed the balance of the English constitution in favor of parliament. Pym realized that until the Scottish army was disbanded an English army would have to be kept together. This cost a great deal and there was the constant danger that the army might be subverted by the king to use against parliament. The act for the £400,000 provided the money needed to pay off the English soldiers and to give the Scots more than £80,000 in cash in return for their departure from England. Once the two northern armies were disbanded, Charles ordered his Irish army to disband.[37] When one looks at the political struggles between the king and his opponents in Britain in 1640-1, it is clear that the existence of the Scots army shaped politics by providing the parliamentarians with the armed force needed to prevent Charles from dissolving parliament. Without those armies there would have been no 'Long Parliament.'

Shortly after Strafford's execution Charles announced his intention to travel to Scotland to be present at the ratification of the peace treaty. This news disturbed the opposition leaders who feared that the king might still subvert the Scottish or English army in the north, and use it against his English opponents. Charles certainly had every intention of attempting to do so.[38] Parliament asked the king to change his travel plans. However, after the disbandment of the armies had been agreed upon, and the treaty settled, there were no grounds to prevent the king's journey.

After an extraordinary Sunday session of the House of Commons, parliament accepted the king's decision to go to Scotland, which he did on 14 August. However, before parliament recessed it appointed six commissioners to accompany him and established a committee to act in the absence of parliament and the king if there was any danger to the country. Since Charles had already departed London, parliament could not use the normal legislative process to appoint its commissioners. Therefore it enacted an 'ordinance.' An ordinance was a declaration by both Houses that had the force of law without the royal assent.[39] Parliament's increasing use of ordinances, in place of traditional parliamentary acts assented to by the monarch, demonstrated the revolutionary shift taking place in the constitution.

The Irish revolt

Charles arrived in Edinburgh on 17 August, where he presided over his Scottish parliament and accepted the Covenanters' settlement of Scotland. He failed to split the Covenanter movement, even though Montrose and other nobles plotted to undermine Argyll's control.[40] He also failed to find military support to use against his English opponents. He had finished his business and was preparing to return to London when, on 28 October 1641, he and the Scots learned that a Catholic revolt had broken out in Ulster and that an Irish attempt to seize Dublin castle had been foiled. Charles asked the Scots for an army to send to Ireland to crush the rebellion, and then rode south. When he arrived in London he was greeted with popular acclamation.

The Long Parliament learned of the Irish insurrection on 1 November. Charles's arrival amidst popular fanfare disturbed Pym and others who suspected Charles of complicity in the Irish revolt. They had good reason to do so since the king had been in correspondence with the Earl of Antrim in the spring of 1641 to arrange for the movement of the Irish army to England. Charles had instructed Antrim, and possibly Ormond, the commander of the army in Ireland, to keep 8,000 soldiers together in readiness to support the king. These secret attempts to retain those soldiers came to nothing, because the Protestant Ormond was unwilling to keep Catholic regiments together, and Antrim was incapable of doing so.[41] However, the English parliament forbade the recruitment and transportation of the disbanded soldiers by their colonels for service with the Spanish army. Consequently, those soldiers were available to form the cadre of Irish Catholic armies.[42]

The Irish insurrection of 1641 was not led by Antrim or designed to aid Charles. It was a rebellion by Irish Catholics opposed to further Protestant inroads in Ireland. The heart of the conspiracy had formed in February 1641, when Roger Moore of Kildare contacted Connor, Lord Maguire, an Old Irish peer in the Irish parliament, and suggested the two meet. Maguire and Moore met in Dublin and agreed to coordinate resistance to further encroachments on Catholic lands and rights. A number of prominent Ulstermen joined them and they soon were in communication with Irishmen serving in continental armies.[43] By August, several officers had returned to Ireland from the Spanish army, prepared to help lead the insurrection. The conspirators obtained promises of support from both France and Spain and set 22 October as the date for the uprising.[44]

Seeing the successful Scottish armed resistance to domination from London, the Irish conspirators hoped to force concessions for Irish Catholics from the English government. Failing this, they believed that if they united all Catholics in Ireland, they stood a chance of driving the English forces out and of defending themselves from a British invasion until the king accorded them autonomy similar to that which he had granted the Scots.[45] At no time did the Irish claim that they fighting for an independent Ireland.

Just as the Scottish wars had profoundly shaped English politics from 1639 to 1641, the Irish insurrection affected British politics from 1641 to 1652. The Scottish and English parliaments agreed that armed force was needed to crush the 'rebels.' The existence of such an army, however, made the political struggles between the king and his opponents intractable to any solution short of civil war. Neither the Covenanters nor the English parliamentarians were willing to trust Charles I with the command of an army in Ireland because they feared he would use that army to crush his opponents in Britain. They also believed that the king was in secret league with the Irish insurgents.[46]

The Irish insurgents achieved significant initial successes, capturing Charlemont, Newry, and Dungannon (see map 4). However, their plan to seize Dublin failed miserably because it was betrayed to the Lords Justices a few hours before it was to have been implemented. The Justices reinforced the Castle's garrison and seized the two insurgent leaders in Dublin, Hugh Mac Mahon and Lord Maguire. The next morning, 23 October, they proclaimed a state of rebellion, as the Irish insurgents swept the interior of Ulster of Protestant garrisons. The Lords Justices also called on James Butler, Earl of Ormond, to command the king's forces in Leinster.[47] The king confirmed his appointment on 10 November. Ormond recruited three infantry regiments from among the refugees flooding into Dublin, ending the immediate risk to the capital.

Sir Phelim O'Neill emerged as the Irish military commander in Ulster. He realized that the insurgents needed a seaport if they were going to receive reinforcements and arms from overseas. However, because Scottish settlers held the Ulster seaports, the Irish had to expand their attacks to include Scottish enclaves, losing any chance that the Covenanters in Edinburgh might stay neutral.

In November, unable to dislodge the Scottish garrisons, O'Neill marched his army south to the border of Leinster and laid siege to Drogheda. For the next five months the Irish military effort in eastern Ulster was directed toward the capture of that seaport.[48] The English attempted to lift the siege, but O'Neill's army won some notable tactical victories, such as when it routed a relief column near Julianstown, County Meath, on 29 November. Generally, however, the Protestant regiments that had been raised among the settlers defeated Irish attempts to capture towns like Derry and Coleraine. The war in Ulster quickly settled down to one characterized by Protestant cattle raids into the Irish-held interior and half-hearted sieges of Protestant garrisons by the insurgents.[49]

It was nearly inevitable that atrocities would be committed by the loosely organized Irish troops. Although Phelim O'Neill tried to prevent looting and murder by his soldiers, there was too much pent-up hatred against the settler population by the Irish for them to resist the chance to even the score. As many as 5,000 Protestant settlers perished in the first months of the rising. Bands of roving Irishmen in search

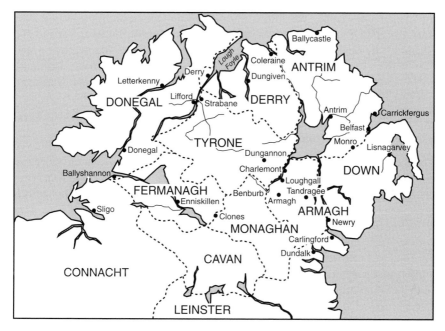

Map 4 Ulster, 1641–2

of loot and revenge tortured and killed settlers who resisted or who were suspected of hiding valuables. Thousands of Protestants fled to the ports seeking passage to Britain. As they arrived in Britain they spread tales of the 'massacres' they believed the Catholics were conducting as a matter of policy.[50] Such accounts heightened the belief that there was a Catholic conspiracy to extirpate Protestantism in the three kingdoms. Pym used this fear to great effect in his efforts to impose parliamentary control over Charles I.

The Irish insurgents were less successful in Leinster than in Ulster. The Old English Catholics remained aloof from the initial rising, fearing the violence of the Irish peasantry more than they feared the English Puritans. The Lords Justices organized Dublin's defenses, appointed Henry Tinchborne to command in Drogheda, and launched Ormond and Sir Charles Coote on punitive expeditions against the Irish insurgents. Ormond's stature amongst his Catholic relatives and friends initially restrained many of them from joining the rebellion. However, by early December, the virulent anti-Catholicism of the Long Parliament and the Lords Justices and the indiscriminant nature of the government's punitive expeditions drove the Old English into the arms of the insurgents. After meetings at Knockcrofty and Tara, the Catholic gentry of Leinster joined the rebellion.[51]

The accession of the Old English to the insurrection was crucial to its chance of success. They controlled the majority of Irish land and were the leaders of most of the population. The important towns of Wexford, Waterford, Kilkenny, and Galway also joined the insurgency, giving the Catholics the ports they needed to receive foreign aid and supplies. Wexford and Waterford provided bases for powerful Irish naval forces that soon were attacking English shipping in the Irish Sea and the Channel.[52] Kilkenny became the capital of the insurgency. The Old English provided most of the leadership in Leinster and Munster, with Lord Mountgarrett, Ormond's uncle, head of the Leinster movement, and Donogh MacCarthy, Viscount Muskerry, and Colonel Garrett Barry the leaders of the army in Munster.

Scottish and English reactions

The response of the Scots to the news of the Irish rebellion was one of anger and resolve. The Scottish parliament responded to the king's request for aid to help crush the rebellion by agreeing to send an army to Ulster. This decision fit with Scottish ambitions to control Ulster as well as to reinforce the Scottish settlers who were defending the Ulster seaports. The Committee of Estates soon was in communication with the parliamentarians in London, asking them to pay for the Scottish forces to be sent. The Long Parliament agreed to this request since it would ensure the rapid reinforcement of troops to Ireland while the English debated their own military contribution. Ultimately the Scots sent more than 10,000 soldiers to Ulster. The first contingent of 2,500 men landed in Carrickfergus in April 1642, while the remaining troops arrived by the end of July.[53]

The arrival of the well-equipped Scottish units turned the tide of war in eastern Ulster. Scottish columns recaptured Newry, Dundalk, and Dungannon in May and cleared counties Antrim and Down of organized resistance (see map 4). To the west, an army of settlers known as the Laggan army broke the siege of Coleraine and cleared much of the area around Derry of Irish forces. These actions were accompanied by brutal treatment of Irish prisoners and bystanders.[54] From then until early 1643, the Scots conducted few major military operations inland, restricting their activity to the defense of their enclaves. The Irish were in no shape to fight the Scots in the open or to attack their strongholds due to their lack of training and artillery. They just barely managed to hold on to Charlemont as their major strongpoint in Ulster.

The English reaction to the uprising was complex, primarily because of the deep gulf between the king and the parliamentary leaders. Just days before learning of the Irish insurrection, Pym had notified the Commons about a second army plot. When news of the Ulster rising reached Westminster it confirmed the fears of many about a Catholic conspiracy. Such a conspiracy pointed directly to the royal court, and especially to the chambers of the Roman Catholic Queen Henrietta Maria. News of the king's machinations in Scotland reinforced the idea that Charles was willing to use any tool to defeat the parliamentary opposition.

Phelim O'Neill added to the king's difficulties by claiming that he possessed a royal warrant for the seizure of Ireland by the insurgents. While the document he displayed was a forgery, it influenced English opinion.[55] Consequently, as the Long Parliament debated how to crush the Irish rising, many members concluded that they could not entrust command of the army to the king. Because the issue of command could not be resolved, the English did not send a sizable army to Ireland until 1647. Instead, during the next six months, parliament ordered separate regiments to be recruited and shipped to Ireland to join their forces already in operation.

These reinforcements joined Ormond's army in Dublin and the army led by Murrough O'Brien, Lord Inchiquin, in Munster, bringing their troop strength to about 16,000 men.[56] While these armies, like the Scots in Ulster, were chronically short of money and supplies, they were strong enough to stabilize the situation and to roll back the insurgents around Dublin. Probably their most important triumphs in Leinster were Ormond's relief of Drogheda in March and his victory over the Catholic forces of Kildare at Kilrush in April.[57] In Munster, Inchiquin was able to retain Cork, Youghal, and Duncannon, while the settler forces in Ulster defeated Phelim O'Neill's army at Kilwarin Wood, near Lisburn (19 April 1642).

If the English had deployed adequate forces and resources to Ireland in early 1642, in conjunction with the Scots, they probably would have crushed the insurrection quickly. They did not do so. Instead, the Irish rebellion brought to a head the political struggle between the king and his parliamentary opponents. This confrontation led to the formation of a Royalist party in parliament and, after the parliamentarians defeated the Royalists in the Commons, helped lead to the formation of a royalist army and the beginning of the English Civil War. As in 1639–40, warfare directly influenced political events in London.[58]

The origins of the first English Civil War

In early November 1641, John Pym opened a discussion about a remonstrance that the Commons could give the king. This 'Grand Remonstrance', as it came to be known, was a catalogue of all of the mistakes made by Charles I since he had become king.[59] A number of the central issues in the remonstrance related to religion and reflected the opposition's belief that Charles and Henrietta Maria were at the center of a popish plot. The remonstrance also attacked the bishops, characterizing them as key players in that plot.

As Pym worked the Grand Remonstrance through the Commons, the king returned to Whitehall without the support he had hoped the Scots would give him to use against his English parliament.[60] Charles mistook his warm welcome by Londoners as a sign that his position had strengthened, rather than as relief that the monarch was back in the capital to help face the challenges in Ireland.

Consequently, the king ordered the guards removed from around parliament where they had been placed to protect its members from toughs who had taken to swaggering about Westminster. Many of these 'reformadoes' were officers formerly employed in the English army who were looking for employment. Charles also replaced Sir William Balfour as Governor of the Tower of London with Sir Thomas Lunsford, a noted rake of unsavory character from Sussex.[61] The London Common Council and parliament protested these moves, seeing them as signs that the king was preparing to use force against his opponents. After several days of protest the king relented. Lunsford resigned and Sir John Byron, who was acceptable to the

Commons, became the Governor of the Tower. The damage was done, however, because such moves by Charles undercut his supporters in parliament in their attempts to stop the attacks on the king and the bishops.[62]

As bad news flooded in from Ireland, Pym pushed the Remonstrance through the House of Commons and took other measures to disable the king's ability to use force against his opponents. The final struggle in the Commons for the Grand Remonstrance came on 22 November, when the debate raged into the night over whether or not it should be passed and published. In the early hours of 23 November Pym and Hampden secured a slim majority of eleven votes in favor of the document. The remonstrance denounced

> 1. The Jesuited Papists who hate the laws as the obstacles of that change and subversion of religion, which they so much long for. 2. The Bishops, and the corrupt part of the clergy, who cherish formality and superstition, as the natural effects, and more probable supports of their own ecclesiastical tyranny, and usurpation. 3. Such counsellors and courtiers, [who] … for private ends have engaged themselves to further the interests of some foreign princes or states, to the prejudice of His Majesty, and the State at home.[63]

On 1 December, the parliamentarian leaders presented the Grand Remonstrance to Charles. Four days later, against the king's express wish, they published it.

Concurrently, throughout late November and December 1641, Pym brought forward measures to reduce the king's authority over the armed forces. The first of these was a bill that allowed the king to impress men for service in Ireland during the current emergency, but specifically forbid him from doing so for any other emergency other than an active invasion of England. This measure was opposed in the Lords and probably would not have been passed had the king not made inappropriate remarks about it in a speech to parliament. His remarks, while they indicated that he would accept the current bill as long as it did not apply to future situations, outraged the House of Lords, which saw his words as interference with parliamentary privilege. The bill passed and Charles felt compelled to assent to it.[64]

The initial reluctance of the Lords to pass the impressment bill convinced Pym that as long as the twenty-six bishops sat in the upper House the crown stood a chance of defeating such measures. Therefore, the bill was revived in the Commons for the exclusion of the Bishops from parliament. This bill fit nicely with the sections of the Grand Remonstrance that had attacked the actions and roles of the bishops during the personal rule. This outraged the king, who made it clear that he would never accept such a measure, thus drawing a clear line against the opposition.[65] This royal defense of the Church of England as it was then constituted became the major unifying point of the Royalist cause in 1642.

Outside parliament, tumultuous demonstrations added to the heat and confusion of the debates about the Grand Remonstrance and the bishops' exclusion bill. Former officers of the northern army rallied around the king. These men clashed in the streets of Westminster with mobs of London apprentices, intimidating members of parliament. The king used this situation as an excuse to order the trained bands of Westminster, who were royalist in sympathy, to guard the Houses. His opponents saw this as a threat and ordered the Westminster forces removed. The popular demonstrations increased, with the crowds so menacing that twelve bishops refused to attend. These bishops then petitioned the Lords and the king to protect their access to Westminster Palace. They also declared that all actions taken by the Lords in their absence were null and void. Both Houses saw this petition as a breach of parliamentary privilege. The Commons reacted by impeaching the twelve bishops and committing them to the Tower. The Lords agreed.[66]

Amidst continuing bad news from Ireland, the government of England had become paralyzed by the struggle for sovereignty in Westminster. The king believed the tide was running with him. For the first time he had a following in parliament that had resisted the Grand Remonstrance (passed by only eleven votes) and that was resisting the exclusion of the bishops. He had gathered around him many former army officers and other young 'Cavaliers' who were ready to crack skulls. With his wife's encouragement, since by this point he had few other close advisors, Charles decided to take the offensive against what he believed to be a small group of plotters. His decision was prompted in part because he and the queen feared that Pym was preparing to impeach the queen, a move she had every reason to fear since she had been at the center of most of the plots against parliament.[67]

Consequently, Charles ordered the Attorney General to draw up treason charges against five of the parliamentary opposition in the Commons and one in the Lords. Attorney General Herbert complied, delivering a bill with seven charges against Pym, Denzil Holles, John Hampden, Arthur Haselrig, William Strode, and lord Kimbolton to the Lords on 3 January 1642.[68] The House of Lords received the charges and considered them the next day. Meanwhile, on 4 January, Charles sent the Sergeant at Arms to the Commons to demand the surrender of the indicted members. The accused members were prepared for this move since the king's agents had already visited their lodgings and seized their papers. The House responded resolving that no member could be arrested until the House had been acquainted with the charges and evidence against him, and that if an attempt was made to arrest him, the member could defend himself.[69] The Sergeant at Arms withdrew empty-handed.

Charles's attempt to arrest the accused men before the House of Lords had a chance to act was a major mistake. The Lords joined the Commons to request that a reliable guard be deployed to Westminster. Where there had been some hope of a sympathetic majority in the Lords for the king, there now was only a royalist minority incapable of defending the bishops' position or the king's prerogative. As bad as this situation was, Charles made things worse for himself.

Outraged that the Sergeant at Arms had been rebuffed, the king decided to go to the Commons and personally arrest the five members. Unfortunately for him, Charles decided to be accompanied by a large number of the reformadoes. When the entourage arrived at the door of the House, on 4 January, the king entered accompanied only by the Prince Palatine and the Earl of Roxburgh. Outside, visible through the door, he left his escort, many of whom were fondling their weapons and murmuring against the parliamentarians. When he looked about the chamber he realized that none of the accused were present. He then sat in the Speaker's chair and asked the Speaker, William Lenthall, 'whether any of those persons were in the House.' Lenthall replied with the famous lines that

> I have neither eyes to see nor tongue to speak in this place, but as the House is pleased to direct me, whose servant I am here; and humbly beg your Majesty's pardon that I cannot now give any other answer than this to what your Majesty is pleased to demand of me.[70]

Charles, in response, observed that 'the birds are flown' but that he expected the House to send them to him. At this the king and his armed followers withdrew. As they did so members of the House shouted 'privilege,' while many felt they had come close to being attacked by the king's retinue. This poorly conceived and miserably executed breach of parliamentary privilege transformed the situation. It united parliament against Charles, confirmed the accusations that he intended to use force to crush legitimate opposition, and ensured that London remained loyal to the parliamentary opposition.

Fearing another visit by the king's men, the Commons passed motions to recess to the safety of the City until 11 January and to appoint a committee to represent parliament in its brief adjournment. The members then withdrew to London where the London Common Council and the newly elected mayor were able, with the London trained bands, to protect them. By this time the City had become a hotbed of opposition against the bishops, and the king's menacing visit to the Commons had aroused widespread anger against him. None the less, Charles courageously rode to London and visited the Lord Mayor and several aldermen on 5 January, hoping they would take his side. They did not, leaving the king in a bad situation.

Charles next proclaimed the accused men as traitors by royal warrant. When ordered to issue the proclamation in London, Lord Mayor Gurney refused, saying that it was illegal. The standing parliamentary committee agreed and defiantly ordered the accused to resume their seats when the Houses reassembled in Westminster. It also resolved that the City could raise forces to restore order and to protect parliament. The Common Council quickly appointed Philip Skippon to serve as Sergeant Major General and commander of the City's trained bands. He was to take all necessary measures to restore order and ensure parliament's safety.

Charles was running out of alternatives. His threat of force against his opponents had made it dangerous for the royal family to remain in Westminster. Fearing for the Queen's safety, he decided to leave Whitehall and move to Hampton Court on 10 January 1642. It was the beginning of a long exile from his capital. The next day, parliament reassembled, with a guard from the London trained bands. Parliament was master of the capital and Pym was the leader of a united parliament. Together they faced two immense challenges: how to defeat the Irish rebellion and how to deal with the king.

The Irish war

Parliament so far had done little to affect the war in Ireland, short of sending limited reinforcements to Dublin and Cork.[71] Once the immediate dangers from a royal coup had receded, efforts were revived to find the money and men needed to crush the Irish insurgents. The Long Parliament negotiated the treaty with the Scots that allowed the Covenanters to send 10,000 soldiers to Ulster. The English undertook to pay this army. In February and March 1642, the Long Parliament attempted to solve the financial problem of how to pay for the conquest of Ireland while also paying for the costs of an increasingly likely English civil war.

On 11 February, a committee of the Commons met with London financiers to discuss how to pay for the conquest. This committee developed a bill known as the 'Act for Adventurers', that received the royal assent on 19 March 1642. This measure solicited £1 million in investments for the conquest in exchange for 2.5 million acres of land to be confiscated from the 'rebels.' This exchange of English money for Irish land produced some cash for the Protestant forces in Ireland, but it failed as a financial measure. Investors subscribed only about £300,000 by 1650, most of which was diverted to parliament's war effort in England.[72]

Parliament also passed an 'Ordinance for the Sea-Adventure to Ireland' in June, encouraging private financing of an expedition commanded by Lord Forbes. Forbes sailed with 1,600 soldiers to Munster in July 1642, with London financial backing. He did little damage to the Catholic forces but depleted the supplies of Lord Inchiquin's Protestant garrisons. His final contribution was to visit Galway, pushing that Catholic city to join the rebellion.[73] Having failed in his mission, Forbes returned to England in the late fall.

Ormond held his own against Mountgarret's troops in Leinster throughout the spring. A string of Catholic defeats indicated that the insurgency was uncoordinated and possibly doomed. In the face of this situation the Roman Catholic hierarchy of Ireland met in Kells and discussed the need for a united Catholic effort. Important laymen soon joined the movement that culminated with the establishment in Kilkenny, on 10 May, of a Catholic Confederation. This organization gave the insurgents a supreme council of twenty-four representatives to coordinate military strategy and to articulate the political goals without which the military struggle would mean little.[74] The supreme council also established diplomatic relations with France, Spain, and the Papacy. These relations were very important, not least of all because the Confederates were able to solicit financial and military support from those powers.[75]

The Confederates created four councils to organize and sustain military forces in each of the Irish provinces. They established county councils to support their war effort, a pattern reminiscent of the Covenanters' efforts in the Bishops' Wars. The supreme council also fielded an army of 4,000 foot and 400 horse.[76] On paper this was an impressive military force. However, the Confederation lacked the ability to enforce its will and probably would have been crushed in its infancy had a number of Irish professional soldiers not returned to Ireland with weapons and the skills needed to train and lead Irish armies.

The Irish struggle for religious autonomy in a Stuart kingdom received its greatest boost with the arrival of two contingents of Irish soldiers from the Low Countries. Their arrival was timely, as Phelim O'Neill was on the verge of disbanding his defeated and dispirited troops. These professionals transformed the Irish levies into reasonably adept soldiers, allowing Confederate armies to challenge the Protestants for control of Leinster and Ulster.[77] By late 1642, Catholic troops commanded by Thomas Preston had turned the tide against Ormond in western and southern Leinster, in no small part because Ormond was receiving only a trickle of financial and material aid from England. Unable to sustain his army in the field long enough to bring Preston to battle, Ormond was lucky to maintain his hold on Dublin and the Pale.[78]

The Irish war continued to affect English political developments. Parliament refused to accept the king's offers to go to Ireland to lead the army. Instead, the parliamentarians demanded that he approve a militia bill conferring on parliament the power to appoint all military officers. The issue of command was central to the struggle for sovereignty in the English state. If parliament controlled the armed forces, the king would have no recourse but to accept parliamentary sovereignty. The parliamentary opposition felt that it was essential to their safety and parliamentary privileges that Charles be denied control of the forces they were certain he would use against them. Charles's attempt to seize the six members and his withdrawal from Westminster was evidence that they were right.

An English civil war approaches

In spite of his past blunders, Charles I created a royalist party, a royalist army, and a royalist government in the first half of 1642.[79] The royalist party consisted of people like Edward Hyde who were convinced that the Long Parliament had gone too far in its reforms. The exclusion of the bishops from the House of Lords in February and the growth of a Presbyterian movement in London seemed ample proof that further religious innovations would follow. Hyde joined the king's cause in February, although he remained in parliament for several months longer, hoping to facilitate a reconciliation of king and subjects.[80]

The king had abandoned hope of conciliation in January. He soon demonstrated his intent to use force when he attempted to gain control of Hull and Portsmouth. Hull held the weapons and munitions that had been gathered for the English army in 1640. Control of Hull would have given him these materials and a port through which he could receive foreign aid. Charles appointed the Earl of Newcastle as governor and secretly sent Captain William Legg to Hull to announce the appointment and to take charge.[81] Pym got wind of this and countered it by sending Sir John Hotham to assume command and to reinforce Hull's garrison with Yorkshire militia. Lord Digby, meanwhile, failed to secure Kingston for the king because the forewarned parliamentarians ordered the Surrey trained bands to garrison the place and deny royalist entry.

Royalists' attempts to seize Hull and Kingston were accompanied by the queen's departure from Dover to the Continent, where she was to pawn the crown jewels for money for arms, and where she was to solicit military support from the Prince of Orange and the King of Denmark. She succeeded in pawning the jewels, but the European powers chose not to intervene on the king's behalf. This situation forced Charles to look harder in Britain for support, first by asking the Scottish government for military support, and finally by working to create a royalist army. The Scots refused, but Charles succeeded in raising an army.

Parliament reacted to the king's machinations by passing ordinances placing the militia in the hands of parliamentarians and by ordering the Lord High Admiral to appoint the Earl of Warwick, a staunch Puritan, as Vice Admiral. Parliament also passed the Bishops' Exclusion Bill, weakening the royalists in the Lords and stiffening the resolve of Hyde and others to take the king's side. Civil war was increasingly likely. In late February, Charles's refusal to accept parliament's appointment of new county Lord Lieutenants was the final royal act in the breakdown of relations. The Long Parliament reacted by passing an ordinance putting the kingdom in a state of defense on 5 March.[82]

The armies gather

The king and the parliamentarians began to gather money and arms in earnest by mid April 1642. The parliamentarians had a distinct advantage because they controlled the machinery of government and the major hub of financial and commercial activity in London. They also possessed the arsenal in Hull and the main naval dockyard at Chatham. Charles, on the other hand, lacked a financial or military base comparable to London, forcing him to seek support in a variety of places.

Charles again attempted to secure the arsenal at Hull on 23 April, appearing in person to appeal to Sir John Hotham to let him in. Hotham refused and the king found out that parliament had ordered the munitions removed to the Tower of London. Foiled in this attempt, Charles returned to York, where he earlier had met with the Yorkshire gentry and appealed for their support. From then until the end of the civil war, Charles's message was that he was the defender of the established church and constitution, and that the parliamentarians were attempting to change both radically.

Once he had found out that the Scots and Dutch would not help him, Charles issued commissions of array to his supporters, authorizing them to muster the trained bands. It quickly became apparent, however, that most trained bands were unwilling to serve outside of their counties, and many were parliamentarian or neutral in their political sympathies. Consequently, the royal commissioners proceeded to recruit new regiments.[83] In some counties these efforts were successful, and in some they failed. None the less, by early October 1642 the king's army consisted of ten regiments of cavalry and nineteen of infantry.[84]

The commissioners of array established royalist administrations in counties where the king's forces were strong enough to keep parliamentarians out. Committees of leading royalist gentry raised money and supplies and helped with recruitment. These committees generally met weekly and oversaw tax assessors, constables, and justices of the peace. They also played a leading role in the confiscation of the rents and properties of parliamentarians, although such sequestrations never proved to be a major source of royalist revenues.[85]

Charles was the Commander in Chief of the royalist forces throughout the war. He appointed the Earl of Lindsay as Lord General of the marching army and Patrick Ruthven, the Earl of Forth, as Chief of Staff in his council of war. Charles tried a number of command relationships over the next three years to make the machinery run smoothly, and he progressively assumed more of a personal command role as his experience increased. He was advised in his military affairs by a council of war, an executive body that could discuss and prepare a centralized strategy. However, the royalist council of war never lived up to its potential, largely due to the rivalries of prominent men surrounding the king.[86]

Charles relied on several types of officers to command his regiments. Some were nobles who had paid for the equipment of the unit, but who were otherwise amateurs in arms. Professional soldiers from the Continent, to include the king's nephews from the Palatinate, Prince Rupert and Prince Maurice, served as colonels and company commanders in many regiments. Hundreds of professional soldiers who had served in English regiments in the Dutch army joined the king's army as well.[87] Throughout the war, a significant percentage of the royalist officer corps was composed of Catholics with professional military experience, in large part because that was one of the few professions open to an English Catholic gentleman in the seventeenth century. As the war wore on, and pikes splattered many an officer's blood, many noblemen left the command of regiments to the professionals, changing the nature of the Cavalier army.[88]

The royalists collected the arms of county militias and reissued them to their troops. They imported arms from the continent and established a number of manufacturing centers to provide small arms and cannon.[89] Royalist soldiers also used weapons captured from parliamentarians in battle. The king's armies did not lose any battles during the First Civil War due to a shortage of arms, although gunpowder was always in short supply.

Paying for the raising of the royalist regiments was a difficult task. It was important that the king's forces remain disciplined and not take free quarter from the population during the summer of 1642, because of the adverse propaganda effects such action would have. Initially, Charles depended on wealthy supporters for money to pay his troops. Thirty-five nobles joined the king in York in June, providing him with important moral support and financial help. For example, the Earl of Worcester and his son Lord Herbert provided £122,000 to the royal coffers in April and June, and eventually gave the king at least £318,000. The queen raised another £180,000 by pawning the crown jewels in the Netherlands, using this money to buy arms and munitions.[90] Other nobles and Oxford University brought their silver plate into the newly established royal mint to provide bullion for coin, and the Catholic community provided additional sums in advance of their recusancy fines. These sources paid for the initial organization of the royalist army.

Parliament faced similar challenges in raising an army. Its initial response was to pass ordinances to raise money through voluntary subscription, to recruit regiments, and to appoint officers. Money was the crux of the successful raising of regiments. In June 1642, parliament passed ordinances asking for a loan of £100,000 from the City and of silver plate for bullion from individuals. Another ordinance appointed the Earl of Essex Captain General of the parliamentary army.[91]

Parliament initially relied on the trained bands for manpower, although militia units seldom were willing to serve outside of their county, with the notable exception of the Londoners. Commissioners mustered the trained bands in areas well affected to parliament and solicited volunteers for the twenty regiments being raised for Essex's army. Parliament promised to reimburse the counties for the weapons it borrowed from county magazines to arm the new units, and it freely imported arms. More important for the long haul, parliament could rely on the domestic arms industry to produce weapons and gunpowder.[92]

Regiments on both sides contained men familiar with their weapons and with rudimentary military maneuvers. These soldiers had drilled with the trained bands and some had served in the two Bishops' Wars. Parliamentarians recruited such men, and especially the officers, from the trained bands to form the regiments of Essex's army. Many of the officers were prominent gentry to whom parliament granted commissions to raise and command their units. Some of these officers had foreign military experience, like the Earl of Essex, but many were novices. However, novices such as Oliver Cromwell were not ignorant of military affairs, having taken a keen interest in the exploits of the great Protestant warrior Gustav Adolphus. Further, literature about how to train and command military units was readily available.[93]

The armies collide

Neither the king nor the parliamentarians initially had a military strategy, although both understood the importance of securing London and of controlling the resources of those regions loyal to their cause. The king gathered his army in Yorkshire and moved south to Nottingham. The Earl of Newcastle in the north and the Earl of Worcester in the west secured the magazines and militia in those regions and forwarded munitions and men to the royalist army. However, as late as 22 August, when the king erected his standard outside Nottingham, he had fewer than 3,000 soldiers. In the following six weeks this force swelled to at least 13,000 men. This remarkable surge in recruitment was due to the efforts of leaders such as Rupert, Hopton, and Newcastle, and to the realization by many gentry that parliament was as unwilling as the king to resolve the conflict peacefully. With the arrival of over 5,000 Welsh infantrymen, in early October, the royalist army had become a potent force.[94]

Essex's army was the first in the field. By October it was larger and better equipped than the king's. Essex moved cautiously because he needed time to train his men and because he was uncertain of the king's intentions. Neither the king nor Essex anticipated how, when, or where hostilities would occur and their initial moves can be seen as groping to find a plan. This period of uncertainty ended on 23 September, when Prince Rupert with about 1,000 cavalrymen engaged a slightly smaller parliamentarian force of dragoons at Powick Bridge, near Worcester. After a sharp fight the Roundheads, as the royalists derisively called the parliamentarians, were routed. Rupert did not pursue them since he knew that Essex's army was marching toward Worcester. Casualties were light, with the parliamentarians losing the most.[95] Rupert withdrew through Worcester, evacuating the town the next day to join the royal army.

The importance of the fight at Powick Bridge was that Rupert's audacious charge established his reputation as a cavalry commander and convinced many of the king's horsemen that they were naturally superior to the parliamentary cavalry. In war, self-confidence and reputation are invaluable to enhanced performance and the royalists' apparent superiority in cavalry lasted for nearly two years. Rupert reinforced his reputation when the two main armies met at Edgehill.

In mid October, Charles moved his army from Shrewsbury toward London. By this time he had nearly 24,000 men, although over half of these were on detached service. The army moved slowly, as it gathered recruits, but the main reason for its slow advance was the inexperience of Charles as a commander and due to the fact that his three generals, Rupert and the Earls of Forth and Lindsay, would not work together efficiently. Rupert refused to take orders from anyone but the king, while Forth, the Field Marshall, and Lindsay, the Lord General, were schooled in different military systems (the Swedish and Dutch respectively), making it hard for them to agree on how to deploy the regiments.

By 22 October, Charles's army was near Banbury, having eluded Essex. This put the king closer to London than Essex's army, giving Charles a chance to move on the capital before Essex could stop him.[96] The parliamentarian leaders in Westminster recognized this danger and ordered another army to assemble to protect the capital.[97] The king, however, turned his army south when he learned that some of Essex's soldiers were in the village of Kineton, near the topographical feature known as Edgehill. By the evening of 22 October, the two armies were poised to face one another in what each side hoped would be the decisive battle.

The armies deployed between Kineton and the Edgehill the next morning. The king's troops faced west and slightly north (see map 5), while the parliamentarians faced east. There were about 13,500 soldiers in each army, although Essex had another 4,000 men within half a day's march. Essex's army occupied a low ridge about a mile from Kineton, giving the advantage of higher ground and the wind to the king. Essex's force was arranged in two lines of infantry regiments, eight men deep, in the Dutch style, with most of the cavalry stationed on the flanks. The infantry regiments were further organized in three brigades commanded by Meldrum, Charles Essex, and Ballard. Only two small regiments of horse were retained near the center rear as a reserve. Several field guns supported the infantry brigades in the center.[98]

The royalists occupied the higher terrain to the south, arranged in the Swedish style with the infantry in five separate brigades with cannon interspersed between the units. The Earls of Lindsay and Forth had delayed deployment because Lindsay opposed this alignment. Charles overruled him and the Earl resigned his position as Lord General in pique, joining his infantry regiment as Colonel. It was at least one

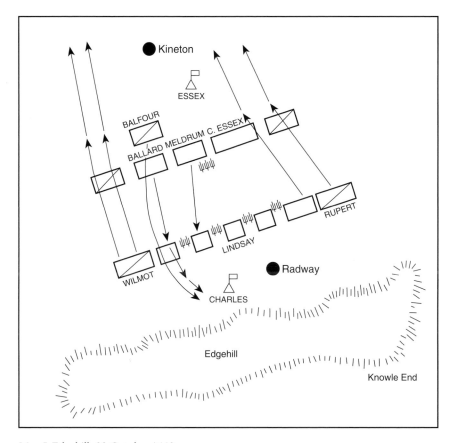

Map 5 Edgehill, 23 October 1642

o'clock in the afternoon before the two armies were in position, and then a tense silence fell over the field.

At this point, a parliamentarian cannoneer recognized the king on the high ground behind his army and fired a shot in his direction. Charles responded by ordering an attack. The forces collided first on the royalists' right, where Prince Rupert commanded the majority of the royalist cavalry. Rupert ordered his regiments to charge, barreling down the slope against the Roundheads to their front. As the royalist onslaught approached, one troop of parliamentarians advanced a short distance, fired their pistols into the ground, and switched sides. Rupert pressed his attack, smashing apart the parliamentary cavalry. This success initiated a pursuit by Rupert's regiments and the second wave of royalist cavalry commanded by John Byron.

At about the same time the royalist cavalry on the king's left, commanded by Lord Wilmot, attacked cavalry on Essex's right. Wilmot's troopers, with the aid of Arthur Astley's dragoons, broke the parliamentarian horse and initiated a pursuit similar to Rupert's. The second line of royalist cavalry on this wing, commanded by

Lord Digby, joined the pursuit. Thus the battle became an infantry struggle in which it appeared that the royalists had the upper hand because Charles Essex's brigade of four infantry regiments had been broken by Rupert's attack on the parliamentarians' left.

All might have been lost for Essex had two things not happened. First, the royalist cavalry left the field in pursuit of the retreating parliamentarians; second, Essex had retained a small reserve of cavalry behind the right flank of his infantry. This reserve attacked the royalist infantry, accompanied by four regiments of infantry in what was the first coordinated infantry-cavalry attack of the Civil War. The parliamentarians penetrated the royalist lines, mortally wounding the Earl of Lindsay and capturing the royal standard and several cannon. The return of Rupert and his cavalry and the exhaustion of the Roundheads saved the Cavaliers from total defeat. As darkness fell, the king's infantry withdrew toward the Edgehill, where the royalist line was re-established. As they did so, Captain John Smith recovered the royal standard and returned it to Charles, who knighted him on the spot. Total losses may have been as high as 1,500 killed and wounded.[99]

The armies remained on the field during the cold night, amidst the carnage. The next day neither side was willing to resume the fight. The king left the field to the parliamentarians, ordering his regiments back to the quarters they had occupied on the night of 22 October. Essex withdrew his exhausted army to Warwick. Both claimed victory, but Charles was able to continue his march toward London.[100]

The race for London

As Essex withdrew, the royalist cavalry maintained contact, giving Charles intelligence about his enemies. When Rupert's cavalry returned from near Warwick in the afternoon they viewed the carnage and misery of the battlefield. They found a number of wounded Cavaliers who had remained unattended for two bitterly cold nights. Roundheads had stripped most of the dead, and Essex had done little to recover enemy wounded from the battlefield. The viciousness of civil war was apparent.[101]

At a rendezvous on 26 October, the king found that most of the stragglers from the battle had rejoined their regiments, giving him a powerful force to continue with to London. The next day the royal army moved east toward Banbury, then held by a parliamentarian regiment (see map 6). The royalists deployed in front of Banbury Castle and planted their artillery in preparation for a bombardment and assault. At this point the garrison asked for terms. The king allowed it to march out unmolested, although disarmed. Two days later, the king's soldiers passed Woodstock and marched into Oxford.[102]

Oxford greeted the king enthusiastically. The colleges provided him with badly needed cash to pay his troops, and the king and his newly appointed commander, the Earl of Forth, established a hospital and a supply depot in what was to become the royalist capital. The king's advance to Oxford caused consternation in London, especially since Essex did not seem to be stirring his army in pursuit.

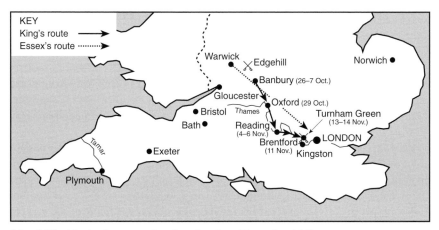

KEY
King's route →
Essex's route ┈┈>

Warwick • ╳ Edgehill   Norwich •
        • Banbury (26–7 Oct.)
Gloucester •
        Oxford (29 Oct.)
• Bristol   Thames
Bath •   Reading   Turnham Green
        (4–6 Nov.)   (13–14 Nov.)
        Brentford • LONDON
• Exeter   (11 Nov.) Kingston

Plymouth

Map 6 The king's advance on London, October–November 1642

The accounts of the Battle of Edgehill that reached London initially had been confusing and contradictory. Emotions in the City and in parliament swung wildly for several days before accurate information arrived. In the process, a 'peace party' emerged, especially in the House of Lords. This group, led by the Earls of Northumberland and Pembroke, called for the resumption of negotiations with the king. After debate, the Lords proposed that a petition be sent to the king. The Commons agreed to this request on 2 November.[103] John Pym kept his wits about him, allowing peace feelers to be put forward while ensuring that a new call for recruits went out.

Pym also convinced the Commons to appeal to the Scots for military aid. This was shrewd, making it difficult for the king to derive help from Scotland, especially since the Scots knew that Charles would never agree to Presbyterian conformity between the two kingdoms. A parliamentarian victory was the Scots' best hope of achieving the goal that had eluded them in the peace treaty of 1641.[104]

Parliament's petition for negotiations reached Charles in Reading on 4 November. Parliament asked for safe conduct for commissioners. Charles hesitated two days before answering that he would give safe conduct to all but one of the parliamentary commissioners. His slowness in answering was due to the fact that he was using the negotiations to delay the parliamentarians' efforts to stop his advance. This became evident when Rupert attempted to take Windsor Castle on 7 November and the king advanced to Colnbrook two days later. On the night of 11 November, Charles ordered an attack against Brentford, then occupied by Lord Brooke's and Denzil Holles's regiments.

The royalist attack the next day was important for several reasons. It was a hard-fought action, as Holles's regiment gave ground only grudgingly, well supported by Lord Brooke's musketeers. Just as the Cavaliers broke the defenders' cohesion, John Hampden's regiment arrived to cover the Roundheads' retreat, demonstrating that the parliamentary forces were anything but dispirited. None the less, Holles's regiment was shattered and Brooke lost over half of his men. After their victory, the royalists brutally sacked the town, stiffening Londoners' will to defend their city from the royalists.

As the king's forces were nearing Brentford, Essex finally got his troops moving east. Charles's delays at Oxford and Reading allowed Essex to pass around the northeastern flank of the royalist army and to arrive in the outskirts of the capital by 9 November.[105] After two days of rest and replenishment, the parliamentarian army was ready for battle.

Charles alerted his enemies to their danger in a letter he wrote to the House of Lords on 11 November, telling them that he would expect to receive messages from them in Brentford the next night. The Londoners and the parliamentarian leaders knew that from Brentford it was an easy march to London by the road through Turnham Green. In response to this intelligence and to the news of the sack of Brentford, Essex's army deployed on Turnham Green during the night of 12–13 November. He was reinforced by 12,000 men of the London trained bands, commanded by Philip Skippon. Another 3,000 parliamentary soldiers defended the bridge over the Thames at Kingston.[106]

Charles brought his army to Turnham Green on the morning of 13 November, and undoubtedly was surprised to find such a large force arrayed against him. During the afternoon cannon shots were exchanged, but neither side attacked. Essex and Skippon understood that their well-drilled but inexperienced trained bands would give a good account of themselves on the defensive, but would have a difficult time in the attack. The king and his senior commanders saw it as too risky to attack a force twice as large as their own. The king blinked first in this face-off, marching his army back through Brentford and then to Kingston. When he approached the bridge at Kingston he found it unguarded, as Essex had ordered Colonel Ramsey to withdraw his 3,000 men to Southwark.

Charles chose, prudently, not to march across the Thames and toward Kent or London Bridge, realizing that his foes had interior lines and could move to block his access to London before he could get there. Essex demonstrated this tactical fact of life when he put a pontoon bridge across the river at Putney. If Charles had moved across the Thames, Essex could have thrown a force into Kingston, cutting the royalists off from their western base. The bulk of the parliamentarians then could have confronted Charles south of the Thames.[107] After several days in Kingston, the king withdrew to Reading, leaving a garrison there before continuing to Oxford and winter quarters. By the end of November, Essex had placed his regiments in winter quarters around Windsor. Major operations in the Thames valley were over for the year.

Both sides resolve to continue the war

The standoff at Turnham Green was a decisive action. Both sides had raised armies, and these armies had demonstrated the will and the capacity to fight. The king won the battle of Edgehill, giving him control of western England and Wales. The parliamentarians won at Turnham Green, protecting their critical base of London and southeastern England. More important, the king's duplicity in the negotiations undercut the peace party in parliament because it was evident that he would use negotiations to cover his military maneuvers. The sack of Brentford showed all parliamentarians what they might expect from a royalist victory.

Pym, consequently, was able to win the political struggle in parliament and London that was needed to organize his cause on a solid basis. London offered to recruit an additional 4,000 soldiers, as long as parliament promised to repay its financial outlays. Parliament passed measures in the following months that gave it the ability to finance its forces.

The final major act of the 1642 campaign season in England was an exchange of messages between the king and the Long Parliament that showed the gulf between the two sides. Parliament insisted that Charles disband his army and return to Westminster, where he could be with his parliament and, coincidentally, under parliamentary control. Charles responded with a proclamation blasting his foes and refusing to come to London as a supplicant. Instead, he called on his people and the loyal members of his parliament to join him. He also demanded that laws be passed to protect the liturgy of the church and to return his garrisons and revenues to his control.[108] Too much blood had been spilled to make such a settlement possible. Both sides prepared for another campaign in the spring of 1643.[109]

Notes

1   C. Russell, *The Fall of the British Monarchies, 1637–1642* (Oxford, 1991), 157.

2   Gardiner, *History of England*, ix: 209–14.

3   A. Clarke in Moody, ed., *New History of Ireland*, iii: 271–6.

4   H. Kearney, *Strafford in Ireland*; M. O'Siochru, *Confederate Ireland, 1642–1649* (Dublin, 1999), 17–18. O'Siochru argues that the traditional ethnic boundaries in Ireland 'became increasingly blurred, especially among the upper classes, through intermarriage and a common interest in land and political power.' But his book amply demonstrates that the traditional labels are still useful for understanding Irish politics and conflict in the seventeenth century.

5   C. Falls, *Elizabeth's Irish Wars* (Syracuse, 1997).

6   A. Clarke, *The Old English in Ireland, 1625–42* (Ithaca, NY, 1966), 15–23.

7   T. W. Moody in Moody, ed., *New History of Ireland*, iii: xlii–xliii.

8   Sharpe, *Charles I*, 908.

9   Ibid., 933–9; Gardiner, *History of England*, ix: 224–6.

10   A. Fletcher, *The Outbreak of the English Civil War* (London, 1981), xix–xxx.

11   Clarke in Moody, ed., *New History of Ireland*, 278–9.

12   Russell, *The Crisis of Parliaments* (Oxford, 1992 edn.), 329–31.

13   Russell, *The Fall of the British Monarchies*, 155.

14   Gardiner, *History of England*, ix: 220.

15   Ibid., 229–36.

16   Fletcher, *The Outbreak of the Civil War*, 37–9; L. Glow, 'The Manipulation of Committees in the Long Parliament, 1641–1642', *JBH*, 5 (1965), 44–5.

17   Glow, 'The Manipulation of Committees'; Russell, *The Crisis of Parliaments*, 329–30.

18   Gardiner, *History of England*, ix: 260.

19   Russell, *The Fall of the British Monarchies*, 228–32; Gardiner, *History of England*, ix: 243–7.

20   Clarendon, *The History of the Rebellion*, i: 204–6, 275–6; Russell, *The Fall of the British Monarchies*, 230–4.

21 Clarendon, *History of the Rebellion*, i: 195; Gardiner, *History of England*, ix: 263–4, 290.

22 Gardiner, *History of England*, ix: 289.

23 Russell, *The Fall of the British Monarchies*, 342; Clarendon, *History of the Rebellion*, i: 275–6; Gardiner, *History of England*, ix: 287–8.

24 Russell, *The Crisis of Parliaments*, 330.

25 Clarendon, *History of the Rebellion*, i: 243–8; Whitelocke, *Memorials*, 43; C. Wedgwood, *The King's Peace* (New York, 1991 edn.), 439–40; Russell, *The Fall of the British Monarchies*, 291–5.

26 Clarendon, *History of the Rebellion*, i: 245–8; Gardiner, *History of England*, ix: 313–14.

27 Gardiner, *History of England*, ix: 316.

28 Ibid., 326–30; Fletcher, *The Outbreak of the English Civil War*, 12–13.

29 Fletcher, *The Outbreak of the English Civil War*, 14.

30 Whitelocke, *Memorials*, 43–4; Gardiner, *History of England*, 331–69; Wedgwood, *A Coffin for King Charles* (New York, 1991).

31 Clarendon, *History of the Rebellion*, i: 260–2; Whitelocke, *Memorials*, 44.

32 Wheeler, *The Making of a World Power*, 121–2; Fletcher, *The Outbreak of the English Civil War*, 29–31.

33 Fletcher, *The Outbreak of the English Civil War*, 29.

34 Stevenson, *The Scottish Revolution*, 215–17.

35 Ibid.

36 Ibid., 219–33.

37 Clarendon, *History of the Rebellion*, i: 260, 264–5, 274, 281; Whitelocke, *Memorials*, 45.

38 Gardiner, *History of England*, ix: 384–400.

39 Ibid., x: 3–5.

40 Stevenson, *The Scottish Revolution*, 233–38; Russell, *The Fall of the British Monarchies*, 304–29.

41 Ohlmeyer, *Civil War and Restoration*, 96–9; P. Corish in Moody, ed., *New History of Ireland*, iii: 290–91; Clarke, *The Old English in Ireland*, 158–60.

42 Clarke, *The Old English in Ireland*, 154–5; Corish in Moody, ed., *New History of Ireland*, iii: 24.

43 Clarke, *The Old English in Ireland*, 156–7.

44 Ibid., 56–8; Corish in Moody, ed., *New History of Ireland*, iii: 290–91; B. Mac Cuarta, ed., *Ulster, 1641* (Belfast, 1993).

45 N. Canny in J. Ohlmeyer, ed., *Ireland: From Independence to Occupation, 1641–1660* (Cambridge, 1995), 26–30; Ohlmeyer in Ibid., 1–3.

46 The T[homason] T[racts], E110 (9), *A Remonstrance of the Beginning and Proceedings of the Rebellion … * (May 1642). The place of publication for all Thomason Tracts was London unless otherwise noted; E. Shagan, 'Constructing Discord: Ideology, Propaganda, and English Responses to the Irish Rebellion of 1641,' *JBS*, 36 (1997), 4–34; K. Lindley, 'The Impact of the 1641 Rebellion Upon England and Wales, 1641–5,' *IHS*, 18 (1972), 143–75.

47 Corish in Moody, ed., *New History of Ireland*, 291–3; J. Wheeler, *Cromwell in Ireland* (Dublin, 1999), 8–15; J. Beckett, *The Cavalier Duke: A Life of James Butler, The First Duke of Ormond* (Belfast, 1990), 23.

48 TT, E149 (34), *An Exact Relation of all Such Occurrences … in the North of Ireland Since the Outbreak of This Horrid, Bloody, and Unparalleled Rebellion*, (4 June 1642).

49 Wheeler, *Cromwell in Ireland*, 8–13.

50 Ibid.; One of the worst anti-Catholic tracts was TT, E508, J. Temple, *The Irish Rebellion*, (London, 1646).

51 Corish in Moody, ed., *New History of Ireland*, iii: 293.

52 Ibid., 294; J. Ohlmeyer, 'The Dunkirk of Ireland: Wexford Privateers during the 1640s', *Journal of the Wexford Historical Society*, 10 (1988–9), 23–49; J. Ohlmeyer, 'Irish Privateers during the Civil War, 1642–50', *MM*, 76 (May 1990), 119–33.

53 D. Stevenson, *Scottish Covenanters and Irish Confederates* (Belfast, 1981), 72–98; H. Hazlett, 'The Recruitment and Organization of the Scottish Army in Ulster, 1642–49', in T. Moody, *et al.*, eds, *Essays in British and Irish History in Honor of James Eadie Todd* (London, 1949), 107–09, 123.

54 TT E149 (12), *A True Relation of the Proceedings of the Scottish Army Now in Ireland*, (13 May 1642), 2–6; E. Hogan, ed., *The History of the War of Ireland from 1641 to 1653, by a British Officer of the*

Regiment of Sir John Clotworthy (Dublin, 1873), 25–7.

55 Whitelocke, *Memorials*, 46.

56 National Archives of Ireland, M2450–1, *The Order Books of the Lords Justices and Council*, (2 vols., Dublin, 1 August–30 November 1642); I. Ryder, *An English Army for Ireland* (Belfast, 1987), 14–15; Wheeler, *Cromwell in Ireland*, 48–52.

57 TT, E146 (14), *A True Report of the Late Good Success in Ireland*, (2 May 1642), 2–6; TT E145 (16), *Captain Yarner's Relation of the Battle Fought at Kilrush Upon the 15th Day of April*, (4 May 1642), 1–7.

58 C. Russell, 'The British Problem and the English Civil War', *History*, 72 (1987), 395–415.

59 TT, E181 (2), *The Grand Remonstrance*, (1641), 8–19.

60 Russell, *The Crisis of Parliaments*, 336–7; Russell, *The Fall of the British Monarchies*, 304, where Russell concludes that Charles was probably not seeking Scottish military assistance, but was trying to get the Scots disengaged from English affairs. He acknowledges that Gardiner, *History of England*, ix: 418, and Stevenson, *The Scottish Revolution*, 223 disagree.

61 J. Kenyon, *The Civil Wars of England* (New York, 1988), 26.

62 Clarendon, *History of the Rebellion*, ii: 32; Gardiner, *History of England*, x: 108, 112.

63 TT, E181 (2), *The Grand Remonstrance*, 5–6.

64 Clarendon, *History of the Rebellion*, ii: 326–9.

65 Ibid., 333–8.

66 Clarendon, *History of the Rebellion*, ii: 350–4; Gardiner, *History of England*, x: 125; Russell, *The Fall of the British Monarchies*, 443–4.

67 Gardiner, *History of England*, x: 128–33.

68 Ibid., 158–9; Clarendon, *History of the Rebellion*, ii: 355–7.

69 Clarendon, *History of the Rebellion*, ii: 357–8.

70 Whitelocke, *Memorials*, 50.

71 Kenyon, *The Civil Wars of England*, 26–7.

72 K. Bottigheimer, *English Money, Irish Land* (Oxford, 1971), 40–41, 54.

73 TT, E121 (44), *A True Copy of Two Letters Brought … .From My Lord Forbes in Ireland*, (12 October 1642).

74 O'Siochru, *Confederate Ireland*, 40–4; J. Gilbert, ed., *A Contemporary History of Affairs in Ireland, from AD 1641 to 1652* (Dublin, 1879–80), i: 37–41; R. Elkin, 'The Interaction between the Irish Rebellion and the English Civil War' (PhD Dissertation, University of Illinois, Urbana, 1971), 106.

75 Ohlmeyer, in Ohlmeyer, ed., *Ireland From Independence to Occupation*, 89–111.

76 Gilbert, ed., *A Contemporary History*, i: 41.

77 N. Perry, 'The Infantry of the Confederate Army of Leinster', *IS*, 61 (1983), 233–35.

78 TT, E125 (15), *A Journal of the Most Memorable Passages in Ireland* (19 October 1642), 1–3.

79 R. Hutton, *The Royalist War Effort* (London, 1982), 3–22.

80 Gardiner, *History of England*, x: 169–70.

81 *CSPD, 1641–43*, 253–4, William Legg to Secretary Nicholas, 14 January 1642.

82 C. Firth and R. Rait, eds, *The Acts and Ordinances of the Interregnum, 1642–1660* (London, 1911), i:1.

83 Hutton, *The Royalist War Effort*, 3–21; M. Bennett, *The Civil Wars in Britain and Ireland, 1638–1651* (Oxford, 1997), 130–31.

84 I. Roy, 'The Royalist Army in the First Civil War,' (PhD Dissertation, Oxford, 1963), 101, 162–3.

85 Hutton, *The Royalist War Effort*, 87–9; Barratt, *Cavaliers*, 8–10.

86 I. Roy, 'The Royalist Council of War, 1642–6', *Bulletin of Historical Research*, 35 (1962), 150–68.

87 P. Young and A. Burne, *The Great Civil War* (Moreton-in-Marsh, 1998 edn), 15.

88 Roy, 'Royalist Army', 3, 103–7; Barratt, *Cavaliers*, 11–17.

89 Hutton, *Royalist War Effort*, 29, 53, 60–1, 76; C. Firth, *Cromwell's Army* (London, 1992 edn.), 15–22.

90 J. Engberg, 'Royalist Finances During the English First Civil War, 1642–46', *Scandinavian Economic History Review*, 14 (1966), 73–96.

91 Firth and Rait, eds, *Acts and Ordinances*, i: 6–8, 14.

92 P. Edwards, *Dealing in Death: The Arms Trade and the British Civil Wars, 1638–52* (Stroud, 2000); PRO SP28/264 contains seven bundles of warrants for the purchase of arms and equipment ordered and paid for by parliament in early 1643.

93 B. Donagon, 'Halcyon Days and the Literature of War: England's Military Education Before 1642', *P&P*, 147 (1995), 65–100; G. Davies, 'The Parliamentary Army under the Earl of Essex, 1642–5', *EHR*, 49 (1934), 36, fn. 1; Barratt, *Cavaliers*, 3–6.

94 I. Gardiner, *The History of the Great Civil War, 1642–1649* (London, 1894), i: 13–27.

95 Young and Burne, *The Great Civil War*, 18–22.

96 Ibid., 41–4; J. Kenyon and J. Ohlmeyer, eds, *The Civil Wars: A Military History of England, Scotland, and Ireland, 1638–1660* (Oxford, 1998), 130–2.

97 *A & O*, i: 36.

98 I. Gentles in Ohlmeyer, ed., *The Civil Wars in England*, 130–2; Young and Burne, *The Great Civil War*, 32–1; Gardiner, *Civil Wars*, i: 43–51; Davies, 'The Parliamentary Army', 36–8; Clarendon, *History of the Rebellion*, i: 44–9; Whitelocke, *Memorials*, 61; TT, E128 (13), *A Full and True Relation of the Great Battle* …, (4 November 1642); E124 (18), *A True Copy of a Letter* …, (26 October 1642); E124 (21), *A Letter Sent from a Worthy Divine* …, (27 October 1642); E124 (26), *An Exact and True Relation of the Dangerous and Bloody Fight* …, (28 October 1642); E126 (39), *A Most True and Exact Relation* …, (9 November 1642).

99 Gentles in Ohlmeyer, ed., *The Civil Wars*, 132–3; Young and Burne, *The Great Civil War*, 28–31.

100 Young and Burne, *The Great Civil War*, 29–31.

101 Clarendon, *History of the Rebellion*, iii: 57.

102 Gardiner, *Civil Wars*, i: 57–9.

103 Ibid., 52–4.

104 Ibid., 54–5; Clarendon, *History of the Rebellion*, iii: 59–64.

105 Young and Burne, *The Great Civil War*, 31–3; Gardiner, *Civil Wars*, i: 16–18.

106 Whitelocke, *Memorials*, 61–3; Clarendon, *History of the Rebellion*, iii: 74–6; Gardiner, *Civil Wars*, i: 58; Young and Burne, *The Great Civil Wars*, 32–3.

107 Whitelocke, *Memorials*, 62–4.

108 Ibid., 64; Clarendon, *History of the Rebellion*, iii: 79–83.

CHAPTER THREE

The wars expand

During the fall and winter of 1642–3, the English protagonists divided their nation into military regions as their garrisons and field forces proliferated. In Scotland the Covenanters faced a growing royalist party seeking to overturn the Scottish revolutionary settlement. Additionally, the Covenanters saw the possibility of affecting the outcome of the English war by political and perhaps military intervention, hoping that their entrance into that struggle would leave a victorious English parliament in their debt. In this way the Scots could possibly achieve religious uniformity in Britain. For the Irish Confederates, the continuation of the English Civil War meant that neither the royalists nor the Westminster government could send sufficient military resources to crush their insurrection. Thus, Irish Catholics had a reasonable chance of achieving political autonomy or of driving the English and Scottish forces out of Ireland.

The struggle for the Provinces

When the struggle for control of England commenced in the summer of 1642, the nation divided along geographical lines dictated by how close or far counties were from the centers of royalist and parliamentarian power and by the inclinations and politics of the leading county families (see map 7).[1] The process of sorting out who was going to control specific localities was messy and varied.

In general, a majority of the nobility sided with the king and worked to bring their localities into the royalist camp. The Earl of Newcastle secured the trained bands of the northern counties for the king and raised a superb regional army around his regiments known as the Whitecoats, from the color of their uniforms. Newcastle defended the north from York and was one of six magnates whom Charles appointed as regional Lieutenant Generals. Similarly, Charles appointed the Marquis of Hertford to command royalist efforts from Wiltshire and Hampshire west to Wales and he commissioned the Earl of Derby to lead royalist efforts in Lancashire. These nobles and others served as the military leaders for regional groupings of counties that provided Charles with men and money during the first half of 1643. Ultimately, these magnates failed to maintain royalist control in their regions, but initially they gave the king's cause a tremendous boost.[2]

Map 7 Counties of England

Not all nobles supported the king. The Earl of Warwick commanded the parliamentary navy, the Earl of Essex commanded parliament's army, and six of Essex's regimental commanders at Edgehill were noblemen.[3] Many younger sons, such as Sir Thomas Fairfax, also served parliament in its central and regional armies. However, the peace party was strongly represented in the House of Lords after the battle of Edgehill, and only the king's unwillingness to resume sincere negotiations for a settlement kept many parliamentarian lords from changing sides. As the war intensified in 1643, a number of formerly parliamentarian nobles left London and found their way to Oxford. Others, such as the Earl of Manchester, were forced out of the increasingly radical parliamentary cause in 1645. By then, the House of Lords was a shadow of its former size.

The gentry split more evenly than the nobility, although they were more susceptible to the pressure of whichever side was nearest and strongest in their localities than were the nobles. Both sides recruited their officers and much of their cavalry from this critical social class, although royalism seems to have been the stronger and more prevalent view of a majority of the gentry. Most of the towns and cities, on the other hand, displayed strong parliamentary sympathies, in large part because puritanism and anti-episcopal feelings were strongest amongst them. London was the most important urban center, but places like Gloucester, Manchester, and Hull displayed strong parliamentarian loyalties. This situation meant that the royalists lacked access to most seaports and to the commercial wealth that was so necessary to their war effort. Hence, Rupert's capture of Bristol and the royalist success in Chester in 1643 were extremely important.

In the final analysis, as long as parliament held London, Charles's chances of winning a protracted war were slim. London's population dwarfed that of any other city in Britain or Ireland, where the largest cities had populations of no more than 30,000 people. The London trained bands could muster 16,000 soldiers. The citizenry rose to the occasion when Charles threatened the city in November 1642 by voluntarily serving on the work gangs that established a ring of fortifications around the capital. And Londoners provided most of the cash that paid for the recruitment and arming of Essex's army. Charles, by not following Rupert's advice to make a quick and strong lunge for London in late October, lost one of his best chances to capture the center of the revolution.[4]

English Catholics did not split their loyalties. Catholics had nothing to gain if parliament won. They had some hope of toleration if the king won, especially since they constituted as much as forty per cent of the royalist officer corps. Their adherence to the king was a mixed blessing for Charles. He gained many competent professional soldiers and some remarkably wealthy supporters. However, his decision to allow Catholics to serve in his forces confirmed to many that Pym was right about the connection of royalism and Catholicism, thus stiffening the resolve of many parliamentarians.[5]

Scotland divides and decides

Scotland enjoyed a year of relative domestic peace and calm after the end of the Second Bishops' War. From the time of Charles's return to London in November 1641 to the outbreak of the Civil War in August 1642, Scotland stayed out of the English Civil War, but she was deeply involved in the war in Ireland. The Scots sent 10,000 soldiers to Ulster, but only after the English parliament promised to pay them at the higher English rate. Charles did not ratify the treaty between the Covenanters and the English parliament agreeing to these terms, but the Scots ignored this point and sent their troops to Ireland anyway. From their earliest days in Ulster, the Scots received only a trickle of the promised support from England. Their commander, the Earl of Leven, stayed only a brief time in Ireland because he found it impossible to control his unpaid soldiers. Command of the Scottish army therefore fell to Major General Robert Monro.[6] None the less, the Scots maintained their army in Ulster for the next four years at a strength of between six and ten thousand men.[7]

The Scots proved repeatedly that the Irish could not defeat them in a stand-up fight. Consequently, they secured a base encompassing Antrim, Down, and Armagh, and they established a close working relationship with the garrisons of British settlers in Ulster. The Scots could not push their authority into the interior of Ulster because they lacked the horses, wagons, and food needed to sustain a long field campaign.[8]

Unhappy with the breakdown in English affairs that weakened the campaign in Ireland, the Scottish council encouraged the king to accept the good offices of Scottish commissioners in negotiations between him and the English parliament. Charles refused these offers brusquely, telling them to tend to their work in Scotland.[9] Meanwhile, the Covenanters' attention was focused on the prosecution of the leading 'incendiaries and plotters' from their previous struggle with the king. While pursuing their political foes, they fostered resentment against themselves and support for the king among the Scottish nobility. By the summer of 1642 a growing number of nobles were drifting toward royalism. Charles was slow to encourage them, relying instead on the Marquis of Hamilton to keep the Covenanters out of the parliamentarian camp.[10]

After his failure to seize Hull, in April 1642, the king showed signs that he wanted to mobilize Scottish resources against his English foes. His hand was forced by a group of Scottish royalists who petitioned the Scottish council to declare its support for the king. The Covenanters recognized the danger of such a step and the ministers and lairds organized demonstrations in Edinburgh against such action. The Scottish council bent to the wind of political protest and refused to enter the propaganda fray in England. In response to this setback, the king sent Hamilton to Edinburgh to rally royalism and to ensure that the Covenanters did not lead Scotland into an alliance with his English opponents.[11]

An increasingly strong Scottish royalist faction coalesced. This group included the Marquis of Huntly, the Earls of Airlie, Montrose, and Nithsdale, and Lord Aboyne. They did not advocate military resistance to the Covenanters, or armed assistance for the king. They provided, however, a powerful counterpoise to the extreme Covenanters, such as Argyll, who believed that they never could trust Charles to live up to his agreements and, therefore, that they needed to assist a parliamentarian victory in England. Events in England clearly destabilized Scottish affairs, making a Scottish civil war increasingly possible.

In February 1643, Scottish commissioners traveled to Oxford to convince the king to accept Scottish mediation in England. They also sought to get him to take steps toward the unity of the two nations' churches and to call a Scottish parliament to discuss the dangerous situation. Charles refused to summon a parliament and again firmly rejected Covenanter mediation. The commissioners received rude treatment in the streets of Oxford as well, leaving them with a bitter taste in their mouth for royalists. Further, the king refused to give the commissioners permission to travel to London to discuss affairs with the parliamentarians. None the less, one commissioner traveled to London where he joined two other Scottish commissioners in a diplomatic delegation to the Long Parliament. Their mission was to get English financial support for the Ulster army and to convince the parliamentarians to agree to religious uniformity.[12]

Charles saw the growing danger of Scottish collusion with the parliamentarians. Thus he shifted his political strategy to keep the Scots preoccupied with Ulster and home affairs. This worked until the Covenanters learned of a plot, centered on the Queen and her court at York, for an Irish invasion of western Scotland by Irish Catholics. This plot was discovered when the Scottish forces in Ulster captured Antrim as he entered the province. This discovery, along with strong Covenanter suspicions that the Earl of Montrose was involved, increased Argyll's support among the burghers, lairds, and ministers. Thus he was able to overcome resistance to negotiations with the English parliament for an alliance.[13] Finally, the king's council in Edinburgh found it difficult to resist Covenanter calls for a convention, in lieu of a parliament, to meet in June 1643.

Stalemate in Ireland

As the English Civil War expanded, the situation in Ireland improved significantly for the Confederate Catholics. In Ulster, the Irish professional soldier Owen Roe O'Neill and his officers organized and trained a fighting force of about 4,000 men. This army became an effective military organization just as the Scots army was forced, through the lack of money and supplies, to remain in its coastal enclaves. O'Neill soon controlled Ulster's interior and operated with increasing success in northeastern Leinster against Protestant garrisons (see map 8).[14]

In Leinster, Thomas Preston and his Irish veterans of Spanish military service created a Catholic army of six infantry regiments.[15] During the fall and early winter Preston's forces ground away at the Protestant strongholds constituting Dublin's outer ring of defenses. These raids narrowed Ormond's logistical base. Ormond, with a Dublin garrison of six to eight regiments of foot, and two of horse, consistently defeated Preston's units in small skirmishes.[16] However, as long as Preston avoided a major battle against Ormond's army, his troops were able to control large areas of central and western Leinster. By the fall of 1642, little support was reaching Dublin from England, as the king and parliament diverted the money intended for Ireland into their war chests.[17] As a result, Ormond was unable to pay his soldiers and faced mutinies in his outlying garrisons, making it difficult to maintain a field army.[18]

Things were less hopeful for the Confederates in Munster, although the adherence of Wexford and Waterford to their cause balanced the situation somewhat. Munster was dominated by the Protestant forces commanded by Murrough O'Brien, Lord Inchiquin. Inchiquin had garrisons in Cork and Youghal, and his troops proved more

Map 8 Provinces of Ireland, 1640s

than a match for the Catholic army led by Lord Muskerry. In August 1642, when Muskerry tried to face Inchiquin's regiments at Liscarroll, County Cork, Inchiquin's men made quick work of the fight, killing hundreds of the Irish. In Munster, as in the north, when the English Civil War diverted money, men, and supplies to armies in England, the anti-Catholic forces could not sustain the operations needed to defeat the Confederates. The war in Munster settled down to one of raid and counter-raid, marked by mutual brutality.

Parliament gropes to find the sinews of war

As the antagonists in England settled into winter quarters in 1642–3, they faced the daunting task of finding resources to sustain the war. Efforts by the parliamentary peace party failed to end the war, although the peace party continued throughout the winter to advocate negotiations. Only after it became clear that Charles would never accept the abolition of episcopacy nor grant parliament a voice in the appointment of his advisors, did the parliamentarians discontinue active discussions about a settlement.[19] Although in hindsight it appears that these efforts were futile, they proved important in keeping the parliamentarian coalition together. Pym believed that Charles would never accept parliamentary interference with the church nor give up his prerogative to name his counsellors. However, by supporting the peace process Pym kept the parliamentary peace party loyal to the cause. Charles never developed an effective peace strategy to support his military plans. Instead, he used negotiations as a cover for military maneuvers and political intrigue. Each time he did so he strengthened the resolve of his opponents.

The frustrations of the Long Parliament with the king's unwillingness to compromise allowed Pym to pass measures laying the financial and administrative foundation for a military victory. Parliament enacted crucial ordinances between 9 November and 15 December 1642 that were a reaction to the dangerous military situation and essential to the future existence of its forces. These included measures giving Essex increased judicial authority over his soldiers, ordering the seizure of horses in London for army use, and one '… for assessing of all such as have not contributed … for the raising of money, plate, horse, and horsemen.' The preamble of an ordinance of 26 November reiterated the view that 'Whereas the king seduced by wicked counsel hath raised an army and leveled war against the parliament, and great number of forces are daily raised under the command of papists and other ill-affected persons, by commissions from His Majesty … ,' it was necessary for parliament to raise an army to defend itself and the religion, law, and liberty of the whole kingdom.[20]

This November ordinance was the first of many that punished those who did not voluntarily support the cause. It established the principle of future confiscatory measures that would be used against 'malignants', the name applied to those who supported the king. The parliamentarians recognized that their army was going to cost a great deal of money. Therefore, they levied a tax called an assessment on Londoners who had not contributed to the costs of raising Essex's army up to five per cent of the value of their estates.[21]

The military situation had again, as during the Bishops' Wars, shaped political affairs. Parliament had usurped powers it never dreamed of having. Its use of ordinances was revolutionary. The parliamentarians justified the practice as necessary because the king had removed himself from his parliament. It created an army, signed a treaty with the Scots, and now was penalizing Londoners who refused to contribute. However, only a small proportion of the money raised by the Westminster governments during the next eighteen years came from fines levied on their opponents. Instead, John Pym recognized the need for taxation to support the war effort. Therefore, he created the components of a fiscal system that was to endure in England for the next two hundred years.[22]

Pym faced the daunting task of providing at least £695,000 for the pay of 20,000 English soldiers for one year, plus additional sums for munitions. Furthermore, parliament needed to support at least another 20,000 soldiers in Ireland, including the Scots.[23] The expenses of the navy were soaring, as parliament used its fleet to interdict royalist lines of communication and to escort forces and supplies along the coasts and to Ireland. Navy expenditures rose from £41,000 in 1642 to £320,000 in 1643, swallowing the customs revenue of £165,000.[24] For the first time in history, parliament was forced to provide adequate financial support for its armed forces or see many of its members executed. This situation focused thought in a remarkable way.

Parliament experimented with fiscal legislation in December 1642, as it passed ordinances extending the principles of the 26 November ordinance to the rest of England. It appointed committees to assess property, to levy and collect taxes, and to provide support to parliamentary forces in the counties.[25] None of these measures resolved the financial question of how to pay for the army and navy, but they established the practices that would be elaborated upon successfully over the next six years. The Commons also tried a number of expedients that made things worse. For example, it authorized customs collectors in ports outside of London to pay their receipts directly to their garrisons. Similarly, the House ordered the Treasurer of the Navy, Henry Vane, to divert £10,000 from the customs for the pay of the navy to the army.[26] Such actions shifted but did not solve the problem of insufficient revenue to support the war effort.

The Long Parliament resolved to discontinue the use of the Exchequer as the central treasury for state money for several reasons. The Exchequer had issued tallies in anticipation of revenues to pay the pensions of noted royalists. If revenue continued to flow through the Exchequer it would have been difficult to ignore the prior claim of these creditors. Also, the Exchequer had not performed efficiently during the Bishops' War and there had been criticism of the Exchequer and its procedures for the past thirty years. Finally, parliament had decided to designate certain taxes for certain purposes, such as the customs revenue for support of the navy and, therefore, it had ordered the collectors of the customs to pay their receipts directly to the Treasurer of the Navy.[27] Over the next two years parliament established a number of treasuries in London to receive and disburse the revenues from its various fiscal schemes. This seemingly decentralized system was to prove remarkably effective.

Passing new tax ordinances was one thing, collecting the money was another. The five per cent tax on those who had not contributed was difficult to collect and had a limited utility. Hoping to provide a steady flow of money for its forces and to repay its creditors, parliament resolved, on 18 February 1643, to impose a 'weekly assessment.' This decision came just after the Houses resolved that they would not accept a cessation of hostilities that did not first require the disbandment of the armies. The weekly assessment was levied on all of England and Wales. Designed to raise £33,886 per week, the ordinance levied a fixed amount on each county in a fashion similar to ship-money. Parliament established committees to oversee the implementation of the tax. These committees were to appoint assessors, collectors, and treasurers to carry out the requisite work. The tax was levied on nearly all property save church ornaments and servants' wages, and its payment was to continue for three months.[28]

The February assessment ordinance established the machinery used to collect all future assessment taxes. Perhaps of greatest importance, the Long Parliament adopted the principle that such direct taxes should be paid according to county quotas fixed in London, not as rates assessed locally. This ended the use and abuse of the old subsidies and went a long way toward making state revenue a reasonably predictable amount.[29] This last characteristic was very important because only with predictable revenues could the Westminster governments borrow cash in anticipation of tax receipts.

The rise of regional associations and the strategic environment, 1643

While the main armies contended for control of the Thames Valley, both sides raised regional armies to fight for control of the rest of the nation. Charles entrusted his regional commands to leading nobles such as Newcastle. The Long Parliament created its regional armies and associations of counties with a series of ordinances, beginning in December 1642. The first of these was the association of the counties of Northampton, Leicester, Derby, Rutland, Nottingham, Huntingdon, Bedford, and Buckingham for 'the mutual defense one of another.' This ordinance, like all subsequent measures, appointed a committee to raise money, horses, men, etc. 'for suppression of rebellion,' and it appointed a military commander, in this case Lord Gray of Groby, to serve as regional Major General.[30]

Parliament created three other associations in 1643. The first was the Eastern Association of Norfolk, Suffolk, Essex, Cambridge, and Hertford. This became the most famous of the associations because it was the most successful and because Oliver Cromwell was transferred from Essex's army to the new Eastern Association's army to raise a cavalry regiment. The next association ordinance linked Warwickshire and Staffordshire.[31] The Long Parliament passed a similar ordinance 'for the preservation of the western parts of the kingdom,' associating Cornwall, Devon, Somerset, Dorset, Wiltshire, Bristol, and Oxford, but royalist forces controlled most of this region.

As a result of the regionalization of the war, the Long Parliament decentralized its war effort. These associations defended themselves against local royalists and fended off raiding parties, but most of them were unable to prevent royalist armies from crossing their territory and seizing their major towns. The Western Association was the first to fail, as Sir Ralph Hopton organized a strong royalist army in Cornwall and defeated the local parliamentarians at Braddock Down, on 19 January 1643. The royalists pushed on to Plymouth, where they besieged a parliamentary garrison that was supported by sea from London. In Warwickshire and Staffordshire, the

Association's forces under Lord Brooke initially made progress against the royalists, driving them out of Stratford and laying siege to Lichfield. When Brooke was killed during the siege, he was replaced by Sir John Gell who successfully completed the operation. Gell, however, was unable to stop the steady growth of royalist control in the region as the royalists picked off one strongpoint after another.[32]

The creation of regional associations reflected both sides' lack of a coherent military strategy to win the war. Charles understood that London was central to his enemies' war effort and vaguely planned to cut the city off from the sea by some sort of pincer movement of his armies that would meet east of London. Then his cavalry could interdict London's food supply. But he did not have a grand design to have his forces in the southwest cooperate with the army in Oxford, or for Newcastle's northern army to converge on London and help crush Essex's army.[33] The dynamics of the military situation pushed the royalists toward two contradictory strategies. One was regionally focused, while the other was nationally focused.

Charles could only win the war by taking London and destroying the main parliamentary army. But he could not afford to lose Cornwall, Wales, or the north in the process. If the Cavaliers failed to hold these areas, their ability to wage war would be undermined and they would not have the resources necessary to conquer London. Therefore, royalist military efforts in 1643 focused on clearing the Roundheads away from the base areas and on capturing the important towns and routes between them to facilitate further operations.

The parliamentarians also lacked a clear military strategy. Their resort to regional associations stemmed from their lack of a central executive strong enough to focus political and military energies on the task of destroying the king's army and his base in Oxford. The Earl of Essex had been unable to conduct the type of operations in the Thames Valley needed to defeat the king. He lacked effective control over the other parliamentarian military forces, although he was their titular commander. Consequently, the Long Parliament adopted a military strategy in 1643 that was predominantly defensive. Regional associations supported regional forces that could accomplish this task, while parliament hoped that Essex would be free to move against Oxford. Unfortunately, hope is not a plan.

Although John Pym was unable to develop or implement a military strategy to destroy the king's ability to fight, he did pursue a political strategy that promised, in the long run, to doom Charles. The first part of Pym's strategy was to keep parliament united. He did this by allowing the peace and middle 'parties' in the Houses to pursue negotiations with the king.[34] The second important part of Pym's political strategy was to bring the Scottish Covenanters into the English Civil War on parliament's side. Charles greatly facilitated these efforts.

The king's rejection of any terms short of parliament's surrender prevented the parliamentary peace faction from convincing the middle group in the Houses to trust the king. As the military situation shifted against parliament in June, Charles became even more unwilling to compromise. His rejection of Scottish mediation, along with the revelation of the royalist plots to invade Scotland, enabled Argyll to convince his fellow Scots that their best hope for the safety of their revolutionary settlement lay in an alliance with the Long Parliament. The king's order to Ormond, in January 1643, to negotiate with the Irish Catholics for a cessation of hostilities in Ireland, also had become common knowledge by May. The Scots recognized that a cessation in Ireland would allow Ormond to send troops to England. By June, the Covenanters had summoned a national convention to ratify an agreement with the Long Parliament. Only English reluctance to commit to religious uniformity delayed the alliance.[35]

Royalist victories, May to July 1643

While these political machinations were taking place the Civil War continued. During the winter of 1642–3, a confused pattern of local conflict characterized operations in England. Brooke's and Gell's successes in the Midlands and Sir William Waller's victories in the south were offset by royalist achievements such as Hopton's consolidation of Cornwall and Newcastle's victories in Yorkshire. By mid spring, the balance of military power shifted toward the royalists, due in part to the arms and money sent to England by Queen Henrietta Maria.

In the Midlands, Prince Rupert led a cavalry force against the Cheshire parliamentarian leader Sir William Brereton and Gell. On 3 April he sacked Birmingham and on 21 April captured Lichfield, after an eleven-day siege. These achievements cleared communications between Wales and Oxford, allowing the king to draw Welsh levies more easily. These maneuvers were offset somewhat by William Waller's capture of Hereford with his parliamentary troops on 25 April.

In the Thames Valley it initially looked as if Essex was going to conduct a major offensive against Oxford. His advance was made possible by parliament's efforts to provide Essex with the money, munitions, and recruits needed to bring his regiments up to strength. Leaving winter quarters in Windsor, Essex encircled the royalist garrison in Reading and forced it to surrender, on 26 April. Charles was unable to break Essex's siege and was forced back on his posts around Oxford.[36] Essex, however, did not push on to Oxford. Instead, he went into camp near Reading and called on London for more money for his men. The conditions in his camp were unsanitary and his soldiers poorly sheltered, leading to a major outbreak of typhus that quickly sapped his army's strength and Essex's will. For the remainder of the spring Essex failed to maintain pressure on the royalists in the central theater of the war, allowing them to shift forces from Oxford to other regions.

By early May the balance of power in the southwest also began to swing in favor of the royalists when Sir Ralph Hopton and his tough Welsh infantrymen crushed the Earl of Stamford's Roundheads in a battle near Stratton, on 16 May. Stamford lost 300 men killed and 1,700 captured, along with his artillery and ammunition. This victory, along with Rupert's success in the Midlands, forced Waller to evacuate Hereford and Worcester. On 19 May Prince Maurice left Oxford with a cavalry brigade to reinforce Hopton. By the end of May this combined force, under the titular command of the Marquis of Hertford, had overrun most of Devon and was threatening Dorset.[37]

Essex remained inactive as his army wasted away due to disease. His failure to act allowed the royalists to shift more forces to other regions and encouraged London royalists to attempt a coup against Pym and his allies. This plot, led by Lord Conway, Edward Waller, and the Earl of Portland, came to a head in late May. These men hoped to use a royal commission of array to secure the obedience of the Westminster and the London trained bands. This force then was to let the king's army into the city. The plot was discovered and quickly foiled by the arrest of the ringleaders, but it indicated the strength of royalist sympathy in London. In the long run it convinced many men in the peace party in the House of Lords that nothing short of a parliamentary surrender was acceptable to Charles. Pym used the outrage engendered by Charles's plot to prod the Lords to accept the impeachment of the Queen and to pass the National Covenant, an oath to stand against the king 'as long as Papists were in arms.'[38]

Pym's political victories were the only good news for his cause for several months. In mid June Essex again stirred himself to action, but failed to take Islip, north of Oxford. Shortly after this, Rupert's royalist cavalry killed John Hampden in a skirmish at Chalgrove Field and raided close to London, unnerving parliament and disrupting the flow of food into the capital. Only London's extensive fortifications, which had been built with an enormous expenditure of effort by the Londoners during the spring, prevented the royalists from entering the suburbs.[39]

As Essex's offensive stalled, the Queen arrived in Oxford with 1,500 soldiers, money, and 300 barrels of gunpowder. This convoy was only part of the results of Henrietta Maria's mission to the continent over the past winter, where she had pawned jewels to procure as much as a £1 million worth of arms, munitions, and coin. She had returned to England on 23 February, landing near Bridlington Town. She spent March and April in York, rallying support and conferring with Montrose and Hamilton about the situation in Scotland and the options available to deter the Covenanters from entering the English war. She had favored Montrose's and Antrim's invasion schemes, but her husband decided to continue to trust the ineffectual Hamilton to convince the Scots to stay neutral. The Queen's return to Oxford on 13 July was an indication of how well things were going for the royalists.

In Yorkshire, Newcastle led his 16,000-man army in a string of victories (see map 9), beginning with his defeat of the Sir Thomas Fairfax and his father Ferdinando at Adwalton Moor, on 30 June. This battle was hard fought by both sides. Sir Thomas led his outnumbered troops in a series of charges that kept the Cavaliers off balance. Eventually numbers told, as Newcastle's troops routed the Fairfaxes' 4,000 men. Newcastle now cleared the West Riding and continued south toward Lincoln and Nottingham. The royalists also came very close to gaining possession of Hull through the treachery of the Hothams, who plannedd to surrender the city when Newcastle arrived. At the last minute, on 28–29 June, their plot to surrender was uncovered by the mayor, who arrested the Hothams. Lord Ferdinando Fairfax become governor of Hull after his flight from Adwalton Moor, securing it for parliament. Now Newcastle had to decide whether to drive south toward the Eastern Association or to capture Hull first. Initially he decided to march south, after protecting the Queen's march to Oxford.[40]

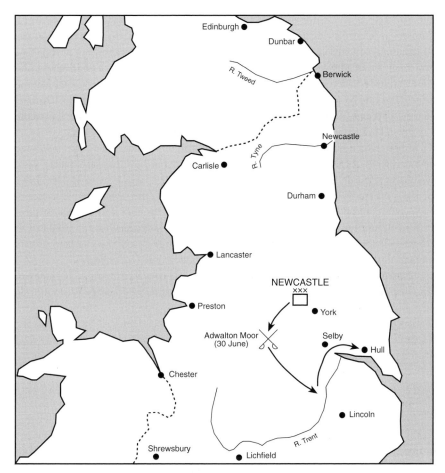

Map 9 The Northern Campaign, 1643

While Newcastle was driving the parliamentarians out of Yorkshire, Hopton and Maurice were maneuvering against Sir William Waller's Roundheads near Bath. Waller's army was parliament's last hope to prevent the royalists from securing the southwest. Waller and his opponents each commanded about 7,000 men, although the royalist troops were qualitatively superior to the parliamentarians.[41] By 5 July, after several weeks of maneuver, Waller established his army on Lansdown Hill, a good defensive position about five miles northeast of Bath. This position blocked the royalists' route to Bath and appeared to be too strong to storm successfully.

Hopton and Maurice decided to withdraw and seek another route into Bath. As they did so, Waller attacked their rearguard. This attack initially succeeded, forcing Hopton and Maurice to counterattack. By 2 p.m. the royalists had driven Waller's cavalry back to its initial positions. At this point Hopton's tough Cornish infantrymen asked their commander to allow them to attack Waller's entrenched troops on the hill, 500 feet above. Hopton agreed, and Maurice threw his cavalry forward in a simultaneous attack on the flank. After a fierce fight the Cornishmen pushed the parliamentarians out of their positions, forcing Waller to withdraw his troops to a stonewall about 400 yards behind their initial positions. By evening both armies were exhausted. In the night Waller withdrew to the fortifications of Bath, leaving lit matches on the stonewall to deceive his foes. The royalists had achieved a narrow victory, although it became more costly when an ammunition wagon accidentally exploded, badly wounding the charismatic Hopton.[42]

Waller remained in Bath long enough to supply his troops. Then, on 10 July, he marched toward Devizes, where Sir Ralph Hopton and his Cornish infantry were awaiting a critically needed supply of gunpowder from Oxford (see map 10). Waller saw an opportunity to trap the royalists in Devizes while they were unable to fight a major battle and perhaps to starve them into submission. Therefore he marched his army to Roundway Down, three miles north of Devizes, from where he could isolate Hopton's force. While these maneuvers took place, Maurice led his exhausted cavalry brigade to Oxford, where he remounted his troopers with fresh horses.

Charles, learning of Hopton's situation, ordered two fresh cavalry brigades to march immediately to Devizes. This column, commanded by Henry Wilmot, rode west and then southwest, arriving at Roundway Down on the morning of 13 July. Waller, with about 2,500 infantry and 2,000 cavalry, had deployed his army on the north slope of the Down, facing the royalists as they advanced west along the road from Marlborough. Wilmot immediately attacked Waller's army, even though his men had been in the saddle all night. His attack struck the parliamentarians' right flank where Sir Arthur Haselrig's cavalry regiment was posted. After a fierce collision and melee of horsemen, Haselrig's soldiers gave way and were driven from the field by the victorious Cavaliers. On the northern flank, Sir John Byron led the charge against Waller's cavalry regiment. Waller's men proved to be no match for Byron's troopers and soon fled. As the two cavalry wings of Waller's army streamed west they unintentionally rode over a steep bluff, and hundreds were killed or wounded in the crush of falling horses and men.

After the royalists had defeated his cavalry, Waller's infantry remained isolated but unbroken in the center of the field. Wilmot lacked the infantry needed to assault such a force of pikemen and musketeers. Hopton, however, had watched the development of the battle and decided to lead his Welsh regiments from Devizes against the rear of the parliamentary infantry two miles to the north. Hopton's pikemen fell on the Roundheads with a vengeance, quickly breaking their cohesion. Waller's infantry, most of whom had been recruited in the past month, put up little resistance before surrendering.[43]

Waller's army was destroyed at Roundway Down, leaving the southwest in royalist hands and opening the way to further royalist advances. Charles and his council saw the opportunities this victory opened. Rupert led the bulk of the remaining cavalry in Oxford west to join Maurice and Hopton before Bristol. Bristol was the kingdom's second largest port and offered the Cavaliers improved access to Ireland and the continent. Its capture would complete the conquest of the west, minus Plymouth

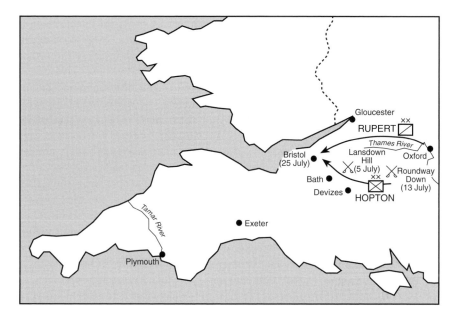

Map 10 The Western Campaign, 1643

and Exeter, giving the king access to the financial resources of a considerable commercial community.

Bristol was well-fortified, with the town protected on the east by the River Avon, and on the west by the Fromme River and a series of fortifications along the hills. The parliamentarian governor, Nathaniel Fiennes had 100 cannon mounted in his forts and redoubts, but his garrison of 1,800 men was too small to man properly the three miles of defenses.[44]

The royalists' council of war determined a course of action on 25 July. Hopton and the Cornishmen favored a siege to starve the place into submission, rather than to risk a costly assault. Rupert pushed for an assault, believing that the garrison was too small to withstand one and convinced that the place had to be taken quickly.[45] The council agreed with Rupert and decided to launch the main attack with five columns against the forts on the west side. Maurice was to lead a supporting attack against the defenses on the east side of the city. Although the attacks were scheduled to commence at daybreak, 26 July, Hopton's Cornishmen jumped the start, assailing their objectives at 3 a.m. Rupert, hearing their gunfire, ordered an assault by the three brigades of infantry on the north and west of the city.

The defenders fought hard to prevent the royalists from breaching their works, and for the first few hours repulsed every assault. However, Wentworth's brigade of royalist infantry found a gap in the western defenses and opened a breach. Rupert reacted to this success by ordering all reserves to be thrown through the breach and toward the city's inner defenses. The defenders were too few to eject the royalists and, after several hours of hand-to-hand fighting, Fiennes determined that further

81

resistance was futile. Fiennes surrendered on lenient terms, giving the king possession of the greatest prize he had yet received from his military efforts. Charles paid dearly for this triumph, losing as many as 500 men killed, including many important officers.[46]

The day after the assault on Bristol a battle was fought near Gainsborough, in Lincolnshire, between a Roundhead force of 1,800 cavalrymen, led by Sir John Meldrum and Colonel Oliver Cromwell, and about 2,000 royalist cavalry led by Charles, Lord Cavendish, Newcastle's younger brother. The parliamentarians won the encounter, driving the royalists from the field and killing Cavendish and a number of his troopers. The battle was not decisive and Newcastle's main army drove the parliamentary force away from Gainsborough and captured that town three days later.[47] What was significant in this skirmish was that for the first time the Cavaliers found themselves faced by an enemy whose cavalry was at least qualitatively equal to their own. Further, Cromwell, who had never heard a shot fired in anger before his forty-second birthday, demonstrated his ability to maneuver troops in offensive and defensive actions. Cromwell's growing reputation as a trainer and organizer was enhanced in the Gainsborough fight and explains why he was selected to serve as one of four cavalry commanders in the new army that parliament ordered raised by the Eastern Association in August.

Newcastle was influenced by the fight at Gainsborough in his decision to stop his advance toward the Eastern Association and to move north to Hull, where he besieged the Fairfaxes and their garrison. The death of his brother Charles Cavendish and the rough handling of his cavalry by Cromwell and Meldrum convinced Newcastle that he could not advance further until he had cleared the enemy from his lines of communication. His siege of Hull, beginning on 5 September, gave Pym time to find the resources to create the Eastern Association's army under the command of the Earl of Manchester. Newcastle had missed his opportunity to crush the Eastern Association.[48]

The turning point, August to September 1643

The royalists enjoyed a military superiority in August 1643 that they had not known before. Newcastle had cleared Yorkshire of all parliamentarians except those in Hull. Maurice, Hopton, and Rupert had crushed Waller's western army at Roundway Down and captured Bristol. Charles had stymied Essex's advance in the center, forcing that timid commander to assume a defensive stance as the king shifted troops to the western campaign. Scotland remained neutral and Ormond was close to concluding a truce with the Irish Confederates that would allow him to dispatch regiments to the king through Bristol and Chester. At this point, if Charles had turned all of his forces toward London, he might have crushed Essex's army before the parliamentarians could react.

The king's victories also gave him a second chance to achieve a negotiated peace. On 5 August the House of Lords proposed to the Commons that another peace proposal be presented to the king. This offer would have given Charles control of the navy and the fortifications of the kingdom in exchange for his promise to negotiate a settlement with a parliament to which all former members, a majority of whom were active royalists, could return and vote. These terms would have been suicidal for the parliamentary cause, but Pym and his allies in the Commons failed by 29 votes to prevent that House from taking up the Lords' proposal on 5 August.[49]

The Common Council of London responded to the urgings of Henry Marten and others of the House's war party to call out thousands of demonstrators to rally in Westminster and to petition against the peace proposals. These demonstrations had their desired effect. Several members of the Commons changed their minds and, along with other members who had been absent earlier, voted against the peace proposals by a margin of eleven votes, on 7 August.[50] This close-run contest between the peace and the war parties demonstrated to Pym that another royalist victory probably would be fatal to his cause. It also showed the tremendous importance of London in the struggle.

Charles and his counsellors sensed their advantage but were uncertain about how to reap the rewards of their successes. After discussions with his war council, Charles decided to continue the process of defeating his enemies regionally, before advancing on London. This meant that Hull in the north would be besieged by Newcastle and Maurice would invest Exeter and Plymouth in the southwest. Charles's main army was to capture Gloucester, the parliamentarian's stronghold in the west midlands. Once Gloucester was taken there would be little threat to royalist communications between Wales and Oxford, nor any major Roundhead garrisons behind the king's army when it marched east. With these towns in their hands the royalist forces could then move against Essex's army and London.[51]

In the southwest the royalists continued to advance. By mid August the Earl of Carnarvon had taken Weymouth, Portland, and Dorchester, leaving only Poole and Lyme in Dorsetshire in parliamentary hands. In Devonshire, Maurice overran the county and laid siege to Exeter. During the last two weeks of August the parliamentary naval commander, the Earl of Warwick, failed in his attempts to supply the city from the sea. After losing three ships, he was forced to withdraw. On 4 September Exeter surrendered to Maurice.[52] Plymouth remained the last major parliamentarian bastion in Devon, and it was under siege. Plymouth, unlike Exeter, was open to easy approach from the sea and, therefore, could be sustained by the parliamentary navy, thus tying down significant royalist forces.

Gloucester, whose parliamentarian garrison was commanded by the professional soldier Edward Massey, was poorly supplied for a siege. Massey also had to contend with a population that was not enthusiastic about the prospects of being surrounded by the royalist army, although he enjoyed the support of the aldermen. The parliamentary cause could only survive if the town held out long enough for Essex to arrive with supplies and reinforcements. When Charles reached Gloucester, on 10 August, one of the most important campaigns of the Civil War commenced.

The king needed to capture Gloucester before Essex could intervene or threaten his position in Oxford. A long siege was not in his interest; however, because the assault on Bristol had been so costly in royalist lives, Rupert was unable to convince

Charles that such a direct approach should be used. Instead, the royalists settled down to a siege to starve the garrison into submission. This did not seem a risky decision, since many royalists thought that parliament could not field an army strong enough to relieve Gloucester. If the parliamentarians did attempt a relief, the royalists believed that they would expose their army to defeat in a battle fought a long way from their London base.[53]

> Thus the king was engaged before Gloucester; and thereby gave respite to the distracted spirits at London, to breathe, and compose themselves; and, more methodically than they hoped to have done to prepare for their preservation ....[54]

The parliamentarians rally

As the cacophony of royalist victories reached a crescendo in early August it looked as if the parliamentarian cause would collapse under the weight of its internal disunity. Calls for Essex's removal came from a radical faction in London and Westminster typified by Henry Martin. This group wanted to create a new army commanded by Sir William Waller. Further, they sought a general levy to field this force. The radicals from one side and the peace party from the other threatened to pull apart Pym's alliance of the moderates in parliament and London. Due in large part to Pym's leadership and to the Lord's disdain for Martin and the radicals, the parliamentarians refused to take counsel of their fears.[55] In spite of the peace party's attempt to reopen negotiations with the king, Pym was able to convince the Commons to support the measures needed to rebuild the flagging fortunes of the cause.

Money shortages remained the crux of the military problem. Parliament again attempted to solve this problem. It renewed the weekly assessment, although it still levied the tax on all counties, including those controlled by the royalists. Consequently, people remained reluctant to loan money to the Westminster government on the credit of the assessment. The parliamentarians also attempted to make royalists pay for the war by passing a series of sequestration ordinances. However, sequestration revenues did not pay for much of the costs of the Roundheads' war effort. In fact, the London-based treasurers received less than £378,000 from this source over the next ten years.[56] This did little to pay for a military establishment that cost at least £1.5 million annually. Obviously parliament still had to tackle the old wartime financial problems of Stuart governments with new fiscal methods.

On 22 July, John Pym finally persuaded parliament to enact an excise ordinance. Excise taxes had long been a mainstay of Dutch finance, and the English had always considered them 'foreign' and alien. However, parliament's growing difficulty in borrowing money to support its forces, coupled with the battlefield disasters, convinced reluctant parliamentarians that it was necessary to tax consumption items. Although it took several months to work out the problems of collection and supervision, the excise became an important source of cash and credit, with over £249,000 in loans secured by its anticipated receipts in its first year. All but £30,000 of this money was used to buy supplies for the armies fielded in August and September 1643.[57] The Oxford regime quickly copied the parliamentary excise system, providing its forces with an important additional revenue.[58]

In the crisis brought on by military defeat, parliament passed ordinances to conscript soldiers to fill the depleted ranks of Essex's army and the new regiments of the armies for Waller and Manchester. These measures called for 6,500 horse and 10,000 foot for Manchester's Eastern Association army, and 5,000 fresh troops for Waller in the west.[59] Each county received a quota of men and horses. In return, parliament promised to repay the counties for the costs of clothing and arming the conscripts. The first 2,000 men raised in London helped to fill Essex's depleted ranks. As the danger to Gloucester became evident, London's Common Council agreed to loan six regiments of its trained bands to help relieve Gloucester. In return, parliament gave the London government command of the garrisons in the Tower and the fortifications surrounding the city.

These financial and military measures enabled Essex to muster about 14,000 men at Aylesbury on 26 August. From there he set out to the northwest, escorting a long wagon train of supplies destined for Gloucester. By 1 September he had reached Aynho, north of Oxford. The king and his advisors disregarded the initial reports of Essex's advance, and only after these reports persisted did they send Wilmot east with a brigade of cavalry to shadow his column.

By 5 September Essex had reached the Severn Valley, near Prestbury, just east of Gloucester. Charles lifted the siege and concentrated his army at Painswick so that his regiments could not be attacked by Essex while dispersed around Gloucester. This consolidation gave the royalist army a good chance to engage Essex's troops before they could make their way back to London. If they won such a battle, the Cavaliers would have a superb opportunity to march on London with overwhelming force. By 7 September the king had moved his army to Sudeley Castle, a point from which he thought he could intercept Essex on his way east (see map 11).

Essex entered Gloucester on 8 September, delivering supplies and reinforcements to an elated populace and garrison. He had no intention of remaining longer than necessary, since he faced the risk of being cut off and defeated far from London. This was exactly what Charles hoped to do. Essex, however, outwitted the royalists by eluding their cavalry patrols, and then starting for London along a route that took him well south of the royalist garrisons around Oxford.[60] The royalists misread Essex's intentions, marching north to Evesham on 14 September. Only with Essex's capture of a supply magazine in Cirencester, on 15 September, did the king realize what was happening. Reacting quickly, he led his army south through Faringdon and Wantage, reaching Newbury, along Essex's direct route to London, ahead of the parliamentarian army on the 19th.

Essex moved methodically, partially because Rupert's cavalry was harassing him, but also because he was careful to keep his ammunition wagons and artillery safely in his column. This was a wise precaution since Rupert tried unsuccessfully to pinch off isolated units near Hungerford. On 19 September, Essex's advanced guard and quartermasters reached Newbury, where they planned to establish quarters for the

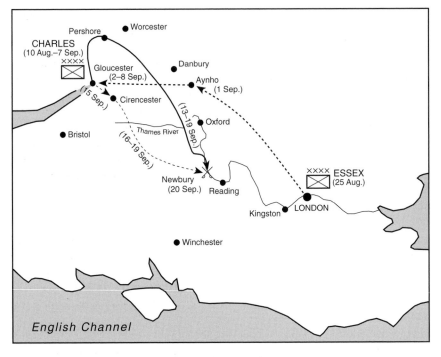

Map 11 The Gloucester Campaign, September–October 1643

night. There they met royalist soldiers who captured a number of the quartermasters. The direct route to London was blocked and the parliamentarians' food and water were running low, prompting Essex to decide to fight his way through Charles's army.

On 20 September the two armies faced each other just west of Newbury. Charles and his commanders failed to secure the key terrain feature of Round Hill, a small ridge about a mile south of the River Kennet. This oversight allowed Essex to advance some of his infantry and cannon to a commanding position among the enclosed fields on the hill. At the same time, Essex pushed infantry forward on his left, near the Kennet. A force of foot and horse led by Sir Nicholas Byron and his nephew Sir John Byron countered this move. For much of the remainder of the day the royalists suffered heavy losses, especially in officers, as they tried to push Essex's men off Round Hill.[61]

Although Charles had intended to let the Roundheads attack his troops, making them pay the cost of an assault in such close terrain, he was forced by Essex's advance to launch Byron's attack on the north side of his line. But he still was in a position on the southern flank to wait for the parliamentary regiments to move forward to the open terrain of Newbury Wash, where Rupert and his cavalry waited to attack. However, the fire from Essex's cannon sited near the Wash Farm galled Rupert into launching a premature attack before the parliamentarians were in the open.

Rupert's initial assault went well, as he drove the leading Roundhead cavalry back across the open ground of Enborne Common and off the battlefield. He decided not to pursue them because two regiments of the London trained bands threatened his left flank on the open ground of Biggs Hill. At this juncture the nature of the battle changed. The London infantry refused to panic in the face of cavalry attacks. Instead, the pikemen presented a wall of steel to prevent the Cavaliers from riding over them, while their well-drilled musketeers poured murderous volleys of shot into Rupert's cavalry. Try as they did in repeated charges, the royalist troopers could not break the infantry formations, only succeeding in forcing the infantry back to even more defensible terrain.

Charles and his senior commanders had exerted too little control over his army's movements during the battle. They failed to secure the critical ground before the fight and to coordinate their attacks on the flanks. Consequently, Rupert's attack was not part of a concerted effort by the whole army to drive the parliamentarians out of their positions. On the other hand, Essex displayed a sure tactical sense in his choice of ground and in his deployments. In addition to seizing Round Hill, he advanced infantry on his left into enclosed fields from which his musketeers could fire at Sir Nicholas Byron's advancing troops. Sir John Byron, unlike Rupert on the southern flank, could not mass his troopers in a coordinated attack to support his brother's infantry. Instead he had to fight his way painfully forward, one field at a time. As they advanced, the flanking fire of Essex's cannon on Round Hill hit Byron's men. By the end of the day, after twelve hours of fighting, losses on both sides had been heavy, but neither army had achieved a decisive advantage.[62]

Essex retired to bed expecting a stiff fight in the morning. His army was intact, but the way to London remained blocked. The next morning, when he sent patrols forward, he was surprised to learn that the king's army had abandoned the field and marched north, leaving the dead and wounded to the parliamentarians. Charles withdrew, over the objections of Rupert, mainly because his gunpowder supply was nearly exhausted. This situation allowed Essex to resume his march to London, which he triumphantly entered on 25 September. The king's best chance of destroying Essex's army and then driving into London was lost.

Essex's relief of Gloucester and his safe return to London did not change the immediate military situation. But he had bought time for the parliamentarians to rebuild their forces. The royalist victories in the summer had forced parliament to enact legislation to place its war effort on a firmer fiscal foundation. The passage of the assessment and excise ordinances, along with the sequestration measures, demonstrated the parliamentarians' resolve. The rapid reinforcement of Essex's army and the creation of new armies for Waller and Manchester provided the forces needed to challenge the king's advance on London. But the royalist successes from Adwalton Moor to Roundway Down demonstrated that the Westminster government, acting alone, lacked sufficient strength to defeat the king. To win, both sides sought help from the other Stuart kingdoms.

The Irish cessation

Ireland remained a major concern to Charles and his opponents throughout the spring and summer of 1643. For Charles, Ireland was a source of additional regiments then serving in Dublin and Munster, which could be sent to join his army in England if a truce were arranged in Ireland. To the parliamentarians, Ireland posed a danger for the same reason. However, because both sides were fully occupied finding the resources for their war efforts in England, little assistance reached the Protestant garrisons in Ireland. In February, things had become so bad that the officers of Dublin's garrison petitioned Ormond and the king describing their shortages of money and provisions and asking for immediate succor.[63]

At the same time, the Catholic Confederates continued to improve their political situation, with their supreme council acting like a sovereign authority, even sending representatives to the major Catholic capitals of Europe.[64] While their military forces remained inferior in pitched battles against the Protestant forces, as they did at New Ross (18 March) and Clones (13 June), the Catholics steadily improved their logistical base by capturing Barre in Leinster (February) and the Fort of Galway (20 June). As long as Preston, O'Neill, and Muskerry refused to stand and fight a major engagement, they could successfully carry on a Fabian strategy that promised to reduce the Protestant garrisons to penury, misery, and mutiny.

Things were equally bad for the Scots in Ulster. Monro complained to Ormond that the English parliament had failed to send the money or supplies promised for his army in the 1642 agreement. Thus he had curtailed operations.[65]

Well before this, the king had set in motion negotiations for a treaty with the Confederates in Ireland. On 12 January 1643, he ordered Ormond to approach the Confederate supreme council in Kilkenny with a proposal for negotiations. After an exchange of letters between Ormond and the supreme council, a meeting was arranged in Trim, on 17 March.[66]

The Confederates offered to accept a treaty ending the war in exchange for a royal promise to meet fourteen demands. These included free worship for Catholics in Ireland; suspension of Poyning's law during a meeting of a free Irish parliament; the Irish parliament to settle all disputes and to redress grievances; protection of Catholics' economic rights; repeal of the penal laws; and the return to Catholics of lands confiscated since 1607. As a carrot, the Confederates hinted that they would support the king's war effort in Ireland and England.[67]

Charles and Ormond recoiled from these demands. They saw that openly to tolerate Catholic worship in Ireland would play into the hands of those who claimed that the king's cause was the Catholic cause. Second, Charles refused to rescind Poyning's law of 1494, which required royal permission for the convening of the Irish parliament and the sovereign's approval of all bills before their introduction in that body.[68]

Realizing that he could not accept the Confederate terms, Charles ordered Ormond to seek a ceasefire. In return, he would promise to conduct further negotiations with Confederate representatives in Oxford.[69] Ormond had little choice but to seek a truce. His garrisons were short of food and his subordinates were calling for relief. He knew that royalist fortunes in England were improving and that reinforcements from Ireland might prove decisive in the English Civil War. The Scots in Ulster, however, refused to condone or join a cessation of hostilities.[70]

Ormond handled the negotiations well, in spite of his deteriorating logistical situation. By May he had convinced the Confederate supreme council to accept a armistice. On 24 June negotiations for the truce commenced, with the approval of the general assembly. Ormond's task was facilitated by the growth of an 'Ormondist' faction within the Confederation, composed mainly of Old English and many of Ormond's relations. These men believed that the best hope for Irish Catholics lay with Charles I. On 15 September, with little foreign assistance available, and with a victory in England by the Westminster parliament clearly their worst option, the Confederates accepted the cessation. This would allow them to concentrate their efforts against the Scots, but it opened fissures in their ranks that would weaken their resistance to future English attacks.[71]

Ormond's negotiations were driven by military necessity. Even before the truce was concluded, Charles had ordered Ormond to select Protestant regiments in Ireland that could be sent to England to serve in the royal army.[72] Ormond and Inchiquin sent as many as eight thousand soldiers to England and Wales during the next six months.[73] Their arrival did not prove decisive, partially because they arrived poorly equipped and with large arrears in pay due them, and partially because many deserted at once rather than fight against parliament. Furthermore, the rumors of their shipment proved useful to the Roundheads' anti-Catholic propaganda efforts, especially in Scotland.

Scotland enters the English Civil War

The Covenanters had watched events closely and realized that the parliamentarians were having an extremely rough time. They had asked Charles to summon a Scottish parliament to discuss the Irish and British situations, but the king refused. The Covenanters went ahead and called for a national convention to meet in June. Charles belatedly granted permission for this gathering, on Hamilton's advice, hoping that Hamilton was right that the convention could be controlled through the nobles, a majority of whom were either royalist sympathizers or luke-warm Covenanters. Once the convention assembled, however, Argyll controlled its agenda with the overwhelming support of the lairds and burghers who made up a majority of the unicameral body.[74]

The Covenanters were deeply concerned about the Ulster situation, where Monro's army was finding it difficult to subsist.[75] By May they had concluded that Antrim, the Queen, and Montrose were plotting an invasion of western Scotland by Catholic forces from Ulster and royalist Scots from England. The evidence came when Monro's soldiers captured Antrim, traveling to Ulster. Interrogation of Antrim and his servants and a search of his papers confirmed the Covenanters' worst fears.[76] Monro relayed this information to Edinburgh and Westminster. Thus the wars in the three kingdoms steadily converged.

The Scots were disappointed that the English had not lived up to the spirit or the letter of the treaty of 1641 that had ended the Second Bishops' War. The English had promised that an assembly of clergymen would be held to which the Scots would be invited to send representatives. This 'assembly of divines' had convened in Westminster, but the Scots had not been invited nor did the agenda seem designed to lead to religious uniformity in Britain. The Scots also were disgruntled because the English had failed to pay all of the 'brotherly assistance' promised in the treaty. But common dangers overcame Scottish irritation.

The news of Ormond's negotiations with the Confederates, along with the deteriorating parliamentarian position in England and royalist plotting against Scotland, led the Covenanters to offer assistance to the Long Parliament. They sent a message to Westminster asking the parliamentarians to send representatives to Edinburgh to discuss ways to face the common danger posed by papists who 'were now in arms under pretext of serving the king.'[77] After strenuous efforts to overcome the Lords' reluctance to ask for Scottish assistance, Pym got parliament to agree to send a delegation to Edinburgh. Ultimately, only members of the Commons traveled north. This group negotiated the Solemn League and Covenant with the Scots. This political-religious-military pact bound the fortunes of the two representative bodies together against their king, turning the tide in the English Civil War.

The Solemn League and Covenant laid out a program of resistance to everything Charles I stood for. Religiously, the signatories promised 'to bring the churches of God in the three kingdoms to the nearest conjunction and uniformity in religion, confession of faith, [and] form of church government … ' and to extirpate all forms of 'popery, prelacy … and whatsoever shall be found to be contrary to sound doctrine.' Politically, they agreed to 'endeavor with our estates and lives mutually to preserve the rights and privileges of parliaments …' Militarily, the two nations agreed to mutually defend one another.[78] Once the covenant was confirmed by the Edinburgh convention it was sent south for approval by the English parliament, while the English delegates and Argyll worked out the details of the military alliance. The Scots promised to send an army into England to support the parliamentarians. In exchange, the English promised to bring the kingdoms closer together religiously and to pay for the Scottish armies in England and Ulster.[79] The Long Parliament accepted the agreement on 25 September, eleven days after Ormond signed the Irish cessation.

The Anglo-Scottish alliance did not immediately bring a Covenanter army into England, but when it did march south in early 1644, that army consisted of 21,000 men, making it the largest force in Britain. At the same time, the 10,000 Scottish soldiers in Ulster remained the largest army in Ireland. Argyll and the Covenanters held the balance of power in Britain and Ireland at the beginning of September 1643.

The royalist tide recedes

The boost in the parliamentarians' morale in the fall of 1643 was an important factor in their successful resistance to the royalists at Gloucester, Plymouth, and Hull, where Roundhead garrisons broke the advance of the king's armies. Newcastle lifted the siege of Hull on 12 October, after the Fairfaxes inflicted a minor defeat on his troops and parliament demonstrated its ability to keep the garrison supplied by sea. The Cavaliers were unable to prevent the parliamentary navy from sustaining Plymouth, and were unwilling to risk an assault against that town's defenses. Finally, the Battle of Newbury ended the king's success in the center, demonstrating that disciplined infantry could beat royalist cavalry.

The Battle of Newbury, which was a strategic victory for parliament because of its effects on Charles's overall war effort, made it easier for Pym to gather the necessary votes to pass the Solemn League and Covenant; it did not solve the underlying problems in parliamentary political and military organizations. Parliament lacked a central military command and continued to dissipate resources regionally without a clear plan of how to defeat the king. Thus, the Scottish alliance was critical to parliament's survival. It would take another year of indecisive warfare before these organizational problems were resolved.

Notes

1 J. Morrill, *The Revolt of the Provinces* (London, 1976), 42–56; Fletcher, *The Outbreak of the English Civil War*, 322–46.

2 Hutton, *The Royalist War Effort*, 50–83.

3 Davies, 'The Parliamentary Army', 34.

4 C. Wedgwood, *The King's War* (New York, 1958, 1991 edn.), 140.

5 J. Malcolm, *Caesar's Due: Loyalty and King Charles, 1642–1646* (New Jersey, 1983), 94–6; E. Shagan, 'Constructing Discord', 4–34.

6 Stevenson, *The Scottish Revolution*, 243–46.

7 H. Hazlett, 'A History of the Military Forces Operating in Ireland, 1641–9', (PhD Dissertation, Queen's University, Belfast, 1938; Hazlett, in Moody *et al.*, eds, *Essays in British and Irish History*.

8 Ibid., 245–6; Wheeler, *Cromwell in Ireland*, 11–12.

9 Stevenson, *The Scottish Revolution*, 246–8.

10 Ibid., 247–9.

11 Ibid., 249–51.

12 Ibid., 261–2.

13 Ibid., 264–70.

14 J. Casway, *O'Neill and the struggle for Catholic Ireland*, 54–63; Stevenson, *Scottish Covenanters and Irish Confederate*, 120–5.

15 N. Perry, 'The Infantry of the Confederate Army of Leinster', *IS*, 15 (1983), 233–6.

16 National Archives of Ireland, M2450–2451, *The Treasury Order Book of the Lords Justices and Council* (2 vols., Dublin, 1 August– 30 November 1642).

17 W. Abbott, ed., *The Writings and Speeches of Oliver Cromwell* (Oxford, 1937, 1988 edn.), i: 165; J[ournals of the] H[ouse of] C[ommons], ii: 698.

18 TT, E108 (15), *Bad News from Ireland* (28 July 1642).

19 Ibid., 89–101.

20 *A & O*, i: 38.

21 Ibid. 38–40.

22 Hexter, *King Pym*, 19–26, 31, 134–5; Wheeler, *Making of a World Power.*

23 *CSPD, 1640*, 373, for an estimate that an army of 11,000 men would cost £262,796 for one year; Firth, *Cromwell's Army*, 21–4: Essex's army's strength is listed as 24,000 foot and 5,000 horse.

24 Bodleian Library, Rawlinson MS A223, fos. 12–16 and 75–6.

25 *A &O*, i: 47, 'Ordinance for taxing several counties for the support of the army', 8 December 1642.

26 *Journals of the House of Commons*, ii: 889, 934, 950–51, 965.

27 G. Aylmer, *The State's Servants* (London, 1973), 24, 182–203; Fissel, *Bishops' Wars*, 137–51; F. Dietz, 'The Receipts and Issues of the Exchequer During the Reigns of James I and Charles I', *Smith College Studies in History*, 13 (1928), 120–3.

28 *JHC*, ii: 922, 927, 944–5, 950–1, 958, 960, 970–1; *A & O*, i: 85–100.

29 Clarendon, *History of the Rebellion*, iii: 171–2, where Clarendon recognizes the importance and magnitude of the assessment ordinance.

30 *A & O*, i: 49–51.

31 Ibid., i: 52–4.
    Gardiner, *Civil War*, i: 97–9.

32 Gardiner, *Civil War*, i: 97–9.

33 M. Ashley, *The English Civil War* (London, 1980 edn.), 79, makes this point, as does Bennett, *The Civil Wars*, 167; Young and Burne, in their book *The Great Civil War*, 47, point out that in the spring of 1643 'signs of a more comprehensive strategy became evident in the royalist camp.'

34 Bennett, *The Civil Wars*, 164–6.

35 Stevenson, *The Scottish Revolution*, 276–90.

36 *JHC*, iii: 51, 53–5, 61; Gardiner, *Civil War*, i: 128–30.

37 Gardiner, *Civil War*, i: 136–45.

38 Ibid., i: 145–9.

39 Clarendon, *History of the Rebellion*, iii: 172; Kenyon, *The Civil Wars of England*, 67–8.

40 Burne and Young, *The Great Civil War*, 55–64; Gardiner, *Civil War*, i: 160–5.

41 Kenyon, *The Civil Wars of England*, 68–70.

42 Burne and Young, *The Great Civil War*, 78–84; Gardiner, *Civil War*, i: 169–72.

43 Gardiner, *Civil War*, i: 169–74; Kenyon, *The Civil Wars of England*, 71–3; Burne and Young, *The Great Civil War*, 86–92.

44 Burne and Young, *The Great Civil War*, 93; Clarendon, *History of the Rebellion*, iii: 293, states that the garrison of Bristol was composed of 2,500 foot and one regiment (300 to 600 men).

45 Clarendon, *History of the Rebellion*, iii: 294–5.

46 Ibid., 294–8; Burne and Young, *The Great Civil War*, 93–6; Gardiner, *Civil War*, i: 179–80.

47 Abbott, *Oliver Cromwell*, i: 240–3.

48 *A & O*, i: 215–19, ordinance to raise 6,500 horse; i: 248–9, ordinance to raise 20,000 foot, all to be commanded by the Earl of Manchester.

49 Gardiner, *Civil War*, i: 184–5; see Clarendon, *History of the Rebellion*, iii: 318–20 for the peace terms.

50 K. Lindley, *Popular Politics and Religion in Civil War London* (Aldershot, 1997), 317–19.

51 Clarendon, *History of the Rebellion*, iii: 312–15.

52 Ibid., 334–9.

53 Ibid., 316–17.

54 Ibid., 315–17.

55 Lindley, *Popular Politics and Religion*, 314–18; Hexter, *King Pym*, 122–32.

56 PRO, E351/440, the declared accounts of the collectors for sequestrations, 1643 to 1653; J. Pringle, 'The Committee for Compounding with Delinquents, 1643–1654', (PhD dissertation, University of Illinois, 1961).

57 *A & O*, i: 202–14, and 274–82 for the first two excise ordinances of 22 July and 8 September 1643; *JHC*, iii: 265, 273–4, 296, 299.

58 Clarendon, *History of the Rebellion*, iii: 453; Hutton, *The Royalist War Effort*, 93.

59 *A & O*, i: 215–19 for the horse, and 248–9 for foot for Manchester.

60 Ashley, *The English Civil War*, 84–5; Clarendon, *History of the Rebellion*, iii: 343–7; Burne and Young, *The Great Civil War*, 97–9; Gardiner, *Civil War*, i: 205–8.

61 Gardiner, *Civil War*, i: 209–14.

62 Burne and Young, *The Great Civil War*, 99–105; Kenyon, *The Civil Wars of England*, 82–4.

63 T. Carte, *The Life of James, Duke of Ormond … with a Collection of Letters* (Oxford, 1851 edn.), v: 395–9, 'Remonstrance of the officers of the army', (February 1643).

64 Ohlmeyer in Ohlmeyer, ed., *Ireland From Independence to Occupation*, 89–96.

65 Bodl., Carte MS 6, fos. 118–9, Robert Monro to Ormond, 25 July 1643.

66 Carte, *Ormond*, v: 1, Charles I to Ormond, 12 January 1643, 401–3, supreme council to the lords commissioners, 9 February 1643; 409–24, 'The Remonstrance of the Catholics', sent to Ormond on 17 March 1643; O'Siochru, *Confederate Ireland*, 61–8; P. Corish in Moody, ed., *New History of Ireland*, iii: 305–8.

67 Carte. *Ormond*, v: 408–24, 'The Remonstrance of the Catholics', 17 March 1643.

68 O'Siochru, *Confederate Ireland*, 58–9, 61–3.

69 Carte, *Ormond*, v: 444, Charles I to the Lords Justices in Dublin, 23 April 1643; Bodl., Carte MS 6, fos. 129–31, Charles I to Ormond, 30 July 1643.

70 Bodl., Carte MS 6, fo. 198, Lord Moore, Commander in Drogheda, to Ormond, 11 August 1643; fo. 235, Inchiquin to Ormond, 19 August 1643; fo. 512, Clanricarde to Ormond, 15 September 1643; Carte, *Ormond*, v: 455–6, Charles I to Ormond, 2 July 1643; ibid., v: 461–2, Secretary Nicholas to Ormond, 1 August 1643.

71 Corish in Moody, ed., *New History of Ireland*, iii: 305–8; O'Siochru, *Confederate Ireland*, 65–8.

72 Bodl., Carte MS 6, fos. 404–5, Charles I to Ormond, 7 September 1643.

73 Wheeler, *Cromwell in Ireland*, 21–2; J. Malcolm, in her article 'All the King's Men: The Impact of the Crown's Irish Soldiers on the English Civil Wars', *Irish Historical Studies*, 22 (1979), 239–64, claims that over 20,000 soldiers were sent over to England. The evidence does not support this view. See for example, Bodl., Carte MS 6, fo. 376, The Lords Justices to Charles, 5 September 1643, where Borlase and Tichborne inform the king that they can send only 1,200 foot and 100 horse, or see Carte, *Ormond*, v: 465–6, Charles I to Ormond, 7 September 1643; Ibid., v: 498–500, Inchiquin to Ormond, 29 October 1643; ibid., Ormond to Orlando Bridgman, 11 November 1643, stating that 3,000 infantrymen were going to be sent from the garrisons in and around Dublin.

74 Stevenson, *The Scottish Revolution*, 276–80.

75 Bodl., Carte MS 6, fo. 277, Robert Monro to the Scottish Council, 28 August 1643.

76 J. Ohlmeyer, *Civil War and Restoration*, 117–23.

77 Stevenson, *The Scottish Revolution*, 278–80.

78 S. Gardiner, ed., *The Constitutional Documents of the Puritan Revolution, 1628–1660* (Oxford, 1889), 187–90.

79 Stevenson, *The Scottish Revolution*, 283–89; Gardiner, *Civil War*, i: 229–35.

CHAPTER FOUR

Stalemate, turning point, and disillusionment

The Solemn League and Covenant and the Irish cessation of September 1643 transformed the strategic situation in the Stuart Kingdoms. The Scottish Covenanters became inextricably committed to the parliamentarian cause and further militarized their nation. The Irish Confederates hitched their fortunes to those of the English king. For the next two years, the Irish and Scottish revolutions depended on the results of the English Civil War. Whichever side won in England would have the power to affect the military and political outcomes in the other kingdoms. At this juncture, the opposing forces in England each possessed strategic advantages that balanced the military odds. Consequently, the outcome of the conflict remained uncertain and unpredictable as the war entered its second year.

The strategic situation, fall 1643

The events of September brought to a dramatic close the first phase of the English Civil War and the Irish insurrection. The king found himself in an ambiguous strategic situation. On the positive side, Charles possessed three major and several minor field armies in England, each with a history of tactical success. In the north, Newcastle, newly created a Marquis, led about 14,000 soldiers in his efforts to secure Lincolnshire and to capture Hull for the king. His troops had soundly defeated the Fairfaxes at Adwalton Moor and had driven Cromwell's and Meldrum's contingents back to the edge of the Eastern Association.

Charles commanded his main army from Oxford. This army had cleared most of the midlands of parliamentary garrisons and had provided columns of nearly invincible cavalry to support the royalists in Cheshire and the southwest. In the southwest, these troopers had joined Sir Ralph Hopton's army in the total defeat of Waller at Roundway Down, and then in the capture of Bristol.

Royalist affairs in Ireland were significantly dimmer than in England, but they were not without hope. The leading royalists, Ormond, Clanricarde, and Inchiquin, held enclaves in the three southern provinces. Ormond's bastion in Dublin was the most important, followed by Inchiquin's bases in Youghal and Cork. The cessation protected these positions. The cessation also made available to Charles a significant number of Protestant troops whom he quickly ordered sent to Bristol and Chester.

Negotiations with the Confederates also offered him hope that he might convince them to send 10,000 soldiers to England or Scotland. His biggest challenge in Ireland was to find a way to reap the fruits of Irish aid without losing the support of those Englishmen who could not stomach the idea of serving alongside Irish Catholics.[1]

The king's situation in Scotland was worse than it was in Ireland or England. The Covenanters controlled the country. Argyll had brought his nation into the English war on parliament's side. During the fall, the Covenanters mobilized their resources, fielding an army of 21,000 men to send to England. This mobilization was a remarkable feat, given the fact that another Scottish army of 10,000 men was already in Ulster.[2] It was a difficult undertaking to field so many soldiers for foreign service in a nation with a population of less than one million people.

The king desperately needed a political and military strategy to prevent the Scots' intervention in England. Such a strategy required significant and rapid help from the Irish. Consequently, he agreed to meet a Confederate peace delegation in Oxford in the spring of 1644. Charles, however, was unwilling to make the concessions needed to convince the Confederates to send a large force to Britain in a timely manner.

Militarily, Charles needed to concentrate his forces against the parliamentarian center of gravity, to use a Clausewitzian term. That objective was Essex's army and London. But to defeat Essex and to capture London would have required the rapid assembly of the three major royalist armies, which would risk leaving the north and southwest uncovered. The royalists were unwilling to adopt this risky strategy, preferring instead to continue their efforts to secure their regional bases before dealing with London.

Although Essex had been able to resupply Gloucester, the parliamentarians faced a grim strategic situation in the fall of 1643. The Westminster government lacked an army capable of staying in the field long enough to break the royalist position in the Thames Valley or to defeat the king's main army. The parliamentary cause had been saved in October only by the willingness of the London militia to march to Gloucester. Those units fought well at Newbury, but they could not be kept from their jobs and homes in London long enough to win the war. Conscription was the Long Parliament's answer; however, it would take time to train new soldiers to defeat the royalist veterans.

Parliament's greatest weakness was its lack of a centralized military command that would enable it to concentrate against the king's center of gravity – which was his headquarters and army in Oxford. The parliamentary Committee of Safety attempted to fulfill this role but it lacked the necessary authority. This Committee included Pym, Sir Henry Vane, and Oliver St John, three of the most important members of the middle party in the Commons. Essex, Waller, Cromwell, and Manchester were among its prominent military members. However, the Committee resided in London and the military members seldom attended, being occupied with leading the forces. The Committee was unable to coordinate operations and Essex and Waller, the senior officers in the field, often ignored its orders. Until a stronger executive was created, parliament would continue to have difficulty directing its armies.[3]

Charles's hopes for victory depended on his exploitation of the situation in England before the Scots arrived. He had to seize and maintain the initiative and break his English enemies. They, on the other hand, had to hang on until the Scots arrived, and then they had to organize their superior resources to win the war. From September 1643 to July 1644, the outcome remained in the balance.

The royalist offensives

The Battle of Newbury did not end the wave of royalist victories in 1643. On 3 October Charles recovered Reading and installed Sir Jacob Astley as Governor with a strong garrison. In the south, Prince Maurice took Exeter (4 September) and Dartmouth (6 October) and established a siege against Plymouth. At the same time, Sir Ralph Hopton formed another army that the king hoped would enable him to drive into Wiltshire and Hampshire. Hopton had about 2,000 foot and 1,500 horse, including at least 500 men in two regiments shipped to Bristol from Munster. However, Hopton had to quell a mutiny in these units from Ireland by shooting the ringleaders. By November he was ready to relieve Basing House near Reading, which Waller was besieging with the army of the Southeastern Association.[4]

Waller's army demonstrated the strength and the weakness of the parliamentary military position. Most of his infantry were militia. The London trained bands had played an important role at Turnham Green and during the Gloucester campaign and Battle of Newbury, defending their homes and saving the cause when it was clear that they were its only hope. The disadvantage of the use of the trained bands in a marching army was that they were reluctant to campaign far from home and they usually refused to remain in the field for extended operations. Waller found this out in November when his militia regiments refused to assault Basing House, and then demanded to go home. This forced him to lift the siege and return to Farnham.[5] His withdrawal allowed the royalists to seize Winchester and Arundel Castle.

Hopton's royalist army in the south, however, was over-extended by early December. He had too few soldiers to garrison the towns and castles taken while still fielding a marching army. The Roundheads thus were able to strike back, destroying royalist regiments at Romsey, near Southampton, in a surprise attack, and then overrunning Hopton's garrison at Alton in a major battle on 13 December. In this fight, four regiments of London's trained bands performed magnificently, helping Waller capture 700 prisoners. Waller went on to capture Arundel on 6 January, before putting his tired soldiers into winter quarters. Hopton was forced to withdraw to the west, having lost a significant portion of his army with little to show for it. The king lost faith in him and sent the Earl of Forth to assume command in the south.[6]

In the north Newcastle remained in front of Hull while the Earl of Manchester organized the Eastern Association's army. The Hull defenders, commanded by Lord Ferdinando Fairfax, took the initiative against their besiegers by cutting the levee along the Humber, flooding the low ground around Hull. They also sallied against the royalists' positions. On 11 October, parliamentary soldiers and townsmen sortied out against the Cavaliers' main artillery battery. After a fierce fight, the parliamentarians captured the position and one of the largest siege guns in Britain. The next day Newcastle lifted the siege and marched his army north. The royalists had lost thousands of men to disease and desertion while accomplishing little.[7] More important, Newcastle gave parliament time to organize new units by not moving into the Eastern Association.

The Roundheads respond

The fruits of the parliamentarian efforts to raise new armies started to ripen in September 1643, when Manchester captured Lynn, in Norfolk, from a group of royalists who had seized that port for the king. Manchester next moved his army to the support of Hull, clearing most of Lincolnshire of royalists as he did so. In early October he reinforced Hull, while on 11 October, the Earl, Sir Thomas Fairfax, and Oliver Cromwell defeated a strong force of royalist horse at Winceby. These royalists, commanded by Sir John Henderson, Governor of Newark, had attempted to lift the Roundheads' siege of Bolingbroke Castle. In the battle that ensued, the royalists found out that the cavalry of the Eastern Association was superior to theirs. This was a vindication of Cromwell's training methods and of parliament's decision to create the Army of the Eastern Association.

After Newcastle's withdrawal from Hull, the parliamentarians cleared Lincolnshire of royalists. This shift in the military initiative continued as Thomas Fairfax went on the offensive with his small army. On 20 December, Fairfax captured Gainsborough on the Trent River, providing a bastion to protect the western flank of Lincolnshire. Then he received orders from Westminster to march west to Cheshire, where a royalist army led by Sir John Byron threatened the last parliamentary garrison in that county.

The king had created Byron's army to supplement Newcastle's efforts to meet the expected Scottish invasion. The royalist war council directed five regiments from Dublin to land in Chester to join Byron. These veterans formed the infantry core of the new army, to which Byron added about 2,500 cavalry. By late December Byron had pushed Sir William Brereton's forces out of Cheshire, leaving only Nantwich in parliamentary hands in that county.[8] Hoping to save Nantwich, Fairfax set out for the west on 29 December with several thousand horsemen. Along his route of march he was joined by many of his former soldiers from the West Riding of Yorkshire and Lancashire, giving him over 6,000 veterans by the time he got near Nantwich on 24 January.

Byron tried to take Nantwich before parliamentary help arrived. He surrounded the town on 13 December, and launched a bloody but unsuccessful assault on 18 January. Fairfax's advance, however, caught him off guard, with his forces divided by the River Weaver. Fairfax saw the opportunity and quickly marched his army toward Byron's isolated infantry on the west side of the river. Byron was slow to react to Fairfax's advance, allowing him to fall on his infantry on the morning of 25 January. Once he recognized his dangerous situation, Byron led his cavalry from his camp on the east side of the river ten miles to the village of Hurleston on the west side, where he hoped to join his infantry.[9]

Within a mile of Colonel Gibson's royalist infantry, near the village of Acton, Fairfax learned of Byron's approach. He did not let this news deter him from exploiting his opportunity to defeat the royalists in detail. Instead, Fairfax detached two regiments to slow Byron near Hurleston while he slammed the rest of his army into Gibson's infantry. After a sharp fight the Roundheads broke through Gibson's position, just as a sortie by the garrison of Nantwich struck the royalists from the rear. Fairfax seized his chance, ordering his troops to turn outward to take Gibson's remaining regiments in their flanks. The royalists broke and ran, losing over 1,500 prisoners. Byron's army was crippled, even though he got away to Chester with his cavalry.[10]

The Battle of Nantwich demonstrated Thomas Fairfax's growing skill as a general and the improved quality of his soldiers. He had skillfully handled a force of infantry and cavalry in a march across central England in the winter. He outmaneuvered Byron and defeated his army in detail. Fairfax destroyed several of the king's regiments from Ireland and forced Charles to dispatch Rupert to the north. There, Rupert was to take command and organize a new army to prevent the total collapse of the royalist cause in Cheshire and Lancashire. Rupert arrived in Shrewsbury on 19 February and set about his tasks.

In Oxford dissension amongst the royalists leaders had grown steadily since the Battle of Newbury. The setbacks in the south and the north made matters worse. Due to a shortage of money, the royalist garrisons around Oxford and Reading also mistreated the civilians upon whom they depended for shelter and sustenance. As Clarendon, an eyewitness and the great royalist historian later wrote,

> ... upon the king's return to Oxford [from Newbury], there appeared nothing but dejection of mind, discontented, and severe mutiny in the army, anger and jealousy among the officers, every one accusing another of want of courage and conduct in the actions of the field; ...[11]

The breakdown of discipline among the royalist garrisons sapped the king's ability to support and control his war effort. In early 1644, the royalist system weakened, due to the behavior of garrisons which acted licentiously while taking free quarter from their environs and to the system's decentralized nature.[12] The pressures of war steadily militarized royalist administration, just as they had forced the parliamentarians to institute taxes and organize their efforts in ways that were unthinkable before 1642.

The death of John Pym was one of the few pieces of good news for the king in December 1643. However, Pym's death had no appreciable effect on the parliamentary war effort, although there was heated debate within the House of Commons in the next few months between a peace party and a war party. On 16 February, facing a divided parliament and a precarious military situation, Pym's successors as leaders of the middle group in the Commons, Henry Vane and Oliver St John, convinced parliament to establish a committee of the Lords and Commons to sit with the Scottish commissioners in London. This 'Committee of Both Kingdoms' gave their cause some of the benefits of a central administration, with the power 'to order and direct whatsoever doth or may concern the managing of the war …'[13] It was the first British executive body in history and a major step forward in parliament's assumption of responsibility for the executive functions of the state. In the short term it coordinated parliament's forces in the north with Leven's Scots, leading to the decisive campaign in the English Civil War. In the longer term, it helped maintain the Solemn League and Covenant long enough for the thorough defeat of the royalists.

The Scottish advance in the north

The Scottish army assembled on the border near Berwick in early January 1644. Berwick had been garrisoned by English parliamentarians to prevent it falling into royalist hands, giving the Scots a forward base in England. On 19 January, Leven led his troops across the Tweed, in part because he could not feed them much longer in the border area in winter.[14] The Scots advance into Northumberland was hampered more by harsh weather than by royalist resistance, taking two weeks to march from the Tweed to the town of Newcastle on Tyne. The Marquis of Newcastle, meanwhile, hurried his army north, barely entering Newcastle before the Scots arrived. Leven sat for three weeks before the town while his quartermaster established a depot at Morpeth to supplement the one at Berwick. At the end of February Leven left seven infantry regiments before Newcastle and marched the rest of his army west, along the north side of the Tyne, hoping to outflank Newcastle. The Marquis, with about 10,000 soldiers, was badly outnumbered, even after Leven had split his force. Consequently, he only was able to skirmish with the Scots, hoping to delay their advance. By 8 March Newcastle had withdrawn to Durham, with Leven following on the 12th (see map 12).[15]

Newcastle retreated skillfully, destroying food supplies between Newcastle and Durham. As a result, Leven was unable to carry on a siege of Durham and was forced to withdraw northward. On 20 March Leven captured a fort on the mouth of the Tyne, giving the Scots control of most of the Durham coalfields. For the next month the armies sparred between Durham and Newcastle, until the Marquis received word of a disaster that had befallen John Belasyse, commander of the royalist garrison at Selby. Newcastle immediately marched his army south to protect York from the advancing parliamentarian armies of Manchester and Fairfax.[16]

Search for a peace with the Irish

The cessation in Ireland provided Ormond with breathing room, endangered the Scots army in Ulster, and gave the Confederates a chance to negotiate a peace with the king that would protect Irish Catholics' rights. In November 1643, the general assembly approved the cessation and granted the supreme council authority to negotiate with Charles. The supreme council, heavily dominated by Old English Ormondists, selected representatives who were willing to accept terms well short of full independence. The Irish presented their demands to Charles after their arrival in Oxford, on 24 March 1644. Their terms, including several allowing the free exercise

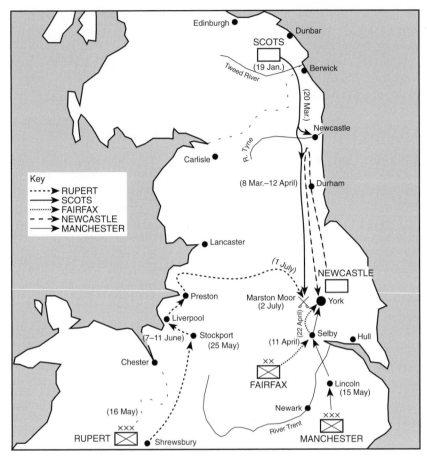

Map 12 The Northern Campaign, 1644

of Catholicism in Ireland, were more than the King could grant without alienating most of his Protestant subjects in Ireland and England.[17]

Charles was in a difficult situation. On 28 March the Confederate representatives presented demands for the repeal of anti-Catholic acts and statutes in Ireland and for the cancellation of the land transfers imposed in the 1630s by Stafford. They further asked that land titles dating back to 1584 be recognized. Most important, they wanted all concessions made by the king confirmed in an Irish parliament free of the restrictions of Poyning's law. This would give them legislative independence similar to that gained by the Scots and the Long Parliament in 1640–1. Only then would they provide 10,000 Irish soldiers to fight for the king in Britain.[18]

The king was outraged by these demands, which were 'truly so unreasonable as to drive us rather to thoughts of breaking with them … than of giving them any satisfaction.'[19] The royal dilemma in Ireland became more evident when a delegation of Irish Protestants arrived in Oxford. These men adamantly opposed the concessions demanded by the Confederates, making it clear to Charles that what he might gain from the Catholics would probably be offset by what he would lose with the defection of Irish Protestants.[20]

The Oxford negotiations took place amidst a deteriorating royalist military situation in England. Charles soon turned his attention to the parliamentarian advances in the north and south, summoning Rupert to confer with him on 25 April. By mid May 1644, the king was in the field with his army, ending talks in Oxford for an Irish peace. Seeing no other way out of the impasse, Charles referred the Confederate delegates to Ormond to whom he granted authority to come to terms if possible. From that point on, Charles never dealt in good faith with the Confederates. The failure of the Oxford discussions did not deter the general assembly of July 1644 from selecting the same men to meet with Ormond in Dublin. However, there were growing tensions within the Confederate assembly and the military between the Old English and the Old Irish.[21]

While talking with Ormond and Charles, the Confederates attempted to pursue a strategy that would drive the Scots out of Ulster and provide some help to the royalists in western Scotland. The attempt to affect Scottish affairs was carried out by Antrim. By April 1644, he had raised 2,000 soldiers to serve in Scotland with Alasdair MacColla. Supply and shipping difficulties, however, delayed their dispatch from Ballyhack, in County Wexford, until 24 June.

Due to a shortage of arms, only about 1,600 men sailed with MacColla, but their impact on Scottish and British affairs was out of all proportion to their numbers. In response to MacColla's arrival in Scotland and the extraordinary help these men provided to Montrose's royalist army, three of Monro's Scottish regiments and his artillery returned from Ulster to protect western Scotland. Further, as Montrose won six victories in Scotland, the Covenanters were forced to raise thousands of additional soldiers to defend themselves, diverting resources from England.[22] Unfortunately for Charles I, MacColla's force arrived in Scotland too late to force the transfer of any Scottish regiments out of northern England until after the Battle of Marston Moor (2 July 1644). MacColla's expedition to Scotland also failed to weaken Monro's army in Ulster sufficiently to allow the Confederates to overwhelm it.

The second and major part of the Confederates' military strategy in 1643–4 was to unite their Ulster and Leinster armies in a campaign to drive Monro out of Ulster. However, the cessation came too late in the year to allow them to support a campaign in the north until the summer of 1644. Further, each of the Confederate generals, Owen Roe O'Neill and James Preston, refused to serve under the other. Eventually, the supreme council selected the Earl of Castlehaven, an English Catholic, to command the operation, causing further resentment and delay. By the time the Confederates had worked out their logistical and command problems, in late June 1644, Monro had launched an offensive of his own. After rampaging through northern Leinster and seizing Belfast from Ormond, Monro returned his troops to their garrisons in eastern Ulster.[23]

The Confederates' delay in attacking the Scots undermined their position in western Ulster and Munster, where those Protestants who had accepted Ormond's lead in agreeing to the cessation now opted to join the Scots and the parliamentarians. Consequently, some of Preston's troops had to remain in the south to help Muskerry guard against an attack by Inchiquin from Cork. By the time Castlehaven's offensive against Monro got underway in July, he had only 11,000 Catholic troops, divided into two armies. Castlehaven's advance was met by Monro who, recovering from his initial surprise at the offensive, put 10,000 Scottish and British troops into the field (see map 13). O'Neill's and Preston's forces finally united to meet Monro's advance, establishing a strong defensive position near Charlemont. The Irish had missed their opportunity to attack Monro's garrisons before he could field a united Protestant army. Thus, they lost one of their best chances to drive the Scots out of Ireland, a move that would have profoundly affected their fortunes and those of their king. After a standoff lasting seven weeks, the Confederates withdrew. For the next two years the major Ulster towns remained in Protestant hands, and warfare there receded to the level of vicious raids.[24]

The advantages Charles I might have reaped from the Irish cessation failed to materialize. His unwillingness to give Catholics political and religious autonomy made them reluctant to risk 10,000 soldiers in Britain. The growing fissures within the Irish cause were exposed by the different views of how to deal with an heretical king in the peace negotiations. Further, the ethnic and personal divisions highlighted by the unwillingness of Owen Roe O'Neill to serve with the Old Englishman James Preston in the Ulster campaign revealed the fragility of the Confederation. Consequently, Charles I remained on his own in England, receiving only limited military help from Ormond's Protestant regiments.

Maneuvers in central and western England

In January 1644, the Scottish campaign in the north and Fairfax's initiative in Cheshire put the royalists in a strategic bind. If they concentrated against these northern threats they opened Oxfordshire to attack by Essex and Yorkshire to attack by Manchester. If they ignored these threats, they could lose their positions in the north, opening Wales to invasion. Meanwhile, Hopton's defeat and withdrawal from Hampshire enabled Waller to move his army to where it could support an advance by Essex toward Oxford.

In early March, a new threat to royalist communications between Oxfordshire and Yorkshire materialized when Sir John Meldrum appeared before Newark with about 6,000 Nottinghamshire and Lincolnshire Roundheads.[25] Newark, on the Trent, was defended by Sir Richard Byron with 2,000 royalists. His mission was to keep open the route to the north and to prevent the parliamentarians from driving into Nottinghamshire and Derbyshire, both royalist recruiting and supply areas. Byron's troops repulsed a strong attack on 8 March, but his supplies were low and the garrison required immediate assistance if it was to hold out. On 12 March, the king ordered Rupert to gather an army and march to the relief of Newark.[26]

Rupert rode to Shrewsbury where he picked up three regiments of foot that had arrived from Dublin. With these veterans and his own cavalry regiment and lifeguard

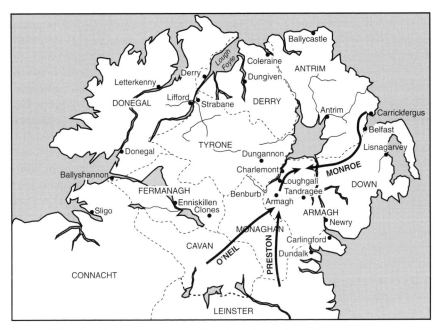

Map 13 The Confederate advance into Ulster, July–September 1644

he pushed east to Bridgenorth, where Major General Nurries joined him on 15 March with several artillery pieces. By the 19th he had linked up with two additional columns of royalists and had reached Bingham, about eight miles from Newark. Meldrum heard rumors that the Prince was advancing, but he took few precautions either to withdraw or to face his approaching enemy. Consequently, Rupert was able to surprise Meldrum on 21 March. Meldrum reacted by pulling his troops out of their siege works and concentrating the bulk of his army at Spittal, northeast of Newark.[27] He also posted a force to hold the Muskram Bridge on the north side of Newark Island, across the Trent from Newark. This move protected his rear and gave him the ability to withdraw across the river to the island if need arose.[28]

Rupert maneuvered his conglomerate force around the south side of Newark, approaching Meldrum's forces over Beacon Hill, to the east of Spittal. At the same time he ordered the commander of the infantry, Colonel Tillier, to march his men to a position northeast of Spittal, cutting off Meldrum's escape in that direction. Once his men were in place Rupert attacked, beginning a fierce cavalry action. Both sides gave a good account of themselves in this melee, which grew fiercer when Tillier's royalist infantry appeared to the northeast and Byron sortied from the town with a strong force of foot. Meldrum's troops, however, prevented Tillier's men from capturing the boat bridge connecting Meldrum's positions with Newark Island.[29]

As Rupert prepared for a second attack against Meldrum he received word that one of Meldrum's units had destroyed the Muskram Bridge on the far side of Newark

Island and retreated, cutting off Meldrum's escape and supply route. The prince decided to hold his forces in position, knowing that the parliamentarians either had to attack him at a disadvantage or starve. Meldrum came to the same conclusion and asked for a parley. Rupert granted it and after a brief discussion agreed to accept Meldrum's surrender. The Roundheads were allowed to march away with their swords and horses, leaving their muskets, cannon, and ammunition.[30] Rupert had demonstrated what could be done when the royalists acted decisively. Newark was to remain royalist for two years and Rupert was free to march his army to the aid of either Newcastle in Yorkshire or the king in Oxford.

In spite of Rupert's victory, the overall royalist position deteriorated as Waller won an important battle at Cheriton in Hampshire, on 29 March, and the Fairfaxes captured Belasyse's army at Selby on 11 April. Waller's defeat of Hopton's army at Cheriton came as a shock to the king since he had sent the Earl of Forth with a brigade of foot and horse to reinforce Hopton after the royalists had been driven from Arundel. Forth, however, allowed Waller to outfight him on the battlefield near New Alresford, after the royalists cut Waller's army off from its lines of communication to the east. After a fierce battle, during which his cavalry regiments were ground up one by one, Forth extricated his army from what could have been a total disaster, making his way back to Reading. Cheriton ended royalist hopes of invading Kent and Sussex and freed Waller's army to operate in support of Essex.

As the king was digesting the news from the south, worse arrived from the north. Following their victory at Nantwich, Fairfax and Sir William Brereton had secured much of Lancashire for parliament. Fairfax then moved east, uniting with a force commanded by his father in southern Yorkshire. Their target was the royalist garrison in Selby, commanded by John Belasyse. This force of about 3,000 men protected Newcastle's army in Durham from a parliamentary advance from the south. The Fairfaxes launched an all-out assault of Selby on 11 April that proved successful, thus avoiding the delay of a long siege. This method of dealing with a fortified town or castle was fast becoming Thomas Fairfax's preferred way of taking such places, saving a great deal of time. The parliamentary victory was complete, with most of the garrison captured and the road to York opened from the south.[31]

Things were bleak in Oxford. Maurice's army remained tied up in Dorset in a siege of Lyme Regis, where Colonel Robert Blake led the defenders. Maurice could not starve out the garrison because it was sustained by sea. Worse, the king's council learned that Essex and Manchester planned a rendezvous in Aylesbury for 19 April, probably in preparation for a move toward Oxford. In the north, Newcastle was cornered in York, as the Scots secured Durham and the Fairfaxes cleared most of Yorkshire after their victory at Selby. In response to this dark news, Charles sent Queen Henrietta Maria, now pregnant with her seventh child, to Exeter on 17 April, where she could escape to France if necessary. He also summoned Rupert to a council of war.

Rupert conferred with the king from 25 April to 5 May. His presence raised the king's morale and stiffened the resolve of his other advisors. The strategy they developed had promise, but it entailed great risk. They decided to strengthen the garrisons around Oxford, making it difficult for Essex and Waller to reach the royalist capital. A strong force of cavalry would maneuver within this fortified zone to protect communications and to harass an advancing enemy. Meanwhile, the armies of Maurice and Rupert would be reinforced. The former would finish the siege in the west against Lyme Regis, while Rupert marched to Newcastle's aid in Yorkshire to help him defeat the Scottish and parliamentary armies. If successful, the Princes could march their armies to Oxford to join the king in a major push against Essex's army.[32]

As it turned out, Essex and Manchester were unwilling to cooperate against Oxford, as they had been ordered to do by the Committee of Both Kingdoms. Waller and Essex also were reluctant to coordinate their operations, maneuvering separately against Oxford in May. In anticipation of their advance, Charles mustered his marching army of 9,000 men at Albourne Chase, north of Oxford, and ordered the abandonment of Reading, so as to add its garrison to his army. This allowed Essex to march directly to the royalist strongpoint at Abingdon, which the royalists evacuated on 25 May. Waller advanced along the south of the Thames, reaching Abingdon after Essex's army had crossed the Thames and occupied Islip, north of Oxford, putting the parliamentary armies into positions from which they could isolate Charles in Oxford. To avoid this, the king decided to leave most of his infantry to defend Oxford and to lead a force of 5,500 foot and horse west to safety. He reached Worcester on 6 June.[33]

The Committee of Both Kingdoms tried to coordinate the efforts of their armies in the Thames Valley by ordering Essex to take Oxford while Waller prevented the king from intervening. This order failed to recognize the chance they had of crushing Charles's army, but it still would have greatly improved the parliamentary military situation. Essex, however, determined that the proper thing for the armies to do was to separate further, with one to march west and relieve Lyme Regis from Maurice's siege. He also decided that his army should do that while Waller screened the royal garrison in Oxford. After a conference with Waller at Stow-on-the-Wold, on 6 June, Essex set out for Dorset. His decision to do so saved Oxford and gave Charles the chance to defeat his enemies piecemeal. In spite of another order from parliament to return to Oxford, Essex marched on, relieving Lyme Regis on 15 June. At that point he decided to continue west into Cornwall. This move put his army well out of the supporting range of Waller[34] (see map 14, p113).

Charles seized the opportunity presented by Essex's movements and turned his army back toward Oxford. He eluded Waller, joining 4,000 soldiers from Oxford at Woodstock on 21 June. He then headed east toward Buckingham, with Waller in pursuit. The news that Charles was in Buckinghamshire threw London into disarray. The Committee of Both Kingdoms ordered the assembly of another force under the command of Richard Browne to protect the capital. Browne mustered fewer than 3,000 infantry, and he lacked cavalry. Fortunately for London, the king turned toward Banbury, allowing Waller to catch up with him. But Charles now outnumbered Waller, and his troops were qualitatively superior to Waller's force that was composed largely of London trained bands. None the less, Waller skillfully placed his army in a position that the king deemed too strong to assault, forcing the royalists to move north along the east side of the River Cherwell.[35]

Waller followed on the west side of the river, parallel to the king's line of advance, looking for a chance to attack at an advantage. On 29 June, he detected a gap in the royalists' column, leaving their rear guard under Henry Wilmot exposed to attack. Waller acted quickly, sending a strong force with Lieutenant General Middleton across a ford a mile south of Cropredy Bridge, while he engaged the king's advanced guard at Cropredy Bridge with the remainder of his army. Middleton initially made good progress against Wilmot, but was brought up short when a large body of royalists doubled back and helped Wilmot crush his attackers, while Charles kept Waller's column at bay. Wilmot routed Middleton's parliamentarians, allowing the royalists to unite to attack Waller's troops at Cropredy Bridge. After a stiff fight the royalists prevailed, capturing Waller's artillery and forcing him to retreat to high ground west of the river. The king, however, did not follow up this victory with another assault, allowing Waller to withdraw toward London the next day.[36]

The Battle of Cropredy Bridge badly weakened Waller's army, allowing Charles to pursue Essex to the west with Oxford secure. If he could destroy Essex's army before the parliamentary and Scottish forces united in Yorkshire, he would stand a good chance to lead his army north and redress the military balance. Time, however, was running out, as his enemies maneuvered against Newcastle.

Decision in the north: the Marston Moor Campaign

Rupert rode north following the conference in Oxford in early May. After picking up his army in Shrewsbury, he drove into Lancashire, planning to punish that hotbed of parliamentarianism and to recruit additional soldiers. On 25 May, Stockport surrendered to the terror of his name. Three days later he took Bolton by storm, killing as many as 1,600 civilians and soldiers in the sack. On 30 May he joined George Goring with most of Newcastle's cavalry. Together, Rupert and Goring drove west, capturing Liverpool on 11 June. While these operations were successful, they failed to prevent Fairfax and Manchester from joining Leven's Scots in a siege of York.

After their victory at Selby, on 11 April, the Fairfaxes faced little resistance to their advance toward York, their assigned objective. On 20 April they reached Tadcaster and joined Leven's Scots, who had followed Newcastle from Durham to York. On 22 April the allied armies began the siege of York, which the Earl of Newcastle defended with about 5,000 infantry.[37]

While Rupert rampaged through Lancashire and the siege of York commenced, Manchester and newly promoted Lieutenant General Oliver Cromwell concentrated the Eastern Association army near Belvoir Castle in Lincolnshire. On 6 May, as Cromwell and the cavalry fended off a royalist relief column, Manchester led the infantry in a successful assault against the garrison in Lincoln. This victory secured the western flank of the Eastern Association, freeing Manchester's army to march north to join the siege of York. By 3 June Cromwell and Manchester had joined the allies and reached the northern capital.[38]

Newcastle's situation in York was desperate. An allied force of about 27,000 men circled the city, and the supplies of his garrison were running low. Charles, realizing the disastrous effects that the loss of York would have on his cause sent the following order to Rupert:

> I must give you the true state of my affairs, … If York be lost I shall esteem my crown little less … ; but if York be relieved, and you beat the rebels' armies of both kingdoms which were before it, then, but otherwise not, I may possibly make a shift upon the defensive to spin out time until you come to assist me; whereof I command and conjure you, by the duty and affection which I know you bear me, that all new enterprises laid aside, you immediately march according to your first intention, with all your force, to the relief of York …[39]

Charles's message indicates that he understood that just lifting the siege would not do much to improve his dismal situation. Rupert and Newcastle must win battles against the armies opposed to them, thereby changing the military balance in the north. If successful, Rupert could join the main army in its efforts to crush Essex and Waller. The order he issued to Rupert is not ambiguous on this score. Rupert read it in the same fashion and immediately set his army in motion toward York.

It was none too soon for Newcastle, who had already sent messengers to Rupert telling him that York could not hold out much longer. The allies captured most of Newcastle's couriers, giving them hope that the garrison would surrender before Rupert arrived. It was not to be, even though the attackers attempted to blast a gap in the walls with a mine filled with gunpowder. The royalist garrison, although short of food, held on, encouraged with news that relief was on its way. Further, the Committee of Both Kingdoms, panicked because of royalist successes in Lancashire, ordered Fairfax and Manchester to leave the siege and march their troops to meet Rupert.[40]

The field commanders, however, decided not to withdraw from before York. They felt it would be better to face Rupert and Newcastle with their combined strength than to have to hunt Rupert down in Lancashire. On 28 June, they received information that Rupert had crossed the Pennines with 14,000 soldiers and was headed toward York. On the 30th, they learned that he had reached Knaresborough, eighteen miles west of York. After a conference, the allied commanders decided to end the siege and move their forces to a favorable defensive position near Long Marston, five miles west of York, on the road toward Knaresborough. There they hoped to intercept Rupert as he moved east and destroy his army before he could link up with Newcastle.[41]

Rupert, however, outmaneuvered his opponents by marching his army north before crossing the Ouse River on a captured pontoon bridge near Poppleton, three miles northwest of York, on 1 July. As Rupert sent word to Newcastle that he had broken the siege, the allies discovered that Rupert had deployed a cavalry screen to mask his movements. This revelation led Manchester, Leven, and Fairfax to overestimate their enemies' strength and to decide to withdraw south to Tadcaster and Cawood, where they could await reinforcements. On the morning of 2 July their infantry, commanded by Leven and Manchester, abandoned their positions on Marston Moor to begin the move to Tadcaster. Cromwell, Fairfax, and the Scotsman David Leslie remained in position with 3,000 cavalrymen to protect the infantry's movement from Rupert's cavalry.[42]

With Rupert's arrival, the royalists numbered as many as 18,000 soldiers. The Prince, following the king's orders and his own instincts, had come to York to fight a pitched battle. When he arrived, Rupert sent a message to Newcastle telling him to lead his infantry to join the army near Long Marston. The allies' withdrawal of their infantry the next day made this seem a wise move, as the royalist had the chance to defeat their enemies piecemeal. Newcastle initially resisted Rupert's desire to fight, believing that the allied armies would break apart once away, and that they then could be defeated one by one.[43] The Scottish army was especially worn out from months of campaigning in the north, and Leven likely would have had to move his army north to refit.[44] Rupert, however, overruled the Marquis, informing him that he had a letter from the king ordering him to engage the allies.

Charles and Rupert were right about the need for Rupert to win a battle. A victory against the allied armies would have divided the Covenanters and the parliamentarians. With Leven's army most likely forced to return to northern England to regroup, and Manchester's army retreating to defend the Eastern Association, the Fairfaxes would have been on their own in Yorkshire. The numerical odds were against a royalist victory: about 27,000 allies against about 18,000 royalists. But military experience favored the royalists. Rupert had never been defeated and Newcastle's soldiers were veterans of more than a year of warfare. Additionally, Fairfax's Yorkshiremen were new levies and Manchester's army had never faced a large royalist army.

The Battle of Marston Moor

Rupert and Newcastle deployed their forces onto Marston Moor, facing south toward their enemies' rearguard, drawn up along a ridge running west to east from the village of Tockwith to Long Marston. Cromwell, Leslie, and Thomas Fairfax observed the prince's cavalry as it assumed positions close to a ditch just to the north. After a brief discussion, Fairfax, as the senior officer, sent a message to Leven asking him to return the infantry to Marston Moor, where Fairfax and the other commanders believed that Rupert meant to give battle. By 2 p.m., most of the allied troops had returned and taken up positions facing the royalists.[45]

While the allied infantry was returning, Newcastle joined Rupert with his troops. The two armies deployed in the traditional manner, with the infantry in the center and most of the cavalry on the flanks. Rupert stationed eight regiments of about 2,100 horsemen, commanded by Lord Byron, on his right. Royalist dragoons were interspersed among the cavalry regiments to provide covering fire. In the center Rupert placed his infantry, with two regiments forward of the main line to block an approach across the ditch. Rupert deployed the main body of the infantry in three lines, with six regiments of foot from his army in the first line and Newcastle's seven infantry regiments in the second and third lines. Two lines of cavalry commanded by George Goring held the left of Rupert's army. These 2,100 horsemen were supported by about 500 musketeers interspersed between the regiments of horse. In reserve, Rupert stationed his lifeguard of 100 men and two regiments of 1,000 cavalrymen.[46]

The allied army, commanded by Leven, was deployed in a similar fashion, with cavalry on the flanks and foot in the middle. Oliver Cromwell commanded the left wing, consisting of the cavalry of the Eastern Association and three Scottish regiments led by David Leslie. This wing was organized in three lines, with Cromwell's units in the first two and Leslie's in the third. Two regiments of dragoons supported Cromwell, giving him about 4,000 men. The infantry brigades in the middle were organized in three parts. On the left center was a 5,000–man brigade commanded by Manchester. Lord Ferdinando Fairfax held the center with two brigades of about 3,000 infantrymen, backed by an identical pair of Scottish brigades. The right-hand infantry units were Scots commanded by the Earl of Lindsay. These Scots were probably the best allied infantry on the field. Sir Thomas Fairfax commanded the cavalry on the right. Fairfax had about 2,800 troopers, including 800 Scots in three regiments.[47]

After about three hours of ineffective artillery exchanges, the field fell silent. By 7 p.m., Rupert, on the strong advice of Newcastle, decided to delay the battle until the next day. Rupert retired to the rear to eat while Newcastle went to his carriage to smoke a pipe. Many royalists followed suit and relaxed. Leven, however, saw the opportunity to launch a surprise attack and ordered an advance at about 7:30 p.m.[48]

On the Roundheads' left, Cromwell sent his dragoons forward to clear the hedges of royalist musketeers. This allowed him to lead his cavalry across the ditch without suffering losses to flanking fire. Once across the ditch, Cromwell's cavalry launched an attack that was met by Lord Byron's royalists. Byron's men were no match for their opponents, who had the advantage of numbers and surprise. During this engagement, Cromwell was slightly wounded and possibly unhorsed before the Cavaliers began to retreat.

Rupert, alerted by the firing, mounted his horse and rode to his right flank to lead a counterattack with his reserve regiment. His courageous attack threw Cromwell's troopers into disorder. Then, however, David Leslie led three Scottish regiments against Rupert's flank, turning the battle once more against the royalists. Leslie's timely attack destroyed the royalist cavalry's cohesion, driving Rupert and his soldiers from the field. By then, Cromwell had remounted and joined Leslie. Together, they decided to have several regiments pursue the defeated royalists while they turned most of their cavalry to face the struggle in the center.[49]

Rupert suffered his first major defeat of the war. He had been caught unprepared, even though the armies were only two or three hundred yards apart when he withdrew for dinner. The horse of the Eastern Association shattered Byron's cavalry, and Rupert's regiment was unable to break Cromwell's troopers in the counterattack. Leslie outmaneuvered Rupert, cutting him off from his lifeguard and forcing him to flee. Rupert's flight left the royalist army without a commander.

On the allies' right wing the battle had gone disastrously for Fairfax. After leading a few troops of horsemen across very difficult ground, Fairfax had succeeded in penetrating the center of Goring's Cavaliers. But Goring's cavalry attacked Fairfax's regiments, 'utterly routing all our horse,' as one parliamentarian account explained.[50] Some of Goring's men pursued the routed Roundheads nearly to Tadcaster, looting their baggage train on the way. The remainder of Goring's horse turned west to attack the Scottish infantry. However, determined resistance by the Scottish Colonel Eglington with his cavalry regiment prevented Goring's men from routing Leven's foot. Meanwhile, Thomas Fairfax, who was cut off behind the royalist lines, threw off his identification ribbon of white and rode around the rear of the royalist army to join Cromwell and Leslie on the left.

In the center of the field an infantry battle commenced simultaneously with the cavalry engagement. On the royalist right center, Manchester's infantry pushed Rupert's soldiers back. After they had cleared the ditch and driven the enemy from their front, Manchester's men turned right, aligning with Leslie's and Cromwell's cavalry. In this process they captured four of Rupert's cannon. In the center, Lord Fairfax's infantry proved no match for Newcastle's veterans, who they encountered after crossing the ditch. Newcastle's Whitecoats quickly routed Fairfax's men, leaving the royalists in command in the center, while several of Newcastle's foot regiments and the royalist cavalry from the left wing attacked Leven's Scots.

The battle hung in the balance. The allies' right was shattered. Their infantry in the right center was under heavy pressure and Fairfax's foot had been routed. Only the determined resistance of the Scottish infantry and Eglington's cavalry kept the allies from defeat. Things were so bad, in fact, that Fairfax, Leven, and Manchester fled, although Manchester soon came back.[51]

At this point, Cromwell, Leslie, and Fairfax, who had kept their cavalry and Manchester's infantry in tight control, launched an attack into the royalists' right flank and rear. Manchester's attack was joined by a number of Scottish infantry regiments in a concentric assault against Newcastle's infantry, while the allied horse swept behind the remainder of Goring's cavalry on the east flank. These attacks were decisive. Goring's men, returning from their pursuit, were driven away, leaving only Newcastle's regiments intact in the center. These soldiers refused quarter, and the majority of them were cut down by allied cavalry and infantry.[52]

The battle was a royalist disaster. They lost most of Newcastle's veteran infantry among their 4,000 casualties. Another 1,500 Cavaliers surrendered. They lost their artillery and ammunition and thousands of weapons. Newcastle gave up the royalist cause in disgrace, fleeing to the continent with most of his officers. This was a particularly heavy blow to the king because only those men might have rallied the northern royalists to further efforts. Rupert escaped with about 6,000 cavalrymen. But he was forced to retreat west, without the infantry and cannon needed to threaten parliamentary garrisons.

Strategically, Charles had lost the north and much of the center of England. He now faced five enemy armies with only his, Hopton's, Rupert's, and Maurice's forces. He lost the strategic initiative, just as he was outmaneuvering Waller and Essex in the south and west. Only a royalist miracle in the west, and failure by his enemies to exploit the new situation, could prevent the destruction of his cause in the summer of 1644. Unfortunately for the suffering people of Britain, that is what happened over the next several months.

Charles's finest hour as a general: the Lostwithiel Campaign

While Rupert was attempting to relieve York, Charles sparred with Waller and maneuvered to defend Oxford. The king's success at Cropredy Bridge, on 29 June, battered Waller's army such that Waller was no longer strong enough to maintain contact with Charles's army without risking further defeat. Thus he fell back to Newport Pagnell to await reinforcements. When ordered to move after Charles he reported that he could not do so, 'our horse being much beaten.'[53]

By early July, it had become painfully clear that the only additional troops available for Waller's army were the trained bands. A number of these regiments, however, had been in the field for a considerable time under the command of Major General Richard Browne and were unwilling to serve much longer. The Committee of Both Kingdoms' attempt to persuade nearby counties to send their militia to join Browne or Waller also failed. This made it impossible for Waller or Browne to take any major action against the king's forces around Oxford.[54]

Charles, freed of the interference from Waller, and certain that Oxford was in no immediate danger, determined to march west in pursuit of Essex's army. By 12 July he was on the road with 8,000 soldiers. This was his best course of action and shows that even after learning of the disaster at Marston Moor, Charles had plenty of fight left. If he could defeat Essex, he might possibly redress the strategic balance. Such a victory also would encourage his supporters in Ireland and Scotland.

Essex, following his decision to move west, had relieved Lyme Regis and continued on to Tavistock, which he reached on 23 July. On 26 July he notified the Committee of Both Kingdoms that he was going to continue west across the Tamar River and into Cornwall, which local parliamentarians had assured him would rise to welcome and feed his army.[55] He was able to continue his advance because the royalist forces in the area, commanded by Maurice and Hopton, were too few to take on Essex's army of 10,000 men. But the royalists knew that the king had set out from Oxford with his army and that their mission was to shadow Essex's movements until Charles arrived (see map 14).

Essex reached Bodmin, Cornwall on 28 July. There he found that the town and region did not welcome him and that Sir Richard Grenville was gathering a force to hinder his supply efforts. On 2 August Essex learned that Charles was nearing a rendezvous with Maurice and Hopton, an event that would give the king 16,000 men. Therefore, Essex retreated south to Lostwithiel, arriving at that small port in southern Cornwall by 4 August. From there he wrote to the Committee of Both Kingdoms, reporting that the royalists were closing in on him and that his army was short of money and supplies.[56] No commander in the civil wars did more than

Essex to allow his enemies to surround his army in an unfavorable situation. He realized the danger to his army but, instead of continuing his march to Plymouth, twenty miles east, he halted for four weeks, allowing four royalist forces to surround him in Lostwithiel.

Charles handled his army and regional forces brilliantly. His task was not made easier by the dissension in his officer ranks by men who had come to the conclusion that a compromise peace had to be sought. Charles faced these men down, replacing Wilmot as cavalry commander with George Goring, one of the few royalists who had done well at Marston Moor.[57] As the Earl of Essex cried for help, the king orchestrated an advance of his forces to within four miles of Lostwithiel, seizing the dominant terrain in the area on 21 July.[58]

The Committee of Both Kingdoms tried desperately to get Waller and Browne to move west to aid Essex. They also sent money and supplies to Lostwithiel by sea. But Waller and Browne found the trained bands unwilling to serve far from home, and the county committees refused to send additional militia to replace those units that deserted en masse.[59] Trained bands again had proven unsuitable for the offensive campaigns needed to win the war.

In the last four days of August the royalists tightened the noose around Essex's position in Lostwithiel by seizing the forts and high ground on the east side of the River Fowey. These moves cut his supply route along that river and made it unlikely that he would be able to evacuate his army by sea. On the night of 30 August Essex decided to send his cavalry out of the trap, through a gap in the royalist lines to the northeast. Commissary General Behr and Sir William Balfour successfully led these men east, to Plymouth.

The next morning the king launched his attack. After two days of fierce fighting the situation became hopeless for the Roundhead infantry, now commanded by Major General Philip Skippon. Essex, unwilling to be captured, escaped in a small fishing boat, after ordering Skippon to get the best terms he could. On 2 September, Skippon surrendered his 6,000 soldiers and 42 cannon. The king allowed the parliamentarians to march away with their swords, in return for their promise not to fight again until they reached Portsmouth. These lenient terms were a mistake, since Skippon's men were the best infantry available to parliament in the south, and could easily be rearmed. Charles, however, had no place to keep so many prisoners.

Lostwithiel was Charles's greatest success in the Civil War. He destroyed parliament's main army and maintained his control of the west. Essex never recovered the trust of parliament. Charles had outwitted and outfought Waller in the Cropredy campaign as well. These successes forced the Committee of Both Kingdoms to give Manchester's army of the Eastern Association the added task of protecting London. Charles, however, had lost far more at Marston Moor than he gained in the south. At Marston Moor, Newcastle's northern army was destroyed, with only its cavalry able to get away. York fell to the allied armies on 16 July. The Marquis of Newcastle left England, not to return until after the wars, depriving the king of the leadership needed to continue a struggle in the north.

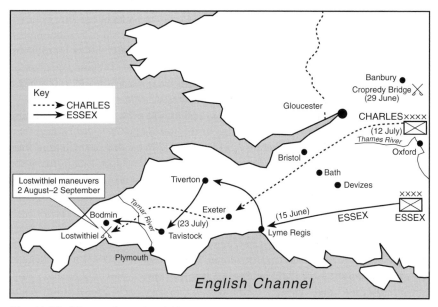

Map 14 The Western Campaign, 1644

The allies go their separate ways

On 30 July, following the fall of York, the three allied commanders—Manchester, Fairfax, and Leven—divided their forces to operate in different regions. Fairfax remained in Yorkshire to defend the West Riding from Rupert, who had led his cavalry to Lancashire after Marston Moor.[60] Leven marched his Scots north to Newcastle, where they joined another Scottish army of about 7,000 men, newly raised by the Earl of Callendar. The Scots then cleared Northumberland and Durham of royalists and besieged Newcastle. For the remainder of the year the Scots stayed in the north, capturing Newcastle on 19 October and sending a strong force west to invest Carlisle.[61]

Manchester and Oliver Cromwell marched south, in part because they were having a difficult time feeding their troops in Yorkshire. As they came south, the soldiers of the Eastern Association captured a number of royalist garrisons, including Sheffield. Manchester, however, decided not to invest the Cavalier-held Newark, in spite of Cromwell's advice to do so. After spending most of August in Lincoln, Manchester finally stirred in response to calls from the Committee of Both Kingdoms to send help to the parliamentarians in Lancashire. This activity ended when he learned that Rupert had led most of his force south to join the king, and that Essex's army had met with disaster at Lostwithiel. The Army of the Eastern Association was now the largest force available to protect London.[62]

Manchester faced a number of serious logistical and financial problems, and he was having difficulty refilling his ranks. But he had more serious problems. He and Cromwell had become estranged politically, and their disagreements about military operations reflected this division. Cromwell, like many parliamentarians, believed that military victory would not be enough to resolve the Civil War. Something had to be done about Charles I, the man whom they felt was the center of their problems. But Manchester, Essex, and parliamentarians like Denzil Holles sought a negotiated settlement with the king because they feared that men like Cromwell might use a thorough parliamentary military victory to depose the king.

Only the perception of a growing danger to London in September and October caused Manchester, Cromwell, and the others temporarily to work together. Manchester acknowledged parliament's unhappiness with the dissension in the armies and promised that, 'Concerning those differences your Lordships take notice to be amongst some of this army, I hope you will find that I shall take such care as, by the blessing of God, nothing of the public service shall be retarded.'[63]

The fall campaign and the Second Battle of Newbury

Charles recognized the opportunity offered by his defeat of Essex. With Waller and Browne unable to raise forces, the royalists had a chance to concentrate and march east. Such a move might allow the king to fight another battle against either Waller or Manchester or to threaten the Eastern Association. In any case, he hoped to relieve his garrisons in Banbury and Basing House, thus protecting his position around Oxford for the coming winter. By 5 September, the royal army was at Tavistock, but it was steadily declining in numbers as many Cornishmen refused to serve outside of their county, and as it became necessary to leave forces to screen the parliamentarian garrisons in Dorset, Somerset, and Devon.[64]

The Committee of Both Kingdoms took the threat from the king's advance very seriously, fearing that he was going to make another attempt on London. Orders were sent to Manchester to march south from Huntington to Abingdon and then on to Reading. The Committee sent messages to Waller, Essex, Manchester, and Browne, urging them to cooperate with one another in this time of peril. London's militia committee agreed to provide five regiments, as long as parliament provided their pay. And the Westminster government sent thousands of weapons to Portsmouth to re-equip Essex's infantry, many of whom had been brought by sea from Plymouth following their march from Lostwithiel. These measures promised to bring together superior forces to face the king's army, if time permitted.

Charles found it impossible to advance rapidly. He lost time providing forces to watch Plymouth and Weymouth, and he paused at Chard from 23 to 30 September to await food supplies. By 29 September, Manchester's army had reached Reading, while Waller led a cavalry force to Salisbury, hoping to block the king's advance. Manchester, however, ignored orders from the Committee of Both Kingdoms and refused to advance further west to join Waller, believing that it was too risky to face the king that far west while outnumbered. Consequently, Waller had to retreat to avoid being trapped by the king.[65]

After receiving supplies, Charles resumed his advance, reaching Salisbury by 15 October. During the next week the Committee of Both Kingdoms succeeded in getting Manchester's, Waller's, and Essex's forces to unite at Basingstoke, just as Charles's army reached Kingscleare. The odds were now decidedly against the king, with his opponents having about 19,000 men, including five regiments of the London trained bands, to use against his 10,000.[66] But the parliamentarians lacked unity of command and their generals were scarcely on speaking terms. The Committee of Both Kingdoms had done a remarkable job pulling together a formidable force, but the best it could do to settle the question of command was to place the army in the hands of a committee composed of Essex, Waller, Manchester, Cromwell, Lord Robartes, Arthur Haselrigg, and two civilian members of parliament.[67] Fortunately, Essex became ill and remained in Reading.

Charles continued his advance, forcing the Roundheads to abandon their siege of Banbury. By 23 October he had arrived at Red Heath, just north of Newbury and near Donnington Castle. In response, the committee in charge of parliament's forces decided to advance toward Newbury in hopes of fighting the king's army before Rupert could join it with reinforcements. Charles, in response, put his troops in strong positions facing northeast, with their right flank anchored on the town of Newbury, their center secured by the River Lambourn and a fortified manor, and their left protected by Donnington Castle. He placed Maurice with a reserve at the village of Speen, south of Donnington Castle, from where he could protect the army's flank and rear and reinforce the main line. From this position Charles felt he could repulse any parliamentarian attack. If none came, he could receive supplies and reinforcements and remain in place while his enemies' forces disintegrated.[68]

Parliament's armies took up positions to the north and east of the royalists while their leaders held a council of war. After deliberation they developed an audacious plan to defeat the king without having to attack his strong position head on. Waller, Skippon, Balfour, and Cromwell would lead over half of the army on a thirteen-mile night march to a position south of Donnington Castle, facing Speen and the rear of the royalist army from the west. Manchester would remain with the remainder of the army in front of the king, making feints to keep the Cavaliers occupied. When the flanking force was in place, it would attack Maurice's position and then the rear of Charles's main line. Once he heard the firing, Manchester was to attack the front, crushing the outnumbered royalists.

This plan showed how far English war-fighting skills had come in the year since the first Battle of Newbury. At that earlier fight no complicated maneuver had been attempted by either side. All tactical movements had been frontal attacks, and no complicated coordination or timing had been used. At the Second Battle of Newbury, a complicated and dangerous maneuver was attempted. It was a scheme that required timing and coordination. It also required a difficult night march in the face of an experienced enemy. It nearly succeeded.

On the night of 26 October, the flanking force marched north from Clay Hill, near Newbury, to Hermitage, then turned west to North Heath, and south to Boxford. From there the Roundheads deployed for the attack. By 3 p.m., after a rest and some food, Waller and his fellow commanders launched their assaults. In the meantime,

Charles got word of their march and sent reinforcements to Maurice, who entrenched his men facing west on a line from Speen to the River Lambourn.

In spite of the strength of Maurice's position, the parliamentarians made steady progress. On the right, or southern, flank, Sir William Balfour and the cavalry from Essex's army drove the royalists back, while Skippon, with Essex's infantry regiments, overran Maurice's fortifications, capturing a number of cannon. Charles reinforced Maurice from his main position, a move that should have played perfectly into his attackers' plan. But Manchester remained inactive, in spite of the urging of Major General Crawford, his infantry commander, to attack. This inactivity allowed the king to stabilize the situation on his left and to stop Cromwell's cavalrymen dead in their tracks when they tried to roll up Maurice's right flank near the Lambourn. Manchester finally attacked half-heartedly at dusk, an attack that Charles easily repulsed.[69]

During the night the king led his army across the Lambourn near Donnington Castle and headed west. His escape from his dangerous position was bad enough, but Manchester refused to join Waller's and Cromwell's cavalry with his infantry in the pursuit. Charles got safely to Oxford where he united with Rupert. The badly divided Roundhead council of war decided to return to Reading after an unsuccessful assault against Donnington Castle, where the royalists had left their artillery and ammunition. On 9 November, Charles and Rupert, whom the king had just made the Commanding General of his army, returned to Donnington Castle to recover their guns. Parliament's armies were too exhausted to prevent this. Worse, the parliamentarian generals were completely at odds with one another, making concerted action impossible, and independent action dangerous.

The news for parliament from the north, however, continued to be good, with the fall of Newcastle, and the steady clearing of royalist garrisons by the Scots and Thomas Fairfax. Hope for a royalist resurgence was shattered, and prospects were bright for future allied operations in Cheshire and Lancashire. However, the campaign in the south left bitter feelings in all participants and exposed deep fissures in the anti-royalist cause. The fighting in the south had shown that divided command, reliance on the trained bands for offensive action, and decentralized administration of the war prevented the parliamentarians from exploiting their material advantages. Even when they won battles like Marston Moor, they could not exploit success because of the ineffectual and bumbling command of parliament's Lord General, the Earl of Essex.

Worse, Manchester and Essex were beginning to fear men such as Cromwell and Vane because the latter sought a total victory over the king. They dreaded such an outcome for several reasons. First, total defeat of the king would undermine the social and political structure that they thought they were fighting to defend. Second, a victory in which Cromwell and his growing body of followers in the armies played a major role might lead to an unsatisfactory religious settlement in which independent sects and congregations could be autonomous within a national church, free from the doctrinal discipline of either bishops or Presbyteries. Finally, the earls saw that it was impossible to defeat the king unless he was willing to accept surrender, because he was still the monarch. Manchester expressed this sentiment perfectly in November.

His lordship replying told the council he would assure them there was no such thing [as a total defeat of Charles], adding (with vehemence) this principle against fighting: that if we beat the king 99 times he would be king still, and his posterity, and we subjects still: but if he beat us but once we should be hanged, and our posterity be undone. Thus it was concluded not to fight, the king suffered to march off unsought (being within a mile of us), and we retreated into Newbury.[70]

The fall campaign was over. Both sides occupied winter quarters. It had been an amazing year of warfare that had militarized the societies of three kingdoms. The Scots had raised at least 40,000 men for their armies in Ulster and England. Royalist armies of at least that many men faced Roundhead forces of more than 50,000 men in England, counting garrisons and trained bands. Military operations touched every corner of England and Ireland, and taxes and conscription touched all three Stuart kingdoms. However, no military decision had been reached, in spite of unprecedented military efforts. The king was too weak to defeat the Scots and parliamentarians, and the parliamentary war effort was not organized in such a way as to exploit its resource and manpower advantages. To do this, and to win, the Long Parliament had to resolve the disputes dividing its generals and emasculating its military forces.[71]

Notes

1 J. Lowe, ed., 'Charles I and the Confederation of Kilkenny, 1643–9', *Irish Historical Studies*, 14 (1964), 1–19.
2 E. Furgol, in Kenyon and Ohlmeyer, eds., *The Civil Wars*, 48–51.
3 Burne and Young, *The Great Civil War*, 145.
4 Gardiner, *Civil War*, i: 247–9; Burne and Young, *The Great Civil War*, 120–1.
5 Burne and Young, *The Great Civil War*, 120–1.
6 Gardiner, *Civil War*, i: 252–4.
7 Ibid., 241–3.
8 Burne and Young, *The Great Civil War*, 132–4.
9 Ibid., 133–5.
10 Ibid., 134–7; Gardiner, *Civil War*, i: 294–5.
11 Clarendon, *History of the Rebellion*, iii: 361.
12 Roy, 'The Royalist Council of War, 1642–46', 155–6; Hutton, *The Royalist War Effort*, 112–28.
13 Gardiner, *Civil War*, iii: 302–7.
14 Stevenson, *The Scottish Revolution*, 297–8.
15 Terry, *Papers Relating to the Army of the Solemn League and Covenant*, xiv–xv.
16 Ibid.
17 Carte, *Ormond*, vi: 74, Muskerry to Ormond, Oxford, 29 March 1644; P. Lenihan, *Confederate Catholics at War, 1641–49* (Cork, 2001), 74–6, 78–81, 84–5; O'Siochru, *Confederate Ireland*, 70–4; Corish in Moody, Ed., *New History of Ireland*, iii: 309–12; Lindley, 'The Impact of the 1641 Rebellion Upon England and Wales', 170–3.
18 O'Siochru, *Confederate Ireland*, 70; Corish in *NHI*, iii: 311.
19 Carte, *Ormond*, vi: 85–6, Lord Digby to Ormond, 2 April 1644.
20 O'Siochru, *Confederate Ireland*, 71–2; Corish in *NHI*, iii: 312.
21 Lowe, 'Charles I and the Confederation of Kilkenny, 1643–9', 1–5.

22 Ohlmeyer, Civil War and Restoration, 132–46; P. Lenihan in J. Young, ed., *Celtic Dimensions of the British Civil Wars* (Edinburgh, 1997), 128–30.

23 Carte MS 11, fo. 117, Council Proceedings in Dublin, forwarded to Charles I, 15 May 1644; J. Tuchet, Earl of Castlehaven, *The Earl of Castlehaven's Review: Or his Memoirs of his Engagement and Carriage in the Irish Wars* (London, 1684), 82–3; Casway, *O'Neill*, 113; Hazlett, 'The Recruitment and Organization of the Scottish Army in Ulster, 1642–9', 102–113.

24 Lenihan, *Confederate Catholics at War*, 81–3; Wheeler, *Cromwell in Ireland*, 21–5.

25 TT, E38 (10), *Prince Rupert's Raising of the Siege at Newark*, March 1644, Oxford, 1–2.

26 Burne and Young, *The Great Civil War I* 138–9; Kenyon, *The Civil Wars of England*, 92–4.

27 TT E38 (10), *Prince Rupert's Raising of the Siege at Newark*, 2.

28 Ibid.

29 Ibid., 2–5; TT E39 (8), *A Brief Relation of the Siege of Newark*, (26 March 1644), 5–7; E39 (9), *Mercurius Veridicus* (19–26 March 1644), not paginated.

30 TT E39 (8), *A Brief Relation of the Siege of Newark*, 7–8.

31 Kenyon, *The Civil Wars of England*, 95; Gardiner, *Civil War*, i: 337.

32 Burne and Young, *The Great Civil War*, 147; Kenyon, *The Civil Wars of England*, 95–6.

33 Kenyon, *The Civil Wars of England*, 94–7; Gardiner, *Civil War*, i: 352–4.

34 Gardiner, *Civil War*, i: 353–5; Kenyon, *The Civil Wars of England*, 97–8.

35 Kenyon, *The Civil Wars of England*, 98–9.

36 Burne and Young, *The Great Civil War*, 149–52.

37 Terry, *The Army of the Solemn League and Covenant*, i: xv–xvi; Gardiner, *Civil War*, i: 337.

38 Abbott, *Oliver Cromwell*, i: 282–3.

39 Quoted in Gardiner, *Civil War*, i: 371, from Forster, *British Statesmen*, vi: 129, Charles to Rupert, 14 June 1644.

40 *CSPD, 1644*, 196–8; Abbott, i: 283.

41 Abbott, i: 284, Scoutmaster General Leonard Watson to the Earl of Manchester, 30 June 1644.

42 TT E2 (14), *A More Exact Relation of the late Battle fought near York*, (17 July 1644), 1–2.

43 C. Firth, 'Marston Moor', *Transactions of the Royal Historical Society*, 12 (1898), 18–79; TT E54 (19), *A Full Relation of the late Victory … sent by the Generals* (11 July 1644); Firth has convincingly argued that Gardiner, *Civil War*, i: 375, got the deployment of the allied forces wrong.

44 D. Laing, ed., *The Letters and Journals of Robert Baillie, 1637–1662* (Edinburgh, 1841), ii: 200–1, Baillie to Mr Spang, 5 July 1644.

45 TT E2 (14), *A More Exact Relation of the Battle*, 2.

46 Firth, 'Marston Moor', 31–5.

47 Ibid., 35–42.

48 Ibid., 43–7; TT E2 (14), *A More Exact Relation of the Battle*, 4–5.

49 Firth, 'Marston Moor,' 44–6.

50 Ibid., 47–50.

51 Burne and Young, *The Great Civil War*, 163–5.

52 TT E54 (19), *A Full Relation of the late Victory*, 8–10; E2 (14), *A More Exact Relation of the Battle*, 6–7; Firth, 'Marston Moor', 50–62.

53 *CSPD, 1644*, 307, Waller to the Committee of Both Kingdoms, 4 July 1644.

54 Ibid., 268, 275, 307, 333, 341, 347–51, for the correspondence between the Committee of Both Kingdoms and Browne, Waller, and the county militia committee in late June and July 1644.

55 Ibid., 379, Essex to Committee of Both Kingdoms, 26 July 1644.

56 Ibid., 398–9, Essex to the Committee of Both Kingdoms, 4 August 1644.

57 Burne and Young, *The Great Civil War*, 170–1; Gardiner, *Civil War*, ii: 10–11.

58 Burne and Young, *The Great Civil War*, 172–4; *CSPD, 1644*, 433–4, Essex to the Committee of Both Kingdoms, 16 August 1644.

59 *CSPD, 1644*, 446–75, for dozens of letters from the Committee to Waller, Browne, and the county committees of Essex, Sussex, Hampshire, and Bedfordshire, in August 1644.

60 *CSPD, 1644*, 385, the Earl of Lindsay and Thomas Fairfax to the Committee of Both Kingdoms, 30 July 1644.

61 Terry, *The Army of the Solemn League and Covenant, 1643–1647*, i: xxiii–lviii; *CSPD, 1644*, 359, Leven, Manchester, and Fairfax to the Committee of Both Kingdoms, 18 July 1644.

62 Gardiner, *Civil War*, ii: 20–6; *CSPD, 1644*, 469, 471, 473, 474, 481, for the correspondence between the Committee and Manchester, 1–7 September 1644.

63 *CSPD, 1644*, 481–2, Manchester to the Committee of Both Kingdoms, 8 September 1644.

64 Gardiner, *Civil War*, ii: 31–5; Burne and Young, *The Great Civil War*, 180–1.

65 *CSPD, 1644*, 541, Committee of Both Kingdoms to Manchester, 28 September 1644; 542, Manchester to the Committee of Both Kingdoms, 29 September 1644; *CSPD, 1644–1645*, Manchester to the Committee of Both Kingdoms, 9 October 1644.

66 Abbott, i: 297.

67 *CSPD, 1644–1645*, 39, Proceedings of the Committee of Both Kingdoms, 14 October 1644.

68 British Library Museum, Additional Manuscript 18,981, fo. 312, Lord Digby to Rupert, 27 October 1644, cited in Gardiner, *Civil War*, ii: 47.

69 Gardiner, *Civil War*, ii: 44–52; Burne and Young, *The Great Civil War*, 182–9.

70 Abbott, i: 310, Cromwell's narrative of the fall campaign 25 November 1644.

CHAPTER FIVE

The creation of the New Model Army and the royalist defeat

The king's withdrawal of his army to Oxford after recovering his artillery from Donnington Castle marked the end of a very long campaign season. Remarkably for the practice of warfare in the mid-seventeenth century, most of the major armies in Britain did not go into winter quarters. Instead, they operated through the winter of 1643–4. For example, the Scots crossed the Tweed on 17 January, beginning a slow advance that took them to York by mid April. Sir Thomas Fairfax campaigned vigorously in December and January in Cheshire and Lancashire and then moved east to Yorkshire. The Cavalier commanders Rupert and Newcastle spent the winter countering these moves. Similarly, the royalist Hopton and the parliamentarian Waller thrust at one another in Dorset and Hampshire during the winter and spring.

The pace of operations of all armies increased in the spring, as both sides sought an advantage. Regiments often marched 200 miles a month, causing tremendous wear on feet and footwear. By 15 November 1644, even the most aggressive of commanders, such as Oliver Cromwell, had to warn the Committee of Both Kingdoms that

> The horse are so tired out with hard duty in such extremity of weather as hath seldom been seen, that if much more service be required of them you will quickly see your cavalry ruined without fighting. The foot are not in better case. besides the lessening of their numbers through cold and hard duty; sickness also is much on the increase …[1]

The miserable condition of the regiments of Essex, Manchester, and Waller was typical of the parliamentary forces throughout the country.[2] The Committee of Both Kingdoms had no recourse but to organize winter quarters for its forces, and to do so in such a way that the royalists could not raid with impunity into the Eastern Association or the counties around London. Waller's units were stationed in towns in a line from the Channel to Farnham. Essex's regiments garrisoned at Reading and the villages around it, while Manchester's men occupied quarters in Henley and Aylesbury. Abingdon was held by a force drawn from all three armies and the London trained bands.[3] With these deployments complete, those commanders who were members of parliament returned to London to fight a different battle.

The royalist military situation was considerably worse than parliament's in late 1644. The Scots and local English parliamentarians had driven the royalists out of the north, with Carlisle and Chester remaining the only substantial towns held for the king. David Leslie besieged Carlisle while Sir William Brereton cleared Cheshire of Cavalier garrisons, isolating Chester. The disaster at Marston Moor had badly demoralized the king's supporters in Lancashire and Shropshire, making them easy prey for their enemies. After several parliamentary victories in the fall, the Roundheads captured Liverpool, overran Lancashire, and made inroads into Wales. These were serious blows to the king's efforts to recruit Welsh infantry to refill his depleted ranks. The siege of Chester also made it more difficult for Charles to receive aid from Ormond in Ireland.[4]

Charles could do little to stem the tide, although he did appoint Maurice as his commander in the Marches and the north. Royalist affairs continued to deteriorate during the winter, even though Maurice outmaneuvered Brereton and slipped into Chester with reinforcements and supplies in late February 1645. Then, on 22 February, disaster struck when local parliamentarians in Shropshire surprised the Cavaliers in Shrewsbury while they slept, capturing the town without a battle. The loss of Shrewsbury compounded the royalists' difficulties in communicating with their base in Wales and their stronghold in Cheshire.[5]

A similar trend of events was evident in Gloucestershire, where Edward Massey, the parliamentary commander of the city of Gloucester, exploited the royalists' preoc-cupation with their campaigns to the north and east during the summer and fall. Massey captured a number of strong points in the Severn Valley, broke the city's isolation and disrupted royalist logistical operations in the surrounding counties. By the fall of 1644 Massey controlled a considerable area astride the royalists' lines of communications.

Charles's efforts to recruit new troops and to raise money were severely hindered by these military reverses. Worse for his hope of victory, war weariness had led to the rise of local associations that refused to support either side. These groups of gentry organized regional police forces to keep order, while a more populist movement known as the 'Club-men' rose to challenge anyone attempting to raise supplies or men. In those regions where there were strong royalist or parliamentarian garrisons, these movements were suppressed. However, the king's need to divert forces to crush such opposition indicated the decline of support he enjoyed and weakened his war effort. The decline in active support for the royalist cause by the gentry was one of the reasons the king turned to professional soldiers to command his armies and garrisons.[6] This ensured firmer royal control of strategically important places, but weakened local support as the professional soldiers used force to extract resources from the surrounding communities.

The king's efforts in Ireland and Scotland

Matters in Ireland were not any brighter for Charles, although the Protestant armies were unable to bring their superior numbers to bear against the Confederates as long as the English Civil War continued. The Irish cessation of September 1643 remained in force in most of Ireland throughout 1644, but permanent peace between the king and his Catholic subjects had not come any closer. Following the abortive negotiations between the Confederates and Charles in Oxford, in May, the king authorized Ormond to continue talks in Ireland. Ormond was well suited for this mission for several reasons. He was a staunch Protestant who was not likely to accept religious terms that would have alienated many Englishmen and his fellow Protestants in Ireland from the king. He also was connected through family ties with many leading Confederates, giving him the ability to deal smoothly with them.

Ormond and the Confederates made some progress in their talks in September 1644 in Dublin. He agreed to allow Catholics to regain property they had held before the war and to remove the indictments of Confederates from court records. Ormond offered to reverse Strafford's plantation schemes in Connacht and promised to reform the court of wards and the customs administration. But he would not agree to dispense with Poyning's law nor accept the independence of the Irish parliament. The main stumbling block to a treaty, however, was religion. The Catholics demanded repeal of anti-Catholic legislation and freedom of worship. Ormond could only promise them the benefits of the king's 'grace and goodness' on these issues after he won the English Civil War. This was unacceptable to the Confederates, and rightly so, given Charles's propensity not to honor the spirit of his promises.[7]

This impasse was not broken for two years, even though negotiations continued intermittently. During this process, Ormond often received secret advice from several of the king's counsellors that he should promise more to the Catholics than Charles could or would deliver. Ormond was only willing to promise the Confederates that they could trust Charles to take care of their interests once he was firmly in charge in London. He even ignored an order from Charles, in February 1645, '… to conclude peace with the Irish whatever it costs, …' because he had to satisfy the demands of the Irish Protestants as well as the Confederates and the king, and because he opposed the religious concessions needed to close the deal.[8]

Ormond had reason for concern about the attitude of Irish Protestants. In July 1644, Lord Inchiquin, the Protestant commander in Munster, condemned the cessation and declared his allegiance to parliament, telling the king there could be no peace with the 'rebel Irish' because of their religion. Inchiquin was convinced that Charles was '… strangely beguiled by the Irish rebels …', and that 'they intend to make such use [of the cessation] so that no English (if Protestant) shall be left.'[9] Inchiquin's defection adversely affected the Confederates' campaign in Ulster in August 1644 because they had to leave substantial forces in Munster to guard against his army.

For these reasons, Charles could not be very hopeful of receiving help from the Irish Catholics. The failure of the Confederate campaign against Monro's Scots made it even less likely that he would receive such aid. The failure of the Catholic generals to work smoothly together and their unwillingness to risk a battle against Monro meant that the Irish war would continue at the level of raid and counter-raid. Ormond's refusal to cooperate with the Confederates against Monro aggravated the situation. By the fall of 1644, Monro was eliminating Ormond's garrisons in Ulster and northern Leinster, limiting Ormond's ability to help Charles in Britain.[10]

The best news for Charles from Ireland was that Antrim had successfully shipped 1,600 Catholic soldiers to Kintyre, in western Scotland, in June 1644. On 26 August, Montrose and MacColla joined forces. Montrose also convinced the Stewarts and Robertsons, who had been sent to stop MacColla's men, to join his campaign against Argyll.[11] Montrose then boldly led his small army to Tippermuir, three miles west of Perth, where, on 1 September, he defeated the Covenanter Lord Elcho and about 7,000 Scottish militiamen.[12]

The Battle of Tippermuir shocked Argyll into action. He led an army from the west in pursuit of Montrose, while another Covenanter force prepared to defend Aberdeen, Montrose's most likely target since the Huntly lands in Aberdeenshire harbored a significant number of anti-Covenanters. Montrose moved too fast for Argyll, arriving just to the west of Aberdeen on 13 September. There his final approach to the city was blocked by the Covenanter garrison of about 2,500 men, arrayed in a good position and backed by artillery and cavalry. Montrose, although outnumbered, summoned the garrison to surrender. He also warned the townspeople to evacuate the place if the garrison refused to submit. Not only did the Covenanters refuse to surrender, one of their soldiers shot Montrose's drummer, who had accompanied the flag of truce.

Montrose wasted no time in drawing up his army of about 1,500 men just to the south of the defenders. The Covenanters, seeing that the royalists had only a few dozen cavalrymen, attacked Montrose's flanks with their horse, hoping to break his infantry formations. MacColla's men, however, did not panic. Instead, as the cavalrymen rode past them, they emptied many a saddle with musket fire and then launched the Highland charge against the Covenanter infantry. The results were the same as at Tippermuir. The inexperienced Covenanters broke and ran for the gates of Aberdeen, closely followed by the Irish and Highlanders. Aberdeen fell quickly. Montrose allowed his men to sack the city before he entered the next day.[13] By this point, Montrose and MacColla's Irish soldiers had unnerved the Covenanters, causing them to divert attention and resources to the defense of Scotland, and away from their operations in England and Ulster.

While developments in Scotland were encouraging to the king, Montrose's operations did not force the recall of more than a few regiments from the Scottish armies in Ulster and England, even after Montrose's victory near Fyvie Castle in October 1644. The Scots capture of Newcastle that month, and their ability to initiate a siege of Carlisle, demonstrated the limits of Montrose's diversion. It did, however, contribute to a growing awareness by the parliamentarians that they needed to find a way to win the war before such unforeseen occurrences snatched victory away.

Dissension in the parliamentary cause

The military results of the campaigns of 1644 favored the parliamentarians, even though the year ended in frustration and embarrassment at Newbury and

Donnington Castle. Charles had lost the north. His attempts to extend his authority toward London had been thwarted. The royalist strongholds of Cornwall and Wales were being exhausted by their efforts on his behalf, and their communications with Oxford were crimped. The king's hopes for an Irish Catholic army had dwindled, while most of Scotland remained under Covenanter control.

The parliamentarians and Covenanters, however, faced a daunting array of problems that sapped their efforts to defeat the king. Parliament's armies saw their best chance to crush the king's army in a single battle thwarted by the inactivity of Manchester at Newbury. The Scots were restless in the north, due to the failure of the English to pay them the £31,000 promised monthly and to a growing fear that the parliamentarians might not accept a Presbyterian church. Parliament's armies also were melting away due to shortages of money, and mutiny was a common problem.[14] Serious dissension in the high command also plagued the war effort, with the senior generals divided over how and why to continue the struggle. In these circumstances, it seemed possible that Charles might yet exploit the fissures within the parliamentary cause.

The divisions within the senior ranks of its armies were the most dangerous problem facing the Long Parliament. This dissension among the generals reflected military, religious, and political disputes that affected the parliamentary cause and which could have fatally weakened it just when victory was on the horizon. However, the immediate and fundamental problems were how to win the war and how to deal with the king.

Parliamentarians like Cromwell favored the prosecution of the war to total victory, while others like Manchester feared such an outcome because it would preclude compromise. This was the issue that Manchester was alluding to in his exclamation at Newbury concerning the futility of fighting the king with all-out vigor. Manchester's view made it impossible for parliament to exploit its material advantages and the current situation to win the war.

The generals also were divided by a religious issue characterized as the 'Independents v the Presbyterians.' All parliamentarian generals professed support for the abolition of episcopacy and the establishment of a Presbyterian church. Some, like Cromwell, wanted such a church to allow for independent congregations within the Presbyterian structure, and for these congregations to be allowed the freedom within a loose order to worship as they chose, based on the Word of God. Further, the Independents, as they were called, did not want to entrust an ecclesiastical hierarchy with coercive power. Presbyterians, like Manchester and Essex, wanted a more centrally supervised national church, with a check placed upon the spread of sectarianism and unlicensed preachers.[15]

The religious issues dividing the generals were connected to the relationship between the Scots and the parliamentarians. Until the autumn of 1644, the Scots had favored men like Waller and Cromwell who pushed for a vigorous prosecution of the war. By November, the Covenanters had come to see Cromwell and Vane and their fellow Independents as almost as dangerous as Charles I. They saw Essex and Manchester as the men most likely to bring the war to an end in such a way as to achieve the goals of the Solemn League and Covenant.[16] How to win the war was the main issue, although below the surface and behind the scenes the religious issues played an important part in the course of events.

The November debacles at Newbury and Donnington Castle convinced the Committee of Both Kingdoms and the House of Commons that their armies needed to be 'new-modeled.' This reorganization would include a new command structure and provisions for a reliable source of money to support the army. The war party leaders, Henry Vane and Oliver St John, understood that the peace party in the Lords and Commons needed to be given another opportunity to negotiate a peace with the king. Such a move would placate the Covenanters who thought that such a peace was the best way to establish Presbyterianism in England and to ensure the safety of their settlement in Scotland.[17]

Therefore, the parliamentarians pursued two seemingly opposite courses of action during the winter of 1644–5. First, they and the Scots participated in peace negotiations with the king's representatives at Uxbridge in January and February 1645.[18] Second, the Commons ordered the Committee of Both Kingdoms to invest-igate the military debacles of the fall and to develop plans for the restructuring of the armed forces.[19]

The simultaneous efforts to secure a peace while overhauling the armies indicate that the majority of parliamentarians probably believed that Charles would never accept parliament's proposals for peace. Therefore, they considered it wise to prepare for war while seeking peace. This was a brilliant maneuver on the part of the leaders of the war party. They remained conspicuously quiet about the chances of peace during the negotiations, giving the king an opportunity to show his utter contempt for their terms.

Parliament's terms for peace were unacceptable to Charles. They included demands for the permanent abolition of episcopacy, the establishment of a Presbyterian church in England, the punishment of his leading supporters and commanders, the exclusion of all papists in England and Ireland from pardon, and parliamentary control of the militia, army, and navy. The king had no intention of accepting these terms, as he told his wife.[20] But he accepted the opportunity to negotiate, believing that the growing religious and political divisions amongst the parliamentarians and the Scots could be exploited.[21] Ironically, because the parliamentarians accepted the Scots' request for another try for a negotiated peace, the Anglo-Scottish alliance was strengthened. Once the king's intransigence during negotiations was manifest, the Scots and the English peace party saw that war was the only option short of abject surrender. As the delegates met at Uxbridge and talked at cross-purposes, both sides prepared to continue the war.

The creation of the New Model Army

While the parliamentarians discussed peace with the king they debated how to reform their military establishment. There were three major issues to be dealt with. First, how should the armies be reorganized so that the full power of the cause could be concentrated against the king? Second, who should command the armies? Third, how should parliament financially support the new army, the navy, and its other garrisons and regional forces?

The question of organization was the easiest to answer. A committee developed the plan for the 'New Model Army', as it soon was called. This committee included Essex, Manchester, Cromwell, Waller, the commissioners of Scotland, and Sir Gilbert Gerard, treasurer of Essex's army. They concluded that the armies of Essex, Waller, and Manchester should be combined into one army of twelve regiments of infantry, each with 1,200 men. Ten, and later eleven, regiments of cavalry, each with 600 troopers, were to make up the horse, and one regiment of mounted infantry, known as dragoons, was to round out the army. Dozens of small regiments in the current armies were to be disbanded and their soldiers put in the new units, saving a great deal of money in officers' pay.[22] The unanimity of this committee ensured the final adoption of this organizational plan in January 1645.

The thorniest issue was the question of who was to command the army. The Scots and Presbyterians feared that Cromwell and his following of sectarians and Independents would get control of the army. Cromwell and Waller feared that Essex or Manchester would retain control, making it unlikely that the New Model would be used to win the war. The struggle for control of the army started in November, when Cromwell, Waller, and Vane criticized Manchester for his failure to win the Second Battle of Newbury. Cromwell expanded his attack against Manchester on 25 November, when he presented a narrative of military events from the middle of July through November to the Commons. In this diatribe, Cromwell rehearsed every mistake and instance of lack of aggressiveness exhibited by Manchester.[23]

Following Cromwell's denunciation, the war party expanded its campaign against Manchester by getting the Commons to take a series of depositions from senior officers during the period 25 November to 6 January. These accounts, to include those of officers who favored a Presbyterian settlement, confirmed the reluctance and inability of Manchester and of Essex to pursue a complete victory. The Earls and their allies responded with attacks against Cromwell's tolerance of the 'schismatic and sectarian beliefs' held by many of his soldiers. By early December the atmosphere in parliament was hardly conducive to compromise, making it unlikely that the New Model Army would be accepted.[24]

On 2 December, Manchester submitted his formal reply to Cromwell's 'Narrative.' He accused Cromwell of being disrespectful of and opposed to the Assembly of Divines and of favoring religious sectarianism. He further criticized Cromwell for his opposition to the social position of the nobility. This charge made the struggle between generals also one between the two houses of parliament, as the Lords sent a request to the Commons that a joint committee of inquiry be formed to investigate Cromwell.[25]

In the midst of this impasse, military opinion largely supported Cromwell's allegations against Manchester, but the division between the two houses threatened to ruin the cause, especially if the king made meaningful concessions in the Uxbridge negotiations. Then, on 9 December, during the debate in the Commons about the past performance of the armies, Cromwell made a masterful and statesmanlike speech.

It is now a time to speak, or forever hold the tongue. The important occasion now is no less to save a nation out of a bleeding, nay almost dying condition, which the long continuance of this war hath already brought it into; so that without a more speedy, vigorous and effectual prosecution of the war – casting off all lingering proceedings like soldiers of fortune beyond the sea [indulge in], to spin out a war – we shall make the kingdom weary of us, and hate the name of a parliament.... But this I would recommend to your prudence, not to insist upon any complaint or oversight of any commander-in-chief upon any occasion whatsoever; ... And I hope we have such true English hearts, and zealous affections towards the general weal of our mother country, as no member of either House will scruple to deny themselves, and their own private interests, for the public good; nor account it to be a dishonor done to them, whatever the Parliament shall resolve upon in this weighty matter.[26]

Zouch Tate, one of Cromwell's political allies, followed this speech with a motion 'that during the time of the war no member of either House shall have or execute any office or command, military or civil, granted or conferred by both or either of the Houses.'[27] This motion was the gist of what became known as the Self-Denying ordinance. If accepted, it would immediately end the debate about the command of the army because Essex, Manchester, and Cromwell would be excluded from serving in the army and parliament simultaneously. The Commons accepted Tate's proposals, since both sides thought it would eliminate their leading enemies from command. On 19 December, the bill was forwarded to the Lords, after attempts to exempt the Earl of Essex from its provisions were defeated.[28]

The Lords reacted predictably, seeing the Self-Denying Ordinance as an attack upon their class and their House. For weeks, the measure languished while other, less complex, problems were addressed. Then, on 13 January the Lords rejected the measure.[29]

As the Committee of Both Kingdoms developed the plan for army reorganization, parliament signaled its determination to carry on the war by stepping up its attacks against the Archbishop of Canterbury, William Laud. Laud had been a prisoner in the Tower for over two years, while his impeachment was carried through the Commons. In the fall of 1644, the House of Lords finally heard the case against him. While Prynne and other former victims of Laud's system proved that they had suffered at the hands of the church's High Commission, they could not prove that Laud was a traitor. In frustration, the archbishop's enemies turned to an act of attainder, the legislative process by which Strafford had been condemned in 1641. The two Houses passed the final measure on 4 January 1645, although it was modified on 8 January to allow him to die by the more humane ax rather than by the barbaric practice of hanging, drawing, and quartering. The executioner beheaded Laud on 10 January.[30]

The legislative murder of Laud was one of a number of executions intended to influence Charles during the Uxbridge negotiations. On 23 December, Sir John Carew was executed for his attempt to betray Plymouth. On 2 and 3 January, the

Hothams, father and son, were beheaded for their attempts to surrender Hull to the king. These executions were ordered by a court martial that parliament set up and used to circumvent common law procedures. Resort to such a process is a good example of the way the needs of war were driving English politics. The House of Lords, however, saw the dangers inherent in the use of court martial proceedings and refused to renew the enabling legislation for longer than one month, on 5 December. The court martial authority lapsed in January, not to be resurrected again until 1646.[31]

The Lords continued to fight a rearguard action to save Essex's and Manchester's military positions and to protect the traditional military prerogatives of their class. The Commons, however, refused to relent in its efforts to put the nation on a firmer war footing. On 3 and 11 January the Commons reviewed and then approved the report of the Committee of Both Kingdoms about the monthly pay of the new army. On 21 January, Sir Thomas Fairfax was selected by the lower House as Commander of the New Model Army by a vote of 101 to 69. Parliament selected Philip Skippon to serve as Major General to command the infantry, leaving the position of Lieutenant General unfilled. The margin of votes in favor of Fairfax's appointment indicate that the tide was running with the war party, in spite of the Uxbridge negotiations.[32] The Commons also ordered the Army Treasurer, Sir Gilbert Gerard, to issue promissory notes known as debentures to the soldiers for their arrears of pay, promising them eventual repayment in full for their service.[33] This important step tied the soldiers' material fortunes to the success of the parliamentary cause.

The creation and support of the New Army

The passage of these measures pushed the Lords forward. From 13 January to 1 February 1645, the Commons enacted the ordinances creating the New Model Army and providing for its financial support. Parliament's most important financial decision was to dedicate the proceeds of the monthly assessment to support its main army, leaving the regional forces and garrisons to be supported by local taxes. The monthly assessment was levied only on those counties under parliamentary control, giving some hope that the money could be raised. The monthly assessment was designed to raise £53,536 per month to pay Fairfax's army. Its proceeds were to be collected by county committees and forwarded to the Treasurers at War in London. Separate ordinances were passed to provide £21,000 per month for the Scots army in England and additional money to support forces in Ireland.[34]

The Lords passed the New Model Army ordinance on 17 February, after amending the procedure by which the officers were to be approved. Fairfax was to nominate all field grade officers, majors and above in rank, while parliament was to approve his nominations. Fairfax submitted his list of officers to the Commons on 1 March. After three days' of debate, the Commons approved all but one of the nominated officers and sent the list to the Lords for approval. The Lords rejected over fifty of the officers on Fairfax's list who were identified as Independents. The Commons, however, refused to concur. After a stand-off between the houses that lasted until 18 March, the Commons won, and the new officer corps was established.[35]

The Commons, by picking Fairfax and Skippon as the two senior generals of the new army, and by approving Fairfax's list of officers that did not contain the names of any members of parliament, circumvented the Lords' rejection of the Self-Denying ordinance. Fairfax and Skippon were as close to non-political generals as could be found. Both had impeccable military credentials. Skippon had stayed with Essex's infantry when the Earl had deserted them at Lostwithiel, and he led them bravely at the Second Battle of Newbury. Fairfax had demonstrated his growing mastery of war at Nantwich, Selby, and Marston Moor.[36] The Lords attempted to limit Fairfax's powers, possibly so that Essex could be retained as Lord General, but the Commons defeated this move and secured the passage of an ordinance on 1 April granting Fairfax full powers as Commander-in-Chief of all parliamentary land forces. Essex resigned his commission the next day.[37]

In a series of ordinances beginning with the New Model Army ordinance of 17 February, parliament created a field army of 22,000 soldiers. Two additional armies were retained as well: one known as the Western Army, commanded by Edward Massey; the second known as the Northern Army, commanded by Sydenham Poyntz. Fairfax retained the authority to direct the operations of these armies, unifying parliamentarian command for the first time.[38] As this was happening, the Uxbridge negotiations failed to bring the warring parties closer to peace, especially since the king refused to give up his church, his servants, and the control of his armed forces.[39]

It was one thing to create an army on paper, and quite another to find the men, munitions and money needed to put one together. Parliament had failed in its efforts to support its three armies in the fall of 1644, and it faced thousands of unpaid, poorly fed, and mutinous soldiers in its garrisons. A 'new modeling' of parliamentary finance was essential if the plans for the new army were to be fulfilled.

Parliament 'new models' its financial system

The parliamentary financial system rested on three pillars in 1645. The first was the customs, largely committed to the support of the navy. The second was the excise, created by Pym in 1643, and obligated to the support of the army. The third was the assessment, originally designed to support the regional forces and Essex's army, and now dedicated to support Fairfax's regiments. Gifts, sequestered royalist rents, and forced loans supplemented these taxes, along with the free quarter and private property stolen by the soldiers. These supplementary sources of revenue, however, had either dried up or were too politically costly to use indiscriminately. Thus, the parliamentarians had to rely on the three 'regular' taxes for the support of their armies and navy.[40]

The customs was the oldest regular tax in English history. Parliament controlled the customs from the beginning of the war because they controlled London, the largest port and the site of the customs administration. From 16 January 1643 to 24 February 1645, the customs revenue exceeded £391,000.[41] Most of this money was spent on the navy. However, the costs of the navy soared in this period as parliamentary warships operated off both coasts, providing supplies to places like Hull and Plymouth, and interdicting royalist shipping. The navy increased from 30 to 44 ships, with squadrons remaining at sea the year round.[42] By early 1645, the commissioners of the navy reported that they needed £79,100 to pay the 'winter guard' then at sea, and another £127,497 to rig out and deploy the 'summer guard.'[43]

The navy commissioners had run out of money and credit. Consequently, the Commons appointed a committee to review the financial condition of the navy. It found that the navy was in arrears by £208,000 for money owed to suppliers of food and supplies, and for wages owed the sailors. In addition, the men who collected the customs in London and the outports no longer were willing to advance money to the Navy Treasurer.[44]

Parliament responded in several ways. It removed the customs commissioners who were unwilling to lend additional funds. It renewed the customs levies for another year. And it appointed new customs collectors who were willing to advance money to the navy in anticipation of the revenue. The new commissioners were supporters of the parliamentary war party as well as wealthy London merchants. They agreed to advance £50,000 to the navy, knowing that their loan was secured by the customs at eight per cent interest per year. Over the next four-and-a-half years, these men collected over £1 million in customs duties, providing the navy with nearly £200,000 per year from the receipts in addition to £110,000 in loans.[45]

Parliament also renewed the excise for another year, making it possible to borrow £437,000 for the army from September 1644 through September 1646. Excise receipts were more important as security for loans than as a source of ready money. This borrowing saddled the excise with over £398,000 of debt by the end of 1646.[46] But the continuation of the excise made it possible to borrow the £80,000 needed to equip Fairfax's new regiments.[47]

The parliamentarians' most important financial action taken in February 1645 was to enact the monthly assessment of £53,536 for the support of the army. This amount, levied on only those counties controlled by parliament, covered the £44,952 needed to pay Fairfax's men their wages and to provide money for arms, munitions, and clothing.[48] The monthly assessment became the largest source of money for parliament's armed forces over the next ten years. It immediately provided an increase in the credit-worthiness of the Westminster government, in large part because the Treasurers at War who were selected to operate the treasury of the assessment were respected members of London's financial community. Six of them had served as city aldermen and most of them were successful merchants before the war.[49]

The monthly assessment ordinance stipulated that county assessment collectors were to send their receipts to London, preventing local diversion of money. Most of the £1 million assessed from February 1645 to October 1646 was collected and was sent to the Treasurers at War in London.[50] Consequently, parliament had sufficient credit in March 1645 to borrow the £80,000 needed to arm and clothe Fairfax's soldiers. By early April, much of this money was in the hands of army treasurer Gilbert Gerard.[51]

The availability of cash and a more certain credit enabled Fairfax and Skippon to amalgamate the troops of the three former armies into a single force. This was no small feat, as the soldiers were on the verge of mutiny and many officers faced the prospect of losing their commissions and livelihoods. Philip Skippon played a pivotal role in this process because of the loyalty and trust held in him by the infantrymen of Essex's army. For example, in early April, when Skippon supervised the dissolution of five infantry regiments at Reading, he talked individually to each unit explaining the need to create a single army. He acknowledged that many officers would lose their rank, but he promised them two weeks in cash for pay arrears if they chose to leave the army. He promised the soldiers that their accounts would be taken and that they would receive debentures backed by the public faith for all money owed for their service. He also announced that all men who joined the new army would receive two weeks' wages on the spot and an issue of new clothing. Skippon was accompanied by two of the Treasurers at War from London with the coin needed to pay the soldiers.[52] The ceremony was a success, and the new army donned its famous red coats.

Even with Skippon's and Fairfax's tact and prestige with the soldiers, there were too few veterans available to provide the 22,000 men needed in the new regiments. Consequently, parliament was forced to pass ordinances for the impressment of men by the county committees. The needs of war had again forced the parliamentarians to do exactly what they had criticized Charles for doing in the 1620s and in the Bishops' Wars. The results were not impressive. The conscripts were unwilling warriors, and there were not enough of them. As a result, the infantry ranks of the New Model Army were not filled until after its victories in the summer. Things in the horse were better, in part because cavalrymen received higher pay than the foot and possibly because many of the men who had served in the cavalry units were committed philosophically to the parliamentary cause. This was clearly the case in the horse regiments of the former army of the Eastern Association.[53]

The Civil War continues

As parliament created the New Model Army, the Uxbridge negotiations broke down and both sides resumed the war with full vigor. Charles knew he needed to regain the initiative before the parliamentarians could get their army organized. But his forces were disintegrating due to the lack of money, with many of his regiments reduced to fewer than 100 men.[54] Although the royalists had lost the leaders and manpower needed to recoup their fortunes in the north, they possessed formidable strength in the west, south, and southwest. Therefore, Charles decided to concentrate his efforts on clearing the remaining parliamentary garrisons out of the south, while sending relief to the few royalist garrisons holding out in the north. He hoped these operations would give him time to come to terms with the Confederates for aid, and for Montrose's campaign to draw the Covenanter's main army back to Scotland.

To implement this strategy, Charles sent Prince Maurice north with cavalry to recruit in the Welsh Marches before continuing on to relieve Chester. Before Maurice had accomplished much, the Roundheads captured Shrewsbury by surprise, on 22 February, forcing the king to send Rupert north with the bulk of his army to redress the situation. The two brothers united on 15 March and marched to Chester with over 5,000 men. Brereton retreated, allowing the Princes to enter the city with reinforcements and supplies. Following this triumph, Rupert led his army to the western Midlands to face Club-men threatening the royalists in the area. After his departure, David Leslie joined Brereton with 4,000 Scottish soldiers, allowing the anti-royalists to again lay siege to Chester.[55]

While Rupert and Maurice operated in the north, the king reorganized his war effort in the southwest by creating an association of Cornwall, Devon, Dorset, and Somerset. Charles appointed his son Charles, the Prince of Wales, as the titular commander of this Western Association. He provided his son with a council in Bristol to oversee the operations in the region. The western army was to consist of Goring's cavalry and the remaining infantry from Hopton's force. This army was expected to capture Taunton, in Somerset, and then take Plymouth.[56]

Things did not go smoothly for the royalists. Rupert found his hands full dealing with a massive uprising of country folk who had grown weary of the depredations and exactions of both sides. These Club-men were concentrated in Herefordshire, Worcestershire, and Shropshire. Few gentry joined the Club-men's efforts to end free quarter and crush the depredations of ill-disciplined soldiers in their regions. The royalists corrected some of the worst abuses of their garrisons and used military force to overawe many of the Club-men. Later in the year the populist movement spread to other parts of England, a sign of war weariness and the steady erosion of traditional social and political discipline.[57]

In Westminster, the Committee of Both Kingdoms did not wait for Fairfax to organize his army before taking action to protect the parliamentary garrisons in the west. In late February 1645, they ordered Sir William Waller to march to the relief of Taunton. Waller quickly found that many soldiers of Essex's and Manchester's armies would not march until they had received two weeks' pay. Even then, the cavalrymen of the Eastern Association's army refused to join Waller until the Committee ordered Cromwell to lead them. Once that was done, Waller and Cromwell moved west with nearly 5,000 men.[58]

Waller and Cromwell relieved the pressure on Colonel Robert Blake's garrison in Taunton. Then, on 22 March, they surprised a force of royalist cavalry at Devizes, alarming the Prince of Wales's council in Bristol. George Goring's western royalist army dueled with them during this period, with both sides suffering small defeats and winning a few insignificant victories. These operations bought time for the organization of the New Model Army and prevented the royalists from completely clearing the southwest. By 27 March, however, Waller's army was exhausted, short of supplies, and mutinous, forcing him to put his soldiers in garrisons before resigning his command in frustration. Parliament accepted his resignation in April and ordered his infantry to join the garrisons in Dorset and Hampshire.

In mid April the Committee of Both Kingdoms ordered Cromwell and his cavalry to operate around Oxford to prevent the royalists from collecting horses to move their artillery train from there to Hereford, where the king was gathering his army.[59] Cromwell readily complied. On 24 April he surprised the Earl of Northampton's cavalry regiment at Islip, capturing 400 horses and 200 men. The same day he convinced Colonel Francis Windebank to surrender Bletchingdon Castle, an act for which Charles I ordered Windebank shot several weeks later. On 27 April Cromwell was operating thirteen miles to the west of Oxford, capturing draught horses and skirmishing with royalist garrisons. After a repulse at Faringdon Castle, he moved east, having completed his mission. Charles could not move his artillery for several weeks due to his shortage of draught horses.[60]

As the measures creating the new army were worked out and the royalist thrusts parried, the war party resurrected the Self-Denying measure in the Commons, on 24 March. They hoped to close off any avenue by which the peace party could insert Essex or Manchester into the military hierarchy. In a sense this was unlikely, since Fairfax had already used the authority given him to drain the existing armies of their troops, leaving the Earls no one to command. The second Self-Denying ordinance was a symbol of the war party's resolve that there would only be one main army to fight the war to a victorious conclusion. The war party leaders softened the language of the original measure, exempting the civil positions of lord lieutenants, deputy lord lieutenants, and justices of the peace from its provisions. Further, the ordinance stipulated that a member of parliament only had to resign his military position within forty days of its enactment, leaving the door open for his future employment if parliament so desired.[61] The Lords accepted the ordinance after the Commons assured them that the measure was not an attack on their class.

The Self-Denying ordinance did not greatly affect the New Model Army since most of its officers were not members of parliament. The loophole was that there was no prohibition for parliament to employ a member of parliament in a military position in the future. The immediate impact of the measure was on the navy. The staunchly puritan Earl of Warwick, who had commanded the fleet since the beginning of the civil war, was forced to resign his command in April. Parliament replaced him with a commission and appointed Captain William Batten to command naval operations. This arrangement lasted for over three years.

The New Model Army in operation

Fairfax and Skippon performed a near miracle in bringing together the new army. On 30 April they set out from Windsor with about 15,000 men. Their goal was to relieve Taunton from Goring's siege. At the same time, Cromwell was to join Major General Browne with his garrison from Abingdon and operate around Oxford to prevent the king from gathering his army. Fairfax was now undisputed commander of the parliamentary forces, while the Committee of Both Kingdoms retained the authority to direct the movements of its armies through Fairfax. Although this system of command ensured civilian control and unity of command, it quickly proved too cumbersome due to the slowness of communications and the inability of the Committee to keep abreast of operations several hundred miles away. The results were predictable.

In early May, Fairfax marched west, leaving 4,000 men to serve with Cromwell and Browne. However, once the Committee learned that Charles and Rupert had joined forces at Stow-on-the-Wold, it ordered Fairfax to reverse course and return to defend the Eastern Association. Fortunately for the parliamentarians, the king's war council was badly divided as to what to do next. Rupert favored marching north to join Maurice and to clear Lancaster and Cheshire of the rebels, before turning south to deal with Fairfax. Lord Digby and Goring wanted the army to concentrate on Fairfax's army first, hoping to crush it as they had Essex's army at Lostwithiel in 1644. Charles made the worst decision. He decided to split his force of 11,000 men and send Goring west with about 3,000 soldiers to contain Fairfax, while the rest of the army marched north.[62]

The Committee of Both Kingdoms saw the danger posed by the royalists in the north, especially since it had received information that Montrose had won another victory over the Covenanters at Auldearn. If Charles went north with his army, the Scots would be caught between two fires, giving the king a chance to crush them before turning south. The Committee ordered Fairfax to return to Oxford, which it thought might be betrayed into Fairfax's hands by the governor. Fairfax besieged Oxford on 21 May, but the governor refused to surrender and Fairfax felt that his infantry were too weak to storm its defenses successfully. These operations did nothing to stop the king from executing his northern strategy.

Things came to a head on 30–31 May, when Rupert assaulted Leicester, opening the town to a brutal sacking. In near panic, the Committee of Both Kingdoms ordered Fairfax to lift the siege of Oxford and move his army to Newport Pagnell to prevent a royalist advance into the Eastern Association. They ordered Cromwell to proceed to Ely to rally the local levies against the royalists as well. Both officers complied, allowing the king to lift the siege of Oxford without a fight. So far little had been accomplished, and the royalists' contempt for what they called the 'new noodle' increased as they observed Fairfax's erratic movements.

The futile movements of Fairfax's army in its first month in the field convinced parliamentarians that the Committee of Both Kingdoms could not direct the daily activities of the field forces. Consequently, on 9 June, Fairfax was given complete control of the army's operations. This allowed him to concentrate his forces against Charles's main strength. Fairfax believed such a strategy would allow him to do in the south what had been done in the north by the defeat of Newcastle's and Rupert's armies at Marston Moor. After that battle, in July 1644, most northern royalist garrisons had surrendered without lengthy sieges.[63]

Meanwhile, Cromwell's commission was about to expire due to the forty-day limitation of the Self-Denying ordinance, for which he had already received a parliamentary extension. This situation was averted when the Common Council of London suggested to the House of Commons, on 4 June, that Cromwell's commission be continued. At the same time, Fairfax and his council of officers unanimously asked that Cromwell be appointed second-in-command of the army. On 10 June, Parliament appointed Cromwell as Lieutenant General of Horse.[64]

The Battle of Naseby

Fairfax now had the defeat of the king's army as his fixed object. On 8 June he learned that Charles was at Daventry with 9,000 soldiers. Charles was again uncertain as to which direction to march. He wanted to pursue the northern strategy, but he feared for the safety of Oxford, not having discovered yet that Fairfax had abandoned the siege. Once he learned that the Roundheads had raised the siege, he started his regiments north, on 12 June. But he had waited too long for his artillery to join him, and his move north was too late. Fairfax closed the distance between the armies to less than ten miles, by 13 June, when Cromwell joined him at Kislingbury. That night the New Model Army advanced to Guilsborough, four or five miles from the king's army at Market Harborough.[65]

The armies now were too close for Charles to get his troops, artillery, and supply columns safely away. Consequently, the king and Rupert decided to stand and fight on a ridge two miles north of the town of Naseby (see map 15). Fairfax and Cromwell welcomed the opportunity to engage the 9,000 royalists with their 15,000 men. The New Model deployed beginning about 3 a.m., on 14 June, establishing a linear position facing north on a ridge running west to east a short distance north of Naseby. The antagonists were arrayed in the traditional manner, with the infantry in the center and the cavalry divided between the two wings. On the royalist side, Rupert and his brother Maurice commanded the right wing of the cavalry and Marmaduke Langdale the left. Sir Jacob Astley marshaled the infantry in the center, while Charles stationed himself with his lifeguard and a small reserve behind the infantry.

Fairfax arrayed his regiments with Cromwell in command of 3,500 cavalrymen on the right and Commissary General Henry Ireton leading 3,000 troopers on the left, opposite Rupert. Skippon commanded five infantry regiments in the center and Fairfax kept a reserve of three foot regiments behind Skippon's forces. Fairfax also deployed Colonel Okey's dragoon regiment along a hedge on the left flank, just to the left front of Ireton's troopers, from where it could fire into the flanks of attacking royalists.[66]

Some time before 10 a.m., Fairfax, on the advice of Cromwell, shifted his army to the west so as to neutralize the wind advantage. Rupert, who was conducting a reconnaissance of the New Model's position, spotted this movement. Rupert, believing that the Roundheads were retreating, ordered an immediate attack by his cavalry. As Rupert's troopers advanced, Henry Ireton launched a counterattack down the slight ridge on which his squadrons stood. However, several of his regiments held back, leading to confusion and evening the odds. Rupert took advantage of the Roundheads' confusion to drive home his attack. The Cavaliers shattered Ireton's leading units, driving many of Ireton's soldiers from the field. Rupert and his victorious cavalry pursued the fleeing troopers three miles south, to Fairfax's supply train near Naseby.[67]

When Fairfax saw Rupert's advance he ordered his army forward. In the center, Skippon's infantry collided with Astley's veteran royalists. Skippon was badly wounded, and the royalists steadily pushed the parliamentary infantry back,

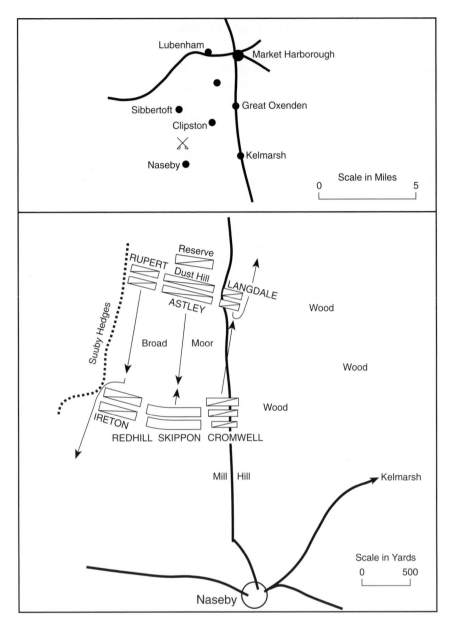

Map 15 The Battle of Naseby, 14 June 1645

threatening to break the New Model's center. Fairfax's reserve infantry regiments stopped the royalist advance, while Cromwell led the first three of his five regiments in a charge against Langdale's outnumbered Cavaliers. The weight of Cromwell's charge shattered Langdale's lines, driving most of the royalist cavalry off the field.

While several parliamentary regiments pursued Langdale's mob, Cromwell wheeled his remaining squadrons to their left to face the exposed flank of the royalist infantry in the center.

At this point Fairfax joined Cromwell and pointed out to him the dangerous situation in the center, where the parliamentary infantry was barely hanging on. Fairfax and Cromwell evidently decided that Fairfax would lead the cavalry on the right against the left of the king's infantry while Cromwell rode to the other side of their army to rally Ireton's troopers. When Cromwell reached the left flank he found that Okey's dragoons had not only held firmly to their hedgerow position as Rupert's men swept past, but also that Okey had mounted his dragoons and joined the attack against the royalist infantry. Cromwell accompanied Okey's charge against Astley's men as Fairfax launched the parliamentary cavalry on the right against their other flank. The outcome of this pincer movement was decisive. Most of the royalist infantry surrendered once they recognized their plight, but Rupert's 'Blue' regiment fought to nearly the last man, accounting for the heavy casualties suffered by the king's army.

Rupert, meanwhile, had been repulsed in his attempt to capture the New Model's supply train and had turned back to the battlefield. When he returned he found Cromwell and Fairfax leading the attacks against the royalist infantry. Lacking reserves, Rupert and the king were forced to withdraw, leaving as many as 4,000 of their foot to surrender or die. Most surrendered. The parliamentary cavalry pursued the Cavaliers nearly thirteen miles, killing as many as 300. They also captured the king's baggage train of 200 carts, 9,000 firearms, ten or twelve cannon, and the king's private papers.

The Roundheads also found several thousand female 'camp followers' in the king's wagon train. After the action had ended, Fairfax's soldiers murdered several hundred of these poor unfortunates in cold blood, claiming that they were Irish whores. The rest were cut on the face with a 'w.' Since few if any of the king's army at Naseby had served in Ireland, these women were more likely Welsh who had followed their men on the campaign. Whatever their nationality, it was murder, and one of the darkest blots on the New Model Army's history.[68]

The Battle of Naseby lasted for less than three hours, from 10 a.m. to 1 p.m. In the process, Fairfax crushed the king's army, capturing most of his infantry, artillery and supply trains, and his correspondence. Many royalist infantrymen agreed to take the Covenant required of parliament's soldiers and to serve in the New Model Army. Of the remainder, those who promised never to serve against parliament again, and who could give security for their future good conduct, were released. Those who could or would not, were sent overseas.[69] Because of his losses, there was little hope that the king could rebuild his army to its former potency, especially since the New Model Army had suffered fewer than three hundred killed. Charles understood the magnitude of his disaster, even to the point where he attempted to lead his lifeguard in a forlorn attempt to save his infantry. His courtiers refused to allow him to endanger himself, turning his horse away from the field.

The 'new noodle', as Rupert derisively had called it, had proven its worth. Fairfax performed brilliantly at Naseby, directing the operations of his army and making the timely decisions. Cromwell demonstrated his worth as a cavalry commander and gave Fairfax sound advice. Ireton and Skippon performed well, although both received wounds from which it would take months for them to recover. Gone was the dissension and hesitancy in the general officer ranks that had wasted the victories of Marston Moor and Second Newbury. The destruction of the king's infantry and the capture of his artillery made it impossible for him to mount another siege. Further, the king's loss of so many officers meant that the parliamentarians no longer had to fear royalist incursions into their territory, allowing them to conduct multiple campaigns against the remaining royalist strongholds. Naseby did not end the war, but it made the outcome predictable.

The destruction of the remaining royalist armies

Thomas Fairfax quickly exploited his victory. After resting and supplying his troops, he moved against Leicester, which the royalists surrendered on generous terms on 18 June. The Lord General then set out for Somerset, where Goring was besieging Taunton. He knew that Charles was frantically trying to assemble another army at Hereford, where he had gathered 4,000 cavalry and 3,000 infantry. Charles was waiting for reinforcements from Wales, immobilizing himself in the process. Fairfax also knew that the Scots army was moving south again, making it unlikely that the king would be able to join Montrose in Scotland or to recruit in Herefordshire. Fairfax's decision to march against Goring was designed to save Taunton and to destroy Goring's army before the royalists could regain their balance.[70]

Royalist fortunes were on the wane everywhere, except in Scotland, where Montrose continued to win victories against the Covenanters. In the north of England, Sydenham Poyntz led parliament's Northern Army into Cheshire, supporting Sir William Brereton's efforts to capture Chester and prevent the Cavaliers from recruiting in the region. In Gloucestershire, Edward Massey used his Western Army to block the royalist communications between their forces in the north and south. As Fairfax moved west, Massey's position was secure enough for him to join Fairfax with 2,000 men in the campaign against Goring. Leven's 12,000 Scots moved toward Hereford, directly threatening the king's position, while David Leslie captured Carlisle, on 28 June. The news from Ireland was equally disheartening for the royalists. Ormond and the Confederates continued to negotiate with no breakthrough in sight, meaning that Charles could not expect Irish reinforcements any time soon.

Fairfax moved remarkably fast in his drive to relieve Taunton and to bring Goring to battle. By 28 June his army was at Marlborough, where it rested on the Lord's Day, after marching 113 miles in one week. This rapid advance was made possible by the ability of the parliamentarians to fund a logistics system that could procure and ship food, shoes, and munitions to its army. Money was the lubricant of such a system, paying for the supplies and the hire of carts, horses, and teamsters. The parliamentary government also employed merchant ships to carry supplies from London to Plymouth and Weymouth, from where they were carted to the army.[71] The system worked well enough during this campaign so that Fairfax was able to prevent the taking of free quarter by his soldiers. To enforce this ban and his prohibitions against looting and desertion, Fairfax hanged a number of soldiers, including a dragoon 'hanged for robbing a countryman upon the highway' and a straggler at Amesbury 'for going from his colors, and endeavoring to seduce another.'[72]

During his advance into Dorset and Wiltshire, Fairfax met several formidable forces of Club-men. These Club-men, led by local gentry, presented a list of demands to Fairfax when he reached Dorchester, in early July. They wanted parliament to renew its negotiations with Charles, to order an immediate truce, and to surrender all garrisons in Dorset and Wiltshire into their hands. They also demanded that soldiers who wanted to leave the army be allowed to do so.[73]

Fairfax handled the Club-men with tact, promising them that his army would be well disciplined, pay for its food, and that his goal was to win the war quickly. He also gave the Club-men copies of the king's correspondence that had been captured at Naseby, proving that Charles hoped to bring 10,000 Irish Catholics into Bristol to use against the parliamentary armies. Fairfax's moderate treatment of the protesters, along with his ability to feed his army without free quarter, convinced most Club-men to allow the parliamentarians to pass unmolested. In the few cases where words failed, Fairfax used force to ensure his armies continued advance.[74]

Goring, hearing of Fairfax's approach, lifted the siege of Taunton at the end of June and began to move his army north, probably intending to join the king. In the process, he closed the distance between his troops and the New Model. Fairfax, not knowing that Taunton was safe, continued west, covering another 85 miles in five hot days of marching. When he arrived at Beaminster, Fairfax learned that Goring had moved toward his army and had established a line along the north side of the River Yeo, from Langport to Yeovil. Fairfax and Cromwell decided to turn this line on its eastern end by sending infantry across near Yeovil, while the cavalry screened the rest of the line to the west. This maneuver, on 7 July, forced the outnumbered royalists to fall back to positions just east of Langport.[75]

Over the next few days Goring decided to retreat to Bridgewater. On 10 July he sent his artillery and baggage train west, screening the movement with his army from a position east of Langport. The Yeo River protected his right flank and a small, but deeply cut, streambed protected his front. His cavalry was drawn up on a hill facing east, with his musketeers and two small cannon covering the only crossing of the stream to his front. Fairfax, learning of the departure of Goring's trains, decided to attack before the rest of the royalist army might withdraw.

On 11 July, Fairfax and Cromwell decided to attack Goring's position head on. They brought up a number of cannon to destroy the guns overlooking the crossing in the stream between the armies and sent musketeers down to the ford to drive away Goring's infantry. Once this was done, Fairfax sent three troops of cavalry across the narrow passage, four troopers abreast. These men, led by Major Christopher Bethel, crossed the stream and attacked the mass of royalist cavalry on the ridge beyond. Remarkably, the outnumbered Roundheads drove deeply into the Cavaliers' ranks before being repulsed. This attack allowed another three troops of Fairfax's cavalry to cross and join the battle. This second squadron, led by Major John

Desborough and supported by musketeers, joined the first wave. Their impact broke the morale of the royalists. Goring's army dissolved into a general retreat that turned into a rout. Most of his infantry surrendered, and his cavalry scattered.[76] Goring departed the country shortly thereafter, without royal approval.

Fairfax resumed his advance west, toward Bridgewater, a royalist base in Somerset, arriving there on 21 July. The place was strongly fortified and defended by a garrison of 2,000 men. The royalist governor, Sir Hugh Wyndham, refused to surrender, forcing Fairfax to order an assault, following a fierce bombardment that set much of the town on fire. The attackers broke into the eastern part of town, forcing Wyndham to surrender on terms on 23 July. Goring's defeat and Fairfax's capture of Bridgewater cut the royalist communications between Cornwall and Hereford, making it impossible for Charles to unite a large force in the southwest. The way was open for Fairfax to move into western Wiltshire to operate against Bath and Sherborne. Fairfax's willingness to storm Bridgewater and to set the town alight greatly impressed other royalist garrisons, a number of which, including Bath, surrendered after token resistance over the next two weeks. At Sherborne, he again launched a successful assault after a fierce bombardment, bringing a rapid end to the siege.[77]

As he moved into Wiltshire, Club-men again interrupted Fairfax's lines of communication, forcing him to deal firmly with them. After several unsuccessful entreaties to them to disperse, Cromwell's cavalry attacked several thousand Club-men on Hambledon Hill, on 5 August. The issue was never in doubt, as the poorly armed country folk faced some of the finest regiments in the New Model Army. Twelve were killed and 300 captured, ending this threat to the movements of the army.

Fairfax next turned his attention to Bristol, held by Prince Rupert with fewer than 2,000 men. By 23 August the New Model Army had arrived at the city and began to deploy. Once his siege guns were in position, Fairfax summoned Rupert to surrender. Rupert played for time, but his luck ran out on 10 September, when the Roundheads attacked. Rupert's men held firm in the south, but the parliamentarians breached the eastern defenses and slaughtered the garrison of Prior's Fort on the north side, after it refused to surrender. As his cavalry deployed through the outer defenses, Fairfax gave Rupert another chance to surrender on easy terms. The Prince accepted, marching out the next day with his cavalry. Most of his infantry chose to join the parliamentary army.[78]

When Charles learned of Rupert's surrender of Bristol he dismissed the Prince from all offices and suggested that he leave England. Cornwall, Wales, Oxfordshire, and parts of Herefordshire and Cheshire remained the last bastions of royalist power. The news from Wales, however, was unfavorable for Charles, especially when he learned of parliamentary victories in Pembrokeshire and that the Welsh were no longer willing to serve in his armies outside of Wales. From August to October, Charles and his small army marched to and fro, trying to find a direction they could go to avoid a major enemy force and to restore the sinking royalist cause.

Charles still received some good news from Scotland after Naseby. There Montrose had followed up his victory at Auldearn with another at Alford, on 2 July. Then, on

16 August, Montrose crushed a Covenanter force at Kilsyth, near Glasgow. The Covenanters lost nearly 6,000 men, leaving Scotland open to Montrose. The Scots immediately recalled David Leslie and the Scottish cavalry from England, relieving the king of one of his pursuers, and forcing Leven to abandon the siege of Hereford. Montrose's success was one reason the king again turned north to Cheshire, in September, hoping to continue on to Scotland.[79]

When the king moved north, he was pursued by Poyntz's Northern Army. After relieving the siege of Chester, Charles allowed his army to engage in a battle on Rowland Downs, just south of Chester, on 23 September. What started as a royalist victory quickly became a disaster when Colonel Michael Jones led a force of infantry from Chester to the field, helping Poyntz's horse to disperse the royalist cavalry. This engagement ended the king's hope of getting to Scotland. He then moved east to Huntington, but was unable to accomplish anything of note due to his lack of infantry and artillery. Meanwhile, Massey drove into southern Wales and Fairfax headed toward Oxford, while Cromwell swung through the south capturing Winchester (28 September) and Basing House (14 October) in addition to a number of other smaller royalist garrisons. The ring was tightening around Charles who, after spending most of October in Newark, slipped back into Oxford on 5 November.

While there was significant mopping up to do, the parliamentarians had won the war. For the next nine months parliament's three armies deployed columns to capture the royalist strongholds in Exeter, Hereford, Chester, and Cornwall. By the spring of 1646, Fairfax and Cromwell would be able to close in on Oxford with the bulk of the New Model Army, prepared to crush the last bastion of royal power in England.

The tale was the same in Scotland, due to a stunning reversal of fortune for Montrose. Montrose had seemed invincible through the time of his biggest victory at Kilsyth, in August 1645. He attempted to exploit this victory by summoning a Scottish parliament to meet in October, and by trying to establish a base near Glasgow. The organization and composition of his army, however, prevented him from turning his military victory into a political triumph. His best soldiers were Irish or Highlanders, and many of them deserted when he did not allow them to sack Glasgow. Worse, few of his troops or supporters were Lowlanders; consequently, he could not recruit many Lowland Scots to join his ranks, and when he was out of the shelter of the Highlands, his army was vulnerable to the powerful forces that the Covenanters had been employing in England.

As David Leslie marched north with a strong Covenanter force in August and September 1645, Montrose decided to trust three leading Earls in the border region to reconstitute his army. These men, the Earls of Roxborough, Hume, and Traquair, promised to raise infantry for Montrose if the Marquis would march to their aid. Montrose accepted their promises and moved his small army from its Highland sanctuary to a position near Kelso, near the eastern border with England. Once there, Montrose realized that few men had joined the Earls, leaving him just his 500 Irish soldiers and about 1,200 horsemen, most of whom were noblemen or gentry. Realizing that without popular support he could not remain safely in the Lowlands, he began to move to the northwest, hoping that he would be better received by the populace.[80]

Leslie crossed the border on 6 September, quickly arresting Roxborough and Hume. Initially, Leslie planned to march north to the Firth of Forth, west of Edinburgh, to intercept Montrose's route to the Highlands. But as he moved north he received a letter from someone within Montrose's army telling him that Montrose was still in the south. Reversing course, Leslie caught up with the royalists on 12 September, near Selkirk, where Montrose had stopped for the night. Thinking that no enemy was near, he placed his Irish infantry at Philiphaugh, a few miles from Selkirk on the Yarrow River.

At about midnight Montrose was roused from bed with the news that Leslie's army of 4,000 veteran soldiers was near. Montrose ordered his troops to form up in a meadow near the encampment at Philiphaugh, on 13 September. In the early morning, Leslie attacked with his cavalry before the royalists could form their ranks. The impact of his charge shattered Montrose's cavalry, leaving only the 500 Irish and Highland infantry and about 150 cavalrymen to face the second Covenanter onslaught. Although Montrose bravely charged Leslie's regiments with his few troops of horse, the battle was hopeless. Leslie cut the royalist cavalry to pieces and then turned his entire army against Montrose's infantry. After over half of the royalists had fallen, the remainder asked for and were granted quarter. After the battle, the Covenanter soldiers and country people murdered them and over 300 Irish women found in the camp in cold blood.[81] Montrose escaped, but he no longer had the cadre of Irish infantry that had made his Scottish army such a formidable force.

With most of Charles's remaining military strength cooped up in Oxford, Chester, and a few other places, the challenge facing the parliamentarians was how to deal with the king and end the war. There were three central issues involved. First, what role was the king to play and what traditional prerogatives and duties could be returned to Charles I? Second, how was the English church to be settled? Third, what was to happen to the royalist leaders?

Notes

1 Abbott, i: 300–1, Cromwell, Manchester, Waller, Balfour, and Skippon to the Committee of Both Kingdoms, 15 November 1644.

2 *CSPD, 1644–1645*, 130–46, for numerous letters from parliamentarian commanders complaining about the condition of their units and the need for money and recruits.

3 Ibid., 161, Proceedings of the Committee of Both Kingdoms, 26 November 1644.

4 Hutton, *The Royalist War Effort*, 145–52.

5 Ibid., 154.

6 Ibid., 155–65.

7 O'Siochru, *Confederate Ireland*, 77–80.

8 Carte, *Ormond*, vi: 219–21, Lord Digby to Ormond, 16 December 1644; ibid., 233–4, Charles I to Ormond, 22 January 1645; ibid., 257–8, Charles I to Ormond, 17 February 1645.

9 Bodl., Carte MS 11, fos. 491–2, Inchiquin to Charles I, 17 July 1644; fos. 533–4, Inchiquin to St Leger, 21 July 1644.

10 Bodl., Carte MS 11, fos. 148–53, Ormond to Charles I, 8 June 1644; Wheeler, *Cromwell in Ireland*, 21–5.

11 C. Wedgwood, *Montrose* (New York, 1995 edn), 58–63.

12 Ibid., 64–6; Gardiner, *Civil War*, ii: 132–42; Wedgwood, *The King's War*, 364–7; P. Lenihan, 'Celtic Warfare in the 1640s', in J. Young, ed., *Celtic Dimensions of the British Civil Wars*, 128–30.

13 Gardiner, *Civil War*, ii: 142–8; Wedgwood, *The King's War*, 375–6.

14 *CSPD, 1644–1645*, 126, for example see Committee of Both Kingdoms to Manchester, 15 November 1644.

15 J. Hexter, *Reappraisals in History* (Chicago, 1979 edn), 219–40, 'The Problem of the Presbyterian Independents.'

16 Ibid., 238–40; I. Gentles, *The New Model Army in England, Ireland, and Scotland, 1645–1653* (Oxford, 1992), 4–8.

17 Gardiner, *Civil War*, ii: 76–81.

18 Ibid.; *A & O*, i: 609, Ordinance of 28 January 1645 empowering commissioners to treat for peace with the king's commissioners at Uxbridge.

19 *JHC*, iii: 703; *CSPD, 1644–1645*, 204–5, Proceedings of the Committee of Both Kingdoms; Abbott, i: 321–32.

20 TT E292 (27), *The King's Cabinet Opened*, (14 July 1645), 2, Charles to Henrietta Maria, 30 March 1645.

21 TT E292 (27), *The King's Cabinet Opened*, 1, Charles to Henrietta Maria, 9 January 1645.

22 *CSPD, 1644–1645*, 204–5, Proceedings of the Committee of Both Kingdoms, 31 December 1644; 231–3, Proceedings of the Committee of Both Kingdoms, 6 January 1645.

23 Abbott, i: 302–11; *CSPD, 1644–1645*, 143–4.

24 *CSPD, 1644–1645*, 146–61; Gentles, *New Model Army*, ch. 4, 'The Importance of Religion.'

25 Abbott, i: 311–13.

26 Ibid., 314–15.

27 *JHC*, iii: 718.

28 Gardiner, *Civil War*, ii: 89–92.

29 Ibid., 92, 118.

30 *A & O*, i: 608; *CSPD, 1644–1645*, 228–9, 241.

31 *A & O*, iii: 5 December 1644, ordinance renewing martial law for one month.

32 *JHC*, iv: 10, 15–16, 31–4.

33 Ibid., 13.

34 Ibid., 24–6, 28, 30–1, 39; *A & O*, i: 531 for support of armies in Ireland and i: 614–25, for the ordinance creating the New Model Army and the monthly assessment that supported it. For more on assessment taxes see Wheeler, *Making of a World Power*, 173–96, and M. Braddick, *The Nerves of State: Taxation and the Financing of the English State, 1558–1714* (Manchester, 1996), 91–106.

35 Gentles, *New Model Army*, 16–21; I. Gentles, 'The Choosing of Officers for the New Model Army', *Bulletin of the Institute of Historical Research*, 67 (1994), 264–85; M. Kishlansky, *The Rise of the New Model Army* (Cambridge, 1979), 26–51.

36 J. Wilson, *Fairfax, General of Parliament's Forces in the English Civil War* (New York, 1985), 43–66; Gentles, *New Model Army*, 12–13.

37 Ibid., 21–3; *A & O*, i: 660–1.

38 *A & O*, i: 685, ordinance of 24 May 1645 appointing Massie as commander of the Western Army; *CSPD, 1644–1645*, 473, minute of an ordinance creating the Northern Army; See J. Jones, 'The War in the North: The Northern Parliamentary Army in the English Civil War, 1642–1645', (PhD dissertation, York University, Ontario, 1991).

39 Gardiner, *Civil War*, ii: 86.

40 Wheeler, *Making of a World Power*, 118, table 5.2.

41 PRO E351/643–4, account of the customs, January 1643 to February 1645.

42 Bodl., Rawlinson MS A223, fos. 11, 21, 25–8; Rodger, *Safeguard of the Seas*, 411–20.

43 Bodl., Rawlinson MS A223, fos. 25–7.

44 *JHC*, iv: 22, 30, 34.

45 Lindley, *Popular Politics*, 188n, 191n, 193n and V. Pearl, *London and the Outbreak of the Puritan Revolution, 1625–1643* (Oxford, 1961), 121, 130 for a discussion of the political affiliation of the new customs commissioners; *JHC*, iv: 50–1, 55, 68–9 for new customs collectors and the terms of

their employment; *A & O*, i: 627–30 for extension of customs; PRO E351/645–9, accounts of the customs, February 1645 to July 1649.

46 Wheeler, *Making of a World Power*, 153.
47 PRO SP28/350/5/2, account of the loans advanced for Fairfax's army.
48 *CSPD, 1644–1645*, 232–3.
49 Wheeler, *Making of a World Power*, 184–5.
50 PRO E351/302, account of the assessment, February 1645 to December 1651; SP28/334, for a number of county collectors' accounts that show they paid most of their receipts to the London Treasurers at War; *A & O*, i: 614–25 and *JHC*, iv: 692 for the amounts assessed.
51 PRO SP28/350/3, fo. 45, list of the people who advanced the £80,000 and the amount each loaned.
52 TT E277 (8), *Several Letters to the Honorable William Lenthall, Speaker of the House of Commons*, (9 April 1645), 3–4, a copy of Major General Skippon's speech; E277 (12), *Mercurius Civicus* (3–10 April 1645), 882–4.
53 Gardiner, *Civil War*, ii: 191–6; Gentles, *New Model Army*, 31–4.
54 Burne and Young, *The Great Civil War*, 193.
55 TT E276 (15) *The Scottish Dove*, (28 March–4 April 1645), 594; E276 (7), *A Diary or an Exact Journal*, (27 March–3 April 1645), no pagination.
56 Hutton, *The Royalist War Effort*, 172–3.
57 Ibid., 155–65; TT E292 (5), *The Scottish Dove*, (27 June–4 July 1645), 699.
58 TT E276 (15), *The Scottish Dove*, (28 March–4 April 1645), 598.
59 Gardiner, *Civil War*, ii: 182–92.
60 Abbott, i: 339–40, Cromwell to the Committee of Both Kingdoms, 25 April 1645; 341–2, Cromwell to Fairfax, 26 April 1645; 342–4, Cromwell to the Committee of Both Kingdoms, 28 April 1645.
61 TT E276 (16), *The Self-Denying Ordinance*, (4 April 1645); *A & O*, i: 664–5.
62 Burne and Young, *The Great Civil War*, 196.
63 Ibid., 197; Gentles, *New Model Army*, 53–5; Gardiner, *The Great Civil War*, ii: 236–8.
64 Abbott, i: 351–5.
65 TT E288 (25), *A Relation of the Victory obtained by Sir Thomas Fairfax*, (16 June 1645), 1–2; E288 (27), *Three Letters, from … Fairfax, … to The Committee Residing in the Army*, (17 June 1645), 2; Abbott, i: 355–7, 359–60, Cromwell to William Lenthal, 14 June 1645.
66 The best secondary accounts of the confusing battle are Gentles, *New Model Army*, 55–7; Burne and Young, *The Great Civil War*, 198–202; Gardiner, *Civil War*, ii: 242–5; Wilson, *Fairfax*, 67–75.
67 TT E288 (38), *A More Particular and Exact Relation of the Victory …*, (19 June 1645), 1–2, for George Bishop's account and 4–6 for Colonel John Okey's account; E288 (26), *An Ordinance of the Lords and Commons for a day of Thanksgiving* (17 June 1645), 2–5 for John Rushworth's account. Rushworth was Fairfax's military secretary and at the battle.
68 TT E288 (26), *An Ordinance of the Lords and Commons*, 3–5; E288 (28), *A More Exact and Perfect Relation of the Great Victory …* (17 June 1645), 3–5; Gentles, *New Model Army*, 55–60. Gentles says they murdered about 100 women.
69 TT E292 (5), *The Scottish Dove*, (27 June–4 July 1645), 700.
70 Ibid., 702–3.
71 A. Nusbacher, 'Civil Supply in the Civil War: Supply of Victuals to the New Model Army in the Naseby Campaign, 1–14 June 1645', *English Historical Review*, (February, 2000), 145–60.
72 TT E292 (16), *The Proceedings of the Army*, (1–6 July 1645), 3–5.
73 Ibid., 4–7.
74 Ibid., 5–8; Gardiner, *Civil War*, ii: 264–5, 305–6.
75 Burne and Young, *The Great Civil War*, 210–11.
76 Ibid., 213–15; Gentles, *New Model Army*, 67–9.
77 Gardiner, *Civil War*, ii: 305–6; Kenyon, *The Civil Wars of England*, 148–9.
78 Gardiner, *Civil War*, ii: 311–17.
79 Ibid., 295–300.
80 Ibid., 348–54.
81 Ibid. 354–6; Wedgwood, *Montrose*, 110–15.

Plate 1 Charles I, by Daniel Mytens the
Elder (National Maritime Museum
Picture Library)

Plate 2 Henrietta Maria, unknown artist
(National Portrait Gallery)

Plate 3 Archibald Campbell, First Marquess
of Argyll, by David Scougall
(National Portrait Gallery)

Plate 4 Robert Devereux, Third Earl of
Essex, by Barcus Gheerearst the
Younger (National Maritime
Museum Picture Library)

Plate 5   William Cavendish, Duke of
Newcastle, by T.A. Dean after Van
Dyck (National Portrait Gallery)

Plate 6   Prince Rupert, Count Palatine, by
Sir Peter Lely (National Portrait
Gallery)

Plate 7   James Butler, First Duke of
Ormond, by William Wissing
(National Portrait Gallery)

Plate 8   Oliver Cromwell by Sir Anthony
van Dyck (National Maritime
Museum Picture Library)

CHAPTER SIX

Parliament's victory and search for a settlement

Parliament's spectacular victory at Naseby, in June 1645, was militarily and politically decisive. The destruction of the king's veteran infantry and the parliamentarians' capture of so many royalist officers meant that Charles could not rebuild his army into a force that could stand up against the New Model Army in open battle. Cromwell's superb handling of the parliamentary cavalry and his defeat of Rupert's mounted regiments removed the aura of superiority that had surrounded the royalist cavalry since the beginning of the Civil War. Henceforth, the Ironsides, as the royalists derisively had called Cromwell's troopers, seldom lost a skirmish against Cavalier horsemen. This situation allowed Fairfax to march most of his army to the southwest while leaving a relatively small force to hold in check the royalist garrison in Oxford.

The fruits of Naseby came fast and furious. Bristol fell to Fairfax on 10 September and the royalists were confined to southern Wales, Dorset, Cornwall, and Oxfordshire, with a few garrisons scattered across northern and central England. Such a dismal military situation encouraged dissension within the royalist ranks. The king no longer trusted Rupert with military command, a number of nobles deserted Oxford and made their way to London to submit to parliament, and the remaining Cavalier military commanders refused to work together.[1]

The royalist defeat in England was accompanied by the Covenanters' defeat of Montrose at Philiphaugh and the destruction of the royalist army in Scotland. Montrose remained a fugitive in search of new forces, while the Covenanters brutally slaughtered the soldiers and leaders they had captured at Philiphaugh.[2] This situation freed Leven's army in northern England from any fear of a royalist army in its rear, allowing Leven to march south again.

In Ireland the Confederates suffered a major defeat three weeks after Naseby when Sir Charles Coote, the Protestant commander in Derry, marched a British force across western Ulster and captured Sligo, on 8 July 1645. This ruptured the Confederates' defensive line in Connacht and made Owen Roe O'Neill's supply problem more difficult.[3] News of the anti-royalist victories at Naseby and Philiphaugh also changed the situation in eastern Ulster, where Monro's army no longer needed to send regiments to Scotland to operate against Montrose. Monro could hope for greater support from Scotland and England. Finally, the parliamentary victory at

Naseby made it clear that it might not be long before the Long Parliament could send powerful reinforcements to Ireland to crush the Catholics.

The tide of anti-royalist victory in Britain changed the political situation in the three kingdoms as well. For the parliamentarians, the steady deterioration of the royalist cause raised the question of how to end the war and to deal with the defeated king. This was an especially thorny question because Charles did not seem to understand how hopeless his cause was. Instead, he continued his armed resistance while attempting to raise new forces by intriguing with the Scots, the Irish, the Danes, the French, and the Dutch to obtain military aid in England.[4] These political developments unfolded as the New Model and Covenanter armies crushed the remnants of the royalist field forces and captured the remaining Cavalier strongholds in England.

The last campaigns of the First Civil War in the west

Following Fairfax's destruction of the royalists' western army under Goring at Langport (10 July), and the capture in quick succession of Bridgewater (22 July), Bath (29 July), Sherborne (15 August), and Bristol (10 September), Fairfax detached Cromwell with a strong column of cavalry and infantry to operate against the royalist bases in Wiltshire and Hampshire. At the same time, Fairfax led most of the army west to operate against the royalists in Exeter and Ralph Hopton's Cavaliers in Cornwall. Fairfax's decision to focus his army's efforts against the royalists' field forces and their western strongholds rather than against the remnant of the king's army or Oxford was shrewd strategically. If Fairfax had moved directly against the king before he destroyed the royalists' armed forces, Charles would have been able to use those assets in any negotiations. Without them, the king had no tangible strength to back his bargaining position. Once the royalists were destroyed in the west and Wales, the English Civil War would be over.

Cromwell did his job well, capturing Devizes, Winchester, and Basing House by the middle of October. During these operations Cromwell used a train of artillery very effectively, battering breaches in the defenses of Winchester and Basing before their royalist governors would surrender. He then turned his column west to rejoin Fairfax, capturing Langford House without firing a shot on 17 October. By 24 October Cromwell was again at Fairfax's side as the army's council of war debated whether or not to relieve the parliamentary garrison in Plymouth or recapture Exeter from the royalists.[5]

Fairfax continued to ignore Charles's army, focusing instead on the encirclement of the royalists in Exeter, preparatory to a campaign into Cornwall. Pausing for several weeks to refresh his troops in early December, Fairfax established outposts around Exeter from which his troops interdicted supplies coming into the city. This pause was timely, as wet weather was taking a toll on the soldiers. In early January 1646, Fairfax received a shipment of badly needed money, shoes, and stockings for his men, allowing him to muster his regiments for field duty on the 8th. On 9 January Cromwell led a surprise attack against a Cavalier outpost in Bovey Tracy, capturing 400 horses and fifty men. This small victory and the movements of the New Model Army completely unnerved the royalists, who retreated west.[6]

Fairfax responded by leaving Sir Hardress Waller with several regiments to mask Exeter while he marched the army to Dartmouth, which fell on 18 January 1646. The moral and physical ascendancy of the New Model Army was so great that Fairfax wrote in a letter to his father that '… three red coats could chase one hundred of the enemy.'[7] Fairfax cleverly released 120 Cornishmen captured in Dartmouth and sent them home after giving each two shillings.[8] In response to the loss of Dartmouth, the royalists abandoned the siege of Plymouth and retreated to Launceston, a town near Cornwall's border. As the Roundheads prepared to pursue them, parliament renewed Cromwell's commission for another six months, on 23 January.

Meanwhile, Hopton collected about 5,000 royalist soldiers and marched to Torrington, in western Devon, hoping to relieve Exeter. To do so, he would need to fight Fairfax's much larger army. His situation was desperate. His men were ill-disciplined, the country folk were tired of the depredations of the royalist soldiery, and he was short of arms and ammunition. None the less, he hoped to prevent the New Model from taking Exeter and from entering Cornwall. This was not to be, as Fairfax concentrated his army at Chumleigh, Devon, on 14 February, and then advanced toward Hopton's army. Hearing of Fairfax's approach, Hopton fortified Torrington and prepared for battle.

After several days of skirmishing, Fairfax ordered his troops to move up to the town. As they did so on the evening of 17 February, a reconnaissance party of Roundheads attempted to enter the town, triggering a battle. After two hours of fierce fighting at the barricades, the parliamentarian infantry forced their way into the town. Cromwell's cavalry followed and prepared to charge Hopton's cavalry on the main street. The Cavaliers, having no stomach for further battle, galloped out of town towards the west. Fairfax's troops captured hundreds of prisoners whom they placed in the church, along with most of Hopton's supply of gunpowder. Somehow a spark ignited the powder, blowing the church up and killing over two hundred prisoners. Fairfax lost about twenty dead and a hundred wounded.[9]

The battle of Torrington destroyed the last of the royalist infantry in the south, leaving Hopton in a hopeless situation. On 21 February, Fairfax and his council of war decided to cross the Tamar into Cornwall while establishing a series of garrisons to cut communications between the king in Oxford and his son in Wales. In preparation for his advance, Fairfax again ordered Cornish prisoners to be released to go home, each with 2 shillings. This leniency, and the dispatch of a double agent to Bodmin to inform the royalists of the good condition of the parliamentary army, proved effective psychological tools in the final conquest of Cornwall.

When Fairfax entered Cornwall, Launceston and Bodmin surrendered to him with minimal resistance, on 25 and 27 February. Five hundred royalist soldiers joined the New Model Army at Launceston, while Hopton found it impossible to recruit new soldiers from the war-weary population. The gentry also changed sides, glad to see the depredations of the royalist garrisons replaced by the regularly paid parliamentarians. By 4 March Prince Charles had escaped by ship to the Scilly Isles, just ten days before Hopton surrendered all royalist forces in Cornwall.[10]

In less than a year, from June 1645, the New Model Army crushed three royalist armies and overran the major royalist bases outside of Oxford and Newark. The news of the final victory in Cornwall was accompanied by the good news that Chester, the last English port in royalist hands, had surrendered on 3 February. On 21 March, Sir William Brereton smashed the last large royalist force outside of Newark and Oxford at Stow-on-the-Wold. Exeter surrendered to Fairfax on 9 April. By then, the king had no military options remaining to him in England. His only hope was that the victorious allies would fall out amongst themselves. Such a development was not impossible, as Sir Jacob Astley said, after his defeat at Stow-on-the-Wold, 'You have done your work, and may go to play, unless you fall out among yourselves.'[11]

Scottish operations and attempts for a settlement, 1645–6

The triumph of the New Model Army was facilitated by the efforts of the Covenanter armies of Leven and David Leslie during the previous year. Leslie's defeat of Montrose at Philiphaugh in September 1645 removed any option for the king to lead his English forces to Scotland to join Montrose. Leven's army, rejoined by Leslie after Philiphaugh, kept the royalists in the north quiet while also establishing a siege of Newark on 27 November. But the Scots rightly felt that their efforts were unappreciated. Worse, they feared that the Independents in the English parliament and army would settle the English church and state in a manner they deemed dangerous to the Scottish political and religious settlements.[12]

Relations between the parliamentarians and their Scottish allies had been strained for some time. The Scots resented the way they were being treated by the English. They especially resented that their army was forced to take free quarter in England because the English consistently failed to provide its pay as promised. The English, and especially the Independents in parliament, criticized the Scottish army for its lack of achievements and its depredations in England. Probably of even greater concern, the Covenanters recognized that their dream of religious uniformity between the two kingdoms was not going to be realized. This became especially clear in October when the English parliament opted for an Erastian settlement of an English Presbyterian church, rather than to copy the more clerically directed Scottish Kirk.[13]

English criticism of Leven for his army's lack of success during most of 1645 was justified. Once Montrose's army was routed at Philiphaugh, Leslie rejoined Leven with the Scottish cavalry, but the army still remained inactive. Leven moved south only after the English parliament promised the Scots £30,000 if they established a siege against Newark. From late November until May 1646, the Scots blockaded the north side of Newark, while Sydenham Poyntz and the English Northern Army covered the south side. Unlike Fairfax at Bristol, Bridgewater, or Sherborne, Leven did not risk an assault, preferring instead to keep his army unscathed for other military and political purposes.[14]

Scottish fears of the Independents in the army and parliament were well-founded. The fundamental issues dividing Independents from Presbyterians in England concerned religious authority and toleration within a Presbyterian church of England. The Presbyterians sought a church in which the power to define and punish heresy would lie with the clergy. Such a church would require a strict conformity of belief and worship from all congregations and would not tolerate congregations outside of the established church. The Independents accepted the Presbyterian organization but opposed giving the power of defining heresy and of excommunicating members of the church to the clergy alone. They favored an Erastian settlement in which parliament would define those offenses for which a member could be barred from communion by the ministers and presbyteries. For a person to be excommunicated for any offenses not listed by parliament, a parliamentary standing commission would have to approve of the action of the clergy.[15] Finally, the Independents favored religious toleration of individual congregations and 'tender consciences', as Cromwell eloquently proposed in his letter to parliament after the capture of Bristol, on 10 September 1645.

> It may be thought that some praises are due to these gallant men, ... Presbyterians, Independents, all had here the same spirit of faith and prayer; the same pretense and answer; they agree here, know no names of difference: pity it is it should be otherwise anywhere. All that believe, have the real unity, which is most glorious, because inward and spiritual, in the body, and to the head. As for being united in forms, commonly called uniformity, every Christian will for peace-sake study and do, as far as conscience will permit; and from brethren, in things of the mind we look for no compulsion, but that of light and reason. In other things God hath put the sword into parliament's hands, for the terror of evil-doers, and the praise of them that do well.[16]

The House of Commons omitted this paragraph from the version of Cromwell's account that it published, indicating the split in parliament and in London between Independents and Presbyterians. This omission prompted London Independents to distribute handbills containing the entire letter.[17]

Robert Baillie, one of the Scots commissioners in London during the war, reflected in his letters the fear by Scottish and English Presbyterians of the New Model Army as a hotbed of sectarianism and Independency. He concluded, in October 1645, that the only weapon the Scots possessed that could affect developments in England was Leven's army.[18] How could such an instrument be used to bring about an English religious settlement that did not endanger the Scottish settlement?

The answer was to make some sort of deal with the king that included the establishment of a strict Presbyterian church in exchange for the preservation of the monarchy with most of its powers intact. This was feasible, especially after the Earl of Holland proposed to the French ambassador in London, in early October, that the king should take refuge with the Scots. This was one of several approaches Charles made to the Scots after Naseby. The Scottish commissioners replied, through the French ambassador, that a deal could be made, but only if the king agreed 'to establish ecclesiastical affairs in the manner agreed on by the Parliaments and Assemblies of both kingdoms.' If he accepted this demand, the Scots would 'use all their power in his support.'[19]

The Scots' proposals to the king were prompted by their belief that Charles and the English Independents in the New Model Army were negotiating a settlement in which the army would restore the king in exchange for religious toleration in England, thus threatening Scottish interests.[20] Nothing came of the communications between the king and the Scots before May 1646, mainly because it was clear from captured letters that Charles would never accept the permanent establishment of Presbyterianism. However, relations between the English and the Scots continued to deteriorate, with only the need to win the war keeping them together.[21] As Baillie noted,

> ... we see no appearance that the king, for all his desperate condition, is minded to yield what both kingdoms has (sic) concluded to have; but is going on in his old plotting way, to destroy the remainder of his subjects; his messengers are still dealing with Denmark, for men to come over; the queen is daily agenting with the court and clergy of France, and the Prince of Orange for men, money, ships, and arms; ... But that which troubles us most is Ireland.[22]

Stalemate and negotiations in Ireland, 1645–6

Even before Charles's defeat, Ireland was a major concern to the warring parties in Britain. The parliamentarians had dealt with the royalist regiments sent from Ireland to England after the cessation of 1643, and they continued to fear that a Catholic army would follow. The Scots faced Montrose's army, which had received substantial military aid from Ireland. Irish soldiers, commanded by Alasdair Mac Colla, were the backbone of Montrose's army until his defeat at Philiphaugh.

Because of their fear of Montrose's army the Covenanters were unable to exploit their success at Marston Moor, therefore prolonging the war in England. The resultant stalemate in southern England led to the creation of the New Model Army and the passage of the Self-Denying ordinance in early 1645, giving the English Independents the military force that ultimately destroyed Presbyterian and Scottish hopes for religious uniformity in Britain. Montrose's continued success in 1645 prevented the Scots from executing an offensive strategy in England until after Fairfax and Cromwell had destroyed the royalist armies, giving the New Model the credit for the final victory.

Encouraged by the performance of the Irish soldiers serving with Montrose, Charles I hoped the Confederates would provide him with an Irish army. Before his defeat at Naseby, the king had ordered Ormond to conclude a peace, even if it meant promising to annul the penal laws. Ormond, however, was unable or unwilling to conclude an agreement with the Confederates that would have granted them religious freedom, frustrating the king's hope for reinforcements.[23] This impasse prompted Charles to send the Earl of Glamorgan to Ireland to speed the negotiations with the Confederates. Glamorgan, an English Catholic, reached Dublin after the Battle of Naseby, when Charles's military situation had become desperate.[24]

The Confederate's war effort had not gone well in 1644, ending that year with their fruitless offensive in Ulster.[25] In early 1645 they achieved some success with the capture of the fortress of Duncannon, near Waterford, and Bunratty Castle on the Shannon River approach to Limerick. However, they lost Sligo in northern Connacht in July, and were unable to prevent Monro from rampaging as far south as Athlone, in Leinster, in August 1645.[26] At the same time, the Confederates were divided over whether or not to come to terms with Charles. Their ultimate question was whether or not they needed an alliance with the royalists badly enough to trust an heretical king who had a long history of double-dealing.

Ormond refused to deviate from the king's instructions during his intermittent negotiations with the Confederates. His task was to achieve a political settlement that would leave the religious issues to be resolved after the royalists had won the English Civil War. Limited religious toleration would be granted in the meantime, and the insurgents would be given a full pardon for all actions since 1641. The confiscation of land undertaken by Strafford in the 1630s would be reversed and the property of Catholics protected. The Confederates demanded a great deal more.

In May and June 1645, as both sides prepared for negotiations in Dublin, the Confederate general assembly declared its terms: Poyning's law and the penal laws were to be revoked; Catholic legal and property rights were to be protected; Catholics were to retain church property occupied since 1641; and Catholics were to receive religious freedom, to include freedom from non-Catholic ecclesiastical jurisdiction. This declaration nearly wrecked the negotiations since Ormond refused to consider it. But last-minute maneuvering by those Confederates on the supreme council who favored a compromise with Ormond succeeded in removing the demand for the retention of all reoccupied church property, and negotiations continued.[27]

Parliament's victory at Naseby increased the king's need for help from Ireland and his willingness to make concessions. This trend was a major factor in the drama that unfolded as the Earl of Glamorgan arrived in Dublin and attempted to find a shortcut to a settlement.

Glamorgan was dedicated to two conflicting principles: loyalty to his king and dedication to his Roman Catholic faith. He knew that Charles desperately needed an Irish army to redress the situation in England. He believed that he could secure freedom for his church in Ireland by providing that army. He came to Ireland with a commission from the king giving him a tremendous amount of discretion in his negotiations with the Irish. This commission was dated 12 March 1645, well before the disaster of Naseby.[28] Finding that the Ormond negotiations were going nowhere, Glamorgan traveled to Kilkenny to continue discussions with the Confederates.

Within several weeks he concluded a treaty with the Catholics, on 25 August. This treaty promised Catholics full religious liberty and the retention of church property they had reoccupied since 23 October 1641. In exchange, the Confederates were to send an army of 10,000 soldiers to England as soon as possible.[29]

This 'First Glamorgan Treaty' was to be confirmed in an Irish parliament and the king was to promise that the concessions would be honored. The negotiators also agreed that the Confederates were to pursue a political treaty with Ormond and that the Glamorgan agreement was to be kept secret until Ormond's treaty was concluded and an Irish army had reached England.[30]

Glamorgan then wrote to Ormond telling him that it was likely that the Confederates would accept a political agreement while trusting the king to take care of their religious concerns after a royalist victory. It is uncertain whether or not Ormond knew of the religious concessions made by Glamorgan. It is clear that Charles never authorized such sweeping concessions, nor would he ever confirm them, as he made clear to Ormond after his defeat at Naseby.

> … I absolutely command you (what hazard soever that kingdom may run by it) personally to bring me all the forces what sort soever you can draw from thence. … But you must not understand this as permission for you to grant the Irish (in case they will not otherwise have a peace) any thing more in matter of religion than what I have allowed you already, except in some convenient parishes where the much greater number are papists. … But I will rather chose to suffer all extremity than ever to abandon my religion, and particularly either to English or Irish rebels.[31]

Glamorgan exceeded his discretionary powers by agreeing to terms that Charles would never accept. In his defense two points can be made. Glamorgan knew that the king was in a desperate situation in which 10,000 Irish soldiers might have turned the tide in his favor. Second, it made sense to a Roman Catholic to grant Irish Catholics and their clergy religious liberty and the rightful possession of their church property.

Ormond knew that some sort of compromise on religious issues had been worked out by Glamorgan, although it is impossible to prove that he knew the exact terms of the treaty.[32] He certainly could not disclose such terms and he continued to reject the inclusion of religious concessions in his own treaty with the Confederates. Consequently, Ormond failed to conclude a treaty in 1645. But Glamorgan assumed that the deal was done and that he could convince the king to accept his terms once 10,000 fresh soldiers joined Charles in England.

While Glamorgan recruited and Ormond negotiated, the Irish situation changed with the arrival of a papal nuncio in Ireland. Giovanni Battista Rinuccini, Bishop of Fermo, arrived in Kilkenny on 12 November, where large enthusiastic crowds greeted him. His mission was 'to restore and reestablish the public exercise of the Catholic religion in the island of Ireland.' To do this he brought money, arms, and papal authority.[33]

Rinuccini rejected the Glamorgan treaty because of its dependence on the approval of the king only after an Irish army was in England, and because its provisions were to be separate from a political treaty with Ormond. As this position became clear to the Confederate supreme council, Glamorgan returned to Kilkenny to meet with the nuncio, on 12 December. Rinuccini quickly won Glamorgan's loyalty and the two of them negotiated a new treaty giving Catholics concessions that would have, if accepted by the king, ended royal authority in Ireland. This 'Second Glamorgan Treaty' was signed on 20 December. It stipulated that the Lord Lieutenant of Ireland would henceforth be Catholic, that the Catholic bishops would sit in the House of Lords in the Irish parliament, and that an army would be sent to England only after Charles publicly accepted the provisions of the first and second treaties.[34]

Glamorgan returned to Dublin where he was summoned to appear before the king's council on 26 December. He was asked to comment on the recently published news that he had signed a treaty with the Confederates in August, the terms of which had been published. Caught red-handed by these revelations, Glamorgan was imprisoned and his treaty disavowed by Ormond and the king.[35] Although Glamorgan was released from prison within a month, his agreements with the Irish were ruined. On 7 February the general assembly rejected the treaties, while Ormond reported to Charles I that the whole affair had set back his negotiations with the Confederates.[36]

Complicating matters further and making the Irish Catholics, sometimes described as nuncioists, even more reluctant to accept less than the Second Glamorgan Treaty, word had reached Ireland that the Queen's representative to the papacy, Sir Kenelm Digby, had negotiated a treaty allowing Catholic independence in Ireland and for religious toleration for English Catholics as well. Although Charles quickly disavowed this treaty, it made it certain that no treaty would be agreed upon in Ireland in time to help the royalists militarily in England.

At about the same time, the English parliamentary Committee for Ireland formally proposed that a major expedition be sent to reconquer Ireland. This force was to consist of 6,840 soldiers, with a siege train of fourteen cannon, supported with a war chest of £30,000 and with another £12,000 provided monthly. More bad news for Charles followed when he learned that Chester had fallen to the parliamentarians, cutting off the last port in which an Irish army could be landed in England.[37] In the face of these tidings, the Confederates allowed Glamorgan to recruit 6,000 men for service in England, while they and Ormond continued to negotiate.

Ormond concluded his first treaty on 28 March 1646, but it was not to be published until ratified by Charles I. The treaty, with its provisions for an army of 10,000 men to serve in Britain, was too little and too late to help the king. It offered too little certainty for the protection of Catholic religious liberty for Rinuccini and the majority of the Confederate general assembly to accept it. These Irish Catholics saw clearly that Charles and Ormond were only trying to use the Irish, with no intention of granting their religious demands. Further, they realized that the royalist cause in England was finished militarily, making it unlikely that the king could deliver the promised concessions.

On 5 May events in Ireland were overtaken by the king's arrival in the Scottish camp before Newark. Then, on 5 June 1646, Owen Roe O'Neill and his Ulster army crushed Monro's army at the Battle of Benburb, transforming the situation in Ireland. Militarily, the Catholic armies enjoyed, for the first time, true superiority over the Protestant forces. Politically, Rinuccini had O'Neill's army available to use to overawe the Ormondists in Kilkenny. Seeing the handwriting on the wall, Ormond forced the situation to a climax by publishing the terms of the Ormond Treaty on 30 July. The supreme council followed suit on 3 August 1646.

Refusing to accept this as the final solution, Rinuccini and the church synod, then meeting, condemned the Ormond Treaty and threatened to excommunicate anyone who accepted it. O'Neill marched his army to Kilkenny to back the nuncio with force if necessary. As a result, on 1 September, Thomas Preston, Commander of the Confederates Army of Leinster, submitted to the nuncio, denying the Ormondists the strength they needed to resist. By 18 September, Rinuccini had purged the supreme council, placing himself as the head of a new sixteen-member council.[38]

While the royalists and the Confederates tried and failed to reach a settlement that would have allowed them to present a common front to their enemies, the parliamentary and Scottish armies crushed the remaining centers of royalist military power in England. This struggle in England profoundly affected the future of Ireland as well as Britain.

The king's flight ends the English Civil War

Fairfax's victories in Cornwall in the spring of 1646 ended the war in the west, denying the royalists one of their two best recruiting grounds. Exeter and Barnstaple, the last two major places in the southwest held by the king's forces, capitulated to Fairfax on 9 and 12 April, respectively. Fairfax granted liberal terms to the defenders, allowing the royalist garrisons to march away or to disband. Most disbanded. This triumph was shortly joined by the surrender of all royalist garrisons in the southwest except for Pendennis Castle, allowing the New Model Army to begin its march toward Oxford and the final major siege of the war.[39]

As Fairfax's army closed in on Oxford, the Scots and the English Northern Army continued the siege of Newark, preventing the royalists from rallying for a last effort. Charles faced certain military defeat, forcing him to redouble his efforts to divide his enemies – Scots from English and English Presbyterians from Independents – hoping to win politically what he could not gain militarily. The Scots and the Presbyterians were responsive to his overtures, both hoping to use the king to gain their political and religious goals.

Charles's approach to the Scots through Leven and their commissioners in London in the fall of 1645, and their overtures to him, had been discovered by the English parliamentarians. However, a rupture between them and the Scots was avoided by the Scots' denial of all secret contacts with the king and by the parliamentarians' acceptance of those declarations. Charles continued to scheme to win the Scots over by offering toleration of Presbyterianism in England and by promising to give them Irish land in payment of the money owed their armies. In these offers he demonstrated his misunderstanding of the depth of religious feeling that had motivated the Covenanters during the past seven years. The Scots, realizing that such proposals left the door wide open for the maintenance of episcopacy in England, which in turn would threaten its possible reestablishment in Scotland, refused his offer. Instead, they countered with the proposal that he accept the Uxbridge proposals as a first condition to a settlement.[40]

Charles also continued to send proposals to parliament for negotiations in Westminster, to which he requested safe conduct. Parliament, seeing this offer as the king's attempt to gain time for his numerous schemes in pursuit of foreign aid to mature, rejected his proposal. In response, Charles offered to accept a settlement that would restore the church to its status in the reigns of Elizabeth and James I and to discuss the control of the militia and the reconquest of Ireland. This unacceptable offer ignored the fact that parliament had already decided to establish an English Presbyterian church.[41]

The king concurrently opened negotiations with Independents in London and the parliament in the fall and winter of 1645–6. These approaches produced no results, nor was there much to be gained by them since parliament's armies were firmly loyal to parliament and the Independents were still a majority in the House of Commons.[42] The king's willingness, however, to negotiate with every conceivable faction and foreign power indicated his desperate situation and his unscrupulous nature. Before long, every faction that he had approached learned of his dealings with the other groups, especially since much of the king's correspondence fell into his enemies' hands.

By April, Charles saw that his hopes of foreign or Irish aid were groundless. At that point he had to decide how to play out his weak hand. He had obvious choices. He could try to leave England, but parliamentary regiments had thrown a noose of garrisons around Oxford and all English ports were in his enemies' hands. He could stay in Oxford and fight to the end, but that would accomplish nothing politically and it would leave him in Fairfax's hands and, therefore, in parliament's control. This option was unsatisfactory because it would leave him little choice but to accept parliament's terms which included, as a minimum, abolition of episcopacy, establishment of a Presbyterian church, parliamentary control of the militia for twenty years, and a parliamentary settlement in Ireland.

Facing these choices, Charles decided to try again to come to terms with the Scots. He was encouraged in this course by a letter from the French ambassador, Montreuil, then in Leven's camp, that 'the disposition of the Scottish commanders was all that could be desired.'[43] Thus he decided to leave Oxford secretly and ride north, hoping to win the Scots over to a compromise peace. He saw this as his best chance to split the coalition of Covenanters and parliamentarians, especially in the light of the steadily deteriorating relations between the two. The overtures from the Scottish commissioners in London also had convinced him that a deal could be reached that would leave him in a position to save episcopacy and royal power in England.

To cloak his plans, Charles wrote to Commissary General Henry Ireton, the senior parliamentary commander nearest to Oxford, offering to surrender to the army. Ireton forwarded the letter to Cromwell, who had returned to his seat in the Commons. Cromwell presented the letter to the House of Commons on 25 April and chastised Ireton publicly for accepting it from the king.[44] The letter was a ruse to sow dissension between parliament and the army. Meanwhile, Charles departed Oxford on 29 April, arriving at David Leslie's headquarters near Newark on 5 May 1646.

The king joins the Scots and the Civil War ends

The Scots knew that Charles was on his way to their camp. In anticipation of his arrival, they told Montreuil 'that they should secure the king in his person and his honor' and 'that they should press the king to do nothing contrary to his conscience.' They further promised 'that if the parliament refused, upon a message from the king, to restore the king to his rights and prerogatives, they should declare for the king, and take all the king's friends into their protection.' In return, they expected Charles to accept Presbyterianism in England.[45] The message they expected Charles to send to parliament was one accepting a Presbyterian church. If the Scots intended to keep their promises, they certainly underestimated the king's aversion to Presbyterianism.

Once they had the king in their hands the Covenanters wasted no time in demanding that Charles order the surrender of Newark, sign the Solemn League and Covenant, order the establishment of Presbyterianism in England and Ireland, and require Montrose to surrender. The king ordered the Governor of Newark to surrender, but refused the other demands. David Leslie, now in command of the Scottish army, tactfully arranged for Newark's Governor to submit to the English Commander Sydenham Poyntz, on 6 May, while Leslie started the process of marching his soldiers north. This withdrawal was prompted by Scottish fears that the English armies would surround them near Newark in order to capture Charles.[46] By 13 May the Scots army had reached Newcastle with the king in tow.

The English were outraged, assuming that the Scots had made a deal with the king. Their immediate impulse was to break with the Covenanters, with the House of Commons passing a resolution on 6 May ordering the king's imprisonment in Warwick Castle and another on 19 May declaring that 'this kingdom hath no further use of the continuing the Scots' army within the kingdom of England.'[47] The House of Lords, now with a Presbyterian majority, refused to accept the first resolution, and calmer heads soon prevailed concerning the second. The Scots also calmed English fears by sending a message to London swearing that they had not anticipated the king's arrival, nor did they plan to take advantage of the situation at the expense of their allies.[48]

The military result of the king's surrender was the capitulation of nearly all remaining royalist strongholds over the next three months. Fairfax's decision to crush the remaining royalist armies in the southwest earlier in the year made it impossible for royalists to hold on to any region of England. Once Oxford surrendered, on 20 June 1646, there no longer was a need for Fairfax to maintain large concentrations of troops. Peace in England and Scotland now seemed possible, and with it the end of war-time taxes and committees and a return to pre-war normality.[49]

The issues of peace: the king, religion, and Ireland

The destruction of the royalist armies ended the Civil War, but it did not settle three fundamental problems facing the Scots and the English. First, what position should Charles I play in their post-war governments? Second, how should the English church be settled and what role were parliament, the king, and the clergy to play in the new church? Third, how was the war in Ireland to be won and what sort of settlement were to be imposed on that kingdom?

The settlement of Ireland affected the Scots as well as the English. There was agreement that the papist threat on Britain's back door must be eliminated through conquest and a new Protestant settlement and ascendancy in Ireland. However, a number of important details needed to be worked out, such as where the soldiers and officers needed to carry it out should come from and how they should be paid. The other major concerns about the king's position and the settlement of religion were much thornier, and many Englishmen did not believe the Scots should have much say in either.

Charles's decision to surrender to the Scots gave the Covenanters the opportunity to deal in the most important political and religious problems of the day. From the moment the king arrived in their camp, the Covenanters had bombarded him with demands that he accept Presbyterianism for England and for the royal family. Charles resisted their entreaties and threats while trying to spin out the discussions to give his agents time to convince the French to intercede on his behalf. After several weeks of debate the Scots gave up in their efforts to convert the king, deciding instead to remain allied with the English parliament. This change in Scottish strategy was symbolically demonstrated on 25 June, when the leading Covenanter, Argyll, spoke to the assembled houses in Westminster, promising them that the Scots fully accepted the Erastian Presbyterian church that parliament had settled upon in October.[50]

Argyll also told his parliamentary audience that the peace terms that the English parliament had proposed to the Scottish commissioners were acceptable, opening the way for the allies to present a common front to the king in Newcastle. Two Lords and four Commoners carried these nineteen terms, known as the Newcastle Propositions, to the king in late July. A copy also was sent to Charles earlier for his consideration. When the parliamentarians officially presented the Propositions to Charles, it became apparent to him that the terms were final, rather than negotiable.

The Newcastle Proposals contained terms that Charles had rejected in the negotiations in Uxbridge, in February 1645. Episcopacy was to be abolished and Presbyterianism established. Catholics were to swear an oath renouncing the Pope and most Roman Catholic doctrines, and their children were to be raised as

Protestants. The militia and navy were to be controlled by parliament for twenty years. All peers created by the king since May 1642 was barred from sitting in the House of Lords without the approval of both houses of parliament. All treaties between England and Scotland were to be ratified by the king and agreements made by the king with the Irish Catholics were to be null and void. Finally, a long list of royalists, to include Montrose, Newcastle, Rupert, and nearly all of the king's principal military and political advisers, were excluded from pardon. Charles was expected to take the Covenant and to accept a parliamentary act imposing it on his subjects. All future acts of parliament implementing the propositions were to be immune from the royal veto, making the king, at best, a constitutional monarch.[51]

Charles had no intention of submitting to such terms, as he told his wife in a letter on 1 July. Instead, he determined to spin out talks with his foes as long as possible to allow for Irish or French intervention. He had no chance of coming to terms with the Scots unless he accepted Presbyterianism, and this he steadfastly refused to do, seeing that form of ecclesiastical organization as anti-monarchical as well as heretical.[52] Charles replied to the Newcastle Propositions with a letter to parliament in early August. In his view, the terms were so far-reaching that 'it is very difficult to return a particular and positive answer before a full debate.' However, to his disappointment, the parliamentary commissioners were forbidden by parliament to make any concessions. Consequently, Charles asked to be allowed to come to London to have his 'doubts cleared, and these difficulties explained unto him.'[53]

The king's inflexibility with the Scots and the parliamentarians forced the two closer together. Measures were taken by parliament and the London Common Council to punish anyone who wrote offensive things about the Scots. A Presbyterian church structure was established in London, and plans made to set it up in the rest of England. For their part, the Covenanters offered to withdraw their forces from England as soon as they were paid the money owed them and, in return, promised a consultation between the two nations to decide what to do with the king. In the meantime, he remained in captivity with the Scottish army in Newcastle.[54]

While the king continued to resist submission to the logic of the war's results, the English parliament moved on with its revolutionary changes in church and state. In a series of ordinances, parliament exercised its control over the armed forces by disbanding garrisons and units all over England. The most important force disbanded was the Western Army commanded by Edward Massey. This was accomplished by Fairfax, acting on the command of the House of Commons only, since the Lords attempted to keep Massey's Presbyterian-leaning force in being. Both houses also agreed to provide funds for the reconquest of Ireland (23 May and 22 July) and to abolish episcopacy in England (9 October 1646), pledging the credit of the Bishops' lands to repay the large loan needed to pay off the Scots.[55]

One of the most important things that parliament did in the fall of 1646 was to come to an agreement with the Covenanters that provided for the withdrawal of the Scottish forces from England. The heart of this agreement was a financial settlement of the money owed to the Scots under the terms of the 1643 alliance. In return, the English parliament would be entrusted with the care of the king. On 27 August, the House of Commons received the bill for Scottish participation in the war. The Scots claimed that a total of £1.93 million was owed them. They admitted that they had received £684,000 of this in cash, goods, and free quarter, leaving £1.25 million still due. The English commissioners saw things differently, claiming that only £992,000 was due to the Scots for their pay, at £31,000 per month since January 1644, and that their army had received £1.46 million in cash, free quarter, goods, services, and taxes taken by the Scots in northern England during the war, 'not counting plunder.'[56]

The English initially offered £100,000 to settle the Scots' financial claims but, after negotiations lasting into October, they agreed to pay £400,000. Half of this money was to be given to the Scottish army before it left England, and the remainder was to be paid once it was in Scotland and the king was in parliament's hands. The English found it difficult to raise this money, delaying the agreement until December 1646.[57] Only after pledging the proceeds of the sale of the Bishops' lands and allowing current creditors of the state to 'double' on the purchase of these lands was parliament able to put together the loan in London that provided the first £200,000 to be sent north to York and Newcastle.

Throughout the summer and fall Charles continued to hope that his foes would fall out amongst themselves. However, he refused to make the concessions needed to gain the support of the Scots and the Presbyterians in England. On 30 September he finally submitted counter-proposals to the Newcastle Propositions. He offered to accept Presbyterianism for three years, at the end of which an assembly of clergy would recommend to him whether or not to keep Presbyterianism. He would retain his position of king, with his legislative veto intact. This offer was unacceptable to his opponents. On 12 and 15 October he tried to make it more acceptable by offering to concede control of the militia to parliament for ten years and to accept Presbyterianism for five, as long as the Presbyterians would accept a 'regulated episcopacy' at the end of that period. At the same time he continued to seek foreign aid to use against his subjects.[58]

His enemies continued to read the king's letters to the Queen, Montrose, Ormond, and others seeking foreign assistance. These missives contained his declaration that he did not intend to keep the bargain he had offered to the Scots. Not surprisingly, the Covenanters accepted the English offer of £400,000 to evacuate northern England in December 1646. The Scots also refused to allow Charles to come to Scotland, although they reaffirmed his position as their monarch, giving notice to the English that they expected to be consulted before a final decision of what to do with Charles Stuart was made.[59]

On 30 January 1647, the English took charge of the town of Newcastle and the king, in exchange for £200,000 in cash. Parliamentary commissioners told Charles that he would not get his wish to be moved to or near London, but instead would be housed in his residence at Holdenby. By 11 February 1647, all Scottish troops had left England. However, the question of what to do with the king remained unresolved, with only a few people, like Henry Marten, calling for the abolition of the monarchy. Charles would remain a prisoner for the remainder of his life, continually trying to sow dissension amongst his peoples.

Attempts to disband the English army and to reconquer Ireland

With the departure of the Scots from England there appeared to be no reason to keep the New Model Army in existence. Beyond that, the Presbyterian majority, fearing strong independent sympathies in the New Model, had political motives to disband Fairfax's army. Most parliamentarians agreed that a number of garrisons were required to prevent royalist uprisings, and that a substantial force needed to be sent to Ireland. On 18 and 19 February the majority of the Commons resolved that all infantry units, save those needed for garrison duty or service in Ireland, should be disbanded. This meant that only 8,400 infantrymen were to be kept on duty in England, scattered throughout the country. Another 8,400 infantry and 4,200 horse were to be sent to Ireland. Finally, the only general officer to be kept on active duty in England was to be Sir Thomas Fairfax.[60]

Most of the New Model's cavalry units were to be maintained to serve as a mobile reserve, but the parliamentary Presbyterians reasoned that such a force, lacking infantry, would pose little threat to the infantry of the trained bands due to the superiority of infantry over cavalry in battle. If the House of Lords had passed the assessment bill sent to them by the Commons the previous October there might have been enough money available to pay off the soldiers and carry out the disbandment. But the Lords rejected that assessment bill on 4 March. This shortsighted act was followed by an attempt in the Commons the next day to remove Thomas Fairfax from command of the army. This motion failed, in part because Fairfax assured parliament that he would cooperate with the dispatch of an army to Ireland.[61]

The biggest obstacle facing parliament in its efforts to disband the army was financial. On 26 March 1647, the army committee reported to the Commons that the current forces required £46,756 in pay every 28 days. From 28 March 1645 to 1 March 1647, the Treasurers at War had received £1,118,551 for Fairfax's army, but the soldiers' pay was £331,000 in arrears. The large amounts that had been paid to the soldiers had come mostly from the assessments (£758,359), with the remainder provided by the excise and loans. However, the committee reported that the assessment receipts were £310,000 in arrears, and the House of Lords had ignored the assessment re-authorization since October 1646.[62]

The Presbyterian majority that emerged in parliament over the winter risked much in its plan to disband and send a large part of the army to Ireland.[63] This was especially true because it did not plan to pay the soldiers their arrears and it was determined not to employ officers in Ireland who had displayed any evidence of supporting the Independents. Such a move would reduce the amount of money needed to disband the forces while removing most of the rank and file from England. Once in Ireland, the soldiers would have little choice but to serve parliament in its anti-Catholic conquest, while there no longer would be a large military force in England that was decidedly pro-Independent in its sympathies.[64]

The decision to send reinforcements to Ireland was timely for the English military interests there. Ormond, following Rinuccini's takeover of the Confederate government in September 1646, had approached the English parliament concerning his surrender of Dublin. He believed that he could not hold out against the Confederate offensive that had commenced in late September, and no help was forthcoming from Charles I. After months of negotiations, Ormond agreed to surrender Dublin to parliament in exchange for payment of his debts and a safe conduct pass to Holland.[65]

Ormond retained his hold on Dublin and Drogheda in the fall, mostly due to the disunity and lack of logistical support of O'Neill's and Preston's Confederate armies. Thus the Westminster government was given time to find reinforcements and a new commander for Ireland. But parliament's attempt to disband the New Model Army by force and to impress many of its soldiers involuntarily for Irish service in March failed, and delayed the dispatch of reinforcements. With Ormond facing another crisis in the spring of 1647, parliament selected Colonel Michael Jones to serve as its Lieutenant General in Dublin. Between his appointment on 8 April, and his assumption of command in July, parliament sent some money, food, munitions, and several regiments of infantry and cavalry to Dublin, giving Jones a formidable force by August.[66] In spite of these efforts to reinforce Dublin, parliament persisted in its attempts to disband Fairfax's army.

There was widespread support from all over England for the disbandment of the army, the curtailment of the excise and assessments, and the abolition of the committees that had managed the war effort. This wave of popular opinion was accompanied by a number of instances in which magistrates proceeded judicially against officers and soldiers for acts they had committed during the war. Since an increasing majority of Englishmen supported the political Presbyterians' goal of returning to pre-war normality, the soldiers would be at the mercy of local juries eager to punish someone for their wartime losses.[67]

Initially it looked as if the soldiers would obey parliament's commands and disband and that many would agree to serve under new officers in Ireland. But the threats to the soldiers of unpaid arrears, the dangers of being prosecuted for wartime acts, and the chance of being forced to serve in Ireland triggered significant unrest in the army's ranks. This upheaval took the form of petitioning by the soldiers to Lord General Fairfax and his council. These petitions included three major requests: that a parliamentary ordinance indemnifying the soldiers from prosecution for acts of war be passed; that an audit of arrears be made and the pay of the soldiers secured before their disbandment; and that there was to be no conscription of soldiers for service in Ireland. If parliament had met these demands in March 1647, the army probably would have disbanded peacefully.[68]

Parliament was indignant that the officers and soldiers had petitioned for the redress of their grievances. Consequently, on 27 March 1647, the House of Commons ordered Fairfax to stop the petitioning and send the leading officers involved to

Westminster for questioning. Fairfax tactfully replied that he would send General Hammond and several Colonels to parliament to explain the situation, but he also told the Speaker that the House was misinformed about the nature of the activities and movements of the army.[69]

Fairfax and parliament were surprised by the response of the army to its disbandment. The Commons, however, charged ahead, ordering the disbandment of the northern infantry regiments as a first step toward eliminating all of the foot units.[70] The majority of parliamentary Presbyterians supported this move because they identified the army as the source of sectarianism and social turmoil, a judgment that the evidence supports. For example, on 24 March a tract was distributed in London attacking the parliamentary majority for its attempts to bring the 'Malignants' (royalists) to power. This tract opposed the Presbyterian covenant as an assault on 'tender consciences', and called on all Englishmen to awaken to the threat posed to their liberties by the Presbyterians. Parliament's attempt to disband the army was seen as the essential step in this process: 'And now they have voted the disbanding of the army, let us beware lest they vote away all our rights and liberties, as in divers particulars they have begun.'[71]

Most of the soldiers generally were not interested in the political message that this and many Leveller tracts put forth in the spring of 1647. Instead the average soldier focused on his material concerns. However, many officers agreed with the view that '… in case this army be disbanded … we will condescend to the Scots … in all things relative to the king and church, … [and] that we shall be threatened again with the Scotch blade.'[72] Thus the concern of the rank and file over disbandment without payment of arrears and an act of indemnity melded into the Independents' and Levellers' opposition to the Presbyterian majorities in parliament and the London government.

Parliament dealt with the army's resistance to disbandment and Irish service by threatening action against soldier-petitioners and by promising to settle the arrears of the men who volunteered for Irish service. The Commons also offered command of the Irish expeditionary force to Major General Philip Skippon, a professional soldier with widespread support in the army, and it promised to bring in an act of indemnity. The threats to petitioners came first, with a parliamentary 'Declaration of Dislike' on 30 March, aimed against the practice of petitioning. The positive incentives dealing with the soldiers' material concerns followed during the next four weeks.[73]

By then it was too late. Parliament's attempt to remove Fairfax and the other senior officers of the army, along with its attack on petitioning, made the situation worse. A parliamentary delegation to the army learned of the depth of the discontent at two meetings of the army's council of war at which over fifty officers expressed their unhappiness with the Presbyterians' disbandment scheme. These officers reiterated the army's demands for an indemnity, payment of arrears, protection from impressment, and relief for the families of men killed or maimed in the war.[74]

The officers, in turn, promised to support service in Ireland, but only after four questions were answered: Who was to command the expedition? What regiments were to be sent? How was parliament going to pay for the expedition? How were the arrears and indemnity for past service going to be settled? The officers also presented another petition to the council of the army reiterating the soldiers' material demands and adding these questions about Ireland.[75]

During April parliament continued to proceed with steps to disband the army and to send a force to Ireland that was not commanded by Independents. Its persistence in opposing petitioning by the soldiers stiffened the will of the petitioners' and united Fairfax and the senior officers with the junior officers and soldiers. This was made clear when 151 officers presented a petition to the Commons on 30 April claiming that the soldiers who had won the Civil War had 'not lost the capacity of subjects nor divested ourselves thereby of our interest in the Commonwealth.' Further, after laying out the basic material grievances, the officers claimed the right to petition as 'members of the Commonwealth.'[76]

The Presbyterian counter-revolution, May–August 1647

Fairfax increased the pressure on parliament in April and May by transferring regiments to billets closer to London. The Presbyterians recognized these threatening moves. In response, parliament gave the London government control over the trained bands of the City and its suburbs. The Presbyterians purged Independents from the London trained bands and used militiamen to enforce rules against unlicensed preaching.[77] The Commons stepped up its attack against the army by resolving, on 4 May, 'that whatsoever soldier, or other person shall take free quarter in any county, without warrant or authority of parliament, shall be apprehended by the sheriffs or justices of the peace.'[78] Since the soldiers were not being paid, free quarter was essential to their survival, making this resolution a direct threat to the troops.

As the soldiers' fear of being disbanded without security from arrest and redress of their material concerns grew, a number of the cavalry regiments in East Anglia created an ad hoc council of two agents from each regiment to prepare a letter to Fairfax. This letter, published on 3 May, listed the material demands of the men and asked rhetorically, 'is it not better to die like men, than to be enslaved and hanged like dogs?' The missive demanded that the 'honor' of the army, which had been falsely impugned by the Declaration of Dislikes and by Presbyterian propaganda, 'be vindicated in every particular.'[79] Seeing that the army was slipping out of control, Fairfax summoned representatives from each regiment to meet at Saffron Walden on 15 May to discuss the issues agitating the soldiers.

By then it looked as if parliament would try to win the army over by meeting its material demands. On 14 May the Commons resolved to pay two months' arrears to soldiers who disbanded and to offer another six weeks' pay in advance for those choosing to serve in Ireland. On 21 May Cromwell recommended to the House that it should order the auditing of soldiers' accounts, promise not to force any soldier to serve involuntarily in Ireland, provide 'real and visible security' for the ultimate payment of the army's arrears, and make provisions for the care of maimed soldiers and families of men killed in the war, all in order to calm the army and end the crisis.[80]

The Commons seemed to work to meet the material demands of soldiers with a series of ordinances to include one granting indemnity for acts of war, another providing relief for maimed soldiers and their families, and a third ordinance for auditing the soldiers' accounts.[81] But the indemnity ordinance covered only acts committed before May 1646, leaving the soldiers vulnerable to prosecution for anything done since, and the 'Declaration of Dislike' of 30 March remained in effect, branding soldiers who petitioned as enemies of the state. This, and the knowledge in the army that the Presbyterians were recruiting new regiments, made these concessions of little worth.[82]

When the officers met at Saffron Walden on 15 May they consolidated the regimental reports into a single document. This work included eleven major points, centered on material grievances, but it also demanded the vindication of the army's honor. This list was published on 27 May. More than 240 officers signed it, indicating the breadth and strength of the soldiers' resolve.[83] A delegation from parliament to the army, consisting of Cromwell, Skippon, Henry Ireton, and William Fleetwood, visited the gathering and reported to the Commons that 'we must acknowledge we found the army under a deep sense of some sufferings, and the common soldiers much unsettled.'[84]

The parliamentary Presbyterian leaders Denzil Holles, Sir Philip Stapleton, and Sir John Clotworthy, however, continued to push for the army's disbandment without adequately addressing the soldiers' grievances. The army's patience ended on 25 May, when the Commons voted 136 to 115 to begin the disbandment of the infantry on 1 June. The regiments were to be stood down over the next two weeks. Only four regiments of foot were to be kept, and these were to be sent overseas under new officers.[85] The Commons designated only £40,000 to pay the arrears of the soldiers, while earmarking another £42,000 to pay the newly raised Presbyterian guard units in London. All remaining money owed to the troops was to be paid in promissory notes after the men's accounts had been audited and deductions made for the value of free quarter taken by the troops over the previous three years. This decision set in motion a revolt by the army against parliament and its Presbyterian allies.[86]

The army versus the Presbyterian counter-revolution

While the Presbyterians were trying to disband the army, they continued to negotiate with the king for a peace settlement in which they seemed willing to accept far less from Charles than before. These terms were published on 27 May, increasing the soldiers' fears that a Presbyterian plot uniting the Presbyterians with the royalists and Scots was underway. This fear was increased by the publication of parliament's disbandment order the next day.[87]

Fairfax, in response to the disbandment order and the army's concerns about the Presbyterian dealings with Charles, called for a meeting of the officers at Bury St. Edmunds, on 1 June. He also notified parliament that the army would not disband and that he had to '… take some speedy resolution for the composing of things, …

(though I am forced to yield to some things out of order) to keep the army from disorders.' A letter accompanied this message to the Speaker from Colonel Rains-borough stating that there had been a riot in his regiment at Long Wittenham that was suppressed with force.[88]

In the face of the Presbyterians' efforts to disband it and to secure control of a military force of their own, the New Model Army united. The officers stood by their men and the soldiers continued to take directions from their commanders. This solidarity doomed the Presbyterian counter-revolution because no military force in England could stand against a united army successfully.

The king remained an important consideration during this time of increasing tension. The Independents feared that the Presbyterians and Scots would cut a deal with Charles I that would unite royalists, Covenanters, and Presbyterians, allowing them to impose their settlement upon the nation. On 31 May, Cromwell prevented the king from falling into hands hostile to the army by sending Cornet George Joyce with a cavalry force to Holdenby House to seize the king. Joyce carried out his mission expeditiously, having Charles in his control by 2 June. On 3 June Joyce notified the king that he was to be moved to a safer location, and on 4 June the king set off with his escort to join the army in Newmarket, Cambridgeshire.[89]

Fairfax and Cromwell reviewed the troops on 4 and 5 June at Newmarket. Cromwell had just barely escaped capture by Holles and Stapleton in London on 3 June, and it was becoming evident that the Presbyterians intended to confront the army with force. Fairfax took this opportunity to create The General Council of the Army, composed of two officer and two enlisted representatives from each regiment and all of the general officers. For two days this body discussed its grievances and courses of action. In the process, it prepared two documents to send to parliament and to be published.

The Humble Representation of the Dissatisfactions of the Army and *The Solemn Engagement of the Army* marked an increasing interest by the army in politics, although they still focused on the soldiers' material grievances. The troops declared 'that without such satisfaction and security, as aforesaid, we shall not willing disband nor divide, nor suffer ourselves to be disbanded or divided.' They pointed out that eight weeks' pay was too little to settle their arrears. This especially made sense since parliament was offering only £70,000 toward the repayment of over £1.5 million in arrears. Further, they pointed out that the excise and the fines from delinquent estates were 'already pre-engaged for vast sums' by parliament.[90]

Parliament, in the face of the army's resolve and unity, seemed to back down by ordering that the 'Declaration of Dislikes' be expunged from its records. The London government also showed a willingness to resolve things peacefully.[91] The army's possession of the king, the refusal of Argyll to accept the Presbyterians' invitation to lead a Scottish army south, and the refusal of many members of the London trained bands to answer muster calls, weighed heavily in parliament's decision to attempt to placate the army.

Events took a major turn in another direction, however, on 7 June, when the Commons called on the London trained bands for protection and attempted to bring loyal troops to Westminster from Worcester and the north of England.[92] Fairfax responded to these provocations by massing the army at Triploe Heath, near Cambridge, and then by moving the army and his headquarters to St Albans, just twenty miles from London. Parliament responded, on 11 June, by asking him to remove the army to at least thirty miles from Westminster, while passing resolutions to strengthen its forces around London. Holles and the other Presbyterian leaders again asked the Scots to send their army south.[93]

Military confrontation seemed unavoidable as the army moved closer to the city and the Presbyterians raised regiments of former soldiers known as Reformadoes and deserters into regiments in London and Worcester. On 12 June the army moved closer to London, while parliament made one more plea to Londoners for its defense. But the army had called London's bluff and the City buckled in the face of the undefeated army. On 16 June, parliament and London seemed to capitulate a second time, repudiating the leading eleven Presbyterian members of the Commons and the City's safety and militia committees. Parliament also promised a month's pay to the troops, an offer that was quickly accepted.[94]

Fairfax halted the army and presented parliament with *A Declaration or Representation*. This document included, for the first time, a political agenda drawn up by the Council of the Army on 14 June. The soldiers now demanded, 'in defense of the people's rights and liberties,' that parliament be purged of delinquent and corrupt members, that the king's arbitrary powers be abolished, and that the right to petition be upheld. The declaration included the Independents' demand for 'provision for tender consciences' and a call for an audit of all public accounts.[95]

The Presbyterian leaders responded to this move by attempting again to rouse London and the parliament to defend themselves from the army. The Commons rejected the declaration from the army and voted additional pay to the Northern Army and the Presbyterian forces in London. These decisions were made amidst popular disturbances in Westminster by Reformadoes and London apprentices designed to intimidate the members of parliament.[96]

While the Presbyterians breathed new life into their cause, Fairfax moved his regiments closer to London, in a concentric arch from Windsor to Kingston upon Thames. He also moved the artillery train from Oxford to Windsor, making it clear that he was prepared to use it against London. These moves had their desired effect. The Houses again gave way, ordering the four new regiments in Worcester disbanded and affirming that the New Model Army was 'its own to maintain and respect.' The eleven leading Presbyterians in the Commons withdrew, giving the Independents a small majority. In response, Fairfax stopped his advance at Uxbridge, 15 miles from London, on 25 June.[97]

Holles and the other ten Presbyterian leaders, however, returned to the Commons on 25 June to redouble their efforts to defeat the army, giving their party a majority again. The Commons then rejected the army's declaration, resolved to stand by the eleven Presbyterian leaders, and called for London's militia to defend Westminster.[98] These resolutions failed to bring together sufficient force to stop the army, while the army responded by tightening its quarters between Uxbridge and Westminster.

These moves again brought the House to its senses. The eleven members were given leaves of absence and parliament forbade any soldiers from leaving the army without Fairfax's permission. Fairfax also sent a letter to parliament listing the preconditions needed to prevent the army's further advance.[99]

For the next several weeks things settled down. Parliament again made Fairfax Commander of all forces, militia, and garrisons in England and reaffirmed its responsibility for the maintenance of the army. Fairfax used his authority to remove Sydenham Poyntz from command of the Northern Army, replacing him with John Lambert.[100] But the issue of how to settle the kingdom remained open and the Council of the Army decided to enter that debate with proposals of its own. These terms, known as *The Heads of the Proposals*, were authored in large part by Cromwell's son-in-law Henry Ireton. A delegation of officers presented them to the king at Royston on 23 July.

The Heads of the Proposals contained the most lenient terms offered to Charles I by anyone since his defeat in the first Civil War. They called for an end to the Long Parliament within a year and for biennial parliaments, whose duration were to be limited. The king was to retain the right to call parliament within 70 days of its mandated meeting time, and there was to be a redistribution of seats to equalize representation. Parliament was to be the final court of judicial appeal, and no one could be protected from the penalties of the law by the king's pardon. Parliament was to be given control over the military for ten years, at which time it would revert to royal authority. And parliament could not be prevented by the royal veto from providing the money to maintain the army and navy.[101]

The *Heads of the Proposals* offered relatively lenient treatment to those who had fought for Charles, barring them from office and voting for only five years. A council of state was to be selected by parliament to command the military and conduct foreign policy. Provisions were included to ensure that the army's material grievances were met and that it would be paid regularly. All proclamations made by the king against parliament, its treaties, and actions during the Civil War were to be annulled. Remarkably, the treaty offered to allow episcopacy to continue in England, as long as the Bishops had no coercive powers and the established Presbyterian church would tolerate 'tender consciences.'[102]

The army's proposal included some amazingly modern democratic ideas, to include equal electoral districts, protection of the citizen from arbitrary arrest, and freedom of conscience. These and the terms allowing for episcopacy especially incensed the Presbyterians, convinced as they were that such religious toleration would open a Pandora's box to papists, sectaries, and unlicensed preachers. So it was not surprising that the Presbyterians rejected the proposals. But the king also rejected them and treated the army's representatives in a rude and ill-considered manner.[103]

The army's attempt to settle the nation on its terms galvanized the Presbyterians to one more burst of counter-revolutionary activity, beginning about 20 July, just as the Council of the Army was debating its peace proposals. By 26 July mobs of Reformadoes and London apprentices had disrupted parliament, forcing most

Independents, including the speakers, to flee for their safety. This situation allowed the eleven excluded Presbyterian leaders to regain control of parliament and to pass ordinances repudiating its earlier conciliatory gestures to the army. They also appointed Edward Massey to command the London trained bands and ordered Fairfax to withdraw the army thirty miles from London.[104]

This coup was the last straw for the army. Fairfax ordered his regiments to march on London on 6 August. He rationalized this advance as necessary to restore to parliament those members who had been forced to flee their seats by the mobs on 30 July. The army responded in a united and determined fashion, entering London's defensive lines on 6 August, along with the Speakers of the Lords and Commons and many members of parliament. On 7 August, Fairfax marched the army through the heart of London with flags unfurled, match lit, and swords drawn. This demonstration of raw power succeeded in humbling the army's opponents and heartening its supporters.[105]

The army dominated London for the next eight months. For a brief period, an Independent majority in parliament annulled the anti-army measures taken from 26 July to 6 August 1647. The Houses renewed the assessment at the rate of £60,000 per month and put a great deal of pressure on Londoners to pay their arrears. In return, Fairfax reduced the army's presence in London to a 2,000-man garrison in the Tower of London and offered to select 6,000 foot and 2,000 horse for Irish service, just as soon as the soldiers' arrears were settled. During the fall and winter of 1647–8 England remained in a political limbo. The king refused to accept either the Newcastle Propositions or the *Heads of the Proposals*. While Fairfax and the Council of the Army demanded that he not be allowed to come to London, no one was able to make Charles believe that he would not succeed eventually in again dividing his enemies in Britain, allowing him to retrieve through intrigue what he had lost on the battlefield.

Notes

1 Clarendon, *History of the Rebellion*, iv: 691–2, 694–6, 719–27; D. Laing, ed., *Letters and Journals of Robert Baillie* (3 Vols., Edinburgh 1841–2) ii: 316–18, Public Letter, London, 14 October 1645.

2 Gardiner, *Civil War*, ii: 298–300; Wedgwood, *King's Peace*, 498.

3 P. Lenihan, *Catholic Confederates at War, 1641–49* (Cork, 2001), 89.

4 Laing, ed., *Letters and Journals*, ii: 289, Baillie to Dr. John Strang, 1 July 1645.

5 Abbott, i: 379–87.

6 Abbott, i: 395; Kenyon, *The Civil Wars of England*, 154.

7 Abbott, i: 395.

8 Gentles, *New Model Army*, 80.

9 Ibid., 82; Abbott, i: 396–7; Burne and Young, *The Great Civil War*, 221–2.

10 Gentles, *New Model Army*, 83; Gardiner, *Civil War*, iii: 58–69.

11 Abbott, i: 399.

12 Baillie, *Letters and Journals*, ii: 347–8, Baillie to David Dickson, 31 January 1646; Wedgwood, *King's War*, 468–9.

13 *A & O*, i: 789–96, for the 20 October 'Ordinance concerning Church Government'; For the Scottish reaction see Baillie, *Letters and Journals*, ii: 318–21, Baillie to George Young, October 1645.

14 Gardiner, *Civil War*, iii: 11–12; Baillie, *Letters and Journals*, ii: 328–9, Public Letter in London, 2 December 1645.

15 Gardiner, *Civil War*, iii: 9–12; K. Lindley, *Popular Politics and Religion in Civil War London* (Aldershot, 1997), 356–66, 379–82; Hexter, *Reappraisals in History*, 219–40.

16 Abbott, i: 377, Cromwell to William Lenthall, 14 September 1645.

17 Lindley, *Popular Politics*, 379–80.

18 Baillie, *Letters and Journals*, ii: 318, Public Letter in London, 14 October 1645.

19 Gardiner, *Civil War*, iii: 3–4.

20 Baillie, *Letters and Journals*, ii: 320, Baillie to George Young, October 1645; Gardiner, *Civil War*, iii: 1–2.

21 TT E292 (27), *The King's Cabinet Opened*, (14 July 1645), Charles to Henrietta Maria, 9 January 1645, for example.

22 Baillie, *Letters and Journals*, ii: 335–41, Baillie to Robert Ramsey, 15 January 1645.

23 TT E292 (27), *The King's Cabinet Opened*, (27 February 1645), Charles I to Ormond, 16–17; O' Siochru, *Confederate Ireland*, 87–90.

24 J. Lowe, 'Charles I and the Confederation of Kilkenny, 1643–9', *IHS* 11–14; J. Lowe, 'The Glamorgan Mission to Ireland', *Studia Hibernica* iv (1964), 155–62; O' Siochru, *Confederate Ireland*, 81–4; Corish in *NHI*, iii: 314–20.

25 Wheeler, *Cromwell in Ireland*, 20–5.

26 Bodl., Carte MS 14, fo. 317, 28 March 1645, Ormond to Charles I, for Duncannon; Carte MS 15, fo. 240, Lord Dillon to Ormond, 10 July 1645; ibid., fo. 536, Dillon to Ormond, 30 August 1645; Ibid., fo. 551, Dillon to Ormond, 30 August 1645; ibid., fo. 560, Dillon to Ormond, 1 September 1645.

27 Corish in *NHI*, 314; O' Siochru, *Confederate Ireland*, 88–91.

28 Lowe, 'The Glamorgan Mission', 160–1; Gardiner, *Civil War*, ii: 32–9.

29 Lowe, 'The Glamorgan Mission', 160–7; O' Siochru, *Confederate Ireland*, 92–4.

30 Lowe, 'The Glamorgan Mission', 166.

31 Carte, *Ormond*, vi: 305–6, Charles I to Ormond, 31 July 1645;

32 Lowe, 'The Glamorgan Mission', 164–7; O' Siochru, *Confederate Ireland*, 93–6.

33 Corish in *NHI*, 314, 319.

34 Ibid., 317.

35 Carte, *Ormond*, vi: 347–8, Charles I to Ormond, 31 January 1646.

36 Bodl., Carte MS 16, fo. 405, Ormond to Charles I, 9 January 1646; Corish in *NHI*, 318–9.

37 Bodl., Carte MS 16, fos. 516 and 617, Proclamations of the Committee for Ireland, 16 February 1646 and 3 March 1646; Carte MS 17, fo. 9, George Digby to Ormond, 26 March 1646.

38 Corish in *NHI*, 320–1.

39 Gardiner, *Civil War*, iii: 91–3; *CSPD, 1645–1647*, 469–70, 12 April 1646.

40 *CSPD, 1645–1647*, 188–90, Sir Robert Honeywood to Sir Henry Vane Sr, 13 October 1645; J. MacCormack, *Revolutionary Politics in the Long Parliament* (Cambridge, MA, 1973), 94; Gardiner, *Civil War*, iii: 19–24.

41 Ibid., 7, 26–9.

42 Lindley, *Popular Politics*, 379; MacCormack, *Revolutionary Politics*, 102–5; M. Kishlansky, *The Rise of the New Model Army* (Cambridge, 1979), 57–75, argues that the army was not highly politicized until after May 1646. Cromwell's handling of the king's letter to Ireton confirms the view that the army leadership did not yet see its role as arbiter of the political and religious settlements of the nation.

43 Quoted in Gardiner, *Civil War*, iii: 96–7; MacCormack, *Revolutionary Politics*, 105–8.

44 H. Cary, ed., *Memorials of the Great Civil War in England from 1642 to 1652* (London, 1842), i: 1–3, Ireton to Cromwell, 23 April 1646; Abbott, i: 401.

45 Gardiner, *Civil War*, iii: 99–100.

46 Baillie, *Letters and Journals*, ii: 370, Baillie to William Spang, 15 May 1646.

47 *JHC*, iv: 551.

48 Bodl., Carte MS 17, fo. 299, Scottish Proclamation, 5 May 1646.

49 Lindley, *Popular Politics*, 367, citing the 26 May 1646 'City Remonstrance.'

50 Gardiner, *Civil War*, iii: 115–17.

51 Gardiner, *Constitutional Documents*, 208–22.

52 Gardiner, *Civil War*, iii: 131–6.

53 Gardiner, *Constitutional Documents*, 223–4, 'The King's First Answer to the Propositions', 1 August 1646.

54 Baillie, *Letters and Journals*, ii: 378–9, Baillie to Glasgow, 14 July 1646; ibid., 388, Baillie to Henderson, 13 August 1646; D. Wilson, *The King and the Gentleman: Charles Stuart and Oliver Cromwell, 1599–1649* (New York, 1999), 352–4.

55 *A & O*, i: 848–51, 879–84; iii: xlviii.

56 *JHC*, iv: 654–6.

57 *JHC*, v: 13–15 for the final articles of agreement.

58 Baillie, *Letters and Journals*, ii: 402–5, Baillie to George Young, 13 October 1646; Gardiner, *Civil War*, ii: 165–73.

59 Gardiner, *Civil War*, iii: 178–81.

60 *JHC*, v: 91, 96, 98–101, 103, 104, 106–07.

61 Gardiner, *Civil War*, iii: 218–19.

62 *JHC*, v: 124–6.

63 Lindley, *Popular Politics*, 364–75 and 386–7 for the steady growth of Presbyterian political strength in London's government and in parliament from September 1646 to January 1647.

64 Gentles, *New Model Army*, 145–50; R. Ashton, *Counter Revolution: The Second Civil War and its Origins, 1646–8* (Yale, 1994), 159–66.

65 Bodl., Carte MS 18, fo. 557, Ormond to Clanricarde, 23 September 1646; ibid., fo. 604, Ormond to Charles I, 27 September 1646; ibid., fo. 658, Ormond's Notice to his garrisons; Carte MS 19, fo. 114, Ormond to Monro and the other Protestant commanders in Ulster, 9 October 1646; Carte MS 21, fo. 239, Ormond's agreement to surrender Dublin, 18 June 1647. He was to receive £10,877.

66 *JHC*, v: 136; Bodl., Carte MS 18, fos. 255–6, Account of Jones's August 1647 campaign; Carte MS 21, fo. 215, Resolution of Parliament, 15 June 1647.

67 Ashton, *Counter Revolution*, 43–80.

68 TT E383 (4), *The Petition of Colonels, Lieutenant Colonels … and Other Officers*, (27 March 1647), 2–7; Gentles, *New Model Army*, 148–50.

69 Cary, *Memorials*, i: 185–6, the Speaker of the Commons to Fairfax, 27 March 1647; ibid., 186–7, Fairfax to the Speaker, 30 March 1647.

70 *JHC*, v: 128.

71 TT E381 (13), *A Warning for all the Counties of England*, (27 March 1647), 2–5.

72 Ibid., 11.

73 *CSPD, 1645–1647*, 543, 'Declaration of Dislike', 30 March 1647; *JHC*, v: 138, 140–41, 144, 155, 158.

74 *The Weekly Account*, (24–30 March 1647), no pagination.

75 TT E383 (12), *The Petition of the Officers and Soldiers in the Army*, (2 April 1647); *The Kingdoms Weekly Intelligencer*, (23–30 March 1647), 472–3.

76 TT E383 (19), *The Petition and Vindication of the Officers of the Army*, (27 April 1647). It was presented on 30 April by a delegation led by Colonels Okey, Hewson, and Pride.

77 *A & O*, i: 924, 928; Ashton, *Counter Revolution*, 170–98.

78 *JHC*, v: 162.

79 TT E385 (15), *The Apologie of the Common Soldiers*, (3 May 1647), 7–8.

80 *JHC*, v: 173–4, 181.

81 *A & O*, i: 936, 938, 940.

82 Gentles, *New Model Army*, 157–64.

83 TT E390 (3), *A Perfect and True Copy of the Several Grievances of the Army*, (27 May 1647) Saffron Walden.

84 Cary, *Memorials*, i: 214–16, Cromwell, Ireton, Skippon, and Fleetwood to the Speaker of the House of Commons, 17 May 1647.

85 *JHC*, v: 183–4; TT E390 (2), *Votes of the Lords and Commons*, (27 May 1647), 2–6.

86 *A & O*, i: 938–40, 948; *JHC*, v: 190–92. I have drawn heavily on the following sources for my discussion of the army's revolt that follows below: Gentles, *New Model Army*, 165–90; Gardiner, *Civil War*, iii: 260–345; Kishlanksy, *Rise of the New Model Army*, 179–222; Ashton, *Counter Revolution*, 159–88.

87 TT E390 (4), *Propositions from Parliament to the King for Peace*. (27 May 1647); E390 (6), *A Declaration of the Lords and Commons … Concerning Disbandment*, (28 May 1647).

88 Cary, *Memorials*, i: 219, Fairfax to William Lenthall, 31 May 1647; 221–2, Rainsborough to William Lenthall, 1 June 1647.

89 Gentles, *New Model Army*, 169–72; TT E392 (10), *Letter from Lord Montagu to Parliament*, (10 June 1647). This includes a narrative of the discussion between Joyce and the king.

90 TT E392 (9), *The Solemn Engagement of the Army*, and *The Humble Representation of the Dissatisfactions of the Army*, (4–5 June 1647).

91 *JHC*, v: 203; TT E391 (6), *Petition of the Lord Mayor, Aldermen, … to the Commons*, (5 June 1647).

92 Gardiner, *Civil War*, iii: 285; *JHC*, v: 202.

93 *JHC*, v: 207; Gentles, *New Model Army*, 178.

94 *JHC*, v: 214–5. The vote to repudiate Holles and his associates was 165 to 104 in the Commons.

95 Gentles, *New Model Army*, 178–9.

96 *JHC*, v: 216, 219; Gardiner, *Civil War*, iii: 302.

97 TT E393 (18), *A Letter from T. Nichols to the Lord Mayor*, (21 June 1647); E394 (11), *Three Letters from … . Fairfax*, (28 June 1647); *JHC*, v: 247; Gentles, *New Model Army*, 179.

98 *JHC*, v: 223–4.

99 Ibid., 224–6; TT E394 (19), *The Propositions of His Excellency Sir Thomas Fairfax, … to Parliament*, (29 June 1647).

100 *JHC*, v: 226; Gardiner, *Civil War*, iii: 320–22.

101 Gardiner, ed., *Constitutional Documents*, 232–41, *The Heads of the Proposals*, 1 August 1647.

102 Ibid.

103 Gentles, *New Model Army*, 181–5; Gardiner, *Civil War*, iii: 329.

104 *JHC*, v: 252, 259–62.

105 Ibid., 268.

CHAPTER SEVEN

The defeat of the Irish Confederacy and the second English Civil War

The army's occupation of London did not settle the underlying political and religious questions that divided the nation. Temporarily, the soldiers' use of force restored an Independent majority to both houses of parliament, allowing the army's political allies to annul all ordinances passed since 26 July. However, it took them six tries to get this measure passed, even though two regiments were billeted in Whitehall and the Mews, menacingly close to parliament.[1] Independents in London also achieved mastery in the city's government, ending for a time the threat to the army from the London trained bands.

In spite of the Independents' victories in Westminster and London, the problems of how to settle the kingdom remained. Relations between the Scots and the triumphant Independents continued to deteriorate, while in Scotland the Covenanter movement split between those who favored a new agreement with the king and those who wished to remain loyal to the Solemn League and Covenant. As these developments unfolded, the situation in Ireland took a dramatic turn for the worst for both the Confederates and the royalists.

The struggle in Ireland: the rise and fall of Rinuccini, 1646–7

While the Presbyterians and Independents struggled for control of England, the Confederates in Ireland forfeited their chance to exploit the military superiority they had gained with O'Neill's victory at Benburb in June 1646. The Irish Catholics failed politically because factions within the Confederation refused to present a united front to their enemies. They failed militarily because their three army commanders would not cooperate against their enemies, and because two of those generals, Preston and Taaffe, allowed their armies to be destroyed in battle. These political and military failures took place from September 1646 to November 1647, while their enemies in Britain were distracted by their renewed struggles. The Catholic cause never fully recovered from its military defeats, nor did it ever again have such a good chance of success as it had in 1646.

In the summer of 1646, the papal nuncio Rinuccini defeated the efforts of the Ormondists in the Confederation to honor the peace they had signed with Ormond.

Rinuccini did this through the threats of excommunication and of military intervention in Leinster by Owen Roe O'Neill's army. Confederates like Thomas Preston, commander of the Leinster Army, were prevented from cooperating with Ormond because of the hold the clergy had over the majority of his army and the Irish population. Rinuccini used his power of excommunication to purge the Confederate Supreme Council, imprison his leading opponents, and become the head of a new council in September.

Because of the struggle between the Ormondists and the nuncioists in Kilkenny in 1646, O'Neill was diverted from his opportunity to drive the Scots out of Ulster. Whether or not he could have captured the Scottish garrisons in Ulster, the political struggle in the south was his rationale not to make a concerted effort in the north. In September, he used it as a reason to ignore the nuncio's urging to march against Ormond's garrisons in and near Dublin (see map 16).[2] The occupation of many Leinster towns by the Ulster army further increased the divisions within the Confederacy because the Leinster population resented the Ulstermen's exactions of lodging, food, and money.

After Rinuccini consolidated his position in Kilkenny, he urged O'Neill and Preston to launch a combined campaign to capture Dublin before Ormond could conclude negotiations for its surrender to the English parliamentarians. O'Neill and Preston refused to move until early October, by which time it was extremely difficult to maintain an army in the field for long. This delay was due to each general's unwill-ingness to obey the orders of the other, and because Preston was secretly negotiating with Ormond for an alliance against O'Neill and Rinuccini.[3]

When the campaign finally got underway, the two Catholic armies advanced on separate routes, capturing Ormond's outposts as they advanced. By 2 November, they were within twenty miles of Dublin with over 13,000 men, a force that Ormond could not possibly face in the field. By this time, any hope of Preston defecting to Ormond was gone because, as Preston observed to Ormond, 'the sharp sword of excommunication has so cut my power and means away that I have no forces to bring with me but a troop of horse.'[4]

Ormond's response was to play for time by conducting negotiations with Preston and O'Neill. For two weeks the Confederates remained motionless before offering Ormond terms that he certainly would never accept, to include the Catholic occupation of Dublin, Drogheda, and his other garrisons and the acceptance of Catholic worship in those places as 'free as in Paris.'[5] At the end of November, O'Neill placed his army in winter quarters, explaining to Rinuccini that his lack of supplies and of artillery prevented him from conducting a long siege of Dublin. Preston followed suit, ending the immediate threat to Ormond's control of Dublin.

Ormond knew that he could not maintain his position in Ireland without help from England, and such help could only come from the Westminster government. He decided that it was better to surrender Dublin to the Protestant parliament than to the Catholic Confederation, a decision he explained to Charles in a series of letters. Negotiations with the parliamentarians in England continued for the next three months before Ormond agreed to surrender his garrisons to parliament, on 6

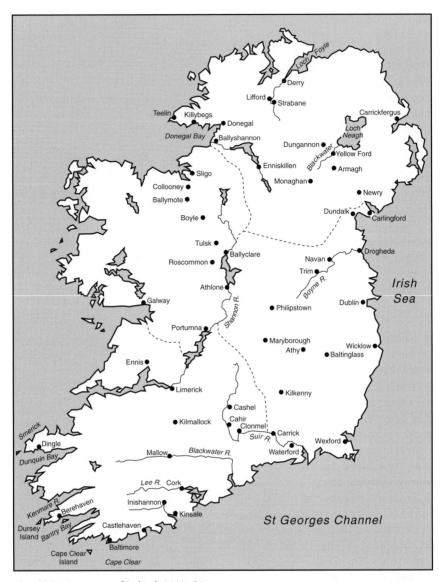

Map 16 Major towns of Ireland, 1641–54

February 1647. In exchange, the Committee of Both Kingdoms promised Ormond a safe conduct for himself, his family, and his closest followers to sanctuary on the continent and £13,000 to pay his debts.[6] With this agreement, the English parliament gained Dublin without firing a shot, providing it with a strategic base for the eventual conquest of Ireland.

The tide shifts against the Confederates,
June–November 1647

Although the English parliament was deeply involved in disputes with the New Model Army during much of 1647, it found the resources needed to send reinforcements and supplies to Dublin and to Lord Inchiquin in Munster. An infantry regiment arrived in Dublin from Chester in April 1647, followed by two more infantry and several cavalry regiments in early June. Michael Jones, who had demonstrated his tactical ability when he routed the king's forces near Chester, in the fall of 1645, commanded these soldiers. Jones, a member of a prominent Protestant family in Ireland, had served in the parliamentary armies in England since 1644, where he distinguished himself on a number of occasions. He now returned to Ireland to serve as the parliamentarian commander in Dublin.[7]

The military situation in Ireland underwent a major transformation when parliament reinforced the Protestant bridgeheads in Ireland and appointed three competent military commanders to lead the war against the Irish Catholics. In addition to Jones, who commanded in Leinster, George Monck, a talented professional soldier, was placed in command of all Protestant forces in Ulster except for Monro's Scots, while Murrough O'Brien, Lord Inchiquin, was confirmed as commander of the Munster Protestants. These men, ably assisted by the ruthless Sir Charles Coote in Connacht and western Ulster, seized the military initiative.

Owen Roe O'Neill, at the urging of Rinuccini, attempted to prevent the parliamentarians' offensive by launching a campaign against Sir Charles Coote's garrisons in northern Connacht, in June. But before he could reach Sligo, O'Neill's soldiers had exasperated the local population with their depredations, and stragglers from his regiments were being attacked in the countryside. Lacking supplies and a proper artillery siege train, O'Neill was unable to take Sligo and eventually retreated to western Leinster. The campaign accomplished nothing, demonstrating and exacerbating the disunity of the Catholic coalition. As O'Neill's biographer observed, 'irreconcilable differences now emerged among the Confederate Catholics.'[8] O'Neill's army would have been far better employed against Dublin, where Ormond was busy settling the terms for the city's transfer to parliament.

Ormond left Dublin with his entourage on 28 July, officially turning the Castle over to Jones. By 1 August, Jones was ready to take the field with 4,300 soldiers and seven cannon, hoping to recapture strongholds to the west of Dublin that O'Neill and Preston had taken the previous fall. He coordinated his offensive with the Protestants in Drogheda and southern Ulster, who joined his column, bringing his strength to 5,000 infantry and 1,500 cavalrymen by 6 August.[9] During the course of his campaign Jones captured six garrisons, including Trim, before turning back toward Dublin (see map 17). His success prompted Thomas Preston to maneuver his army toward Dublin in an attempt to cut Jones off from his headquarters.

Preston's move seemed to succeed, as he positioned his army near Trim, between Jones and Dublin. There Preston put his army of nearly 7,000 men into good defensive positions on a terrain feature known as Dungan's Hill. Jones, enlightened by his

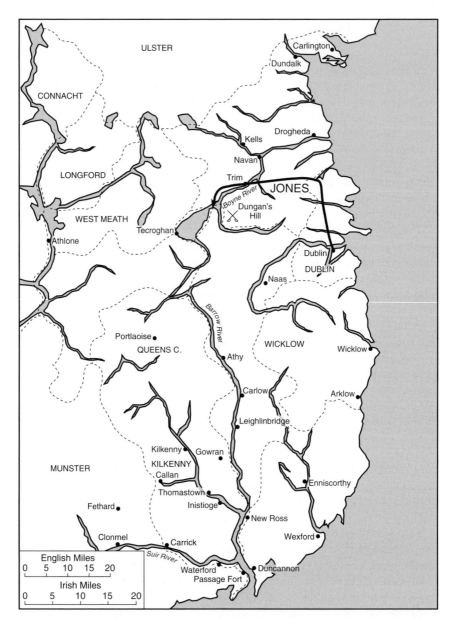

Map 17 Jones's Campaign in Leinster, August 1647

experiences in the English Civil War, where commanders had learned that wars are
won by destroying the enemies' armies rather than by fruitless maneuvers, saw his
opportunity to destroy the Leinster Army. On the morning of 8 August, Jones
deployed his army from Trimbleston to Dungan's Hill. Preston, whose cavalry was

176

outnumbered and badly outmatched by the English cavalry, stood his ground with his 1,000 horse divided on the wings and his infantry deployed in the center of his line.[10]

Jones, having seized the tactical initiative, deployed his seven field guns and infantry in front of Preston's positions and deployed his cavalry on the two wings, facing uphill toward the Irish. A first-hand account describes what followed:

> Under this hill was our army drawn up, the enemy cannon played hot at us, but with little success … About 12 [p.m.] … our two wings of horse, with some foot, having broken both wings of the enemy, our main body advanced and broke theirs. Which upon, about 3,000 of the rebels betaking themselves into a bog, they there drew up in a body, but Colonel Jones commanding the bog to be surrounded with horse and foot, our foot followed into the bog, where they put to the sword and not admitted [any] to quarter … Also put to the sword without mercy all formerly of our side, and all English, though never of our side.[11]

Jones captured Preston's papers, artillery, supplies, and nearly one hundred officers. Preston managed to escape, but Jones destroyed one of the best-trained Confederate armies at Dungan's Hill. The Protestants went on to capture other Catholic garrisons in central Leinster before returning to Dublin for fresh supplies, on 10 August. With the destruction of the Leinster Army, the Confederation was forced to rely more than ever on O'Neill's army for the defense of Kilkenny. With the movement of O'Neill's regiments to south central Ireland, the Confederate pressure on the British garrisons in Connacht and Ulster was relieved.

The annihilation of the Leinster Army was accompanied by the growth in the power of more moderate voices in the Confederate Supreme Council and General Assembly, weakening Rinuccini's position. While this political shift was underway, the Confederates were unable to reinforce their army in Munster in its efforts to face another offensive led by Inchiquin.

Inchiquin was one of the most capable commanders of the Irish wars. He had maintained Protestant enclaves in Munster with limited forces and minimal support from England for six years. He initially accepted the Ormond ceasefire with the Confederates in September 1643, but by July 1644 had switched sides, due to his intense anti-Catholicism and unwillingness to trust the Catholics in any deal made by Ormond or the king. For the next three years Inchiquin hung on precariously, receiving limited logistical support from England.

In July 1647, after receiving reinforcements and supplies, Inchiquin launched a major offensive. By September, while the Catholic Munster Army commanded by Theobald, Viscount Taaffe, stood aside, Inchiquin captured Duncannon, a fortress on the sea approaches to Waterford, and brutally sacked Cashel, where his men destroyed one of the most precious churches in Ireland.[12]

More bad news came to the Confederate Supreme Council in October, when Jones led 7,000 men against their garrisons in central Leinster. On 7 October he attacked Portlester, using artillery to destroy a tower in the defenses before launching his final assault. Most of the defenders were put to the sword, with only a small party able to escape to Athy.[13] Before returning to Dublin for supplies, on 17 October, Jones overran a number of Catholic strongholds, improving his defensive ring around Dublin. By this time, however, the turmoil in England significantly had decreased the flow of money and supplies from there to the garrisons in Ireland, preventing Jones and Inchiquin from exploiting their victories.

O'Neill, following his abortive campaign in Connacht, faced a series of mutinies in his army that prevented him from taking part in the August campaign against Jones. When Jones launched his October expedition, O'Neill still was unable to lead his men into the field. Finally, in early November, O'Neill found enough money to pay his soldiers and regain control. This allowed him to launch an offensive toward Dublin, hoping to recapture some of the places taken by Jones. O'Neill's move surprised Jones, allowing the Ulster general to lead 8,000 men to within seven miles of Dublin. He failed, however, to capture any significant Protestant garrisons, primarily due to his lack of siege artillery. When Jones recovered from his surprise, he attempted to bring O'Neill to battle, but O'Neill eluded him, retreating rather than give Jones another chance to destroy a Catholic army.[14]

While O'Neill was failing to make headway in Leinster, disaster befell the Confederate army in Munster, on 13 November. Taaffe, frustrated by his failure to prevent Inchiquin from rampaging through Confederate territory in September, took a stand against Inchiquin's army at a place called Knocknanuss, near Mallow in County Cork. Although Inchiquin's army of 5,000 men was slightly outnumbered by Taaffe, the Protestant cavalry completely outmatched the Confederate horse, allowing Inchiquin to destroy the two wings of the Confederate army, much as Jones had done at Dungan's Hill. Then Inchiquin used his artillery to goad the Irish infantry into attacking downhill against his foot. The

> rebels began … little by little, to descend from the top of the hill, and then the fight was very fierce, but lasted not long, for in half an hour they were routed and broken. And no quarter was given to the Irish rebels, nor to the Redshanks.[15]

From June to November, Jones and Inchiquin destroyed two major Catholic armies in Ireland, while Jones chased a third Irish army away from Dublin without a great deal of effort. The Confederates never recovered their former power due to the tremendous loss of officers and munitions suffered in the defeats at Dungan's Hill and Knocknanuss. Although sufficient manpower was found to fill the depleted ranks, the officers needed to train and lead those men in battle were not available in sufficient numbers. These military disasters also seriously weakened the political position of Rinuccini and his 'clerical' party, and convinced the Ormondists in the Confederation that their best hope of survival lay with an accommodation with Ormond. Thus, while the Scots and the English slid into another war in Britain, the Irish and the exiled royalists, led by the Queen and Ormond, sought a new alliance in Ireland.

The search for an English settlement, 1647–8

While the Irish situation was being transformed on the battlefields of Dungan's Hill and Knocknanuss, the English and the Scots continued to seek an acceptable political settlement in Britain. The greatest difficulty in this search was that Charles I was unwilling to accept any settlement that would satisfy his subjects' religious and political concerns. He rejected parliament's Newcastle Proposals in the spring, the army's Heads of the Proposals in the summer, and the Hampton Court Propositions in September.[16] As the struggle between Presbyterians and Independents intensified during the summer, Charles negotiated with both sides while also continuing talks with the Scots, Dutch, and French for military assistance.

After the army's occupation of London in August, the king gave up hope that the Presbyterians could restore him to power or that the Independents and the army would. Therefore, his approach to the Scots grew stronger. The Scots responded favorably to his overtures, although the Covenanter movement was badly split over whether or not to remain loyal to the Solemn League and Covenant. Argyll and a majority of the clergy were most concerned with the religious issues and remained reluctant to support Charles until he accepted and took the Covenant. They suspected that if the king won the struggle in England, the Presbyterian church there would not last long. They further reasoned that if Presbyterianism disappeared from England, it would not be long before the king would again try to impose episcopacy on Scotland. On the other hand, many Scots, like the Earls of Loudon, Lauderdale, and Lanark, favored an agreement with Charles I even without ironclad protection for Presbyterianism.[17]

There was growing support in Scotland for the view of the Earls, as many Scots feared the Independents more than the royalists. By late October, the Scots' Commissioners to the king were trying to get him to escape from Hampton Court, where he was held by the army, or to have him moved to London, where they felt he could rally English royalists and Presbyterians against the Independents and the army. Their only stipulation was that he sign the Covenant before receiving Scottish aid.

In the meantime, the failure to achieve a political settlement after the army coup in August 1647 frustrated many soldiers. Without a settlement, the threat from a resurgent royalism in Britain and Ireland made it necessary to maintain a large military establishment. However, without a reduction in the army's size and cost, popular support was difficult to muster to raise the taxes needed to pay the soldiers. The taking of free quarter by the troops undermined support for the army, while embittering the soldiers against the parliamentary Presbyterians. The army became a fertile seedbed for political agitation by the Levellers, who hoped to use the army to achieve their political and social revolution.

By October 1647, the leading Levellers, John Lilburne, William Walwyn, Richard Overton, and John Wildman, were working to infiltrate the army with Leveller ideas and sympathizers. They were remarkably successful, even gaining the support of several senior officers, such as Colonel Thomas Rainborowe.[18] After the king rejected the army's peace terms, known as the *Heads of the Proposals*, the Levellers produced two powerful pieces of propaganda. The first was *The Case of the Army Truly Stated*, an attack aimed at the army 'grandees', such as Cromwell and Henry Ireton, for their attempts to come to terms with Charles I. This polemic struck a cord with those soldiers who believed that the king was 'a man of blood' who should be brought to justice for leading his peoples to war, and who, therefore, should not be restored to his throne by the generals.

The second work was *An Agreement of the People*, which called for 'a firm and present peace upon the grounds of common-right and freedom.' This pamphlet proposed a political settlement based on a written constitution that carefully reserved certain powers that the people did not grant to their government. It affirmed the sovereignty of the people and advocated religious toleration and significant electoral reform.[19] Together, the *Case of the Army* and *An Agreement of the People* challenged the Independents and the Presbyterians and threatened to undermine Fairfax's and Cromwell's hold on the army.[20] In response, Fairfax ordered the General Council of the Army to meet in Putney in early November to reconcile the various declarations of the army and to discuss the Levellers' proposals.

During the fall, a number of regiments elected Levellers to serve as their representatives to the General Council. These Levellers made the Putney Debates lively and easily held their own in the debates over a political settlement with Cromwell and his son-in-law Ireton. In fact Ireton's lengthy defense of the connection between property ownership and the right to vote strengthened the Levellers' arguments in favor of popular sovereignty. In the end, Fairfax and Cromwell ended the debates by ordering the regimental representatives back to their units. To placate the men, Fairfax had his staff prepare a 'remonstrance' for presentation to parliament, asking for increased taxation and adequate pay for the soldiers in exchange for the ending of free quarter. Fairfax succeeded in ending the Putney Debates without resorting to force, due in large part to his immense stature in the army and to the growing concern by many soldiers that the Levellers threatened the army's unity.[21]

Fairfax also ordered three rendezvous of the army to be held so that he could defuse the Leveller propaganda by explaining to the soldiers the steps he was taking to get parliament to resolve their material difficulties. This move signaled the rejection of the Leveller program by the generals. The three separate gatherings of the regiments prevented the Levellers from provoking a massive demonstration of the army at a single rendezvous, while increasing the effect of Fairfax's presence.

In response to the order to hold three musters rather than one, the Levellers organized demonstrations against the Lord General's decision. Fairfax and Cromwell put down the most dangerous of these mutinies, in Robert Lilburne's regiment, at the rendezvous on Corkbush Field, on 15 November. When Lilburne's soldiers refused to remove the Leveller symbols of sea-green ribbons and the *Agreement of the People* from their hats, Cromwell rode into their ranks with sword drawn, intimidating the men and pulling the papers out of their hatbands. Most of the soldiers responded by reaffirming their obedience to their officers, allowing Fairfax to have the ringleaders arrested and court martialled on the spot. He pardoned all but three, ordering those three to draw lots to see who would be executed. Richard Arnold lost the draw and was shot by two of his fellow mutineers before sunset.[22]

Over the next few days Fairfax talked to most of the army's rank and file at the musters. By 18 November, he had restored order and discipline in the regiments, although he and Cromwell recognized that the Levellers had come close to shattering the army's unity, and perhaps to taking it over altogether. The Lord General realized that he needed to solve the soldiers' material problems of pay and sustenance while also purging royalists and Levellers from the ranks. The remonstrance to parliament was the first step. This outlined a plan to settle the army and the kingdom. It included demands for constant pay, the audit of pay accounts, indemnity from prosecution for wartime acts, and provisions for maimed soldiers, widows, and orphans. It also called for a time limit to the current parliament, regular parliaments thereafter, and electoral reform.[23]

Parliament responded by sending a letter to Fairfax promising him that it would 'give satisfaction to the army, in point of their arrears, future constant pay, and for a present month's pay.' Money was rushed to Windsor to pay the troops a month's wages, and pressure was put on London to collect £50,000 of its assessment arrears as quickly as possible.[24] In the longer term, parliament passed ordinances in late December designed to provide money for the army's arrears and the current pay. It also provided for the care of widows, orphans and maimed soldiers, and set the rate for free quarter reimbursement at 4d per day.[25] This last measure simplified the business of determining how much to deduct from the soldiers' arrears for free quarter taken in the past, allowing the balance due to be determined. Once that was done, the soldiers could be issued debentures for future repayment, secured by excise receipts and the proceeds of the sale of the Bishops' lands.[26]

Fairfax energetically set about the process of disbanding units no longer needed. Between January and March 1648, he released 20,000 of the 44,000 soldiers in England from active duty. The demobilized men received two months of their arrears in cash and debentures for the balance. The units selected for disbandment were those that had not been part of the original New Model Army. Most soldiers who had joined the army since 26 July were demobilized as well, eliminating many royalists, Levellers, and Presbyterian sympathizers from the army. By March, the army consisted of one dragoon, fourteen cavalry, and seventeen infantry regiments, composed of 24,000 men. 'It was a leaner, more politically homogeneous, and less costly body of men.'[27] For these reasons, the army was an organization suitable for its coming trials. In return, parliament found the money to pay the army fairly regularly until at least June, greatly easing Fairfax's challenges in maintaining discipline and disbanding unnecessary units.[28]

Scotland prepares for war against England

While Fairfax was ending the Putney Debates and preparing to hold the rendezvous, Charles I escaped from Hampton Court, on 11 November. He did so in part because he feared more radical elements in the army would win the struggle for power within the army. He decided to throw in his lot with the Scots and to move to a place on the coast from where he could sail either north or to France. The king reached the Isle of Wight by 14 November, where he asked Colonel Robert Hammond for protection in Carisbrooke Castle. He would remain there as a prisoner for the next twelve months.

Scottish commissioners joined Charles in Carisbrooke and negotiated the 'Engagement', which was signed on 26 and 27 December 1647. The Scots promised to restore the king to his throne. In exchange Charles promised to 'confirm' the Solemn League and Covenant, to integrate Scots into the English Privy Council, and to open free trade between the two kingdoms. Charles was not required to take the Covenant, nor was anyone else required to do so. Although Presbyterianism would be continued experimentally in England for three years, at the end of that time the Assembly of Divines, reinforced by twenty clerics chosen by the king, would recommend to the king and parliament a permanent English religious settlement.[29]

The Engagement was tantamount to a declaration of war by Charles and the Scots against parliament and the army. The king's attempt to escape from Carisbrooke Castle on 28–29 December made this even clearer. In response, the House of Commons passed a 'Vote of No Addresses' and ordered the dissolution of the Committee of Both Kingdoms. The Lords resisted the Vote of No Addresses until 17 January, when it gave in under pressure from the army, which menacingly had increased the guard around Westminster Hall.[30]

The Scots remained divided over whether or not to accept the Engagement, even after the English abolished the Committee of Both Kingdoms. Opposition centered in the assembly of the Kirk, where a majority of the clergy felt it unacceptable that the king was not required to take the Covenant or to establish a Presbyterian church permanently in England. But the majority of the Scottish parliament that met in late January and a majority of the Committee of Estates favored an alliance with Charles and therefore a war against England.[31]

Argyll was soundly defeated in the debates in the Scottish parliament and the Committee of Estates by a coalition of nobles and lairds led by Hamilton. As Baillie observed, 'never so many noblemen [were] present in any of our parliaments … among whom were found but eight or nine for our way … All the rest and almost half the burghers … ran in a string after duke Hamilton's vote.'[32] By early spring the Scots, led by the Engagers (those Scots willing to sign a treaty with the King), were preparing for war. Scotland, however, remained badly divided, with prominent soldiers such as the Earl of Leven and David Leslie refusing to lead an army against their former allies in a war to restore the man who thrice had tried to destroy the Covenanters.[33]

The outbreak of the second Civil War and the third Anglo-Scots war

In England, Fairfax and Cromwell worked to restore unity to the army, forge political alliances with as many Presbyterians as possible, and prevent royalist uprisings. They did all of this while disbanding supernumerary regiments.

Remarkably, most of the soldiers accepted their disbandment with two months' arrears and went home peacefully. Only in Wales did some soldiers refuse to submit to Fairfax's orders. This armed resistance to the army and parliament commenced on 24 March 1648, when Colonel John Poyer and Major General Rowland Laugharne refused to disband their troops or to surrender Pembroke Castle, then garrisoned by Poyer's regiment.

In response to Laugharne's uprising, Fairfax ordered Colonel Thomas Horton to gather four loyal regiments and march to Pembroke. Horton did so, but approached the mutineers cautiously, knowing that their army outnumbered his, having been reinforced by local royalists. By 1 May, the Committee of Safety, which had replaced the Committee of Both Kingdoms, was concerned enough to order Fairfax to send additional troops west. This he did by ordering Cromwell to march to Pembroke with five regiments. Before Cromwell arrived, however, Laugharne forced a battle against Horton's army at St Fagan's, Wales, resulting in a resounding defeat for the mutineers.[34]

Horton's defeat of Laugharne on 8 May, although he was outnumbered three to one, demonstrated the power of the New Model Army and deterred some royalists from rising. None the less, royalist agents were active throughout England preparing what they hoped would be a coordinated uprising to accompany a Scottish invasion of England. A strong desire for a return to normality and a growing sense of alienation by local gentry against the centralizing activities of the Westminster government aided them in their attempts to ignite a rising against parliament. Parliament's centralizing and disruptive activities were symbolized by the county committees, which the parliamentarians used to collect taxes, enforce laws, and punish royalist delinquents from the first Civil War. The continued taking of free quarter by the army exacerbated this sense of anger, alienation, and frustration in the provinces and provided fuel for the royalist conspirators to use in their efforts. Significant royalist sentiment persisted in many counties as well, providing an ideology around which those discontented with the state of the country in 1648 could gather.[35]

Anti-parliamentarian conflagrations were not long in coming. In April, townsmen in Norwich rose against soldiers sent to arrest their mayor and seized the armory. Troops from Fleetwood's regiment crushed the uprising with difficulty, aided by an accidental explosion in the magazine that killed forty protesters. Disturbances took place in Suffolk, Nottingham, Leicester, Huntingdon, Rutland, Sussex, Surrey, Hampshire, and a number of other places in April and May, showing parliament and the army the breadth of feeling against them. The most dangerous of these disturbances were the London riots, the army revolt and royalist rising in Wales, and a rising in Kent that soon spread to Essex.[36]

Amidst the crescendo of reports of local royalist risings, parliament received word on 11 April that the Scottish parliament had declared that the Solemn League and Covenant was no longer in effect. On 18 April, the Scots selected the field officers for an army of 30,000 men that the Edinburgh parliament had ordered to be raised. On 3 May, the Scottish Committee of Estates, dominated by Hamilton and Scottish royalists, sent a letter to Westminster demanding that the English parliament establish

Presbyterianism in England, allow the king to travel to London to negotiate a settlement, to abolish the New Model Army, and to suppress religious schismatics, heretics,
and Independents. The Scots expected a response within fifteen days.[37]

At this critical juncture of provincial revolts, army mutiny, and Scottish threats, it
was essential for the Independents and the army to prevent the Presbyterians in
London and parliament from joining the royalists and Scots. Their concerns were
well founded. On 2 April, London apprentices gathered in Moorfields to protest.
When the trained bands tried to disperse the crowd, the apprentices attacked and
disarmed the militiamen and started to march toward Whitehall, where they hoped
to eject Colonel John Barkstead's regiment from its billets. Surprised by this move,
Fairfax and Cromwell decided to disperse the mob. Cromwell led several hundred
cavalrymen against the apprentices, and 'fell upon them, killed him who carried the
colors, and one or two more were slain, and divers of them cut and hacked by the
troopers, whereupon they soon fled and were dissipated [dispersed].'[38]

After driving the apprentices back into London, 'the troopers followed them and
cleared the streets.' But 'the rude rabble were again met, and had secured Ludgate
and Newgate' and attacked the mayor's house, driving away his guards. Briefly, it
appeared as if the mob would be able to seize control of the city if it could secure the
armories. Fairfax, however, ordered Barkstead's infantry regiment to move from
Whitehall into the city through the Mooregate to reinforce Cromwell's cavalry.
Once inside, Barkstead's men 'overtook a great part of the rabble as they were going
to seize upon some magazines in Leadenhall, fell upon them in Gracious Street,
[and] charged them.' The soldiers killed eight rioters and wounded many more,
with no losses to themselves. 'After this, they [the apprentices] were driven like sheep
into Leadenhall, the chief of them [taken] prisoners', and the horse and foot soldiers
cleared the streets.[39]

This was a dangerous affair, showing that it would be hard to keep London
occupied unless considerable forces were committed to its garrison, and the army
needed all of its regiments elsewhere. Consequently, encouraged by Cromwell and
Henry Vane, the Independents in the Commons made several important concessions
to the Presbyterians to keep the city quiet. On 27 April the Commons entrusted
command of the London trained bands and of all troops 'within the lines of
communication' to Philip Skippon, a man who enjoyed the confidence of most
Presbyterians. The next day, the House voted 165 to 99 to promise 'not to alter the
fundamental government of the kingdom by King, Lords, and Commons.' This
motion passed the Lords on 6 May, when both Houses annulled the Vote of No
Addresses and resolved that any member could approach the king to discuss a treaty
and that the terms proposed to Charles at Hampton Court were an acceptable basis
for an agreement.[40] Finally, the Independents dropped all efforts to punish the
Presbyterian leaders from the previous summer's struggle, allowing them to return
to the Commons.

These concessions played a crucial role in keeping most Londoners from joining
the revolts in Kent and Essex. Equally important, the parliamentary Presbyterians
realized that if the royalists won the second Civil War, they would be swept away

with the Independents and the army. The London Presbyterians were appalled that the Scots had allied with the royalists and signed the Engagement with the king, even though he had refused to take the Covenant or maintain Presbyterianism in England.[41] Assured that control of the city's militia was in their hands, and given hope that a settlement might be reached with the king, most of the parliamentary Presbyterians supported the renewed war effort.

In the midst of their trials and tribulations many army officers and regimental agitators gathered in Windsor Castle, on 29 April, to seek God's judgment and guidance for the coming campaign. By the third day, the soldiers were deep in open prayer, asking God where they had gone wrong and how they should proceed. Their conclusions as to the Lord's judgment and will were not surprising. They were in their perilous situation because they had attempted to come to an agreement with 'Charles Stuart, that man of blood', and now they must 'go out and fight against those potent enemies … with an humble confidence in the name of the Lord only.' If they were victorious, it was their duty to call the king 'to an account for the blood he had shed, and mischief he had done to his utmost, against the Lord's cause and people in these poor nations.'[42]

The Windsor conclave broke up on 2 May, as Fairfax set in motion the war machine to crush the royalists and defeat the expected Scottish invasion. Cromwell marched to Wales with 6,500 men to recapture Pembroke and extinguish Poyer's and Laugharne's revolt. Fairfax prepared to lead most of the army north, where royalists led by Sir Marmaduke Langdale and Sir Philip Musgrave had just seized Berwick and Carlisle, providing the Scots with bases for the invasion of England. Before Fairfax was able to start north, however, a royalist revolt erupted in Kent, threatening that county, and worse, London.

The Kent royalists had planned to start their uprising after a Scottish invasion had drawn the bulk of the army away from London. Things, however, got out of hands when disturbances in Canterbury blossomed into a full scale popular rising by 21 May. By the end of the month as many as 11,000 men had joined the revolt and had seized control of Rochester, Sandwich, Deptford, and Canterbury. The rebels besieged the parliamentarian garrison in Dover and threatened the approaches to Southwark as well. On top of this, Fairfax and the Committee of Safety learned that most of the navy's crews in the Downs had mutinied and joined the rebellion, on 27 May.[43]

Fairfax mustered seven regiments at Blackheath, south of the Thames, on 30 May. These included regiments that had garrisoned Westminster and the Tower, leaving London in the hands of Skippon and the recently reconciled Presbyterians in the common council. Fairfax's approach caused a number of the protesters to return home, but about 10,000 men remained in arms, spread out in groups from Rochester to Dover. Taking advantage of his soldiers' march discipline and speed, Fairfax sent columns to secure his army's rear at Croydon and the river crossing at Gravesend, and another force to Dover to relieve the siege. With the remainder of his army, now reinforced by loyal militia, Fairfax approached the main body of about 7,000 royalists gathered on Penenden Heath, south of Rochester near Maidstone.

By the evening of 31 May, Fairfax had reached Malling, a few miles west of Maidstone, where a garrison of about 2,000 royalists blocked his route east.[44]

Fairfax maneuvered south of Maidstone on 1 June, crossing the Medway at Farleigh Bridge and reaching the edge of the town around 7 p.m. Recognizing that the royalists had prepared Maidstone for a strong defense, he decided to wait until the next morning before launching a coordinated assault. His advance guard, however, got too close to the town and started a battle. Fighting continued into the night as royalist reinforcements arrived and Fairfax judiciously fed reserves into the battle. After fighting from barricade to barricade, the army veterans eventually overcame the stubborn resistance, securing the center of Maidstone at about 1 a.m. on 2 June.[45]

Most of the royalist army remained on Penenden Heath, where the Earl of Norwich had assumed command by virtue of a commission from the Queen. Seeing the outcome of the battle, Norwich decided to lead his army north, to London if possible, or across the Thames into Essex if the way to the capital was blocked. Skippon and Fairfax anticipated Norwich's move and closed the direct approach to London by fortifying London Bridge and removing all boats from the south side of the Thames. These moves forced the Kent royalists who desired to continue the struggle to retreat into Surrey or cross the lower Thames, which many did in small boats, swimming their horses alongside. Norwich, in the meantime, crossed to Chelmsford ahead of his army, seeking a meeting with the Essex royalists who had just revolted.[46]

Fairfax sent Colonel Edward Whalley with his cavalry regiment in pursuit of Norwich, while he remained in Kent with most of his infantry to snuff out the remaining embers of revolt. Through a mix of judicious conciliation and brute force, Fairfax restored parliamentary control, allowing him to move his army across the Thames at the bridge near Tilbury Fort, and into Essex by 11 June.[47] Norwich, meanwhile, had united with the Essex royalists led by Sir Charles Lucas and Lord Arthur Capel, increasing his strength to over 5,000 men. While this was happening, Skippon managed to keep London under control, although there was a great deal of sympathy for the revolts and many London royalists left the city to join Norwich in Essex.

Cromwell in Wales

In early May, while Fairfax was still planning to march north to meet the anticipated Scottish invasion, Cromwell set out for southern Wales to join Colonel Horton in Pembrokeshire, the center of royalist activity in Wales. On 8 May he reviewed his troops at Gloucester, talking to each regiment to inform the soldiers of the nature and purpose of their mission. He declared 'that he had often times ventured his life with them and they with him, against the common enemy of this kingdom, and a far more potent power and strength than now they are to engage withal; … [and] for his part, he protested to live and die with them.' The soldiers responded enthusiastically, vowing 'that they would venture their lives and fortunes under his conduct and command against any enemy either foreign or domestic.'[48]

With this ceremony complete, Cromwell set out for Wales. On 10 May he learned of Horton's victory at St Fagan's. This meant that Cromwell's task in Wales would be to mop up the remaining royalist strongholds at Pembroke, Chepstow, and Tenby. By 16 May, he was requesting that ammunition and siege artillery be sent to Wales for the bombardment of those three strong fortifications. He also sent part of his cavalry to Cheshire and north Wales to reinforce efforts being made to overawe royalist sympathizers and prevent additional uprisings.[49]

While Cromwell was advancing toward Pembroke, the royalist plot to deploy military forces against parliament in all three Stuart kingdoms was gathering steam. Hamilton was at the head of the Scottish Engagers and was levying an army for the invasion of England. Ormond was traveling from France to Ireland where he hoped to create a coalition of Confederates, Scots, and royalists to drive Jones out of Dublin. The Prince of Wales was preparing to take command of the ships that had mutinied against parliament and use them to blockade London. And the royalist risings in Kent and Essex were soon to erupt, preventing Fairfax from marching north to meet the Scots. Cromwell needed to reduce the Welsh royalists quickly so that he could reinforce Major General John Lambert in the north, where Fairfax had sent him to face the Scots and northern royalists.

When Cromwell arrived in Cardiff he dealt with the prisoners captured by Horton. To set an example and deter future risings, he had two royalists shot because they had violated their parole from the last war, and he sold 240 royalists to entrepreneurs who shipped these poor unfortunates to Barbados to work on the plantations. He then continued his march west, reaching Pembroke on 24 May. At the same time, he sent Horton to capture Tenby Castle. Within a week, both Tenby and Chepstow Castles surrendered, leaving only Pembroke to tie down the parliamentary forces.[50]

Colonel Poyer and as many as 2,000 soldiers defended Pembroke's old, but massive, walls. Although on short rations, Poyer's men were veterans of the first Civil War and mutineers, and they knew that they could expect little mercy from their besiegers. After launching an assault on 4 June, which was repulsed, Cromwell realized that the defenses had to be breached with artillery fire before a successful assault could be launched. Therefore, he had to wait for the arrival of the siege artillery.[51] The siege guns did not arrive until 4 July, after a series of mishaps, including the sinking of the vessel carrying them in the mouth of the Severn River. Adding to his difficulties, Cromwell's troops were short of money and food, and were kept busy repulsing sorties by Poyer's garrison and in suppressing minor insurrections in the surrounding county.[52]

Poyer could not hold out indefinitely due to food and ammunition shortages, but he gave a good account of himself before deciding to surrender on 11 July. By then, Cromwell's cannon were in action and Cromwell had made it clear that when a breach was made and the assault launched, there would be no quarter. As Cromwell wrote to Poyer, 'I know where to charge the blood you spill.'[53] Poyer and Laugharne surrendered to the mercy of parliament, and their officers promised to leave the kingdom for two years. The common soldiers were allowed to return to their homes and the property and persons in the town were protected from a sack. These generous terms expedited the surrender, allowing Cromwell to set off for the north to join Lambert.[54]

The royalist uprising in Essex

While Cromwell was operating in the west, Fairfax followed the Earl of Norwich into Essex. After his quick success in crushing organized resistance in Kent, Fairfax hoped to make quick work of the Essex royalists and then march north to join Lambert. This was not to be, due to the difficulties Fairfax encountered in Essex.

The Essex rising, like that in Kent, was dangerous because, if successful, it would give the royalists a position close to London. Then, if the Prince of Wales arrived with reinforcements from Holland, London itself could be attacked, in conjunction with another uprising in the City. Recognizing these dangers, Fairfax stripped London of all New Model Army regiments, leaving the city in the hands of the city's Presbyterians and the trained bands under Philip Skippon's command.[55]

In early June, when the Earl of Norwich arrived in Essex with the remnant of the royalist forces from Kent, he found that the county committee had been seized by royalists at Chelmsford, and that Sir Charles Lucas, an Essex native, had rallied many of the county trained bands to the king's cause.[56] On 9 June, Norwich's and Lucas's troops united at Chelmsford, watched at a discrete distance by Colonel Edward Whalley's parliamentary cavalry. Knowing that Fairfax had crossed the Thames and was advancing toward them, the royalists decided to retreat to Colchester where the Lucas family enjoyed influence and where they hoped to receive reinforcements from the royalist navy. Over the next three days, they eluded Whalley by marching north and then turning in the night toward Colchester, where they arrived on 12 June.[57]

Although initially confused by the royalists' ploy, Fairfax determined their destination and ordered his army to concentrate at Colchester. After a grueling forty-eight hour forced-march, covering fifty miles, Barkstead's infantry brigade joined Fairfax and his cavalry just west of the town, on the evening of 12 June. The next day, reinforced by the Suffolk trained bands, Fairfax decided to attack the royalist army, which Lucas had drawn up in formation on the London Road, outside the city's western wall. Fairfax assumed his veterans would crush the Essex royalists.

The Battle of Colchester proved one of Fairfax's toughest fights. Lucas's infantry withstood three determined attacks by Barkstead's infantry brigade, and were only forced to retreat after the parliamentary cavalry on the right defeated the outnumbered royalist horse opposite them and turned the flank of the Cavalier infantry. Even then, a rout did not ensue, as Lucas and Lord Capel kept their infantry under control in an orderly withdrawal into the city. At that point Barkstead urged his infantry forward, through the open gates, close on the heels of the royalists. His men responded enthusiastically, unwittingly walking into a trap set by Lucas. Once Barkstead's men were in the town, Lucas's men attacked them from two directions, driving them out of the town with heavy casualties.[58]

After this costly setback, Fairfax recognized that he could not afford to risk his regiments in further assaults against the strongly defended town. Therefore, on 14 June, he ordered his army to begin the laborious process of establishing positions around Colchester to cut the town off from supplies and reinforcements. This process took weeks to accomplish, exposing Fairfax's troops to disease and hardship not much dissimilar to that suffered by the defenders. Ultimately, the siege lasted eleven weeks. By its end, the town was completely isolated and the royalist cavalrymen in the town had slaughtered their horses to feed the garrison. Fairfax refused to let civilians leave the town, forcing Lucas to feed the population.[59]

The royalists in Colchester resisted until there was no hope of relief. By 19 August, with the Scots nowhere in sight, and the Prince of Wales unable to get reinforcements and supplies through the ring of parliamentary garrisons blocking the sea approaches to Colchester, Lucas and Norwich decided to negotiate with Fairfax. Fairfax responded by offering to allow soldiers below the rank of captain, who had not served in the parliamentary army since 9 May, to return peacefully to their homes. All captains and above were 'to submit to mercy.'[60]

Lucas and Norwich rejected these terms and prepared to lead a sortie against the parliamentary positions on the north side of the town, hoping to escape with part of their army. Most royalist soldiers refused to take part in the operation, and some 'soldiers got to the gates and said they would kill their officers if they offered to stir out, and so continued in an high mutiny.'[61] With starvation and mutiny facing them, the royalist leaders accepted Fairfax's terms, on 27 August, ending the bitterest siege in England during the 1640s. The officers surrendered at mercy, and the common soldiers accepted quarter. Fairfax promised the townsmen protection from plunder, but required them to pay a large fine to his army.[62]

After the surrender, Fairfax and his council of war tried Lucas, Sir George Lisle, and Sir Bernard Gascoigne for their roles in the uprising. They found them guilty and sentenced them to be shot. Fairfax spared Gascoigne. Lucas and Lisle, however, had surrendered to the parliamentary army in the first Civil War, promising never again to take up arms against parliament again. They had broken their parole and by the rules of war could be executed. Lucas also was accused of having put 'twenty to forty' parliamentary soldiers to death in cold blood at Stinchcombe, Gloucester in the previous war. Fairfax played an instrumental role in the decision to execute Lucas and Lisle, although his council of officers and parliament supported his decision whole-heartedly. Parliament demonstrated this when it later ordered Lord Capel's execution.[63]

The fall of Colchester ended the Essex revolt and the threat to London. Fairfax was not required to lead his army north after the grueling siege because Cromwell eradicated the Scottish threat to the parliamentarian regime with his stunning victory at Preston, on 17 August.

The Preston Campaign and end of the second Civil War

The Scots invaded England on 8 July 1648. Instead of an army of 30,000 men, as Hamilton and the Engagers had hoped to levy, Hamilton and his Lieutenant General Callander entered England with about 10,000 soldiers. Their invasion had been delayed by their need to suppress an anti-Engager revolt in Clydesdale, and by the refusal of many Scots to pay their taxes. Neither Hamilton nor Callander was a competent commander, and most of the senior officers who had led the Covenanter armies to victory in the previous war refused to serve. The troops were inadequately clothed and equipped. They lacked a steady food supply, forcing them to take free quarter from the people they had supposedly come to free from the English parliament.[64]

Hamilton invaded England along the western side of the border, near Carlisle, rather than to march along the east coast through Berwick, Newcastle, and Durham. He expected to be reinforced by 3,000 Scottish veterans from Ulster, led by Sir George Monro, and by 3,000 English royalists led by Sir Marmaduke Langdale. After lingering in Carlisle for eight days, where Langdale joined him, Hamilton advanced to Kirby Thore, where he waited for Monro and a shipment of arms from France. When ships arrived from France they carried a few arms and no money.

By 2 August, the Scots had reached Kendal, where Hamilton again stopped to wait for his artillery train and additional horses from Scotland. This pause allowed Lambert to fall back from Lancashire into a pass into Yorkshire, to the east along the valley of the Aire, and for Cromwell to move his army from Wales to join Lambert.

Cromwell had started north from Pembroke on 15 July. He sent his cavalry ahead to reinforce Lambert, while he marched with his infantry. His advance was slowed by the miserable condition of his soldiers' footwear and the shortage of money needed to buy provisions along the way. On 24 July he was near Gloucester, from where he wrote to the Committee of Safety at Derby House, pleading for money and shoes. The committee responded swiftly, ordering 3,000 pairs of shoes and stockings to be gathered in Leicester, where Cromwell arrived on 1 August.[65]

By then it was clear that Hamilton was moving through Lancashire, and that Lambert would be able to hold the route between there and Yorkshire open for Cromwell (see map 18). A few days later, on 4 August, Cromwell ordered Lambert to refrain from engaging the enemy before he arrived with his infantry, indicating that Cromwell planned to join Lambert and then strike west across the mountains into the flank of Hamilton's force.[66] Cromwell might now cut off Hamilton's forces from Scotland. As he advanced, Cromwell gathered regiments of trained bands, raising his force to about 5,000 men, while Lambert commanded as many as 9,000. Hamilton's total strength probably was close to 20,000 soldiers, strengthened by the arrival of Monro's troops from Ireland.[67]

Hamilton's army was torn by discord and hampered by supply shortages. Monro refused to accept the orders of Callander, the second-in-command, and Hamilton did little to coordinate operations with Langdale. By mid-August, the royalists were stretched along a route twenty miles long, between Lancaster and Wigan, with the town of Preston on the Ribble River in the center of the column. These deployments gave Cromwell a remarkable opportunity. By 11 August, he was at Leeds, where he and Lambert planned their next moves. On his march to Leeds, Cromwell stopped briefly at Pontefract, where a royalist garrison was holding out against several veteran army regiments. Cromwell took the opportunity to exchange his militia for the veterans, giving him much greater hitting power to use against Hamilton.[68]

The next day, Lambert and Cromwell united and were joined by the artillery train from Hull. After sending the artillery to Knaresborough, from where it could

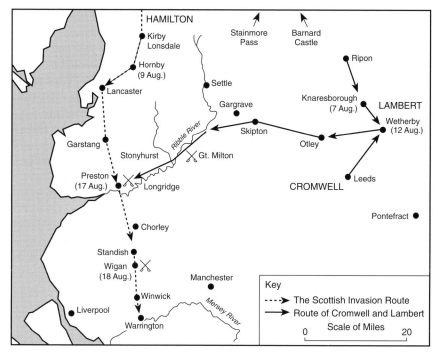

Map 18 The Preston Campaign, August 1648

follow the main road west, Cromwell led his army toward Preston, on the direct route through Otley and Skipton. He reached Skipton on 13 August and Hodder Bridge on the afternoon of the 16th. There he held a council of war at which it was decided to follow the north bank of the Ribble to Preston Bridge, where it was anticipated they would find Langdale's detachment.[69]

The royalists did not detect Cromwell's advance until the evening of 16 August, when Langdale learned that the parliamentarians were three miles to the east, in Stonyhurst. Hamilton's troops were dispersed, with Callander and most of the Scottish cavalry sixteen miles south of Preston, near Wigan, and Hamilton with the infantry just north of Preston. Monro, with about 2,000 men, was well to the north. Langdale, with 3,600 English royalists, was about six miles east, in the path of Cromwell's advance along the Ribble.

On the morning of 17 August, Cromwell launched a coordinated attack against the outnumbered Langdale. The parliamentary cavalry quickly drove the royalist cavalry back on the flanks, but Langdale's infantry in the center took advantage of the constricted terrain to make the Roundheads fight for every foot of ground. The battle raged for at least four hours before Lambert ordered the Lancashire trained bands to attack Langdale's exhausted infantry. The charge broke the defensive line, allowing the parliamentarians to drive Langdale's troops from the field.[70]

While Cromwell was crushing Langdale, Hamilton vacillated. Initially, Hamilton sent his infantry south, across Preston Bridge, as the battle raged. Then, after an appeal from Langdale for help, Hamilton countermanded the order. Finally, however, Callander convinced Hamilton to withdraw the Scots south across the Ribble, leaving their English allies to their fate. This indecision and the final decision sealed the fate of the Scots army as well as that of Langdale's force. Cromwell exploited his victory by advancing to Preston, where his infantry drove the Scots rearguard south of the river and seized the bridge intact.[71] This action cut Hamilton's host off from Scotland and interposed the English army between him and his ammunition wagons.

Driven from Preston and cut off from home, Callander and Hamilton determined that their best hope was to retreat south with about 11,000 men, hoping to reach Wales. They got beyond Wigan before Cromwell caught up with their tired and hungry soldiers, at Winwick, on 19 August. He immediately attacked, killing and capturing as many as 3,000 Scots before the remainder could get away. Cromwell next caught up with Hamilton at Warrington, on the Mersey, where, as Cromwell wrote, '… they possessed the bridge, which had a strong barricade and a work upon it, formerly made very defensive. As soon as we came thither, I received a message from Lieut.-General Baillie, desiring some capitulation; to which I yielded.' Baillie surrendered 4,000 men, the majority of the remaining Scottish infantry, in exchange for quarter, while Hamilton and the cavalry retreated southward.[72]

Leaving a detachment at Preston to guard against an advance south by Monro, Cromwell sent Lambert with a strong force in pursuit of Callander and Hamilton while he prepared to march to Scotland. As the Scots retreated, the local militia and country people attacked stragglers, making life more miserable for the invaders. Lambert overtook the Scots at Uttoexeter, on the River Dove in Strafford, where Hamilton's men refused to march further or to fight, forcing the Duke to surrender. Langdale was captured a few days later, although Callander escaped.[73]

Cromwell's defeat of Hamilton's invasion ended hopes for successful royalist risings in England in the near future. Cromwell moved rapidly north, trying to cut Monro off from Scotland. In this he failed, but his own way into Scotland, along the east coast, was wide open. The destruction of Hamilton's army completely changed the political situation in Scotland, where Argyll and the Covenanters regained control of the government and closed the Scottish borders to English royalists.

The second English Civil War was a near-run thing for the parliamentarians. If the Scottish invasion had come sooner, while Cromwell was still committed in Wales and Fairfax was tied down before Colchester, the royalists might have defeated their enemies in detail. As it was, the Presbyterians regained control of London and parliament and repealed the Vote of No Addresses, opening the way to Charles to continue his attempts to regain his throne through the division of his enemies.

Notes

1   *A & O*, i: 998–9; *JHC*, v: 268–80; Gentles, *New Model Army*, 195–6.
2   Lenihan, *Confederate Catholics at War*, 93–5; O' Siochru, *Confederate Ireland*, 119, fn. 8.
3   Bodl., Carte MS 19, fos. 183–4, Digby to Ormond, 15 October 1646; ibid., fo. 206, William Cadogan to Ormond, 17 October 1646; ibid., fo. 251, Ormond to Clanricarde, 23 October 1646; ibid., 301–2, Walter Bagnell to Ormond.

4 J. Lowe, ed., *The Letter-Book of the Earl of Clanricarde* (Dublin, 1983), 302, Preston to Ormond, 2 November 1646; for the estimated strength of the Catholic armies see Bodl., Carte MS 19, fo. 143, Ormond to the Lords Justices, 11 October 1646.

5 Lowe, *Letter-Book of Clanricarde*, 308–334 for correspondence of the negotiations Clanricarde served as an intermediary in this correspondence; Bodl., Carte MS 19, fos. 311–13, O'Neill and Preston to Ormond, 2 November 1646 for the Catholics' terms.

6 Bodl., Carte MS 20, fos. 260–1, Ormond to Parliamentary Commissioners, 6 February 1647; ibid., fo. 341, Committee at Derby House to Ormond, 22 February 1647.

7 Bodl., Carte MS 20, fo. 367, Derby House Committee to Ormond, 27 February 1647; ibid., MS 21, fo. 188, Parliamentary Commissioners to Ormond, 7 June 1647; O'Siochru, *Confederate Ireland*, 149–51; Corish in *NHI*, iii: 320–4; A. Kerr, *An Ironside of Ireland: The Remarkable Career of Lieutenant General Michael Jones* (London, 1923).

8 Casway, *O'Neill*, 190 for the quote, 183–7 for the Connacht campaign.

9 Bodl., Carte MS 20, fos. 371–4, 'A Diary and Relation of Passages in and About Dublin from the first of August unto the tenth.'

10 Ibid. The English captured Preston's muster books after the battle and the contemporary report cited here lists Preston's strength as 7,300 foot and 1,047 horse.

11 Ibid., fos. 372–3.

12 O'Siochru, *Confederate Ireland*, 157; Corish in *NHI*, iii: 324–5.

13 Bodl., Carte MS 118, fos. 33–4b, 'Diary of the Proceedings of the Leinster Army under Michael Jones from 2 to 20 October 1647'; TT E412 (4), *The Late Successful Proceedings of the Army Commanded by Colonel Michael Jones*, (October 1647), 4–5.

14 Bodl., Carte MS 118, fos. 34–4b., Sir Theophiles Jones to Mr Annesley, 10 November 1647, relating the movements of Jones and O'Neill, 3 to 8 November 1647; TT E416 (22), *News From Dublin*, (November 1647), 3–6.

15 TT417 (14) *A Mighty victory in Ireland*, (29 November 1647) for the quote; E418 (6), *A True Relation of a Great Victory*, (30 November 1647), 2–5.

16 Gardiner, *Constitutional Documents*, 241–2, The King's Answer to the Propositions of Parliament, 14 September 1647.

17 Gardiner, *Civil War*, iv: 1, 14–19, 37–41.

18 Bennett, *The Civil Wars*, 267–8, 272–3.

19 The full title of the Agreement is *An Agreement of the People for a Firm and Present Peace Upon the Grounds of Common-right and Freedom*, ibid., 279; Gentles, *New Model Army*, 204.

20 Gentles, *New Model Army*, 197–202.

21 Ibid., 218–19.

22 Ibid., 219–24.

23 Ibid., 223–4.

24 *JHC*, v: 358, 363–4, 374–7, 383.

25 *A & O*, i: 1,048–55; *JHC*, v: 395–6, 399–403, 415.

26 *A & O*, i: 1,050–2.

27 Gentles, *New Model Army*, 231–4.

28 Ibid., 239–41, Table 8.1 on 240, and note 26 on 509.

29 Gardiner, *Civil War*, iv: 51; Gardiner, ed., *Constitutional Documents*, 259–65, 'The Engagement Between the King and the Scots', 26 December 1647.

30 *JHC*, v: 415–16; Gardiner, *Civil War*, iv: 51–3.

31 Baillie, *Letters and Journals*, iii: 31–40, Baillie to William Spang, 27 March 1648.

32 Ibid., 35 for quote, 38 for outcome of vote; Bennett, *The Civil Wars*, 288–9; Gardiner, *Civil War*, iv: 86–8; E. Furgol in Kenyon and Ohlmeyer, eds, *The Civil Wars*, 63–4.

33 Baillie, *Letters and Journals*, iii: 38, Baillie to William Spang, 27 March 1648, where Baillie tells Spang that the nation was threatened with Civil War.

34 Gentles, *New Model Army*, 242–3.

35 Ibid., 239–42; Ashton, *Counter Revolution*, 205–8, 448–54; J. Morrill, *The Revolt of he Provinces: Conservatives and Radicals in the English Civil War, 1630–1650* (London, 1976), 125–31; D.

Underdown, *Revel, Riot, and Rebellion: Popular Politics and Culture in England, 1603–1660* (Oxford, 1987 edn), 220–31.

36 Gentles, *New Model Army*, 238–42; Gardiner, *Civil War*, iv: 121–36.

37 Baillie, *Letters and Journals*, iii: 31–40, Baillie to William Spang, 27 March 1648; ibid., Baillie to Spang, 26 June 1648; Gardiner, *Civil War*, iv: 111–12, 123–4.

38 C. Firth, ed., *The Clarke Papers* (4 Vols., London, 1891–1901), ii: 1–4, Newsletter from London, 10 April 1648.

39 Ibid., 3–4.

40 The quote is from *JHC*, v: 546–7, 563–4; Gardiner, *Civil War*, iv: 115–7; Ashton, *Counter Revolution*, 40–2.

41 Firth, ed. *Clarke Papers*, ii: 7, Newsletter from London, 12 May 1648. 'The Scots honest [clerical] party declaring against the other [Engagers] very much stuns them here, and puts them to their wits end.'

42 Quoted in Gardiner, *Civil War*, iv: 119–20; Gentles, *New Model Army*, 245–6.

43 Gardiner, *Civil War*, iv: 133–5; B. Capp, *Cromwell's Navy: The Fleet and the English Revolution, 1648–1660* (Oxford, 1989), 17–22.

44 Gentles, *New Model Army*, 247–8; Gardiner, *Civil War*, iv: 136–8.

45 Gentles, *New Model Army*, 248; Gardiner, *Civil War*, iv: 140–1.

46 Firth, ed., *Clarke Papers*, ii: 26–7, Colonel Edward Whalley to Fairfax, 10 June 1648; Gentles, *New Model Army*, 248–50.

47 Wilson, *Fairfax*, 135–6.

48 Abbott, i: 606, Speech to Each Regiment at Gloucester, May 8, 1648.

49 Ibid., 607–9.

50 Ibid., 608–11.

51 Ibid., 613, Cromwell to a Member of the Derby House Committee, 14 June 1648; Whitelocke, *Memorials*, 306, says there were 300 horse and many foot defending Pembroke. Gentles, *New Model Army*, 258, gives the royalist garrisons' strength as 2,000, while Abbott, 612, says it was 300.

52 Abbott, i: 618–19, Cromwell to Fairfax, 28 June 1648.

53 Ibid., 620, Cromwell to Poyer, 10 July 1648.

54 Ibid., 620–1, Articles for Surrender of Pembroke, 11 July 1648; ibid., Cromwell to Fairfax, 11 July 1648.

55 Gentles, *New Model Army*, 246–8.

56 Whitelocke, *Memorials*, 307.

57 Gardiner, *Civil War*, iv: 147–50.

58 Ibid., 150–3.

59 Whitelocke, *Memorials*, 313, 325.

60 Ibid., 326, report of a letter to Fairfax and his reply; Gentles, *New Model Army*, 256.

61 Whitelocke, *Memorials*, 328.

62 Ibid., 328.

63 Ibid., 328–9; Gentles, *New Model Army*, 256–7; Wilson, *Fairfax*, 137–9.

64 Baillie, *Letters and Journals*, iii: 43–6, Baillie to William Spang, 26 June 1648; Gentles, *New Model Army*, 259–60; Gardiner, *Civil War*, iv: 165–6.

65 Abbott, i: 624–6.

66 Ibid., 626, Cromwell to Lambert, 4 August 1648.

67 Gentles, *New Model Army*, 260–1.

68 Ibid., 260.

69 Abbott, i: 630–1.

70 Ibid., 631–3; Gentles, *New Model Army*, 261–4.

71 Abbott, i: 632–3, Cromwell to Committee of Lancashire, 17 August 1648.

72 Ibid., 634–8, Cromwell to William Lenthall, Speaker of the Commons, 20 August 1648.

73 Ibid., 641–2, Cromwell to the Committee at Derby House, 23 August 1648.

CHAPTER EIGHT

The execution of Charles I and the conquest of Catholic Ireland

The royalist strategy for 1648 included the revival of royalist military fortunes in Ireland as well as in Britain. The Marquis of Ormond hoped to unite all anti-parliamentarian factions in Ireland to destroy the parliamentarian garrisons and then intervene in Britain. The king confirmed Ormond's position as Lord Lieutenant and 'commissioned him to try again to reach a peace with the Irish', before sending him on to Paris to confer with the Queen and the French government.[1] Ormond undertook this new effort because of significant changes then taking place in the political climate in Confederate Ireland.

The disintegration of the Irish Catholic Confederation

Rinuccini's victory in Ireland in 1646 over those in the Confederation who favored an Ormond settlement forced Ormond to surrender Dublin to parliament, in July 1647 (see Chapter 7). Michael Jones's subsequent defeat of Preston's army in August and Inchiquin's destruction of the Confederate army in Munster, in November, left the Confederates in a desperate situation. This strengthened the hand of 'moderates' within the Confederation who believed that Ireland's best hope for the future lay with Charles I and a royalist victory.[2]

The Confederates had few good options in early 1648. They could continue the war against Jones, Inchiquin, and the Ulster Scots, but the defeats at Dungan's Hill and Knocknanuss demonstrated the risks of such a strategy. They could find a continental power to serve as a 'protector of Ireland', providing arms, money, and reinforcements with which they could defend themselves from the parliamentarians. The Confederates, however, were deeply divided over who that protector should be (France, Spain, or the Pope), and over what price they would pay for protection. Their third option was to come to terms with Charles I through Ormond.[3] But many Confederates, especially the clergy and Old Irish, were opposed to dealing again with an heretical king who failed to keep his promises to his subjects.

Necessity forced the Supreme Council to decide to pursue the second and third options simultaneously. Two delegations were sent to the continent: one traveled to Rome to solicit papal aid and to get approval from the Pope to make a deal with Charles. This delegation also was to sound out the pontiff about becoming the protector of Ireland. The second embassy went to Paris to offer the Queen and the Prince of Wales the government of Ireland, but only if they would accept the religious concessions made by Glamorgan. They also were to solicit French support. These delegations, with their conflicting objectives, reflected the divisions within the Confederation.[4]

The Confederate agents did not leave Ireland until February 1648. By then, affairs in southern Ireland were taking a dramatic turn as Inchiquin considered abandoning the parliamentarians and joining the royalists. Inchiquin controlled all of the major Munster towns except for Waterford, Clonmel, and Limerick. He had received a trickle of support from England over the years, and a major infusion of reinforcements and money in 1647, allowing him to destroy the army of the Catholic Commander, Taaffe. By the spring of 1648, his support from England was drying up, due to the preoccupation of parliament with the royalist uprisings and the Scottish invasion. Equally important, Inchiquin was disturbed by the army's imprisonment of the king and the growing indications that many soldiers were contemplating constitutional changes, including Charles's deposition.[5]

On 3 April 1648, Inchiquin declared his loyalty to Charles I and denounced the Independents in the English parliament and army.[6] This declaration changed the Confederates' situation because it offered a potential solution to their military weakness in Munster. It also forced a split within the Confederation because Rinuccini refused to condone a truce or an alliance with the fervently anti-Catholic Inchiquin, while the Old English leaders wanted to come to an understanding with Inchiquin.

Rinuccini understood the dangerous situation of the Irish after their defeats by Jones and Inchiquin. He believed that the Confederates' best strategic option was to unite their armies against Inchiquin in Munster, before advancing against Jones in Dublin. He solicited financial aid from Rome, knowing that if he had the money, he could influence the operational decisions of the Irish military commanders. Therefore, the nuncio saw Inchiquin's declaration in favor of Charles I as a threat to his plans and all that he had worked for during the past two years.[7]

In spite of Rinuccini's view, the Supreme Council sent delegates to Dungarvan to parley with Inchiquin, on 22 April. Rinuccini was furious, forcing a confrontation with those seeking accommodation with Inchiquin. In a meeting of the Leinster assembly on 20 April, which included members of the Confederate general assembly, the peace party obtained a majority in favor of a truce in Munster. In response, the nuncio and fourteen bishops signed a declaration condemning the peace initiative. The negotiations with Inchiquin took place anyway, resulting in a draft treaty by 27 April. Rinuccini vetoed the treaty on the grounds that it gave insufficient protection to the Catholic church, but Rinuccini also was convinced that the truce in Munster was the first step toward an agreement with Ormond.[8]

On 9 May, Rinuccini, fearing for his safety, fled Kilkenny and traveled to O'Neill's army at Maryborough (Portlaoise). The stage was set for a civil war between the nuncioists and the peace party in the Confederation. The threat of O'Neill's army to the peace party was offset by Preston's declaration that he and his army supported the Kilkenny government. On 20 May the Confederates signed a truce with Inchiquin.[9] In response, the nuncio and a small committee of like-minded bishops threatened to excommunicate anyone adhering to the Inchiquin cessation. This threat was met by an appeal by the Supreme Council to Rome, and was undermined by the refusal of at least eight bishops to implement the religious sanction. 'The Old English and Rinuccini had reached the stage of mutual incomprehension.'[10]

The formation of the royalist coalition in Ireland

The Inchiquin truce, along with the Scottish Engagement with the king, opened the way for the creation of a broad royalist coalition in Ireland. Ormond, still in France, had been working for an agreement with the Confederates. He communicated with Inchiquin and hoped to win over Owen Roe O'Neill and the Old Irish, although he intended to make as few religious concessions as possible. By April, Ormond was preparing to sail to Ireland, hoping to arrive in time to lead an offensive against Jones that would coincide with the royalists' risings and the Scottish invasion of England.[11]

Ormond was unable to sail until 30 September. By then the Supreme Council had proclaimed that anyone who aided O'Neill would be considered a traitor and that O'Neill was 'a traitor and a rebel against the king and the fundamental laws of the land.'[12] Ormond had learned of the royalist defeats in England and the Scots' disaster at Preston, and he understood that it was only a matter of time before the New Model Army would be unleashed in Ireland. After arriving in Cork, on 3 October, Ormond worked to knit together Inchiquin, the Ulster Scots, and the Confederates in an alliance strong enough to drive the parliamentarians out of Ireland and to create a new foundation for the royalist war effort.

Ormond's negotiations with the Confederates took nearly four months to complete. In the meantime, Ormond and Inchiquin cooperated against O'Neill's forces in western Leinster. By the end of October, Inchiquin had driven O'Neill's garrison out of Fort Falkland, destroying supplies O'Neill needed to sustain his army. In November, Inchiquin thwarted O'Neill's invasion of Connacht, where the pro-royalist Clanricarde was working to bring the Catholics into Ormond's camp. These efforts diverted Ormond from his strategy of driving Jones out of Ireland.[13]

Jones and his allies Charles Coote and George Monck did not sit idle as the threat of an Ormondist coalition loomed. Jones and Coote led expeditions into Catholic territory, expanding their control of the areas around Dublin and Derry and destroying the crops that the Catholic armies relied on for sustenance. Monck surprised the Scottish garrisons in Belfast, Coleraine, and Carrickfergus, securing those towns for parliament. Such operations, along with the Catholic civil war, devastated regions of Ireland that had been untouched by earlier campaigns, impoverishing the people and weakening the ability of anyone to conduct operations.[14]

Ormond was unable to come to terms with the Confederates quickly because he was unwilling to give them the necessary religious guarantees. There seemed to be no way to bridge the gulf between the two sides, with the Catholics demanding 'the free and public exercise of the Roman Catholic religion', the removal of the penal laws, and the retention by their clergy of all property taken in the previous seven years. Ormond was only willing to accept limited religious toleration in Ireland and to promise that the Catholic clergy would be undisturbed in their occupation of ecclesiastical property until the king was able to rule on the property and jurisdictional issues.[15] The negotiations did not get much past this impasse until events in England again intervened in Irish affairs.

Scotland: defeat and civil war

As Ormond was preparing to return to Ireland in August, Cromwell inflicted one of the worst military defeats ever suffered by a Scottish army at Preston, on 17 August 1648. The destruction of Hamilton's army did not complete the tasks that the Derby House Committee had given Cromwell, as he reminded them:

> That I should prosecute the remaining party in the North, and not leave any of them (wherever they shall go) to be a beginning of a new army; nor cease to pursue the victory till I finish and fully complete it, with their rendition of those towns of Berwick and Carlisle.[16]

With these instructions in mind, Cromwell left Lambert to finish off Hamilton while he led 5,000 men north toward Berwick, in pursuit of Monro and his Ulster troops. Monro evaded Cromwell, crossing the Tweed on 8 September. Cromwell was close on his heels, reaching Durham on 7 September and Berwick by 14 September, where he summoned the Scottish commander Ludovic Leslie to surrender.[17] By then, Lambert had finished his work with Hamilton's dispirited troops and was marching to join Cromwell.

Hamilton's defeat changed the political situation in Scotland and the military balance in Britain. Argyll and the Earl of Eglington led an insurrection in southwestern Scotland against the Engagers. The Earl of Leven and David Leslie joined this 'Whiggamore' rising, giving the insurgents competent military leaders. Encouraged by their success, the insurgents marched on Edinburgh, driving the Engagers from the city and capturing Edinburgh Castle. By 26 September, the Engagers had relinquished their positions on the Committee of Estates and retreated to the protection of Monro's army in Stirling.[18]

Cromwell encouraged these developments, promising Argyll military support in the struggle against Monro. This was a timely offer, since Monro's veterans defeated Leven's poorly armed troops near Stirling, killing as many as seven hundred. Argyll and his newly constituted Committee of Estates in Edinburgh accepted Cromwell's offer of aid and reciprocated by ordering the Scottish governors of Berwick and Carlisle to surrender to the English army.[19]

On 21 September, Cromwell crossed the Tweed, meeting with Argyll at Mordington the next day. Simultaneously, Lambert approached Edinburgh with seven regiments of horse to provide Leven's army with sufficient cavalry to face Monro's troops. Cromwell supported Argyll's forces in part because

> I do hear that their infantry consists of men who come to them out of conscience, and generally are of the godly people of that nation, which they express by their piety and devotion in their quarters; and indeed I hear that they are a very godly and honest body of men.[20]

Cromwell calculated that the party of the Kirk offered a much better chance of Scotland leaving the royalist coalition that threatened the parliamentary regime.

Cromwell's calculations were sound. With Lambert's regiments billeted in Seaton, six miles from Edinburgh, Argyll was able to gain control of the situation. On 30 September, Ludovic Leslie obeyed his orders to surrender Berwick to Cromwell. The governor of Carlisle followed suit shortly thereafter. Argyll also got Monro and the Engagers at Stirling to agree to disband their forces in exchange for the disbandment of all other troops in Scotland save 4,000 men, to be commanded by Leven.[21]

With Berwick secured and garrisoned by Sir Arthur Haselrigg's infantry regiment, Cromwell joined Lambert at Seaton, near Edinburgh, on 3 October. Argyll and the Committee of Estates invited him to enter Edinburgh the next day, where he was entertained in the Earl of Moray's house. On 5 October, Cromwell presented England's terms for peace to the Scots. The Committee of Estates was to

> give assurance in the name of the Kingdom of Scotland, that you will not admit or suffer any that have been active in, or consenting to, the said Engagement against England, or have lately been in arms at Stirling ... to be employed in any public place of trust whatsoever.[22]

Loudon, Lord Chancellor of Scotland, accepted Cromwell's proposals the next day, although many Scots, including David Leslie, resented English intrusion into their affairs. Monro's men in Stirling made threats against the English as well, and Monro agreed only reluctantly to take his men back to Ulster, from whence they had come in June. With this shaky start to Argyll's government, Cromwell returned to his army at Seaton. From there he wrote to the Westminster parliament, summarizing his demands to, and agreements with, the Scots and the strategic results of the campaign.

> All the enemy's forces in Scotland are now disbanded. The Committee of Estates have declared against all of that party sitting in [the Scottish] parliament. Good elections are made in divers places, of such as dissented from and opposed the late wicked Engagement; and they are now raising a force of about 4,000 horse and foot, which until they can complete, they have desired me to leave them two regiments of horse and two troops of dragoons. Which accordingly I have resolved, conceiving I had warrant by

your late votes so to do, and have left Major-General Lambert to command them … I am now marching to Carlisle. …[23]

Cromwell moved southwest, reaching Carlisle by 14 October. His first campaign as an independent army commander was completed. Fairfax's trust in his abilities was proven well founded. Cromwell had helped crush the Welsh royalists, defeated a Scottish army, and prevented that defeated army from returning to Scotland. With little bloodshed, he recaptured Berwick and facilitated the installation of a friendly government in Edinburgh, within the remarkably short period of five weeks.

The New Model Army defeated the royalist strategy in 1648 with tough fighting and a great deal of good fortune. Their luck included the poor timing of the English revolts with the Scottish invasion, the continued loyalty of the London Presbyters to the parliamentarian cause, and the internal divisions of the Confederacy in Ireland. Perhaps their greatest fortune was that the naval mutiny in the Downs in May did not spread to the rest of the fleet. Had it done so, the royalists would have gained control of the one military instrument they could have used to bring the army and its London allies to their knees.

The naval mutiny of 1648

The English navy had remained loyal to parliament throughout the 1640s, enabling the Roundheads to protect the London commerce upon which Pym's war effort counted for much of its tax revenue. The navy increased significantly during the 1640s as its missions expanded. By 1648, the fleet had grown to forty-five warships, from thirty 'purpose-built' warships in 1642. The summer guard of 1648 totaled sixty ships, forty-three of which were state-owned vessels.[24] The Westminster government spent over £300,000 annually on the navy from 1642 through 1648, most of which was provided by the customs. In return, the fleet had done a good job in supporting operations ashore, in cutting off royalist supplies, and in protecting English commerce.

By 1648, however, there was discontent in the navy with the way in which the army had purged the Presbyterians from parliament and the offices of the navy. The Independents further aroused the sailors' ire when they replaced the Earl of Warwick, the Lord High Admiral, with an Independent-dominated navy commission. The final irritant to the sailors was parliament's removal of William Batten as commander of the fleet, in September 1647, and the appointment of Colonel Thomas Rainsborough in his place.[25]

The sailors and many of the officers disliked Rainsborough because he was a Leveller and a 'tool' of the army grandees. He symbolized the Independents' threat to the king, the constitution, and the traditions of England in which so many of the seamen believed. When the royalist uprising in Kent exploded in late May, Rainsborough's crew on his flagship, *The Constant Reformation*, mutinied and refused to allow Rainsborough to return to his ship. The crews of eleven other warships in the area joined this revolt. Fearing the spread of the mutiny to other squadrons, parliament reappointed Warwick as Lord Admiral and sent him to talk the mutineers back to their allegiance.[26]

Warwick arrived in the Downs within a few days, offering the sailors full indemnity if they would surrender. They refused, even though Fairfax's rapid victories in Kent deterred the sailors in Chatham and Yarmouth from joining the mutiny. Warwick kept most of the ships elsewhere loyal, although with only nine loyal ships in the Downs, he lacked the means to force the mutineers to surrender. After a week of uncertainty, the mutineers sailed to Helvoetsluys, Holland, where they surrendered their ships to the Prince of Wales. As a result, the royalists acquired a powerful weapon.

During the next month, Warwick attempted to organize a force strong enough to prevent the royalist fleet from returning to the Downs and cutting off London's commerce. He was partially successful, finding enough sailors to man a fleet comparable in size to the Prince of Wales' navy. On 17 July 1648, Warwick was put to the test, when Prince Charles arrived in the Downs with eleven warships. For ten days the royalists operated freely, capturing merchant ships and ransoming them back to their London owners. The royalists, however, did not impose a total blockade of the Thames commerce, allowing London to survive, while aggravating the city's merchants with their financial exactions. Charles was joined in this activity in August by William Batten and his ship *The Constant Warwick*, from Portsmouth. Batten's adherence to the Prince gave the Cavaliers an experienced naval commander to whom they might have entrusted their fleet.[27]

The royalist leadership was badly divided over what to do with their fleet in the Downs. Rupert wanted to lead the ships to Ireland to support Ormond's efforts to create a royalist coalition. Lauderdale, the Scottish representative, hoped that Prince Charles would sail north to Berwick to join Hamilton's army, and use his warships to support the invasion of England. Many of the sailors and their leaders wanted to support the royalists in Essex and to cut off London's trade, but Charles was reluctant to antagonize the Londoner merchant community in this way. There also were tensions between the staunch royalists, like Rupert, and the new converts to the cause, like Batten and most of the sailors.[28]

The royalists attempted to land parties of seamen ashore to open the mouth of the River Colme into Colchester, but they were repulsed by the army. After nearly coming to blows with Warwick's squadron at the end of August, the royalist fleet returned to Holland to replenish its supplies. Warwick followed two weeks later with a superior force, ready to give battle if necessary. Warwick, however, hoped to convince the sailors to return to their previous loyalty peacefully and refrained from opening hostilities.

While Warwick blockaded the mouth of the River Maas at Helvoetsluys, the Dutch navy stood between the two English fleets, preventing a battle. This situation continued until early November, when the Dutch Admiral Tromp withdrew his squadron. During the next two weeks, six royalists ships surrendered to Warwick, forcing Rupert, the newly appointed admiral, to pull his remaining vessels into the inner harbor where they could be protected by shore batteries. On 21 November, Warwick sailed home to England to replenish his supplies. He was confident that the royalists would not be able to outfit their ships for sea duty before the blockade could be resumed.[29] The royalist threat to London's sea lanes was ended for the short term. When Warwick got back to England, affairs took a dramatic turn that soon forced him to resign his commission.

Last attempts for a settlement with Charles I

As Cromwell and Fairfax fought their enemies in the summer of 1648, the Presbyterian-dominated parliament voted to re-open negotiations with the king. These negotiations got underway on 18 September, well after Cromwell's and Fairfax's victories. Support for a settlement with Charles remained widespread, especially among the London Presbyterians, in large part because it seemed that it was the only viable alternative to submitting to army domination.[30]

Fifteen commissioners met with the king at Newport, on the Isle of Wight, just as Cromwell was approaching Edinburgh. Parliament offered Charles once more the terms that he had rejected at Hampton Court, in 1647. Charles continued to hope that his enemies would again fall out amongst themselves, and he played for time to allow Ormond to organize royalist efforts in Ireland. In both these hopes he was foiled. Parliament refused to accept his proposal to establish Presbyterianism for a trial period of just three years, especially since he refused to take the Covenant or to make it mandatory. It was remarkable that he even offered such a proposal, since parliament had passed legislation establishing a Presbyterian system throughout England, in spite of the army or the king, on 26 August.[31]

The Newport negotiations continued until late November, although, by 27 October, it was clear that Charles was unwilling to agree to acceptable terms. The ultimate effect of the Presbyterians' attempts to come to terms with a man no one trusted was to convince most army officers that Charles could not be allowed to escape punishment and that the Presbyterian-dominated parliament must either be replaced or purged. The Newport negotiations also brought the Levellers and the army radicals together against a settlement with the king, making it likely that the army would proceed against him with or without parliamentary sanction.[32]

Radicals within the army reacted to parliament's dealings with Charles by petitioning Fairfax to put an end to the talks and to force parliament to pay the soldiers their badly overdue arrears. These petitions were part of an effort to push Fairfax to break with parliament that culminated with the preparation and discussion of *The Remonstrance of the Army*. This document, written mostly by Cromwell's son-in-law Henry Ireton, was debated by the Council of the Army between 10 and 16 November.[33] At the same time, Fairfax and other moderate officers convinced the council to submit new peace proposals to the king that included biennial parliaments, the establishment of a Council of State to command the armed forces, parliamentary approval of the king's chief officers, and a permanent establishment for the army. No mention was made of eliminating the royal legislative veto or of changes in the church. Charles rejected these terms on 17 November, convinced that his strategy to split his foes was working.[34]

The army leaders then agreed to submit the *Remonstrance* to the House of Commons, while the more radical officers sought an alliance with the Levellers against those willing to come to terms with Charles. On 20 November 1648, a delegation of officers presented the *Remonstrance* to parliament. At the same time, the Levellers published a new version of *The Agreement of the People*. These documents called for a settlement that relied on a written constitution to limit the power of king and parliament, although they differed in how to reach such a settlement. The House of Commons, after listening for four hours to the reading of the *Remonstrance*, tabled it. This irritated the army, producing an 'irrevocable breach with parliament.'[35]

On 27 November, after weeks of fruitless discussions with the king, parliament's commissioners ended the negotiations. By then, the army had given up hope of a deal with the king. The most vocal opponent of any further compromise with Charles was Ireton. He represented the senior officers who thought that the king must be punished for causing the civil wars and that the Presbyterians could no longer be left in control of parliament. Their decision to effect an alliance with the Levellers was an attempt to win over or neutralize opposition to the steps against the king that the senior army officers were contemplating.[36]

Pride's purge and the execution of Charles I

Throughout the fall, while the various negotiations with Charles had been taking place, Cromwell remained in the north to supervise the capture of royalist-held castles and to establish garrisons to deter another Scottish invasion. He stayed informed of events in the south and in close contact with Ireton, Fairfax, Vane, and other army and parliamentary leaders. The surviving correspondence indicates that he was playing a cautious game to prevent the king and Presbyterians from coming to terms and that he planned to bring Charles to justice.[37]

Parliament's refusal to debate the army's *Remonstrance* triggered the army coup of 1648 and set in motion the events that led to the trial and execution of Charles I. The king had refused all offers of a settlement. Parliament continued to show a willingness to restore him with too little protection to prevent his resumption of 'tyrannical' rule. Royalists in Ireland and Scotland continued to work to resume the war, and parliament seemed determined to reduce the army's role and influence in England. The General Council of Officers faced stark choices, and the use of force seemed the only way to cut the Gordian Knot.

On 21 November, Fairfax ordered Colonel Isaac Ewer to replace Colonel Robert Hammond as the king's gaoler and to move Charles from Newport to Hurst Castle, where his escape would be more difficult. Hammond refused to follow his orders to relinquish his post, forcing Fairfax to order his arrest. On 30 November, Ewer occupied Newport with a strong contingent of soldiers and secured the king's quarters. The next morning he moved Charles across the Solent to Hurst Castle, on the first leg of his journey to Westminster.[38]

Parliament, meanwhile, delayed the debate of the *Remonstrance* until 1 December, convincing the army that no favorable action was to be expected. The General

Council of Officers then voted to march on London and to insist on the impartial administration of justice, regular payment of the army, and the speedy enactment of 'salutary laws.' Fairfax also summoned Cromwell to return to the headquarters at Windsor.[39]

Once the officers had decided to march on London, Fairfax wrote to the mayor, notifying him that the army was going to arrive on 2 December and that he expected the city to pay £40,000 of its assessment arrears to the army immediately. On 1 December, Fairfax assembled 7,000 soldiers in Hyde Park, preparatory to their march into London the next morning. Hearing that the army was less than a mile away, the House of Commons sat all night debating a course of action. In the end, parliament backed down, refusing to pass a motion declaring that the army's advance was 'prejudicial to the freedom of parliament.'[40] As the parliamentarians went home, the army occupied Westminster and London.

The Council of Officers seemed uncertain as to what course to follow once they had occupied the capital. They hoped that parliament would purge itself of those who had opposed the army over the past two years. On 4 December, as Fairfax and his senior officers discussed what to do, the Commons resolved, after a long debate, 'that the removal of the king out of the Isle of Wight was without the knowledge or consent of this House.'[41] This resolution was accompanied by another, passed by a vote of 129 to 83, in the early hours of 5 December, that 'the answer of the king to the propositions of both Houses are a ground for the House to proceed upon, for the settlement of the peace of the kingdom.'[42]

These resolutions brought matters to a head between the army and parliament. On 5 December, the Council of Officers decided to purge parliament of those who stood against the army and who now sought to continue negotiations with Charles. The task was assigned to Colonel Thomas Pride and his infantry regiment. A committee of officers and Independent members of parliament prepared a list of those to be excluded and those to be arrested. At 7 a.m. the next morning, Pride, assisted by Lord Grey of Groby, stood at the entrance to the Commons sorting through the arriving members. By the end of the day, forty-one members had been detained and another ninety-six turned away.[43]

The following day, Cromwell resumed his seat in the purged Commons, having arrived in Westminster the night before. He and his fellow soldiers, along with the 'Rump' – as the remaining members quickly became known – of the Long Parliament, still faced the questions of what to do with Charles and how to settle the kingdom.[44] After three weeks of debate about a political settlement the officers produced a new version of *The Agreement of the People* that was published on 15 December 1648 and presented to parliament on 20 January 1649.[45] The Rump tabled it for a future discussion that never took place. This action effectively ended the most radical impulses of the revolution then underway.[46] Following a second debate about what to do with Charles I, the Rump decided to bring him to trial.

The Council of Officers took the first step toward the trial of the king on 15 December, when it voted to bring him to Windsor so that he could be 'brought to justice.' Colonel Thomas Harrison was ordered to take a strong contingent of his regiment to Hurst castle, pick up Charles, and escort him back to Windsor. Harrison complied, arriving in Windsor with his prisoner on 23 December. During his trip to army headquarters, Charles did not suspect that the army was going to take any action against him beyond imprisonment.[47]

The army and its allies in the Rump and London also endeavored to broaden the base of their regime by courting moderate parliamentarians. The army released many of the arrested members and kept a tight rein on the soldiers to prevent looting. Fairfax and the Council of Officers, however, continued to demand that London pay its assessment arrears, and when money was not forthcoming, ordered the seizure of the treasuries at the Goldsmiths', Haberdashers', and Weavers' Halls. The soldiers took £27,000 from the Weavers' Hall, but found little money elsewhere.[48]

The Council of Officers also pressured parliament to rescind those measures that over the past year had so irritated the army. The Rump responded with alacrity, annulling the repeal of the Vote of No Addresses and the resolution of 5 December that had accepted the king's answer to the Newport propositions.[49] The Commons ejected those of the 'eleven members' – the leading Presbyterians – who were still alive, and the Lords, reduced to as few as seven members, banished the Earl of Norwich for his part in the royalist risings and imposed a large fine on the Duke of Hamilton, now the army's prisoner.

While defusing as much opposition as possible, the army tightened its hold on the king and debated its next step. As late as 23 December there was resistance in the Council of Officers, possibly led by Ireton and Cromwell, to the prospect of putting the king on trial. In a last-minute attempt to avert that step, the officers allowed the Earl of Denbigh to visit Charles to offer a compromise that would keep him on his throne, as long as he renounced his veto powers and endorsed the sale of the Bishops' lands to pay the army. Charles refused to see Denbigh.

This royal response forced the officers' hand. On 27 December, the Council of the Army decided to bring the king to trial.[50] In the following week, the Commons passed an act establishing a special court. The Lords refused to concur, forcing the Commons to go it alone. On 4 January, the Commons resolved 'that the Commons of England, in parliament assembled, do declare, that the people are, under God, the original of all just power.' Acts of the Commons henceforth expressed the will of parliament. On 6 January 1649, the Rump passed the 'Act erecting a High Court of Justice for the Trial of the king.'[51]

For the remainder of January, attention was on the trial of Charles Stuart as a 'tyrant, traitor, murderer, and public and implacable enemy of the Commonwealth of England.'[52] The court consisted of 135 commissioners chosen by the Commons to serve as jury and judges. The sessions opened on 20 January, with sixty-eight jurors in attendance. Many of those selected to serve on the court, such as Thomas Fairfax, refused to attend, but this did not stop the proceedings. John Bradshaw, one of the few lawyers, was selected as President of the court.

The heart of the prosecution's case was that Charles had waged war against the English people and had solicited foreign aid in that struggle. He was accused of violating his trust to serve as a monarch 'with a limited power to govern' in accord with the laws, and of having attempted 'to erect and uphold in himself an unlimited, and tyrannical power to rule according to his will, and to overthrow the rights and liberties of the people … .'[53] Charles's actions over the past twenty-four years supported the essence of the charges, although there were no statutes of law specifically violated.

During the trial, Charles refused to recognize the court's authority or to make a plea. He got the better of the argument with the judges, especially when he ironically put his finger on the heart of the nation's dilemma:

> It is not my case alone; it is the freedom and liberty of the people of England; and do you pretend what you will, I stand more for their liberties; for, if power without law may make laws, may alter the fundamental laws of the kingdom, I do not know what subject he is in England that can be sure of his life, or anything he calls his own.[54]

He was right. There was no legal precedent or constitutional basis for his trial. But because he refused to accept the judgments of war, he left his opponents no alternative. It was, as Cromwell is reputed to have said, 'a cruel necessity' to execute the king. Knowing that Charles had bested them in argument, the court concluded, on 26 January, that Charles Stuart 'as a tyrant, traitor, murderer, and public enemy to the good people of this nation, shall be put to death by the severing of his head from his body.' On 30 January 1949, after three days of unsuccessful attempts by the Dutch and French ambassadors to obtain leniency, Charles I was executed.[55]

The rise of a royalist coalition in Ireland

The decisive steps the army took against Charles I transformed the situation in Ireland. It was obvious to most Catholics that the Westminster regime would stop at nothing to crush all opposition in Ireland. This realization got the peace process moving swiftly.

Ormond had returned to Ireland on 30 September 1648, planning to establish a coalition to operate against the parliamentarians. The groundwork for this coalition had been laid with the Confederate-Inchiquin truce in May. Rinuccini's excommunication threat failed to stop the Supreme Council or the Leinster and Munster assemblies from accepting the truce, largely because many bishops refused to enforce the sanction. These men, like the Ormondists in the Confederation, had believed that the best hope for Catholics lay with a royalist victory.[56]

Those Confederates who supported the Inchiquin truce and a peace with Ormond were unwilling to accept less than the full and free exercise of Catholicism in Ireland, to include Catholic jurisdiction of the church property they occupied in 1648 and the abolition of the penal laws. Ormond, however, continued to balk at the open declaration of Catholic religious tolerance and control of their churches. Consequently, negotiations between the Lord Lieutenant and the Supreme Council continued throughout the fall.[57]

Meanwhile, the Irish Catholics fought a civil war that pitted O'Neill and many of the Old Irish against those, mostly Old English, who had rejected the nuncio and accepted the Inchiquin settlement. Neither side was strong enough to win, although the Confederates mustered larger forces than O'Neill. O'Neill's focus on his war against fellow-Catholics enabled Jones's deputy, George Monck, to expand parliamentarian control in Ulster, making it harder for anyone to expel the hated English. Ultimately, the Catholic civil war prevented the Irish from focusing their power against Jones's garrisons.

Irish affairs began to change at this point due to events in England. The *Remonstrance of the Army* of 20 November broke the deadlock in negotiations between the Confederates and Ormond. The *Remonstrance* made it clear that the army intended to bring the king to justice, meaning that Catholics in Ireland were going to receive religious toleration only if they could defend themselves against an English invasion. The Confederates realized they could not do this alone and that a united effort of anti-parliamentarian forces was their best chance. Thus they decided to sign a much-less than satisfactory agreement with Ormond.

The Ormond peace of 1649 promised the

> free exercise of the Roman Catholic religion … And that the Oath [of Supremacy] shall not be tendered unto them, [the Catholics] … they taking the Oath of Allegiance. … That they shall not be molested in the possession which they have of present of the churches … until such time as His Majesty upon full consideration … in a free parliament to be held in this kingdom shall declare his further pleasure.[58]

Details such as who would be allowed to sit in the free parliament, etc., were kept vague. The stage was set for Ormond to gather his coalition together and drive Jones from Ireland. Thus the royalists in Ireland became one of the most pressing concerns of the new regime in England.

The creation of the English Commonwealth

The execution of Charles I did not settle the government of England. Over the next four months the Rump swept away many political institutions, replacing them with structures that proved remarkably successful. This political revolution commenced on 30 January 1649, when the Rump forbad anyone from proclaiming Charles II as king. An act abolishing the monarchy was not passed until 17 March, but the Rump created a new executive, known as the Council of State, on 13 February. The Commons resolved no longer to confer with the House of Lords, on 6 February, abolishing that body on 19 March. This institutional restructuring was completed with an act, on 19 May 1649, 'declaring and constituting the people of England to be a Commonwealth.'[59]

The Commons selected forty-one men to serve on the Council of State. This executive was 'to oppose and suppress' anyone who proclaimed the late king's son

Charles as king, and 'to order and direct all the militias and forces both by sea and land …' Further, the Council was 'to use all good ways and means for the reducing of Ireland, the Isles of Jersey, Guernsey, Scilly, and the Isle of Man, and all other parts and places belonging to the Commonwealth of England not yet reduced.'[60]

The Council of State had at hand two fine instruments to execute this mandate: the army, composed of over 38,000 combat veterans, and the Commonwealth's navy, with more than forty warships. These were easily the strongest forces of their kind in Britain and Ireland. If their power could be brought to bear against the Republic's Irish enemies, the results would favor the Commonwealth. The Council of State made no significant changes in the army. Thomas Fairfax remained Lord General, seconded by Cromwell and the other capable warriors who had led the army to victory.

The navy required significant restructuring and strengthening to ensure its political reliability and to give it enough ships and crews to carry out its expanding missions. The Rump, on the recommendations of the Council of State, removed the Earl of Warwick from his position as Lord High Admiral and replaced him with a commission. Three of the commissioners served as 'commissioners to go to sea' to command the fleet in action. Three army colonels, Robert Blake, Richard Deane, and Edward Popham, served in this capacity. The Rump appointed John Hollond, Thomas Smith, Peter Pett, and William Willoughby to serve as commissioners on land to oversee the naval yards, the procurement of supplies, and the recruitment and maintenance of personnel.[61]

The changes to the navy proved successful over the next eighteen months, as the fleet grew to seventy-two warships and drove the Republic's enemies out of British and Irish waters. To support the costs of this naval activity, which averaged over £350,000 per year, parliament increased the customs rates and assigned money from other sources of revenue to the navy treasurer, Sir Henry Vane. The commissioners at sea, also known as Generals at Sea, and their administrative counterparts ashore, ably directed the fleet against the royalist navy commanded by Prince Rupert and the large number of Irish privateers operating against English commerce from their lairs in Wexford and Waterford.[62]

To remain in power in 1649, the Commonwealth had to deal with the Levellers, who hoped the revolution would enact the *Agreement of the People* that they and the army had submitted to parliament in January. Second, the republic had to solve the perennial financial crisis that had plagued English governments for nearly two years.

By February, it was clear that the Rump had no intention of considering the Levellers' reform agenda. In fact, Cromwell and the other Commonwealth leaders worked to broaden support for the new regime by trying to convince moderate members of parliament to return to Westminster. These efforts brought the membership of the purged Commons to over 200 members. To broaden support the Commonwealth leaders had to limit the revolution to institutional changes at the center. Ironically, '[t]he inauguration of the Commonwealth proved to be the end, not the beginning, of the Long Parliament's revolutionary measures, and the regime left in its wake a trail of disillusionment and resentment among the advocates of social and religious reform.'[63]

The Levellers' failure in parliament made them determined to contend for control of the army. For three months after the regicide, Leveller agitators worked to convince the army's rank and file to refuse to serve in Ireland. The soldiers were receptive to Leveller propaganda, especially since their pay arrears had reached over £1.3 million. The Levellers also argued that it was wrong to conquer the Irish and to impose Protestantism on them by force, since such actions violated inherent human rights.[64]

The Commonwealth solved its financial problems first. The Rump passed acts continuing the customs, excise, and assessment taxes. The assessment rate was raised from £60,000 to £90,000 per month to provide the money needed to support the army. The Rump ordered the army to support collection efforts with force if necessary, and set strict standards of accountability. The results were remarkable. During the period from 26 March 1649 to 25 December 1651, the Treasurers at War received £3.15 million from the assessment collectors. This was one hundred per cent of the amount assessed by parliament.[65]

The Rump's biggest financial difficulty was figuring out how to settle soldiers' arrears and to pay off the £1.5 million owed to people who had loaned money to the parliamentarian cause. The Rump settled these debts by selling church property and the king's personal possessions. The proceeds of these sales retired about £2.7 million of debt. The government issued debentures, secured by the anticipated profits of the land sales, to the soldiers for their arrears. The other creditors of the state were allowed to double the amount owed them by advancing a new amount equal to their original loan, all to be secured by the proceeds of the land sales, thereby receiving a good chance of getting land in exchange for the not-so-certain promise of eventual cash payment.[66]

These fiscal measures restored the credit of the Westminster government by July 1649. This made it possible for it to borrow £200,000 to pay the soldiers headed for Ireland six weeks' of their arrears in cash and to provide the expedition with a treasury of over £100,000.[67] The regular collection of taxes provided the Commonwealth with most of the £1.27 million needed to sustain the army and the £500,000 to support the navy during the next year.[68] The solution of the financial crisis opened the way for the Commonwealth to send an expeditionary force to Ireland.

The Cromwellian conquest of Ireland

The Council of State and army estimated that 19,000 soldiers were needed to conquer Ireland, including Jones's 7,000 men in Dublin. In March, Cromwell was asked to command the expedition. He accepted the offer on 23 March, and was appointed Lord Lieutenant of Ireland as well. He proposed that eight infantry and six cavalry regiments be selected by lot from the army in England to serve in Ireland. He made it clear that this force would not sail until all financial arrangements had been made.

As the English focused their military resources on the conquest of Ireland, Ormond worked to put a royalist army into the field. He received a major boost when the Ulster Scots and the 'Laggan' army of British settlers joined the royalist coalition. Their forces, combined with the Confederate armies, gave Ormond over

14,000 soldiers, not counting garrisons.[69] The royalist war effort got another boost when Rupert arrived in Kinsale with the royalist fleet. Rupert reinforced the efforts of the Wexford and Waterford corsairs against English commerce, forcing the Commonwealth to concentrate its navy in Irish waters.

With things finally going his way, in late March, Ormond sent the Earl of Castlehaven with 6,000 men to force O'Neill out of Leinster. Inchiquin supported this offensive by leading another 4,000 men to Athlone to threaten O'Neill's flank. By May, the royalists had driven O'Neill's army into central Ulster. O'Neill, out of desperation, signed a truce with the parliamentarian Monck, receiving gunpowder in exchange for the assistance and food he provided to Monck. Disaster struck, however, when Inchiquin ambushed a detachment of O'Neill's army near Dundalk, in early July, killing hundreds of men and capturing their cargo of gunpowder. This defeat forced O'Neill to retreat to western Ulster.[70]

O'Neill's retreat allowed Ormond to concentrate against Monck's garrisons in eastern Ulster. By 24 July, Inchiquin had captured Dundalk from Monck, leaving Derry as the only Ulster town in parliamentarian hands. Derry, commanded by Sir Charles Coote, held out only because O'Neill protected Coote from local royalists threatening the town. Thus, the Catholic civil war continued to hamper Ormond's efforts to drive the parliamentarians out of Ireland before Cromwell could get his army ready.[71]

Inchiquin captured Drogheda and Trim in late July, tightening the noose around Dublin, the last remaining parliamentary position in Leinster. While the royalists moved closer, Jones received fresh supplies and reinforcements, bringing his strength to 8,000 men. Jones then launched sorties against the royalists, demonstrating that Dublin would not be captured without a concerted effort. Meanwhile, Cromwell prepared the expeditionary force in England.

Cromwell's biggest problem in getting his army to Ireland, once the financial affairs were settled, was his need to defeat the Levellers who had infiltrated the ranks. In March, soldiers petitioned Fairfax demanding their arrears and radical governmental reforms. In response, Fairfax ordered the malcontents purged from the ranks. Attempts to do so triggered a mutiny led by Robert Lockyer in late April.[72]

Fairfax and Cromwell reacted swiftly, surrounding the mutineers with loyal regiments and arresting the ringleaders. The ringleaders were court-martialled and Lockyer and several others shot. Lockyer's funeral in London, however, triggered demonstrations by thousands of Londoners in sympathy with the Levellers, forcing Fairfax to compromise and allow soldiers who did not want to serve in Ireland to leave the army. During the discharge of these men, several regiments mutinied and refused to go to Ireland until their rights and the 'nations' privileges' were secured. By the end of May, three hundred mutineers had gathered near Oxford, and the movement seemed sure to spread if prompt action was not taken.[73]

Fairfax and Cromwell again responded to this challenge to their authority and army discipline. On 9 May they mustered a force in Hyde Park, where Cromwell convinced the soldiers of the necessity to crush the mutiny and to get on with the business in Ireland. He reminded the soldiers of their years of service together and the blood shed for the new political covenant. With their loyalty assured, Cromwell and Fairfax ran down the mutineers at Burford, west of Oxford. They court-martialled the ringleaders and shot three in the churchyard on 15 May. Resistance to the Irish expedition collapsed, allowing Cromwell to get his units moving to the embarkation ports.[74]

As Cromwell's regiments converged on Milford Haven and Bristol in late July, Ormond moved his army to Finglas, near Dublin, where he and his senior commanders debated their next move (see map 19). Many of them were reluctant to assault the city's defenses. However, they understood that a siege could not starve Jones out since the Commonwealth's navy protected his lines of communications to England. And they knew that Cromwell was on his way, and there was concern that he might land in southern Ireland. Therefore, some of the royalists wanted to send forces south. The majority of the Catholic officers, however, wanted to isolate Dublin by establishing artillery positions overlooking the sea approaches to the city from Dublin Bay.

Ormond accepted a compromise solution. He ordered Inchiquin with two cavalry regiments to ride to Munster to watch for Cromwell, while he moved most of the army to a new camp at Rathmines, south of the River Liffey, where they could threaten Dublin's communications. Lord Dillon, with 2,500 men, remained at Finglas. These deployments were completed by 26 July. On 29 July, Ormond decided to establish an artillery battery near the ruined castle of Baggotsrath, within cannon range of the mouth of the Liffey. Expecting Jones to counterattack, Ormond sent a strong force to Baggotsrath on the evening of 1 August to protect the proposed battery from an attack by Jones.

This force, led by Major General Purcell, got lost during the night, arriving at Baggotsrath at about 9 a.m. Jones, hearing of the royalist movements, led 5,200 men out of Dublin and launched an attack against Purcell's 1,500 soldiers before they could entrench. Jones's attack overwhelmed the royalists, crushing their attempts to stand and fight with flank attacks. Ormond and Purcell tried to rally their men and to bring reinforcements up from the Rathmines camp, just a mile away, but the onslaught was too swift for them to stop it.[75]

The parliamentarians crushed the force at Baggotsrath, killing Major General Vaughan, Ormond's cavalry commander. Then Jones launched an attack west toward the royalist camp at Rathmines. Ormond, his brother Richard Butler, and Colonel Giffard did all they could to rally the royalist troops at Rathmines, but their regiments disintegrated in flight toward the Wicklow Hills. Dillon, at Finglas, refused Ormond's pleas to attack the rear of Jones's army, dooming the royalists to their worst defeat of the war. By evening, Ormond was a fugitive with his army shattered. Jones killed and captured as many as 4,000 royalists, with minor loss to his army. Just as important, he had preserved Dublin for the landing of Cromwell's army.[76]

Cromwell's army arrived between 15 and 23 August, in a fleet of over 130 ships (see map 20). He brought with him a large artillery train, a full treasury, and well-disciplined regiments. After reorganizing Jones's units and dismissing men unfit for

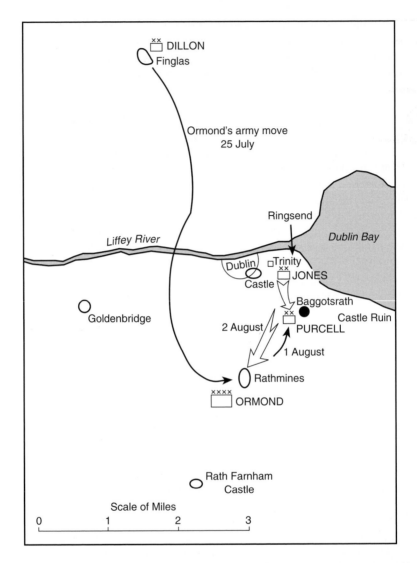

Map 19 Operations around Dublin, 25 July–2 August

duty, Cromwell marched north to Drogheda, with about 9,000 men. The English army arrived before that town on 3 September, joined a few days later by a fleet carrying the siege artillery and supplies. As he moved, Cromwell promised the Irish people fair treatment and cash for food they brought in to sell his soldiers. He also promised to punish any of his men who mistreated them, enforcing this decree with the execution of several looters.[77]

Drogheda was the well-fortified gateway to Ulster, on the Boyne River. It was defended by 2,800 royalists commanded by Sir Arthur Aston. Ormond was powerless

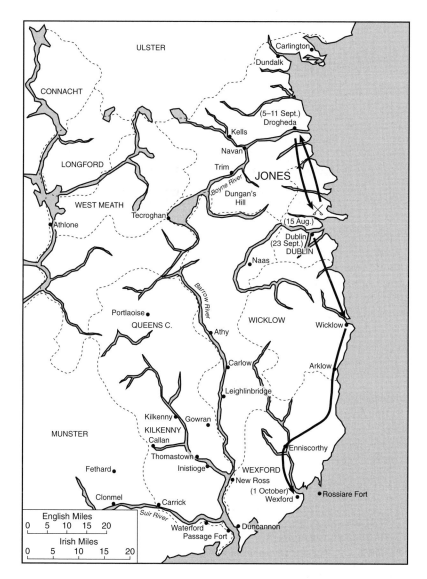

Map 20 Cromwell's Campaign, September 1649

to stop Cromwell's advance, having failed in his attempts to unite Clanricarde's and Monro's armies with the remnants of his forces. Consequently, Ormond observed Cromwell from a distance, hoping that the defenses of Drogheda would force him to settle into a costly siege while he convinced Owen Roe O'Neill to join the war effort.[78]

Cromwell, however, planned to take Drogheda by storm, after his siege guns blew breaches in the walls. To accomplish this, he sited his cannon at two positions

213

on the southeast corner of the town, where assault columns could converge at St Mary's Church (see map 21). The guns were in place by 10 September. After asking Aston to surrender, 'to the end the effusion of blood may be prevented,' and receiving his refusal, Cromwell ordered his guns to open fire the next day.[79]

The artillery fired several hundred shots at the walls, creating two breaches in the 'east and south wall' and demolishing the steeple of St Mary's. Three infantry regiments attacked these breaches at about 5 p.m., and for the next hour a fierce battle raged. Aston's men drove the first wave of Roundheads out of the southern breach, forcing Cromwell to lead another assault into and through the defenses. This did the trick, as the exhausted royalists were driven from their entrenchments inside the walls and their regimental commander was killed.[80]

The parliamentarians pursued closely, preventing Aston's men from pulling up the drawbridge over the River Boyne that connected the main town on the north side with the south-side suburb. Aston and about 200 defenders retreated to a hill known as the Mill Mound where, as Cromwell reported, 'our men getting up to them, were ordered by me to put them all to the sword. And indeed, being in the heat of action, I forbade them to spare any that were in arms in the town.'[81] Cromwell exploited his success at the breaches by pouring cavalry into the town, making it impossible for the defenders to organize a defense. Over the next few hours the attackers killed most of the defenders, including many who tried to surrender. Some innocent townspeople also were killed in the chaotic fighting. Cromwell later explained why he ordered his men to take no prisoners:

> I am persuaded that this is a righteous judgment of God upon these barbarous wretches, who have imbrued their hands in so much innocent blood; and that it will tend to prevent the effusion of blood for the future, which are the satisfactory grounds to such actions, which otherwise cannot but work remorse and regret.[82]

Cromwell ordered the slaughter as a warning to future defenders and as a punishment for actions for which he held Aston and his men responsible. Since as many as half of the defenders were Protestants, Cromwell was punishing them for their part in the royalist war effort in 1648–9 for the same reasons the parliamentarians executed English royalists after the surrender of Colchester. Cromwell also associated the Catholics in Aston's garrison with the atrocities committed in the Irish war. In both cases, it was avoidable bloodshed and a blot on the record of Cromwell and the English army.[83] The evidence does not, however, support the view that Cromwell's army slaughtered many innocent civilians in Drogheda.[84]

Cromwell's capture of Drogheda struck fear into the nearby royalist garrisons, all of which quickly surrendered. With the gateway to Ulster open, Cromwell sent Colonel Robert Venables north with 4,000 men to destroy Monro and the royalists in eastern Ulster. Venables did this efficiently over the next three months, culminating his campaign with the defeat of Monro's army at Lisnagarvy and the capture of Carrickfergus in December. His actions were matched by Sir Charles Coote's ruthless

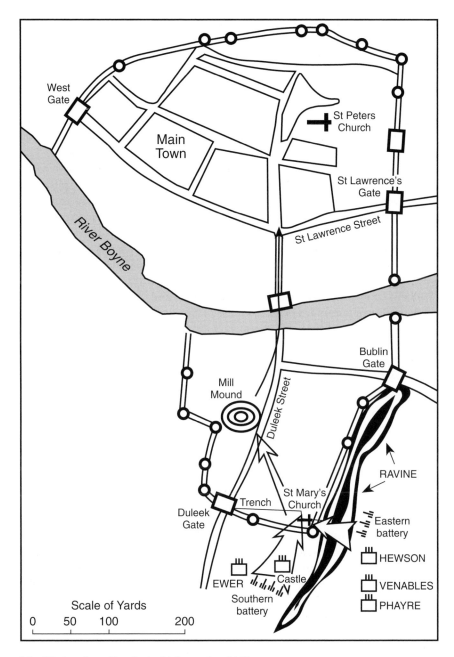

Map 21 Assault on Drogheda, 11 September 1649

campaign against the royalists in western Ulster. By the end of the year, Ulster was firmly in Cromwellian hands.[85]

Following the capture of Drogheda, Cromwell and Lieutenant General Michael Jones marched the main army south, through Dublin and on to Wexford, in southern Leinster. Ships carrying munitions, food, and heavy artillery supported their advance along the coast. Ormond was powerless to stop the advance, and the royalist garrisons in Arklow and Ferns offered only token resistance before surrendering to Cromwell's Ironsides. In each case, Cromwell spared the lives of the defenders and the property of the inhabitants.

The speed with which the Commonwealth's army moved unhinged the royalists. Ormond's strategy after Drogheda was 'Fabian', based on the idea that the royalists would avoid a battle with Cromwell's army while relying on disease and hunger to defeat the enemy through attrition. All armies in Ireland had employed such a strategy during the previous eight years. Such a method only works if the enemy is not sustained with replacements, food, and clothing. Cromwell's forces were regularly supplied and reinforced, allowing him to capture towns that had been the bases for the Catholic and royalist war efforts during the past eight years.

On 1 October, the English army approached Wexford, where a Commonwealth naval squadron commanded by Richard Deane had already arrived. Wexford was an important Irish naval base and commercial center whose loss would grievously wound the royalists. Knowing this, Cromwell prepared to take the town in the same manner he had taken Drogheda, with a bombardment and an assault into breaches created by the artillery. As Deane and Jones opened the approaches to Wexford and landed the siege guns, Cromwell summoned the garrison commander, David Sinnott, to surrender, 'to the end effusion of blood may be prevented and the town and country about it preserved from ruin, …'[86]

Sinnott played for time, hoping that Ormond would reinforce him. Cromwell refused to accept much delay, giving the town one day to decide whether or not to surrender. Sinnott asked for negotiations to take place on 5 October, and then played for more time as Castlehaven approached with 1,500 Irish soldiers. Finally, on 9 October, Sinnott wrote to Cromwell to tell him that he would not surrender. By the next evening, Deane and his sailors had helped Cromwell's men establish a battery on the south end of town and the guns opened fire (see map 22). After about a hundred shots, Sinnott asked for another parley and submitted terms to Cromwell. On 11 October Cromwell rejected Sinnott's proposals but renewed his promise to spare the garrison and inhabitants if Sinnott submitted.

While negotiations were taking place, one of Sinnott's officers surrendered a castle outside the walls to the besiegers. Cromwell's men quickly occupied the castle, which overlooked the town's wall, and launched an assault over the walls. The garrison fought stubbornly against this attack but were driven back into the center of town and overwhelmed. The fighting became a slaughter of the defenders and hundreds of innocent townspeople. Many inhabitants also drowned while trying to escape across Wexford harbor when the attackers sank their boats with heavy fire. Over two thousand townspeople died in the capture of Wexford, leaving the town nearly

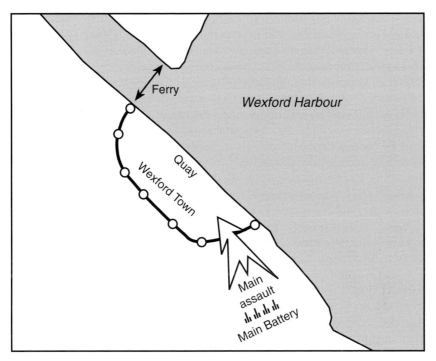

Map 22 Assault on Wexford, 11 October 1649

uninhabited.[87] After Wexford, all garrisons in Ireland thought carefully before refusing Cromwell's summons to surrender.

Ormond lost at least 5,000 soldiers at Drogheda and Wexford. Worse, the Catholics in the royalist coalition lost faith in his military abilities and the alliance frayed as Cromwell continued his relentless advance.[88] Cromwell's capture of Wexford gave the Commonwealth navy a good harbor in southern Ireland from which it could support the army and operate against Rupert's fleet in Kinsale (see map 22). Rupert, seeing how close the parliamentarian army was to Kinsale, decided to sail to Portugal with his seven remaining warships.

From Wexford, Cromwell marched most of the army to New Ross on the Barrow River, arriving there on 17 October. By 19 October, the English artillery had blown a breach in the wall and Cromwell's infantry was preparing for an assault. The governor of New Ross, Lucas Taaffe, then asked for terms. Cromwell offered to allow Taaffe to lead his 2,000 soldiers out of the town unmolested, leaving only his artillery and ammunition. Taaffe accepted. As Taaffe departed, one of Inchiquin's Protestant regiments in the garrison deserted and joined Cromwell's army.[89]

The defection of one of Inchiquin's regiments at New Ross indicated how tattered the royalist coalition had become. In the same week, the Protestant garrisons of Cork and Youghal revolted against Inchiquin and surrendered to English troops led by Lord Broghill. Such defections continued in November, when Protestants in

Bandon and Kinsale surrendered to Cromwell without a fight. His acquisition of these towns was timely, since bad weather had set in, bringing disease and misery to his troops. After receiving his first repulses in Ireland at Duncannon and Waterford in November, Cromwell put his soldiers into winter quarters and awaited the arrival of 9,000 replacements from England.[90]

The only positive development for Ormond in the fall of 1649 was when Owen Roe O'Neill joined the royalist fight against the invaders, in October. O'Neill sent 2,000 men south with Lieutenant General Farrell to aid Ormond, but O'Neill died before he could follow with the rest of his army. O'Neill's reinforcements saved Ormond from complete defeat in the autumn, making Cromwell's task harder. But most of the Ulster army remained inactive during the winter, as the Old Irish deliberated about who should replace O'Neill. Since O'Neill's regiments were the best Catholic troops in Ireland, their absence was sorely missed by Ormond.

During the short pause for winter quarters, from December to late January 1650, the Catholics of the royalist coalition debated whether or not to continue to accept Ormond's leadership. Eventually they decided to stay in the coalition, but they demanded and received greater control of military policy. This was reasonable since, by early 1650, the majority of the troops were Catholics. The royalists also sought foreign aid, but to no avail.[91]

As the news from Ireland worsened, the Queen and Charles II's advisors determined that it was unsafe for him to join Ormond in Ireland, as previously planned. Instead, they concluded that Charles II's best hope of recovering his father's throne was to make a deal with the Scots. Ormond concurred in this judgment. From January 1650 on, therefore, the royalist war effort in Ireland was diversionary, to buy time for an agreement to be reached with the Scots.

By the end of January 1650, Cromwell's expeditionary force had been reinforced to over 20,000 men. The Commonwealth managed to send a steady stream of supplies and money to Ireland, enabling Cromwell to launch a campaign in the mild winter of 1649–50.[92] Cromwell launched this effort on 29 January, catching the royalists off guard. In the next three weeks, the English captured most of the royalist strong points in Munster against negligible resistance. In fact, Ormond found it difficult to get his regiments to leave their comfortable winter garrisons to operate against the English columns then converging on the royalist capital of Kilkenny.[93]

By 20 March, English columns from Munster and from Dublin were near Kilkenny (see map 23). Royalist efforts to respond were hampered by the plague, shortages of supplies, and continued political dissension within the coalition. Thus, Kilkenny was defended by fewer than 600 soldiers and 1,200 townsmen, under the command of Sir Walter Butler, who resolved to 'maintain this city for his majesty, which by the power of God, I am resolved to do.'[94]

The English launched their assault against Kilkenny on 23 March. Over the next three days, the Redcoats overran the Irish Town on the north and the suburb of St John's on the east, putting them in a position to mount their final assault against the outnumbered defenders. At this point Butler asked for terms of surrender. Cromwell granted lenient terms to the garrison and the townspeople, as he had done to all

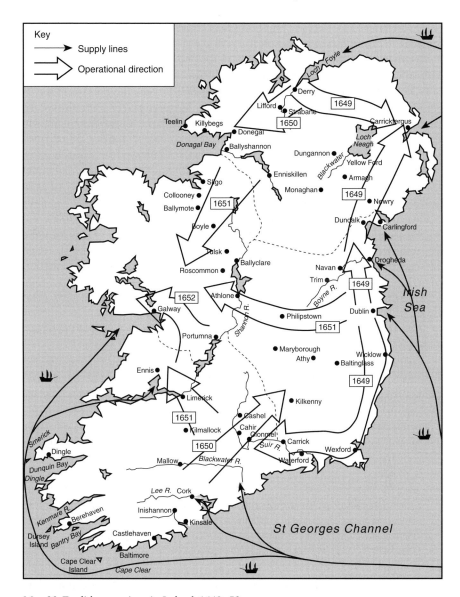

Map 23 English operations in Ireland, 1649–52

towns his army captured in the winter of 1650. Butler and his men were allowed to march out with their arms, and the town was spared a sack. On 27 March, the English army occupied the royalist capital.[95]

Cromwell continued to offer lenient surrender conditions to those Protestants remaining in the royalist coalition. His successful winter campaign convinced most to surrender. By May, Ormond, Inchiquin, and a few faithful followers remained the only Protestants in the royalist camp. From then on, resistance to the English conquest came mainly from the Irish Catholics.

Cromwell made his final contribution to the conquest of Ireland at Clonmel, in May 1650. There the New Model Army met its worst defeat in Ireland when Hugh O'Neill and his Ulstermen killed 2,000 Redcoats in a breach in the town's wall.[96] None the less, O'Neill had to evacuate the place due to shortages of munitions and food, leaving Cromwell to grant generous surrender terms to the mayor. Shortly thereafter Cromwell returned to England to assume urgent duties. Ormond was unable to stop Cromwell's successor, Henry Ireton, from capturing Waterford in August and advancing to Limerick in October 1650. Consequently, the Irish refused to follow Ormond's orders any longer, ending the royalist coalition in Ireland. Ormond sailed to France on 11 December 1650.

After the departure of Cromwell and Ormond, the major ports of Limerick and Galway and all of Connacht still remained in Irish hands. For the next two years, the Commonwealth poured men and resources into Ireland to support the total subjugation of the island. At least 43,000 English soldiers were sent, from March 1649 through December 1651, to join the 9,000 men already there. By 1652, only 37,000 of these soldiers remained alive. Thirty-seven percent, including Michael Jones and Henry Ireton, had died due to various causes.[97] The war ended only after all of the island had been occupied and the English allowed as many as 34,000 Irish soldiers to go overseas to serve in the Spanish armies.[98]

Charles II abandoned his Irish subjects. In May 1650, he signed an agreement with the Scots that included the repudiation of the Irish and any hope of religious toleration for his Catholic subjects. This agreement meant that the greatest threat to the English Commonwealth, henceforth, came from Scotland. For this reason, the Council of State ordered Cromwell to return in May to prepare the army for another war against the Scots.

Notes

1 Bodl., Carte MS 22, fos. 58–9, Ormond's memorandum of 5 April 1648, 'All that I conceive necessary to be done by way of preparations for the business of Ireland'; Carte, *Ormond*, iii: 331–3; Corish in *NHI*, iii: 327, for the quote.

2 Bodl., Carte MS 2, fo. 67, John Barry to Ormond, 15 April 1648; Corish in *NHI*, iii: 324–26; O' Siochru, *Confederate Ireland*, 160–4; Ohlmeyer, *Civil War and Resoration*, 199–202; Lenihan, *Confederate Catholics*, 106–9.

3 Ohlmeyer, *Antrim*, 201.

4 Ibid., 201–4; Corish in *NHI*, iii: 326–8; O' Siochru, *Confederate Ireland*, 166–8; Tadhg O' hAnnrachain, 'The Strategic Involvement of Continental Powers in Ireland, 1596–1691,' in P. Lenihan, ed., *Conquest and Resistance, War in Seventeenth-Century Ireland* (Leiden, 2001), 36–44.

5 TT E452 (10), *The Declaration of the Protestant Army in the Province of Munster*, (Cork, April 1648).

6 O' Siochru, *Confederate Ireland*, 172.

7 Ibid., 169–73; D. Corish, 'The Crisis in Ireland in 1648: The Nuncio and the Supreme Council: Conclusions', *Irish Theological Quarterly*, 22 (July 1955), 230–57.

8 Corish in *NHI*, iii: 328–9.

9 Bodl., Carte MS 22, fo. 99, 'Terms of Agreement Between Inchiquin and Lord Montgarret and the rest of the Supreme Council', 20 May 1648.

10 Corish in *NHI*, iii: 330; Corish, 'Rinuccini's Censure of 27 May 1648', *Irish Theological Quarterly*, 18 (October 1951), 322–37; O'Siochru, *Confederate Ireland*, 173–8.

11 Bodl., Carte MS 22, fos. 58–9, Ormond's memorandum of 5 April 1648.

12 Ibid., fo. 167, Declaration of 13 August 1648; D. Murphy, *Cromwell in Ireland* (Dublin, 1897), 13.

13 Bodl., Carte MS 22, fo. 301, Clanricarde to Ormond, 4 October 1648; TT E536 (14), *Full Satisfaction Concerning the Affairs of Ireland*, (Cork, 30 November 1648).

14 R. Gillespie, 'The Irish Economy at War, 1641–1652', in Ohlmeyer, ed., *Ireland*, 176–8; TT E468 (3), *The Proceedings of the Army … Under Colonel Michael Jones*, (Dublin, 2 October 1648), 2–7.

15 Lenihan, *Confederate Catholics*, 108–10; O' Siochru, *Confederate Ireland*, 190–2; Corish in *NHI*, iii: 332–3.

16 Abbott, i: 657–8, Cromwell to the Derby House Committee, 20 September 1648; Gardiner, *Civil War*, iv: 227–30 for Gardiner's account of Cromwell's northern campaign in September.

17 Abbott, i: 650, Cromwell to Sir William Armyn (?), 14 September 1648; ibid., 650–1, Cromwell to Ludovic Leslie, 15 September 1648.

18 Gardiner, *Civil War*, iv: 228–9.

19 Abbott, i: 651–2, Cromwell to the Committee of Estates, 16 September 1648; ibid., 652–3, Cromwell to Argyll, 16 September 1648; Ibid., 653–4, Cromwell to the Earl of Loudon, Chancellor of Scotland, 18 September 1648.

20 Ibid., 656–8, Cromwell to the Derby House Committee, 20 September 1648.

21 Ibid., 660–2, Cromwell to William Lenthall, Speaker of the House of Commons, 2 October 1648.

22 Ibid., 663–4, Cromwell to the Committee of Estates, 5 October 1648.

23 Ibid., 668–9, Cromwell to Lenthall, 9 October 1648.

24 Bodl., Rawlinson MS A223, fos. 6, 45–8, 75–7, 80–1, 85, 97.

25 Capp, *Cromwell's Navy*, chapter 2; R. Anderson, 'The Operations of the English Fleet, 1648–52', *English Historical Review* 31 (1916), 406–28; Rodger, *Safeguard of the Seas*, 424–6; P. Kennedy, *The Rise and Fall of British Naval Mastery* (London, 1986 edn.), 45–8.

26 Capp, *Cromwell's Navy*, 20–1.

27 Ibid., 29–33.

28 Ibid., 33–6.

29 Ibid., 36–40.

30 MacCormack, *Revolutionary Politics*, 280–4; Gardiner, *Civil War*, iv: 130, 212–14.

31 Ibid., 214–17; Abbott, i: 674–6.

32 MacCormack, *Revolutionary Politics*, 287–92; Gardiner, *Civil War*, iv: 237–9.

33 R. Ramsey, *Henry Ireton* (London, 1949), 115–26.

34 MacCormack, *Revolutionary Politics*, 240–4; Abbott, i: 689.

35 Gentles, *New Model Army*, 274.

36 Abbott, i: 690, 701–4.

37 Ibid., 676–94, 701–3; MacCormack, *Revolutionary Politics*, 300–1; Gentles, *New Model Army*, 283–5; Gardiner, *Civil War*, iv: 247–72.

38 C. Wedgwood, *A Coffin for King Charles* (New York, 1991 edn.), 30–3; Abbott, i: 704–5.

39 Firth, ed., *Clarke Papers*, ii: 61–3; Gardiner, *Civil War*, iv: 262–3; MacCormack, *Revolutionary Politics*, 301–2; Gentles, *New Model Army*, 278–9.

40 Gentles, *New Model Army*, 280.

41 *JHC*, vi: 93. The vote was 136 to 102.

42 Ibid.

43 Gardiner, *Civil War*, iv: 269–71; Gentles, *New Model Army*, 281–3.

44 Ramsey, *Ireton*, 127–36; *Clarke Papers*, ii: 71–135; Gardiner, *Civil War*, iv: 276–8.

45 TT E476 (76), *An Agreement of the People*, 10 December 1648, (London, 15 December 1648).

46 B. Worden, *The Rump Parliament* (Cambridge, 1977 edn.), 39–42.

47 Gardiner, *Civil War*, iv: 278–80.

48 *Clarke Papers*, ii: 67–9, A Letter from Headquarters, 12 December 1648.

49 *JHC*, vi: 96.

50   Gardiner, *Civil War*, iv: 284–6.

51   *JHC*, vi: 111, 4 January resolution; *A & O*, i: 1,253–5.

52   Gardiner, ed., *Constitutional Documents*, 288, 'The Sentence of the High Court of Justice Upon the King.'

53   Gardiner, ed., *Constitutional Documents*, 282–4.

54   Gardiner, *Civil War*, iv: 301 for quote. Pages 287–330 for the 'cruel necessity' of Charles's trial and execution; Wedgwood, *Coffin for King Charles*, 135–66.

55   Gardiner, *Civil War*, iv: 308–30. For the quote see Gardiner, ed., *Constitutional Documents*, 288, 'The Sentence of the High Court of Justice Upon the King.'

56   O' Siochru, *Confederate Ireland*, 177–88.

57   Ibid., 188–93; Lenihan, *Confederate Catholics*, 110.

58   TT E555 (21), *Articles of Peace* …, (London, 16 May 1649), 3–4.

59   *A & O*, i: 1,363; ibid., ii: 2–4, 18, 24; *JHC*, vi: 132, 133, 140–1; Worden, *The Rump Parliament*; S. Kelsey, *Inventing a Republic* (Stanford, 1997); R. Hainsworth, *The Swordsmen in Power: War and Politics under the English Republic, 1649–1660* (Stroud, 1997); S. Gardiner, *History of the Commonwealth and Protectorates* (London, 1913).

60   *JHC*, vi: 138–9; Gardiner, ed., *Constitutional Documents*, 291–3.

61   *JHC*, vi: 138, 144.

62   P. Kerrigan, 'Ireland in Naval Strategy, 1641–1691,' in Lenihan, ed., *Conquest and Resistance*, 160–2; Wheeler, *Making of a World Power*, 43–6; Capp, *Cromwell's Navy*, 41–65.

63   Worden, *The Rump Parliament*, 40–73; Hainsworth, *The Swordsmen in Power*, 22–4.

64   Wheeler, *Cromwell in Ireland*, 68–9, and 254, note 14.

65   Wheeler, *Making of a World Power*, 187, table 8.2, and 257, note 67.

66   Ibid., 111–19.

67   PRO, SP25/118, 'A Particular of the Charges of Raising and Paying the … [Expedition] for Ireland.'

68   M. Braddick, *The Nerves of State: Taxation and the Financing of the English State, 1558–1714* (Manchester, 1996); M. Braddick, *Parliamentary Taxation in Seventeenth-Century England* (Woodbridge, Suffolk, 1994).

69   Bodl., Carte MS 25, fos. 1–18, especially Ormond to Charles II, 1 June 1649.

70   Wheeler, *Cromwell in Ireland*, 55–7.

71   Ibid., 57–9.

72   Gardiner, *History of the Commonwealth*, i: 31–48; Gentles, *New Model Army*, 318–29.

73   Wheeler, *Cromwell in Ireland*, 68–9.

74   Ibid., 69–70.

75   Ibid., 76–9.

76   Ibid., 78–9.

77   Abbott, ii: 110–12, Proclamation issued in Dublin, 24 August 1649; Wheeler, *Cromwell in Ireland*, 81–3.

78   Wheeler, *Cromwell in Ireland*, 79–81.

79   Abbott, ii: 118, Cromwell to Aston, 10 September 1649; Ibid., 125–8, Cromwell to Lenthall, 17 September 1649.

80   Ibid.; TT E533 (15), *Perfect Occurrences*, 28 September-4 October 1649, 1,275–6, for Colonel Hewson's account; Whitelocke, *Memorials*, 412, 'More Letters of the Taking of Drogheda', 1 October 1649; Murphy, *Cromwell in Ireland*, 97–8, and footnote on 98; Gardiner, *C & P*, i: 117–20.

81   Abbott, ii: 126, Cromwell to Lenthall, 17 September 1649.

82   Ibid., 127, Cromwell to Lenthall, 17 September 1649.

83   For a different view, see T. Reilly, *Cromwell: An Honorable Enemy. The Untold Story of the Cromwellian Invasion of Ireland* (London, 1999), 93–130.

84   Wheeler, *Cromwell in Ireland*, 83–8.

85   Ibid., 104–5.

86   Abbott, ii: 135, Cromwell to David Sinnott, 3 October 1649.

87 Ibid., 140–3, Cromwell to Lenthall, 14 October 1649.
88 Bodl., Carte MS 26, fo. 25, Barry to Ormond, 15 October 1649.
89 Abbott, ii: 144–8.
90 Wheeler, *Cromwell in Ireland*, 102–4, 107–15.
91 Ibid., 122–4; J. Ohlmeyer, ed., *Ireland: From Independence to Occupation, 1641–1660* (Cambridge, 1995), 105–7.
92 Wheeler, *Cromwell in Ireland*, 118–20; P. Lake, *Dealing in Death: The Arms Trade and the British Civil Wars, 1638–1652* (Stroud, 2000), 44–8.
93 Abbott, ii: 212–15, Cromwell to Lenthall, 15 February 1650; Corish in *NHI*, iii: 344–6.
94 Abbott, ii: 224.
95 Ibid., 226, Cromwell to Walter Butler, 26 March 1650; ibid., 228, Articles of Surrender of Kilkenny, 27 March 1650.
96 J. Burke, 'The New Model Army and the Problem of Siege Warfare', *Irish Historical Studies*, 27 (1990), 16.
97 *CSPD, 1650*, 570–608; *CSPD, 1651*, 155–60, 168, 171; Bodl., Carte MS 29, fo. 928, list of English garrisons, winter 1650–1; PRO, SP25/118, fos. 137–46; R. Dunlop, ed., *Ireland Under the Commonwealth* (Manchester, 1913), i: 7–8.
98 Gilbert, ed., *A Contemporary History*, iii: 296–335 for surrender terms offered Irish military commanders in 1652; R. Stradling, *The Spanish Monarchy and Irish Mercenaries: The Wild Geese in Spain, 1618–1668* (Dublin, 1994).

CHAPTER NINE

The triumph and failure of the Commonwealth, 1649–53

The English Commonwealth faced daunting challenges in 1649. European governments, shocked at the execution of Charles I, encouraged exiled royalists that they might receive foreign military assistance. The end of the Thirty Years' War increased such hopes because the Dutch and French had considerably fewer commitments, thus freeing resources for other purposes. However, for a variety of reasons, the leading western powers were not forthcoming with military aid. This left Charles II reliant on Ormond's efforts and on the possible resurgence of the Scottish royalists.

While Ireland remained the Commonwealth's military priority until the successful completion of Cromwell's campaign of January to May 1650, the English government faced threats at sea that had to be surmounted if it were to survive. Therefore, while Cromwell fought in Ireland, the newly appointed leaders of the Commonwealth's navy faced the republic's enemies at sea.

The first campaigns of the Commonwealth's navy

The most dangerous naval threat to the republic came from Rupert's squadron, which had retreated to Helvoetsluys in September 1648. By January 1649, Rupert had overstayed his welcome in Dutch waters, mainly because of the lack of discipline of his crews and his privateering activities. On 21 January 1649, Rupert sailed for Ireland, where he planned to join the Irish privateers in their campaign against English commerce. He arrived in Kinsale at the end of January, where he established a royalist naval presence and commenced operations against English merchant ships.[1]

The Rump could not respond to this challenge until April, due to the remodeling of its naval administration and the need to resolve its financial crisis. By May 1649, these actions were far enough along to allow the three Generals at Sea to lead a large fleet to Irish waters, where they established a blockade of Kinsale, bringing an abrupt halt to Rupert's attacks. They also plugged up the approaches to Waterford, making it difficult for Irish privateers to prey on English shipping.[2]

The English blockade of the Munster ports, and especially of Kinsale, was sustained through the summer and early autumn of 1649. Another naval squadron commanded by George Ayscue protected the sea-lanes to Dublin, enabling supplies and reinforcements to reach Jones. These supplies and men saved Dublin and allowed Jones to mount his attack against Ormond's army at Baggotsrath-Rathmines, nearly two weeks before Cromwell arrived. The navy also escorted the transports that carried Cromwell's men and supplies from western England to Dublin, allowing them to land unmolested between 15 and 23 August.

The Westminster government took special pains to ensure the loyalty and effectiveness of its navy. Competent officers loyal to the new regime took command of the ships, and the Council selected navy commissioners for their administrative expertise as well as for their loyalty. The Rump provided sufficient funds to its naval administrators to sustain operations at an unprecedented rate and to begin an ambitious naval construction program that doubled the fleet in the next two years. Under energetic leadership, the navy dramatically diminished privateering in the North Sea, the Channel, and in Irish waters. Without the navy, Cromwell could not have even got to Ireland, let alone sustained his campaign.[3]

The capture of Wexford in October ended one threat to English commerce. The defection of the Munster Protestants from Ormond's coalition forced Rupert to leave Ireland, which he did when bad weather drove Colonel Robert Blake's squadron off station in late October. The defection of the royalist garrison of Kinsale to parliament in November ended another threat to the republic and gave it a base for operations against the Irish privateers in Waterford.

After leaving Ireland, Rupert led his squadron to Lisbon, Portugal, where he arrived with thirteen ships in late November 1649. There he took sanctuary. The Portuguese, however, were reluctant hosts, occupied with a war against Spain. Although their king, John IV, was sympathetic to Charles II, he did not want to provoke a war against the Commonwealth. The English Council of State, after deliberation, was willing to risk a war with Portugal if that was necessary to end the royalist naval threat. On 2 March 1650, Robert Blake and sixteen warships left Portsmouth and sailed to Lisbon to destroy Rupert's fleet. Blake's instructions also allowed him to take action against Portuguese vessels if necessary.[4]

Blake arrived in time to corner Rupert's fleet in the Tagus River. After the Portuguese refused to surrender their guests, Blake led his squadron into the Tagus, hoping to come to blows with the royalists. However, as he got close to Rupert's anchorage the wind died, preventing Blake from consummating his offensive move. The Portuguese then interposed their warships between the two enemies, preventing Blake from engaging the Cavaliers. The English Council of State responded by sending Colonel Edward Popham to Portugal with reinforcements and supply ships. Popham's arrival allowed Blake to maintain his blockade of the Tagus and Lisbon, choking Portuguese commerce as well as bottling up Rupert.

Blake continued his blockade of Lisbon into November 1650. In the process, he defeated two sorties of a combined Portuguese-royalist-French fleet, captured the outward- and inward-bound Portuguese Brazil fleets, and prevented Rupert from hindering English commerce. Blake's successes were possible because the English naval establishment provided a steady stream of supplies and reinforcements to sustain his fleet off the Tagus. It was a remarkable accomplishment, even though Rupert finally escaped, on 12 October, while Blake was replenishing water near Cadiz. Rupert fled into the Mediterranean, where Blake caught up with him in late November and captured or destroyed most of the royalist ships. Rupert again escaped, but with only two poorly maintained vessels. He no longer threatened the Commonwealth. Blake returned to England in February 1651, where he was greeted as a hero.[5]

While Blake pursued Rupert, the Commonwealth's navy continued to protect the supplies and reinforcements sent to Ireland, allowing Cromwell and his successor, Henry Ireton, to increase the army to 37,000 men. Beginning in July 1650, however, the navy received an additional mission that further taxed its capabilities and forced the Rump to provide more resources to the fleet. This occurred just as the Commonwealth increased its army to defend itself from another significant threat from Scotland.

The origins of the last Anglo–Scottish war, 1650–2

When Cromwell left Scotland in October 1648, he was fairly certain that the northern neighbor did not pose an immediate threat to the revolutionary changes that he and the army contemplated in London. Argyll and the party of the Kirk were firmly in control of Edinburgh. The Engagers had agreed to disband their forces, leaving an army of fewer than 5,000 men on foot in Scotland. As a precaution, Cromwell established strong garrisons in Carlisle, Berwick, and Newcastle, blocking the best routes into northern England in case the Scots decided to intervene in England. Cromwell, however, hoped that his 'Scottish brethren' would remain on good terms with England while the army dealt with parliament, the king, and then Ireland.[6]

The Rump's execution of Charles I diminished the chances that Scotland would remain at peace with the Commonwealth. On 5 February 1649, the Scots proclaimed Charles II as 'King of Great Britain, France, and Ireland.' This was a direct threat to the English republic and its plans to conquer Ireland. Scottish commissioners followed this proclamation with a visit to the Commons in Westminster, on 24 February, where they upbraided the Rump for its violations of the Solemn League and Covenant. The Rump retaliated by denouncing the commissioners' outburst, noting that the Scots were laying 'the grounds of a new and bloody war.'[7]

Argyll, meanwhile, maintained his grip on the Scottish Committee of Estates, although he saw that the winds of Scottish nationalism and religious distaste for the English regicide were blowing Scotland toward another war against England. Argyll consolidated his power with the 'Act of Classes', passed by the Scottish parliament in January 1649. This act barred most royalists and many Engagers from participating in government for a period of between five years and life, depending on their roles in the Scottish civil war of 1648. Argyll and his brother, the Lord Chancellor, understood that their grip on the nation was precarious, especially since a majority of the Scottish nobility supported making an arrangement with the new king.[8]

Charles II faced the daunting question of how to regain his father's throne. He hoped that another royalist uprising in England would take place that could topple the new regime. In 1649 this was most unlikely, given the powerful blows inflicted on the royalists by Fairfax and Cromwell in 1648. Therefore, Charles II had to look to either Scotland or Ireland to find the forces and the resources needed to return him to England. Unfortunately for the king, a royalist alliance of Irish Catholics with Presbyterian Scots was beyond the realm of the possible, forcing Charles to decide whom to use. He chose to continue his father's policy of basing his war effort on a royalist coalition in Ireland.[9]

In March, shortly after Charles decided to rely on Ormond and the Irish for help in regaining his throne, he learned that Ormond and the Confederates had come to terms and that all factions in Ireland except for O'Neill's Ulstermen were united in his behalf. This policy was made public before representatives from the Committee of Estates arrived in Holland for negotiations with the exiled royalists. The Scottish commissioners brought demands rather than proposals. Charles was to swear to both the National Covenant and the Solemn League and Covenant, to promise to make England and Ireland permanently Presbyterian, to denounce Montrose and Ormond, and to accept all acts passed by the current Scottish parliament.[10]

Charles rejected these demands, without closing the door on the Scottish option. He commissioned Montrose to lead an expedition to Scotland to raise that nation on his behalf. Meanwhile, the king remained on the island of Jersey, planning to join Ormond in Ireland once the Lord Lieutenant could ensure his safety. Bad news from Ireland intervened in the execution of the Irish strategy, beginning with the battle of Baggotsrath-Rathmines and continuing as Cromwell captured Drogheda and Wexford. By late November 1649, the defection of the Munster Protestants to Cromwell ended hopes of the king going to Ireland or of Ormond expelling Cromwell. On 11 January 1650, Charles II wrote to the Committee of Estates, asking the Scots to be more flexible in their terms.[11]

As he approached the Scots, Charles encouraged Montrose to launch his expedition to Scotland to topple Argyll and the Kirk party. Although they suspected the king's duplicity, the members of the Committee of Estates voted 31 to 19 to reopen negotiations, believing that they played the stronger hand. On 13 February, Charles sailed from Jersey to France, where he met with the Queen on 21 February. He found a strong revulsion by his mother to the idea of abandoning Ormond and the Catholic royalists and against the idea of joining the Scots, who had done so much in the previous twelve years to diminish the power and stature of the monarchy.[12]

Charles ignored this sentiment and the advice of his mother and agreed to receive Scottish commissioners at Breda in the Netherlands. On 25 March, the Scots presented the same demands as before, displaying no inclination to moderation. Negotiations continued for three months, first at Breda, and then wherever the king was as he moved slowly toward Scotland. On 28 April he agreed to renounce Ormond and the Irish Catholics, receiving an invitation the next day to travel to Scotland. On 1 May 1650 he signed the Treaty of Breda, hoping to modify its terms once he was in Edinburgh. In the end, the Scots prevailed and Charles gave in to all of their demands, claiming later that he was absolved of keeping his promises since he agreed to the terms while under duress. His mother was shocked that he promised to accept

Presbyterianism and appalled with his desertion of Ormond and his Catholic subjects in Ireland.[13]

Many staunch Scottish Presbyterians were equally shocked that the Committee of Estates agreed to trust the king. Baillie's assessment of the situation in September 1649 indicates why they still sought an agreement with Charles II:

> It seems you will stay [from an agreement] until Cromwell perfects his Irish conquest; which I think will not take [a] long time, and then I expect him or his deputies in the heart of Scotland … My hopes are only with God.[14]

Whether or not the English intended to invade Scotland once they had crushed Ireland, many Scots believed they would. Therefore, the Scots continued to seek an agreement with the king.

Charles continued to play a double game with the Scots by secretly supporting Montrose's activities. By 9 April 1650, Montrose had raised a small army of mercenaries and landed in northern Scotland. The Edinburgh government reacted promptly, sending David Leslie with a strong force of cavalry to reinforce local militia against Montrose. On 27 April, Lieutenant Colonel Strachan surprised Montrose at Carbisdale, where he annihilated the royalist army. Montrose was captured and sent to Edinburgh. On 21 May, after a swift trial, Montrose died at the hands of the executioner, who hanged, drew, and quartered him.[15] During Montrose's trial and ordeal, Charles II remained silent, abandoning another subject who had ceased to be useful to his restoration.

The English government knew that the Scots and Charles II were negotiating a treaty. It was common knowledge that Charles's motive was to use the Scots army to return him to his English throne. By January 1650, the Council of State was concerned enough about another war with Scotland to order Cromwell to return from Ireland. Cromwell received this order after he had commenced his winter campaign on 29 January. He chose to ignore the order until May, when he was certain that the conquest of Ireland was only a matter of time and a sustained logistical effort.

Cromwell's recall indicated how important he was to the survival of the republic. 'An ever victorious commander with an aura of invincibility, compelling eloquence, profound conviction of the righteousness of his cause and the certainty of its success, and unconquerable resolution, was precisely what the Commonwealth most needed, and what he now provided.'[16] It also indicated that the Rump had lost confidence in Thomas Fairfax, in large part because of his quiet but sustained opposition to the execution of Charles I.[17]

The Commonwealth did not wait for Cromwell's return to prepare for another Scottish war. On 30 March 1650, the Rump reviewed its military strength and costs. The armed forces in England and Ireland required £101,578 per month. There were 28,000 men in twenty-eight regiments in England, with at least that many soldiers in Ireland, needing another £145,000 monthly.[18] On 9 April, parliament ordered the Council of State to prevent all invasions from abroad and directed John

Lambert to gather an army of 16,000 men in the vicinity of Newcastle, from where he could respond to any military threats in the north.[19]

In mid April, as it became clear that Charles and the Scots would conclude an agreement, the Rump set aside £50,000 for the train of artillery and supplies for a 'marching army.' On 2 May, it ordered two months' pay to be collected for this army and the garrisons of Carlisle, Newcastle, and Berwick. By then, the English anticipated launching an offensive against the Scots, rather than waiting for their invasion. To facilitate this strategy, the Rump resolved that:

> In regard the army is now to march northward, and probably into those parts where provisions, especially corn are very scarce and dear, and it not to be had but from places but far remote, and at dear rates, for ready money, that there may be some effectual care taken for their supply.[20]

The Westminster government had also taken precautions to defend London from another royalist uprising by doubling Colonel Barkstead's regiment in the Tower of London to 2,000 soldiers and by raising two new infantry regiments and two troops of cavalry for home defense. It appointed Philip Skippon to command the forces in London, hoping that his selection would placate the London Presbyterians (see Chapter 7). These measures were accompanied by parliamentary acts continuing the assessment at £90,000 per month and renewing the excise and customs. The navy also expanded when the Rump ordered construction of additional frigates and the purchase of other ships to bring the fleet up to 80 warships.

When Cromwell returned from Ireland and took his seat in parliament, on 11 June 1650, England was well along in its preparations for a Scottish war. The only major decisions for the English to make were who was going to command the army and what strategy he was going to follow. Most of the Council of State and senior army officers, including Cromwell, favored striking Scotland before it could invade England and ignite royalist uprisings.[21] There was a clear consensus that Fairfax ought to be offered the command of the marching army. Fairfax, however, refused to lead the army in a preemptive invasion of the northern kingdom. After a last minute appeal to him by Cromwell, Fairfax resigned his commission as Lord General of all English forces.[22]

On 26 June 1650, the Rump appointed Oliver Cromwell as 'captain general and commander-in-Chief of all forces raised and to be raised within the Commonwealth of England.' He remained Lord Lieutenant and Commander-in-chief in Ireland, giving him undisputed control of the English army.[23] Two days earlier, Charles II landed in Scotland, having agreed to the Scots' terms in hopes that they could defeat the English army and restore him to his throne.

The Scottish army was poorly prepared for the forthcoming struggle against the veterans of the New Model Army. Although the Scottish parliament levied 36,000 men for David Leslie's army, fewer than 26,000 men had been gathered near Leith by June. Most of these men were raw levies. Worse, the Kirk insisted on purging many of the Covenanter veterans and any known royalists from the regiments, leaving few experienced soldiers to shape up the new recruits. With this army, Leslie now had to decide how best to defend his country.[24]

The elderly Earl of Leven served as the titular army commander, with his nephew David Leslie performing the actual duties of commander as Lieutenant General. They decided that their best chance to defeat the English was to follow a Fabian strategy. In such a strategy, they refused to give Cromwell the chance to fight a battle at favorable odds while they stripped the country bare of men and provisions that the invaders could use to sustain themselves. Eventually, they hoped, the effects of weather, disease, and hunger would so weaken the English that they would retreat to England. They hoped that such a retreat would trigger royalist and Presbyterian uprisings in the south, allowing the Scots to march into England as liberators.[25]

Cromwell's invasion of Scotland, July–December 1650

Cromwell anticipated Leslie's use of a Fabian strategy. By July, it was reported in the English newsbooks that the Scots had stripped the region between Berwick and Edinburgh of livestock and grain, making it impossible for the English to sustain their army through the purchase of local foodstuffs.[26] Consequently, the Council of State ordered depots in Lynn and Newcastle to be filled with two months' stock of food, in addition to a month's supply of comestibles carried with the army in wagons and in the ships supporting the army along the coast.[27] Eventually, the Commonwealth employed 140 merchant ships to haul supplies of all types to its army in Scotland, enabling Cromwell to counter an important element of Leslie's strategy.[28]

On 22 July, the English army crossed the Tweed (see map 24). They found a country bare of provisions and a population of women, children, and old men. Leslie, meanwhile, maintained his army behind strong entrenchments running from the southern end of Edinburgh to Leith, the port to the north of the Scots' capital. He took special care to prevent the English from taking Leith and using it as a supply magazine.[29] Scottish cavalry shadowed Cromwell's army as it marched north, but they refused to allow a major engagement to develop. By 28 July, the English had reached Musselburgh, fewer than twelve miles from Edinburgh. During their advance, convoys off the coast landed supplies at the small ports of Dunbar and Musselburgh.

Cromwell hoped to fight a battle as soon as possible, trusting that his veterans would defeat the Scottish levies. The withdrawal of the Scots to Edinburgh, and Leslie's refusal to be drawn out of his strong positions, denied the English their chance. Throughout August, the two armies maneuvered from Musselburgh to the west of Edinburgh. Leslie anticipated and parried Cromwell's attempts to cut Edinburgh off from the rest of Scotland. The English, having exterior lines, always had to march farther than the Scots, and the Redcoats slept most nights on the ground, while the Scots sheltered in the houses of Edinburgh and Leith.

During these operations Cromwell was forced to return his army to Musselburgh or Dunbar every three to five days to replenish supplies and drop off an increasing number of sick soldiers. Whenever the English withdrew, the Scots launched small

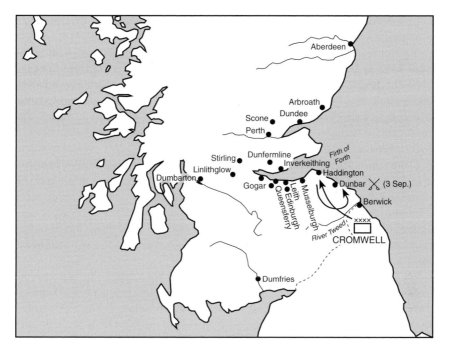

Map 24 Cromwell's invasion of Scotland, 1650

attacks to whittle away their enemy's strength. Although these strikes did little damage to his army, Cromwell was frustrated with his inability to bring on a major battle in which he could destroy the Scots with one sharp blow.[30]

In late August, the English fleet was unable to land supplies in Musselburgh due to high seas and bad weather. Consequently, Cromwell marched his army back to the port of Dunbar, where ships could unload in a sheltered anchorage and take aboard the hundreds of sick from the army. Leslie, with the urging of the Committee of Estates, followed the English with his army, arriving on Doon's Hill, south of Dunbar, on the evening of 31 August. Cromwell intended to recuperate his men and to accumulate supplies and reinforcements in anticipation of renewing the campaign. Dunbar was a good place to do so, since it was located on a small, easily defended, peninsula.

The Scots believed that the English were evacuating their artillery and wounded in preparation for a retreat by the rest of the army south, along the Berwick Road. Based on this assessment of Cromwell's intentions, Leslie sent a force to seize a narrow passage of the Berwick Road known as Cockburnspath, thus cutting off Cromwell's retreat.[31] Cromwell responded, on 1 September, by deploying his army in positions facing south toward Doon's Hill, with a deep ravine cut by the Brock Burn separating the armies (see map 25). The English deployed their smaller cannon across the front with the infantry, placing the heavy artillery in a battery opposite the Scots' positions on Doon's Hill.

By leaving their Edinburgh defenses, the Scots gave Cromwell the opportunity to engage them in the open. However, Leslie's position on Doon's Hill was too strong for the English to attack with much hope of success, especially since there were at least 23,000 Scots on the hill facing about 11,000 Englishmen across the Brock Burn. Although he hoped for a battle, Cromwell continued to load his sick onto the ships while awaiting a move by Leslie. The Scottish council of war, believing that Cromwell was getting ready to cut his way out to the south, pushed Leslie to shift his army down from the hill to cut off the anticipated English retreat.

Leslie reluctantly agreed to this move on the morning of 2 September. This shift of forces brought most of the Scottish cavalry onto the open ground facing north toward the Berwick Road, near its crossing of the Brock Burn, where a strong force of infantry backed them. The troops in the center and left of the Scots' lines were deployed in cramped quarters between the hills and the ravine along the Burn, but since Leslie planned to shift more forces to the right to face an English withdrawal south, he did not see this as a problem.[32]

The English responded by shifting regiments to their left flank, opposite the growing body of Scottish horse and foot. As they did so, Cromwell and Lambert observed that the Scots were placing themselves in a position in which they could be attacked with hope of English success. They determined that if the Scottish right flank could be defeated, Leslie would have difficulty deploying the regiments on his left to face the attackers, because of the constricted terrain. At a council of war that evening, Cromwell and Lambert convinced the other senior English officers that they should attack the Scots the next morning, in spite of their enemy's superiority of numbers.[33]

During their deployment to the right, the Scots captured an English outpost on the south side of the Burn, covering the crossing. This small victory may have helped to convince Leslie that he had a good chance of success the next day. Cromwell and Lambert, meanwhile, planned an attack across the lower reaches of the Brock Burn, where the banks were low and the English horse and foot could get across with little difficulty.

The English moved most of their regiments from their right and center to their left flank during the night of 2–3 September. The night being cold and rainy, the Scottish officers allowed most of their men to settle in for whatever sleep they could get in the wet fields. Cromwell's plan of attack was simple. Lambert and Lieutenant General Fleetwood were to lead six cavalry regiments across the Burn at first light, near the Berwick Road, to be followed by Monck with three infantry regiments supported by light field guns. Colonel Pride was to lead another three infantry regiments across the Burn to the north, closer to the sea where the banks were low, and then was to envelop the Scots' right flank as it was attacked by Fleetwood and Lambert.[34]

The Scots failed to discover the English deployments until dawn, when Lambert's cavalry attacked the Scots at the crossing of the Brock Burn. According to Cromwell's account,

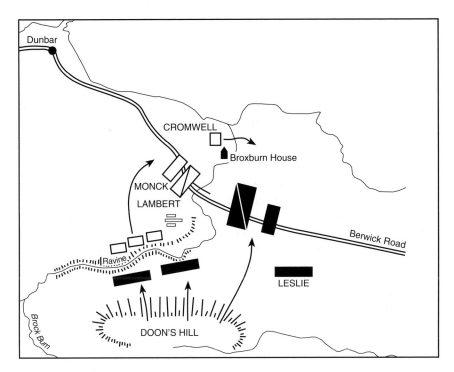

Map 25 The Battle of Dunbar, 3 September 1650

before our foot could come up, the enemy made a gallant resistance, and there was a very hot dispute at sword's point between our horse and theirs. Our first foot, after they had discharged their duty (being overpowered with the enemy), received some repulse, which they soon recovered. But my own regiment … at the push of pike, did repel the stoutest regiment the enemy had there. … The horse in the meantime … beat back all opposition, charging through the bodies of the enemy's horse and their foot; who were, after the first repulse given, made by the Lord of Hosts as stubble to their swords.[35]

While Lambert attacked the Scots' front, Pride and Cromwell led infantry against the Scots' right flank. The results were catastrophic for Leslie's army. 'The best of the enemy's horse and foot being broken through and through in less than an hour's dispute, their whole army being put into confusion, it became a total rout; our men having the chase and execution of them near eight miles.'[36] The English killed at least 3,000 Scots. Leslie lost his artillery, his baggage, and 15,000 weapons in the rout. The English losses were remarkably light, indicating that once the Scots broke, their units lost cohesion and discipline, making resistance impossible.[37] In this situation, the veterans recently purged from Leslie's army would have been invaluable.

Leslie's army disintegrated, leaving the English with 10,000 prisoners, including 5,000 wounded soldiers. Fewer than 8,000 Scots lived to fight another day, and only half that number rejoined Leslie near Edinburgh during the next few days. Cromwell had destroyed a Scottish army, but there was no indication that the Scots or the king were ready to capitulate. Instead, Leslie commenced building a new army and the Committee of Estates gave serious consideration to allowing Engagers to serve the cause, as long as they showed proper contrition for their past 'sinful' conduct.[38]

Cromwell dealt with his prisoners after the battle so that they could not rejoin their army. He released 5,000 wounded Scots to the local population and ordered the remaining prisoners marched to Berwick, where Haselrigg was to deal with them. Many of these men died during the eight days' march south due to the effects of malnutrition and dehydration. Some escaped. The remainder eventually were sold as indentured servants in the colonies. Neither Cromwell nor the Scottish government seemed aware of the tragedy that took place with the death march of these Scots, although Cromwell did order Haselrigg to 'let humanity be exercised towards them.'[39]

After the debacle at Dunbar, the Committee of Estates wanted to relieve Leslie of his command, but no one could be agreed upon to replace him, so he continued as Lieutenant General.[40] He had fewer than 5,000 men to face an enemy who was receiving a large number of replacements even before the Battle of Dunbar. Therefore, Leslie abandoned Edinburgh, whose strong defenses could no longer be manned, and withdrew to Stirling to recruit.

Cromwell exploited his victory by pushing Lambert with a strong force to Edinburgh, which he entered without opposition. Cromwell followed, arriving in Leith on 7 September, where he established the forward English supply depot and naval base in Scotland. This gave the expeditionary force a port through which reinforcements and supplies arrived during the next ten months. From October 1650 to June 1651, the Commonwealth sent 8,500 soldiers to Scotland, increasing Cromwell's army to 20,000 men. The Westminster government provided the expeditionary force with more than 5.6 million pounds of biscuit, 7.6 million pounds of wheat, and 1,928 tons of cheese, all of which was shipped to Leith from London and Lynn. The Commonwealth also sent over £1.2 million to Scotland to pay its soldiers. These financial and logistical efforts were a far cry from the hand-to-mouth support that parliament had provided to Essex's army in 1643–5, or even to the New Model Army in 1645–7. It was a remarkable achievement considering that at the same time the republic supported over 30,000 men in Ireland and a rapidly expanding navy.[41]

Scottish logistical and financial affairs remained precarious for the rest of the war. Most of southern Scotland was a battleground, reducing the resources the Scots could extract to support their war effort. Excise and assessment taxes trickled in, forcing the troops to levy 'voluntary contributions' for their sustenance. 'Whatever order had been up to then retained in public finance quickly vanished.'[42] The new king found himself with a household that received barely one tenth of the money promised by his Scottish hosts, severely restricting his ability to feed his entourage, let alone reward faithful servants.[43]

The shortages of food and money slowed the process of rebuilding the Scottish army. It is a tribute to David Leslie's leadership that he managed to field 10,000 men by mid September. He kept this army in fortified positions near Stirling, realizing that Stirling was the gateway to northern Scotland and a good rallying point for Scottish military efforts. Cromwell realized this as well. On 14 September he led his army west. The weather was miserable, with steady rain. The roads became impassable for heavy guns and wagons, forcing the English to leave their artillery in Linlithglow and to rely on the navy for the shipment of supplies. On 17 September, the English reached Stirling, which they summoned to surrender.

Leslie refused to surrender Stirling, realizing that Cromwell lacked the heavy artillery needed to breach the walls. The garrison also had worked feverishly to reinforce the defenses, making the town difficult to take. Although Cromwell initially intended to have his men assault the city using ladders, he thought better of it after reconnaissance, on 18 September. Perhaps his memories of his army's bloody repulse by the Irish at Clonmel deterred him. In any case, Cromwell withdrew his troops to Linlithglow, where he established a garrison and planned the defenses of what was to be his closest outpost to Stirling during the autumn and winter.[44]

The Scots, the weather, and distance had stopped the English advance, but the Scottish war effort remained hamstrung by the same sort of disunity that had destroyed Ormond's efforts in Ireland. The extreme Covenanters, led by the clerics James Guthrie and Patrick Gillespy, remained opposed to including former Engagers in the war effort. The clerical party was deeply suspicious of Charles II, knowing that he wanted to bring royalists into the Committee of Estates and the army, and that he was offering Argyll lavish rewards if the Marquis would find a way to do so. Ministers such as Johnston of Warriston also were reluctant to retain Leslie as army commander, knowing that he favored national reconciliation and the inclusion of the Engagers to strengthen the army.[45]

Scottish affairs came to a head in early October, when Charles attempted to lead a coup against the Covenanter-dominated Committee of Estates. Word of the planned royalist uprising reached the Committee of Estates before the day of execution. The Covenanters secured Perth and ordered the king's household and lifeguards to be purged. Charles initially refused, fleeing instead to the west, where a strong force of Covenanter cavalry caught up with him on 5 October. Having lost the stomach for flight or a battle, the king submitted and returned with his captors to Perth. 'The Start', as it is called, triggered a brief armed struggle between Charles's supporters and the Committee of Estates. Major bloodshed was avoided, however, when Leslie and the moderate Covenanters accepted the surrender of the royalists, who were then pardoned by the king. 'In appearance a surrender, the acceptance of the indemnity was in reality a coalition between all parties except one [the extreme Covenanters]. It was the substitution of the national for the covenanting cause.'[46]

Cromwell's victory at Dunbar shattered the power of the extreme Kirk party in the Scottish government and demonstrated the need for the Scots to unite. Charles II was, in this sense, the beneficiary of the destruction of Leslie's army. Henceforth, his influence grew in Scottish affairs. The reconciliation of the Engagers, royalists, and moderate Covenanters enabled the Scots to rebuild their army and to hold out against Cromwell for another nine months, forcing the English to maintain a large army in Scotland through the winter.

Cromwell attempted to win over those Scots who opposed national reconciliation with Engagers and Malignants (royalists). He had reason to hope that he could do so, especially after a number of ministers in Dumfries issued a 'Remonstrance' against the government in Perth. In this document, 'the Remonstrants', as they were henceforth known, repudiated the royalist 'Malignants' and those who allied with them. Strong in southwestern Scotland, the Remonstrants created an association and an army, commanded by Colonels Gilbert Ker and Archibald Strachan. This force refused to take orders from the Committee of Estates, posing a direct threat to the national cause.[47]

In late November, the Perth government prepared to destroy Ker's army. Cromwell also found the Remonstrants irreconcilable to his conquest of Scotland, as they demonstrated when Ker tried to surprise Lambert's garrison at Hamilton, on 1 December. Lambert's soldiers repulsed the assault, wounding and capturing Ker. Over the next nine days, the English dispersed the remainder of Ker's army, ending for the short-term resistance to the English south of the Forth and Clyde, with the notable exception of Edinburgh Castle, which capitulated on 24 December 1650.[48]

Cromwell's final campaign in Scotland

The Scots crowned Charles II in Scone, on 1 January 1651. This act reconciled the moderate Covenanters with the Engagers and most royalists. It also marked the growing influence of the king in the Scottish government and army. For Argyll, who had tried to ride two horses during the past few years, the return of Hamilton's followers to the Committee of Estates and army undercut his position. Although Charles II retained Argyll in his offices and courted his daughter, the Campbell leader no longer directed affairs. Over the next few months he drifted from the center of power, withdrawing altogether in July.[49] From January 1651, the government of Scotland was royalist.

The English watched these events from their garrisons, where bad weather and miserable roads forced them to remain during the winter. Their biggest problem during this period was posed by the 'moss troopers', or partisans, who operated against their lines of communications throughout southern Scotland. The moss troopers continued a long tradition of endemic border warfare; however, in 1651, the English had the means to eliminate the threat, since their army now occupied southern Scotland. From January to March, English cavalry and dragoons, supported by artillery, destroyed the raiders' lairs, securing Cromwell's lines of communications.[50]

At the same time, Cromwell maintained tight discipline over his troops, punishing those who stole from or terrorized civilians. Looters paid for their transgression with their lives.[51] Cromwell could enforce such policies because his soldiers received regular pay from England, enabling them to buy food and necessaries in the local markets. This was in strong contrast to the arbitrary requisitioning carried out by the king's army.[52]

Although the English maintained their armies in Scotland and Ireland, these operations put a severe strain on English resources, forcing the Rump to maintain the assessment at a rate of £90,000 per month through the end of 1651. The English people grumbled and the republican government became even less popular, but the assessment collectors collected nearly every penny assessed.[53] This income, along with the excise and customs and the proceeds from the sale of crown and church property, allowed the Commonwealth to support two overseas campaigns simultaneously, in countries where little local support could be expected. But Cromwell and Ireton, in Ireland, understood the importance of ending their conquests as soon as possible.

In February 1651, Cromwell mustered his army at Linlithglow, hoping to march to Stirling and tempt Leslie to fight. The weather was terrible, turning the roads to quagmires. The English got only as far as Kilsyth before turning back to winter quarters to escape the hail, rain, and snow. The exertions exhausted the troops. Worse, Cromwell fell seriously ill and remained sick into May. The absence of his energy, along with the bad weather, ended most operations in Scotland until late spring.

During this hiatus in the campaign, a royalist plot was uncovered in England. The republican government reacted forcefully, hunting down and incarcerating hundreds of royalist, and executing a number of them to deter others. Royalist activities in England in 1650–1 showed how precarious the Commonwealth's hold on the country was. The royalists' failure to carry out an open rebellion, however, also demonstrated that only external force could topple the government.[54]

By April, Cromwell was recovering and the outlines of a strategy to end the military stalemate were emerging. Cromwell and Lambert needed to force the royalist army out of its positions near Stirling. They conceived that this could be done by sending a strong force across the Firth of Forth, threatening Leslie's communications with Perth and northern Scotland. Leslie then would have three choices: stay in Stirling and starve; move north against the English army and attempt to destroy it; or march south to England. Cromwell, however, did not adopt the amphibious strategy until June, due to its risks.

In the meantime, Cromwell led his army back and forth from Edinburgh to Stirling and Glasgow, trying to get Leslie to fight and to undercut royalist operations in southwestern Scotland. The English were unsuccessful on both counts. Leslie kept his army in its nearly impregnable positions. He blocked the routes around Stirling to the west that would have allowed the English to march into Fifeshire and cut the Scottish army off from its supplies. The Scots continued to recruit new regiments, raising their strength to about 20,000 men. By June, Cromwell was driven to adopt the amphibious strategy that would allow him to invade Fife from the south, across the Forth.[55] The risk of such a scheme was that it would divide the English forces on the two sides of the Forth, giving the Scots a chance to defeat the parts piecemeal.

To execute this strategy, Cromwell had to maintain strong positions south of the Forth to protect Edinburgh, and to find a way to cross the Forth. He also had to develop a plan to prevent the royalist army from going all the way to London if Charles and Leslie chose their southern option. It is clear from the actions of the English government and Cromwell that these issues had been under consideration for some time before June.

In April 1651, the Council of State, acting on Cromwell's request, ordered the construction of large flatboats in England and their shipment to Scotland. These boats arrived in Leith in late June, along with a naval squadron commanded by Richard Deane to support amphibious operations in the Forth.[56] While these preparations were underway, Cromwell recovered sufficiently to lead his army to Glasgow on another foray to prevent Leslie from recruiting in the west and in a last effort to win the Remonstrants' support. The English stayed in the west until the end of the month while Cromwell talked religion with the ministers of the Kirk and coordinated future activities with Thomas Harrison, the English commander in northern England.

Cromwell failed to win the Remonstrants over, although his army impressed the Scots with its discipline and decorum. He encouraged Harrison in his efforts to prepare his forces for their part in 'this great business.'[57] This was especially important because if Charles and Leslie led their army into England, as Charles hoped to do, Harrison's mission would be to slow its advance until Cromwell and Lambert caught up. Coordination was carried out with the Council of State to organize another army, commanded by Charles Fleetwood, to defend London.

By June, these preparations were well in hand. During June and early July, Cromwell led his troops to and from Linlithglow and the Scottish positions near Stirling, still hoping Leslie would attack. Cromwell also intended these moves to focus Leslie's attention on his field army while Lambert made preparations for the crossing of the Forth. On 17 July, while the main army was at Linlithglow, a small English detachment crossed the Forth at Queensferry in flatboats. During the next three days, Lambert led 5,000 men over the Forth to Inverkeithing and established a bridgehead.

Cromwell remained south of the Forth waiting to see how the Scots would react. Leslie underestimated the strength of Lambert's force and sent a column of about 4,000 men to drive it back into the Forth. When the Scottish troops reached Inverkeithing, their commander realized that Lambert's troops outnumbered them. Consequently, on 20 July, the Scots retreated to positions north of Inverkeithing, to await reinforcements. Lambert quickly deployed his troops to just south of the Scots and lured them into attacking what they thought was only his advance guard. Once the Scottish infantry was in the open, Lambert launched an all-out assault. The English onslaught shattered the Scottish cavalry, leaving two regiments of Highland infantry exposed to Lambert's entire army. The English killed 2,000 Scots and captured another 1,500 in the rout.[58]

Leslie reacted by starting his army north, across Stirling Bridge, toward Lambert. As he did so, Cromwell observed his move from positions near Torwood and moved his army toward Stirling. This caused Leslie to turn his regiments back to positions south of Stirling, stopping Cromwell's advance. These maneuvers allowed Lambert to exploit his victory and advance toward Perth. Cromwell reinforced this move by sending another 9,000 men over the Forth by 24 July, leaving only eight regiments south of the Forth to defend Edinburgh and Leith from Leslie.[59]

The royal army was caught between two forces. If it moved against Cromwell's 15,000 men in Fifeshire it would have had to fight outnumbered in open ground. If it stayed near Stirling, it would starve or be crushed between the English forces. The royalists' best options were either to attack Edinburgh and Leith or to strike out for England. The first choice offered little chance of success, since Harrison had reinforced Edinburgh with 4,000 soldiers and the English were well entrenched. That left the option that Charles and his English advisors had always favored: the invasion of England.

While Lambert moved toward Perth, and Whalley and the navy cleared the north shore of the Forth, Cromwell remained in the south, visiting Leith and laying plans for his pursuit of the royal army. It took Charles more than a week to convince Leslie to march south. Argyll argued vehemently against such a campaign, losing in the end and withdrawing from the army to his estates. As the royalists debated, Cromwell rejoined Lambert near Perth where, on 1 August, he summoned the Governor to surrender. The royal army marched out of Stirling the same day and headed south.

The royalists' decision to invade England with a predominantly Scottish army was a desperate but not a hopeless strategy. With the best Commonwealth troops in Scotland, the invaders anticipated meeting primarily militia, many of whom might be royalist or Presbyterian sympathizers. The king's presence might ignite another English royalist rising, and it certainly would not hurt recruitment, especially in the west and north, where royalism remained strong. If the army blew through the English militia, picking up strength as it marched, Charles might reach London, where he and his counsellors believed the Presbyterians would rise to welcome him. It was Charles's only way to regain his throne any time soon.

The crowning mercy: the Worcester Campaign

Cromwell learned of the departure of the king's army with a sense of relief, realizing that he could end the Scottish war with a decisive battle. As he said in his letter to parliament, on 4 August,

> It may be supposed that we might have kept the enemy from this, by interposing between him and England; which truly I believe we might; but how to remove him out of this place, without doing what we have done, unless we had a commanding army on both sides of the river of Forth, is not clear to us; ... [In 1648] we chose rather to put ourselves between their army and Scotland: and how God succeeded that is not to be forgotten [Preston]. This is not out of choice on our part, but by some

kind of necessity; and, it's to be hoped, will have the like issue, together with a hopeful end of your work; ...[60]

The royal army had a good start and made steady progress, reaching the border on 5 August and Carlisle on the 6th (see map 26). Carlisle's commander refused to surrender to the invaders, demonstrating what could be expected from the English people for the remainder of the campaign. The Scots reached Penrith on 7 August, with fewer than 13,000 men, due mainly to the desertion of thousands of Scots. After a day of rest, Charles and Leslie led their troops into Lancashire, hoping to recruit large numbers of soldiers. By 15 August they had reached Warrington on the River Mersey, the southern boundary of Lancashire. To that point, few recruits had come in, although the arrival of the Earl of Derby with several hundred officers raised hopes for better recruiting.[61]

The English response to the Scots' invasion was well coordinated. Cromwell sent Harrison to Newcastle to organize a force to march parallel with the royalists' advance. Lambert led 3,000 cavalrymen southeast from Leith, picking up the king's trail south of Carlisle. Harrison mobilized the trained bands of the northern counties, while Lord Thomas Fairfax agreed to command the Yorkshire militia to protect that county. Cromwell swiftly moved 10,000 soldiers across the Forth by ship, pausing in Leith to issue instructions for the defense of Edinburgh. He started south along the east coast on 6 August, leaving George Monck in Scotland with 6,000 soldiers to continue the campaign against Stirling and Dundee.[62]

Cromwell's infantry marched more than 100 miles during the next week, reaching the River Tyne on 13 August. By then, Harrison and Lambert had united their columns and added another 5,000 militia and regulars to their ranks. With 11,000 men, they attempted to block the king's route into Cheshire, at the bridge over the Mersey near Warrington. They were too late, however, to establish a defense or to break the bridge down before the king led his troops across. Unwilling to risk a battle, Lambert and Harrison retreated, lifting the royalist spirits.[63]

Charles's affairs were not prospering, aside from this small triumph. Few Englishmen joined him. His troops were poorly armed and ill supplied. The Earl of Derby, whom Charles had sent into Lancashire to recruit, gathered 1,500 recruits, but on 25 August he unwisely attacked Colonel Robert Lilburne's cavalry regiment near Wigan and was defeated after a sharp fight. Hundreds of Derby's men were captured, and many of the rest dispersed, leaving only a few hundred to join Charles II.[64]

The king's exhausted soldiers reached Worcester on 22 August, where some of the population welcomed them. Knowing that Fleetwood and 12,000 men blocked the way to London, Charles and Leslie decided to remain in Worcester to rest and recruit the army. Three days later, Cromwell and his veterans joined Lambert and Harrison in Warwick, giving them at least 20,000 soldiers to block the king's retreat north. On 27 August, Fleetwood arrived nearby in Evesham, giving the republicans 28,000 men to face the 16,000 royalists in Worcester.[65]

Cromwell and his officers decided to advance against Worcester from the east and the south. According to this plan, Fleetwood and Richard Deane led 11,000

Map 26 The Worcester Campaign, August–September 1651

men to Upton, seven miles south of Worcester, where they captured and rebuilt a bridge over the Severn on 28 August (see map 27). They next crossed the Severn and advanced north along that river to its confluence with the River Teme, two miles south of Worcester. They were accompanied by boats that they planned to use to build two bridges, one over the Severn and the other over the Teme, west of the Severn. For the next several days, Fleetwood's men prepared to build the bridges and to seize another destroyed bridge near Powick, which they planned to repair.[66]

Cromwell and Lambert led the rest of the army to the east of Worcester, where they established positions on Red Hill and Perry Hill, blocking the route to London. Units were dispatched to the west and north of the city to cut the remaining routes

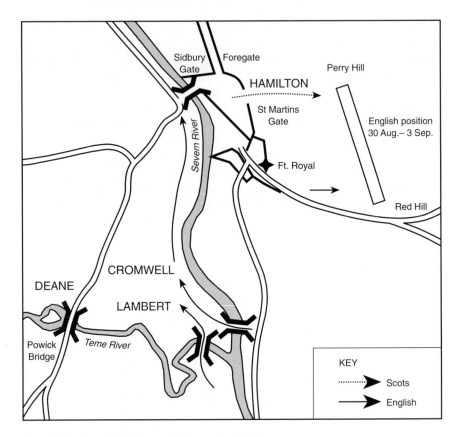

Map 27 The Battle of Worcester, 3 September 1651

of escape. By 2 September, the parliamentarians were in place, having been reinforced to about 40,000 men. Cromwell was poised to lead three brigades of veterans across the Severn to join Fleetwood once the boat bridges were in place.

Early on 3 September, Fleetwood's columns advanced to the Teme, where they captured and repaired Powick Bridge and set up the boat bridges over the Teme and Severn. The Scottish infantry defending the Teme crossings put up a stout resistance against Fleetwood's infantry and artillery. However, once the bridges were in place, Cromwell charged across the Severn bridge with cavalry and infantry. This assault unhinged the Scottish defenses, and the parliamentarians 'beat the enemy from hedge to hedge till we beat him into Worcester.'[67]

Charles, seeing that Cromwell had crossed the Severn with a large detachment, ordered his remaining infantry and cavalry in Worcester to join him in an assault against Lambert's positions east of town. The royalist assault made progress against the trained bands, with the king leading the attack against Red Hill and Hamilton leading the Scots against Perry Hill. But Cromwell brought his veterans back across the river and attacked the king's column, driving the outnumbered royalists back in confusion. The English militia and New Model veterans followed closely on their heels. The battle had swung decisively against the king, allowing the English militia to storm and capture the redoubt known as Fort Royal, opening Worcester to a final assault.[68] The results were catastrophic for the king's army. In Cromwell's words,

> This was fought with various success for some hours, but still hopeful on your part; and in the end an absolute victory, and so full an one as proved a total defeat and ruin of the enemy's army; a possession of the town (our men entering at the enemy's heels, and fighting with them in the streets with very great courage); and took all their baggage and artillery. ... There are about 6 or 7,000 prisoners taken here, and many officers and nobles of quality: Duke Hamilton, the Earl of Rothes, and divers other noblemen ... I do not think we lost two-hundred men. ... The dimensions of this mercy are above my thoughts.[69]

Charles escaped from Worcester, as did about 4,000 Scottish cavalry. The English army and the country people ran the Scots to ground, killing or capturing all of them. Charles wandered about southern England for six weeks before escaping to France. Generals Leslie and Middleton surrendered near Manchester, as did the Earls of Derby and Lauderdale and a number of other senior officers near Nantwich. A total of 10,000 men surrendered, and another 2,000 or more died of wounds. The Duke of Hamilton died of his wounds on 11 September, and many other English royalists were executed over the next few months.

Politically, Cromwell's victory at Worcester strengthened the Commonwealth. The voluntary outpouring of the trained bands to destroy the invaders and the absence of significant royalist activity showed how low the monarchy had fallen. Charles II had associated himself with the Irish and then the Scots against the English, and he paid a heavy price for those decisions. While most Englishmen did not love the republic, they were willing to support and defend it against foreigners. Charles thus learned that the only way he would ever regain his patrimony was through the voluntary acceptance of the English people.

The settlement of Scotland and Ireland

During Cromwell's campaigns in Scotland and England, his son-in-law Henry Ireton continued the English conquest of Ireland. During the summer of 1650, Waterford, Carlow, and Duncannon surrendered to Ireton. In the autumn, Ireton failed to capture Limerick, forcing him to plan for another campaign in the spring and summer of 1651. During this campaign, Ireton, ably supported by Lord Broghill, John Reynolds, and Sir Charles Coote, penetrated the Irish Shannon River defensive lines and overran most of Connacht, leaving only Limerick and Galway to the Catholic Confederates. In October, Ireton captured Limerick, after a protracted and brutal siege.

During the spring and summer of 1652, Galway surrendered and most of the Irish military commanders capitulated in return for safe passage for them and their soldiers overseas, where they took service in the Spanish army. In this way, over 30,000 Irish soldiers and thousands more of their families left Ireland. The eleven years of warfare in Ireland destroyed the Irish economy and directly and indirectly caused the deaths of nearly one third of the 2.1 million pre-war population. This unbelievable misery was compounded for the Catholic landowners by the 'Cromwellian Settlement of Ireland', carried out over the next five years.

During this same period, Scotland suffered at the hands of its English conquerors. In the autumn of 1651, George Monck used his artillery and army of 6,000 men to capture Stirling and Dundee. Over the next two years, the English completely subdued Scotland, opening the way to its incorporation into the English state several years later. Although there was nothing comparable in Scotland to the massive confiscation and transplantation experienced by the Irish, the land suffered at the hands of the conquerors. For the rest of the decade, an English army of 10,000 soldiers garrisoned Scotland, while another 35,000 English soldiers remained in Ireland.

The English Commonwealth won the respect of most of the European powers with its conquests of Ireland and Scotland, and with the growing exploits of its navy. By early 1652, Spain and France had recognized the republic, as had the Dutch and Danes. English naval squadrons established the Commonwealth's control of the Channel Islands, the Scilly Isles, Barbados, and the North American colonies. The cross of Saint George flew for the first time from warships operating in the Mediterranean and the Baltic Seas. English power had reached a point not seen in the history of Early Modern Europe. This power brought new challenges brought on by the ambitions of the Rump and its Council of State. These commercial and political ambitions led to the last war of the republic. This war, known as the first Anglo-Dutch war, would demonstrate both the potential and the limitations of England's new-found power.

Notes

1   Capp, *Cromwell's Navy*, 60; Ohlmeyer, 'The Dunkirk of Ireland', 23–49; J. Ohlmeyer, 'Irish Privateers during the Civil War, 1642–50', *Mariner's Mirror,* 14 (1964), 119–33.

2   Capp, *Cromwell's Navy*, 66–7.

3   Ibid., 52–7; Wheeler, *Making of a World Power*, 43–6; Anderson, 'The Operations of the English Fleet, 1648–52', 409–11.

4   Anderson, 'The Operations of the English Fleet', 411–12; Capp, *Cromwell's Navy*, 63–4.

5   Anderson, 'The Operation of the English Fleet', 412–22.

6   For Cromwell's and the soldiers' views of the Scots and the Irish see Wheeler, 'Sense of Identity in the Army of the Republic', in J. Ohlmeyer, *Awkward Neighbours* (forthcoming 2002).

7   Gardiner, *C & P*, i: 21, for the quote; J. Grainger, *Cromwell Against the Scots: The Last Anglo-Scottish War, 1650–52* (East Linton, 1997), 6; W. Douglas, *Cromwell's Scotch Campaigns, 1650–51* (London, 1898), 1–10.

8   Douglas, *Cromwell's Scotch Campaigns*, 11–26; Grainger, *Cromwell Against the Scots*, 6–8.

9   Gardiner, *C & P*, i: 21–2.

10 Baillie, *Letters and Journals*, iii: 84–5, Baillie to the Commission, 3 April 1649; Gardiner, *C & P*, i: 63–4.

11 Ibid., 183–8.

12 Ibid., 194–5.

13 Ibid., 196–205.

14 Baillie, *Letters and Journals*, iii: 102–3, Baillie to George Winram, 7 September 1649.

15 Wedgwood, *Montrose*, 137–55.

16 Abbott, ii: 260.

17 Wilson, *Fairfax*, 157–68.

18 *JHC*, vi: 425.

19 Ibid., 390–1, 394.

20 Ibid., 400–1, 407–8.

21 Ibid., 431.

22 Grainger, *Cromwell Against the Scots*, 9–13; Abbott, ii: 267.

23 *JHC*, vi: 431–2; *A & O*, ii: 393.

24 TT E607 (18), *Mercurius Politicus*, (11–18 July 1650), 96; Douglas, *Cromwell's Scotch Campaigns*, 31.

25 Douglas, *Cromwell's Scotch Campaigns*, 32–3; Grainger, *Cromwell Against the Scots*, 16–18.

26 TT E608 (6), *A Brief Relation*, (16–23 July 1650), 736; E608 (16), *A Brief Relation*, (23–30 July 1650), 751–2

27 TT E608 (17), *True Intelligence of the Headquarters*, (23–30 July 1650), 10–13; *JHC*, vi: 453, 458.

28 J. Wheeler, 'The Logistics of the Cromwellian Conquest of Scotland 1650–1651', *War and Society*, 10 (May 1992), 1–18.

29 Douglas, *Cromwell's Scotch Campaigns*, 38–48, for the best description of the defenses.

30 Ibid., 48–92; Gardiner, *C & P*, i: 272–6; Grainger, *Cromwell Against the Scots*, 26–36.

31 Gardiner, *C & P*, i: 284–6.

32 Grainger, *Cromwell Against the Scots*, 42–4; Gardiner, *C & P*, i: 284–6; Baillie, *Letters and Journals*, iii: 110–29, Baillie to D. Dickson and W. Spang, 2 January 1651.

33 Abbott, ii: 315–6.

34 Ibid., 321–5, Cromwell to Lenthall, 4 September 1650; Gardiner, *C & P*, i: 290–4.

35 Abbott, ii: 324.

36 Ibid.

37 Ibid.; Grainger, *Cromwell Against the Scots*, 47–50; Gardiner, *C & P*, i: 293–6; Douglas, *Cromwell's Scotch Campaign*, 110–13.

38 Baillie, *Letters and Journals*, iii: 103, Baillie to C. Lowe (?), 20 December 1650.

39 Grainger, *Cromwell Against the Scots*, 55–8; Gardiner, *C & P*, i: 295–6.

40 Baillie, *Letters and Journals*, iii: 111, Baillie to Dickson and Spang, 2 January 1650.

41 *JHC*, vi: 425.

42 Stevenson, 'The Financing of the Cause of the Covenants', 120–1.

43 Stevenson, 'The King's Scottish Revenues and the Covenanters', 38–9.

44 Abbott, ii: 341–3; Grainger, *Cromwell Against the Scots*, 59; Gardiner, *C & P*, i: 332–4.

45 Gardiner, *C & P*, i: 331–4.

46 Ibid., 337–9; Douglas, *Cromwell's Scotch Campaigns*, 135–9.

47 Douglas, *Cromwell's Scotch Campaigns*, 140–53.

48 Gardiner, *C & P*, i: 340–6.

49 Abbott, ii: 385–6, Cromwell to Parliament, 4 January 1651.

50 Ibid., 388–90.

51 Ibid.; Wheeler, 'The Logistics of the Cromwellian Conquest of Scotland', 8–14.

52 Stevenson, 'The Financing of the Cause of the Covenants', 120–1.

53 PRO E351/302, Accounts of the Treasurers at War, February 1645 to 25 December 1651; Wheeler, *Making of a World Power*, 191–4.

54 Gardiner, *C & P*, ii: 8–22; Abbott, ii: 393–407.

55 Grainger, *Cromwell Against the Scots*, 94–102; Gentles, *New Model Army*, 400–2.

56 *CSPD, 1651*, 555–66.

57 Abbott, ii: 411–12, Cromwell to Harrison, 3 May 1651.

58 Grainger, *Cromwell Against the Scots*, 104–7; Gentles, *New Model Army*, 402–3; Abbott, ii: 432–3, Cromwell to Lenthall, 21 July 1651.

59 Abbott, ii: 435, Cromwell to William Bradshaw, President of the Council of State, 24 July 1651.

60 Abbott, ii: 443–4, Cromwell to Lenthall, 4 August 1651.

61 Grainger, *Cromwell Against the Scots*, 114–21; Gardiner, *C & P*, ii: 30–6; Gentles, *New Model Army*, 403–4.

62 Abbott, ii: 443–5, Cromwell to Lenthall, 4 August 1651.

63 Ibid., 448–9.

64 Grainger, *Cromwell Against the Scots*, 123–4.

65 Gardiner, *C & P*, ii: 40–1.

66 Gentles, *New Model Army*, 406–8; M. Atkin, *Cromwell's Crowning Mercy: The Battle of Worcester, 1651* (Stroud, 1998), 65–72.

67 Abbott, ii: 461, Cromwell to Lenthall, 3 September 1615; Atkin, *Cromwell's Crowning Mercy*, 79–90.

68 Atkin, *Cromwell's Crowning Mercy*, 90–100.

69 Abbott, ii: 462–3, Cromwell to Lenthall, 4 September 1651.

CHAPTER TEN

Triumph and tragedy: the first Dutch War and the death of the English Republic

Cromwell characterized his victory at Worcester, on 3 September 1651, as 'a crowning mercy.'[1] It was indeed the culmination of the war effort against the Scots. The Commonwealth's army had saved England from invasion, and through its victories in Ireland and Scotland had removed the threat of outside interference in English affairs. During the year following Worcester, English armies destroyed organized resistance to English rule in Ireland and Scotland so thoroughly that by the summer of 1652 the Council of State felt it safe to demobilize a significant portion of the army. Peace, however, proved elusive for the republic. By May 1652, it was waging a naval war against the United Provinces – the leading maritime power in Europe (see map 28, p. 252) – that would require two years of effort and unprecedented financial sacrifices to win. In the process, hopes that the Rump would reform the English political and legal systems were dashed.

Hopes of reform

The Rump accomplished a great deal in its first two years. It restored norms of civil government and invented effective administrative institutions to replace the monarchy. The Commonwealth carried out radical changes to ensure continuity, although the process included arbitrary courts and the ruthless collection of the taxes needed to sustain the armed forces upon which the regime depended for its existence and England's defense.[2]

Many, even if not a majority, of Englishmen greeted the establishment of the Commonwealth in early 1649 enthusiastically. To the army officers, it promised a solution to the soldiers' material concerns and perhaps significant political reform to protect political and religious freedom. To John Lilburne and the Levellers it offered a chance to establish representative government responsive to the will of the majority. To the religious sects, such as the Quakers or Diggers, it promised a new Eden, characterized by religious 'truth' and social justice. To Independents, it offered congregational freedoms and the propagation of the Word of God. The new dispensation also seemed to offer a chance to reform English law and governmental institutions, thus protecting the inherent rights of freeborn Englishmen.[3]

Expectations of such changes were the basis of what some of the revolutionaries later called the 'Good Old Cause.'[4]

The Rump postponed most of the far-reaching changing desired by its supporters because of its need to win the wars in Ireland and Scotland. After the climactic victory at Worcester it appeared to many that the reforms could commence. Since the Commonwealth had proven so militarily successful in its defense of England and conquest of Ireland, it enjoyed significant popular respect, if not support.

By 18 November 1651, Cromwell was able to convince the Commons to set a date for its dissolution. This was an advance toward reform of the representative institution. It was also a move army leaders considered essential to curb governmental corruption. On 24 February 1652, the Rump passed an Act of Oblivion pardoning people for 'treasons and felonies' committed before 3 September 1651. Although the act did not end the process of sequestrations against former royalists, it broadened the base of support for the Commonwealth.

The Rump made motions toward religious and legal reform by appointing a Law Committee (January 1652) to review the legal system and a Committee for the Propagation of the Gospel (February 1652) to identify appropriate religious changes. Unfortunately, the Rump ignored most of the recommendations of the Law Committee, enacting only the suggestion to pay judges fixed salaries rather than fees. Likewise, the House ignored most of the religious ideas suggested to it. Even the Rump's efforts to deter moral vice, such as the Adultery Act of 1650, had more bark than bite, and few people suffered the consequences of the law for their violation of rules such as those against Sabbath breaking.[5]

The Rump frustrated the expectations of its constituencies for a number of reasons. Most prominently, the Commonwealth leaders focused on their wars in Ireland and Scotland until 1652. Then they became involved in a war with the United Provinces, which was the rationale and the final reason for their failure to carry out far-reaching changes. The voracious appetite of war consumed the energy and resources that might have gone into creating a more equitable republican Commonwealth. By May 1652, as victory appeared certain in Ireland and Britain, the English and the Dutch drifted into a war that would challenge the English navy and establish its tradition of success for the next three centuries. In the process of winning this maritime struggle, the need to devote all of England's resources and energy to war suffocated the impetus for most reforms.

The Commonwealth's navy and the coming of the Dutch War

The Commonwealth's navy played a critical part in the English conquests of Ireland and Scotland by protecting the lines of communication of Cromwell's expeditionary forces, cutting off his enemies from overseas aid and materials, and providing transports for amphibious English operations. The navy also destroyed Rupert's fleet and defended English merchant ships from privateers. These operations forced the Rump to increase the navy from the forty-five ships it inherited in 1649, to over eighty warships by the end of 1651.[6] This expansion of naval power fulfilled Charles I's dream of making England an international power.

The need to send squadrons to Irish and Scottish waters, while deploying flotillas to Portugal and the Mediterranean, forced the English to change the way they thought about naval operations. Until 1650, the navy had deployed separate 'winter' and 'summer guards.' Robert Blake's blockade of Portugal in 1650 and the support of the army year round in Irish and Scottish waters made such a deployment method obsolete. In 1651, the navy commissioners established a 'constant guard' and a 'constant convoy' to provide warships year-round to carry out the tasks of the fleet. In October 1650, the navy treasurer estimated that the service would need 11,500 sailors and £496,514 in the coming year to man its ships and pay for its operations. Another £115,785 was required to build new warships.[7] The Rump raised most of this money from the customs and excise, but the navy's debt increased £128,000 during 1651, to a total of £237,000.[8]

The increased resources provided to the navy enabled it to carry out amphibious operations to recapture the Scilly Isles (April 1651), the Channel Islands (October 1651), and Barbados (January 1652). These operations, along with the capture or blockade of the Irish ports in 1650–1, reduced the threat from royalist privateers to English commerce, contributing to the support the Commonwealth enjoyed amongst the English seafaring community.[9]

The growing power and success of their navy encouraged the Commonwealth's leaders to be more assertive in their dealings with the United Provinces. Relations between the two republics were strained in 1651 for political and economic reasons. The heart of the economic rivalry stemmed from Dutch dominance of the carrying trade of Western Europe, in which they exploited their geographic location and long tradition of commerce. English merchants wanted a larger share of this lucrative activity and resented the near-monopoly the Dutch had of the Far Eastern spice trade. The two nations also competed in the North Sea fisheries, with the Dutch holding a distinct edge in the profitable herring industry.

The political issues between the two states revolved around the support the Dutch gave to the royalists during the civil wars. The English regicides especially resented the sanctuary the Dutch Stadtholder had given to Rupert's fleet in 1648 and to the Stuart court in 1649–50. The refusal of the Dutch to recognize the English Common-wealth until November 1650 exacerbated the ill feelings between the two states.[10] However, the death of the pro-Stuart Stadtholder, William II of Orange, in October 1650, offered an opportunity for the merchant oligarchy of Holland to force the States General to recognize the English republic and to attempt to improve relations. None the less, at the end of 1650 the political tensions between the two states were more dangerous to their relationship than were the economic issues.[11]

In February 1651, the English Council of State responded to Dutch recognition of the English republic by sending a delegation to the Netherlands to discuss a possible alliance between the two Protestant republics. The English ambassadors, Oliver St John and Walter Strickland, sought an association with the Dutch against any enemies who threatened either of the countries. Such an alliance would bind the parties to refuse to harbor enemies of the other and to provide assistance in wartime. The Dutch were reluctant to commit to such vague, yet potentially broad, commitments to support the English in their various wars. They countered with a proposal that neither state would harbor enemies of the other and that the commerce and fisheries of the two nations would be open equally to the merchants of both.[12]

During the negotiations, royalist exiles in the Hague greeted the English ambassadors with jeers and threats that the English felt the Dutch government did too little to prevent. The English plenipotentiaries soon realized that the Dutch were unwilling to accept the political alliance the English offered and that the Dutch proposal for commercial equality was designed to allow their merchants to dominate English trade. St John countered the Dutch proposal by demanding that the States General forbid William II's family from harboring the Stuarts or any royalists and, if they did so, to confiscate the property of the Orange family. The Dutch delayed their response for weeks. When they did respond, they passed over in silence the demands concerning the Orange family, while making their demand for commercial equality more explicit. The English treated this counter-proposal as a rejection of their terms and returned to England on 18 June.[13]

The attempt to bring the two republics closer together had pushed them farther apart. The English were convinced that Dutch commercial rivalry must be met head on. In October 1651, the Rump passed a Navigation Act stipulating that all goods carried to England must be carried in the ships of the nation of origin or in English vessels. The English also insisted that their navy had the right to search any ship for goods belonging to nations with which England was at war and to confiscate such 'contraband.' Finally, the Council of State ordered its warships to force all ships to recognize English supremacy in British waters by dipping their flag in salute whenever they encountered an English warship. These commercial and symbolic measures directly threatened Dutch commerce and prestige.[14]

The Dutch responded by sending a delegation to England in December 1651 to resolve the growing dispute. The Dutch demanded the repeal of the Navigation Act and adherence to the principle that the flag of the merchant ship covered the goods it carried. Negotiations continued in London into February, when the English learned that the Dutch had ordered the expansion of their navy by 150 warships. This expansion convinced the Council of State that war was inevitable, leading it to order its navy to enforce English sovereignty at sea and to prepare for war.

While negotiations continued in London, English privateers and navy ships stepped up their seizure of Dutch and French merchant ships. Most notably, word reached London and the Hague that Sir George Ayscue, the English naval commander in the Caribbean, had captured twelve Dutch merchantmen found trading 'illegally' with the English colony of Barbados in December. English privateers' treatment of Dutch sailors was notoriously barbaric, as English sailors tortured the Dutch to make them confess that their cargoes were contraband, and therefore liable to seizure.[15] Such piracy incensed the Dutch and heightened demands for retaliation by the Dutch navy.

The first engagement of the war took place on 12 May, when an English frigate fired on a Dutch warship in the Channel whose commander had refused to lower his flag in salute to English sovereignty. This incident was followed six days later by a more serious exchange of shots between the Dutch Admiral Cornelis Tromp's squadron and an English squadron commanded by Robert Blake. In this fight, two Dutch ships were captured and the Dutch forced to retreat.

In the mobilizations that followed the English possessed distinct advantages (see map 28). Their battlefleet had expanded during the past two years and English naval administration was centralized, due to the reforms carried out in the late 1640s. The Dutch had demobilized and sold most of their warships after peace was signed with Spain in 1648. The English Council of State exercised control over its navy through a single commission, and Robert Blake was recognized as the 'first among equals' of the Generals at Sea. The Dutch had five admiralties, located in the two maritime provinces of Holland and Friesland, and the United Provinces lacked a central executive comparable to the Council of State. The English ports lay to the west of the Netherlands, giving the English the advantage of the prevailing winds for much of the year, and their ports were deeper, allowing them to use larger warships with a deeper draft. This enabled the English to use warships carrying heavier and more cannon than the shallower-draft Dutch vessels.

The Dutch had a much larger merchant marine, making more sailors available to man their battlefleets. But their merchant marine was a far more lucrative target to an enemy's frigates than was the smaller English merchant fleet. Consequently, the Dutch admirals always had to protect their nation's commerce while trying to fight the English battlefleet. This disparity in merchant wealth prompted one Dutchman to observe that 'The English are about to attack a mountain of gold; we are about to attack a mountain of iron.'[16]

The Anglo-Dutch War, 1652

English mobilization started in April, when Blake asked parliament for £729,000 for the navy for the coming year. This was to support 117 warships, the purchase of 335 new iron cannon, and the expansion of the dockyards to support the enlarged fleet.[17] The Rump also ordered the construction of thirty frigates at a cost of £300,000. However, parliament failed to increase taxes to pay for these commitments, forcing the navy treasurer to borrow another £189,000 and retarding the navy commissioners' efforts to sustain the fleet.[18]

The tempo of operations increased in the summer as Blake destroyed the Dutch escorts for their herring fleet in the North Sea, and George Ayscue destroyed most of a Dutch convoy in the Channel in late June 1652. The Dutch fought back, sending Tromp to sea with nearly 100 warships at the end of July. This fleet, however, was under-manned, poorly victualled, and under-gunned, making it impossible for Tromp to exploit several chances to defeat Blake and Ayscue individually. After a disastrous storm, Tromp was forced to retreat to Holland, where he resigned rather than face criticism.[19]

In August, Ayscue and Admiral Michiel de Ruyter came to blows as Ayscue tried to intercept a convoy carrying silver from Cadiz to Holland. De Ruyter

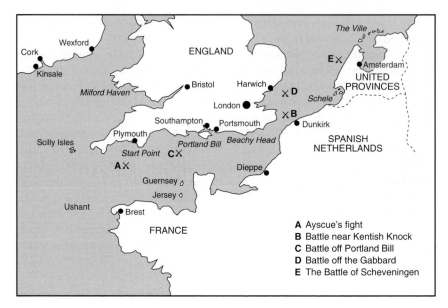

Map 28 Naval battles of the Anglo-Dutch War

successfully defended his convoy in a confusing melee that ended in a draw on 16 August. On 4 September, Blake took advantage of the lull in operations to lead a squadron across the North Sea to engage French warships escorting reinforcements to Dunkirk, then besieged by the Spaniards. Blake destroyed the French fleet, capturing seven frigates and 1,500 soldiers. This victory caused France to recognize the Commonwealth, hoping to avoid further English interference in the Franco–Spanish war.[20]

Meanwhile, Tromp's successor, Admiral Witte de With, put to sea with sixty-eight warships. Blake met de With on 28 September, near the Kentish Knock, in a major fleet action. Part of the Dutch fleet did not engage, giving Blake superiority with his sixty-two warships. After six hours of action, de With escaped, having lost two ships. English superiority in numbers of heavy cannon and in engagement techniques gave them an advantage, as the Dutch shot for the rigging and the English aimed their guns at their enemies' hulls. The English lost no ships and were able to repair their rigging more easily than the Dutch could repair their hulls.[21]

Blake's victory at Kentish Knock gave the English a false sense of superiority, leading parliament and the Council of State to slacken their efforts. Consequently, the navy commissioners were not provided with the money and material needed to repair, revictual, and man the fleet properly. The English also dispersed their strength by sending warships to the Danish Sound and to the Mediterranean, leaving fewer than seventy ships in the vital North Sea and Channel theater. By October, navy debt had soared to £510,000, and £174,000 was needed in cash by 1 November to feed the crews. The results were that Blake's ships were not ready for action in November, when a revitalized Dutch fleet was led into the North Sea.[22]

The Dutch recalled Tromp to duty from his retirement after de With's defeat at Kentish Knock. The Dutch admiralties provided over eighty warships and promised to give Tromp a free hand to direct operations. On 21 November, Tromp entered the North Sea, escorting a large merchant convoy. By 30 November he was in the Dover Straits, where he released the convoy of 270 merchantmen to continue to Bordeaux. Tromp was then free to seek a battle with Blake, whom he assumed would sortie from his base in the Downs against the Dutch fleet.[23]

Blake had no more than forty-two warships ready for action, and many of these were still damaged. None the less, Blake led his ships out, thinking the Dutch would try to escape another action. Tromp was waiting, determined to fight. As the English caught up with the Dutch, nearly half of Blake's ships hung back, especially those vessels whose captains were afraid of battle. Thus, when Blake led his ship into the center of the Dutch fleet, few ships followed, leaving him outgunned and outfought. By the end of the day, the Dutch had destroyed three English warships, with a loss of one of theirs. Blake was forced to retreat into the Downs to refit under the guns of shore batteries.[24]

Blake's defeat was not the only setback the English suffered in 1652. In the Mediterranean, two small English squadrons commanded by Richard Badiley and Henry Appleton took refuge in Leghorn, pursued by superior Dutch forces. When the English tried to escape, on 4 March 1653, they were defeated with most of their ships sunk. The English received bad news from the Baltic as well, where the Danish closure of the Sound stranded English merchant ships carrying naval stores such as tar and masts to England. The English dispatched twenty warships to Denmark, weakening Blake further, but the Danes refused to be intimidated, and the English could not afford to widen the war. Henceforth, the English had to develop their North American colonies as a source of the naval stores formerly procured in the Baltic.[25]

Tromp controlled the North Sea and Channel for two months after his victory. This allowed the Dutch to interfere with London's commerce and her critical coal trade with Newcastle, and it allowed the Dutch merchant marine to pass freely through the Channel rather than to take the long route around Britain and Ireland to the Netherlands. Not since the naval mutiny of 1648 and Prince Charles's blockade of the Thames had the parliamentary government faced such a dangerous situation.

The Commonwealth's resurgence, 1652–3

Blake's defeat at the Battle of the Dungeness shocked the English into action. A special commission, that included Oliver Cromwell, investigated the defeat and determined the steps needed to re-establish English control of British waters. Significantly, there was no talk of a negotiated settlement with the Dutch until the naval balance was redressed in English favor.

The Rump's first step to regaining naval superiority was to find enough money to pay for the fleet. The assessment was raised from £90,000 to £120,000 per month, and £726,000 was allocated from it to the navy over the next two years. The sale of captured Dutch ships and cargo netted £208,000 and, along with the customs and the proceeds of land sales, helped to provide £2.4 million to the navy treasurer in the same period.[26] These measures re-established the credit of the navy, allowing the commissioners to order victuals and supplies on credit. The increased revenue enabled the navy treasurer to repay £269,000 of debt owed victuallers and other suppliers as well, keeping the accumulated debt below £467,000. Thus, the navy treasurer operated a 'funded debt', allowing the English to expand their navy while improving its credit-worthiness.[27]

The Rump also installed a new navy commission that included able administrators, such as Sir Henry Vane, to oversee the efforts in the shipyards, as the navy's logistical establishment became the largest manufacturing operation in Britain. They achieved impressive results. The victuallers provided preserved food sufficient to feed 30,000 sailors during 1653. Although quality always remained a problem, shortages of food no longer hampered the operations of the fleet. In addition, the commissioners hired forty merchant ships to carry supplies to the squadrons at sea, providing one of the earliest 'underway-replenishment' systems in history.[28]

By February 1653, the English had more than eighty warships ready for action. They commissioned George Monck and Richard Deane to serve with Blake in command of the fleet. Blake, who had offered to resign, and the other Generals-at-Sea dramatically changed the way the navy was to fight. Fighting Instructions were issued. The fleet was divided into three permanent squadrons: the Red, White, and Blue. Each was commanded by a Vice Admiral who was to take his directions from the Admiral of the Fleet, in this case Robert Blake. The Instructions required ship captains to conform their ships' movements to those of their squadron commander in battle and provided authority for the Admiral to punish captains who shirked their duty. This organization and the new procedures improved the command and control that one man could exercise over a large fleet, enabling the English commander to direct 100 ships effectively in a battle.[29]

When Tromp returned to the Channel in February, Blake was ready with eighty freshly supplied ships to meet him. Tromp's eighty ships had been at sea for three months and were short of supplies. In addition, Tromp had to protect an inbound merchant convoy, making it impossible for him to avoid battle, even if he had wanted to. At about 8 a.m., on 18 February, the fleets collided off Portland Bill. Tromp was eager for battle, under-estimating his enemy as Blake had done in the previous November. The bigger English battleships heavily outgunned him, a disadvantage he recognized too late.

When the battle opened, the English squadrons were divided by several miles, allowing Tromp to mass his ships against Blake's squadron. But the Dutch tactics of destroying their enemies' rigging and attempting to board proved disastrous in the face of the heavier English firepower, which was focused on smashing holes in the Dutch hulls. By midday, Tromp had lost his numerical advantage as the squadrons of Monck, William Penn, and John Lawson joined the battle. By evening, after the longest gun battle in naval history thus far, Tromp broke away. He had lost twenty warships. The English lost one ship, although a number of vessels had to retreat to Portsmouth for repairs.[30]

For the next two days English frigates pursued the Dutch merchant convoy that Tromp could no longer defend. Only very skillful sailing in the shallow waters off France saved the bulk of the Dutch fleet from total disaster. During the battle and the pursuit, the Fighting Instructions proved their worth as Blake kept his captains focused on the destruction of Dutch warships rather than on chasing prizes. The Battle of Portland restored English control of the Channel.[31]

After the Portland battle, the English added new warships, improved sailors' pay and food, and expanded their dockyards. Hospitals in Dover and Southampton treated wounded sailors, and 1,300 barrels of gunpowder were collected from fortresses throughout the nation to replace that consumed at Portland Bill. The commissioners pressed forty additional merchant ships into service as replenishment vessels and coordinated the dockyards as they repaired damaged warships. These efforts allowed the English fleet to resume operations off the Dutch coast near Texel in May. No longer did warships have to return to England for supplies, keeping the fleet concentrated to face Dutch sorties.[32]

Tromp could not afford to remain in port for long, since the English navy threatened to strangle Dutch commerce with its blockade. In late May, he sailed with over 100 warships, meeting the English off the Gabbard, on 2 June 1653. The battle raged for three days before the superior English organization, weight of guns and ships, and cohesion wore down the Dutch and forced Tromp to retreat. The English also used a new tactic in this battle, known as the 'line ahead', to coordinate the attack of 100 ships in three squadrons. The results were that the entire English fleet engaged the Dutch at about the same time. In the process, Tromp lost at least twenty ships, while the English lost none. The Dutch put forth peace feelers, but the English terms were so harsh that the war continued.[33]

English efforts continued undiminished after the victory of the Gabbard. Only twelve English ships had to return to port for repairs. A steady stream of replenishment vessels supplied the fleet of over 100 warships with food, beer, and munitions. After a series of English attacks along their coast, the Dutch navy was forced to come out and fight another battle. This time, on 31 July, Tromp united his squadron with de With's from a different port, a remarkable achievement considering the communications and the vagaries of winds and tides. Once united, Tromp led 107 warships against the English fleet of 104, commanded by George Monck.

The two fleets collided in what is known as the Battle of the Texel or the Battle of Scheveningen. Monck commanded with great skill, using the Fighting Instructions and his heavier ships and firepower to advantage. Before the fleets engaged, Monck had ordered his captains to sink enemy ships rather than to capture them, to avoid weakening his force by detaching crewmen to take the captured vessels home. Initially, however, the Dutch outsailed the English, gaining the weather advantage.

Although the Dutch outmaneuvered Monck initially, he understood how to exploit his advantages and how to lead a charge. By tacking into the Dutch fleet, he robbed it of the wind advantage and used his heavier broadsides to tear apart the smaller Dutch vessels. After several hours the English had shattered the Dutch fleet, sinking twenty-six Dutch ships and killing over 2,700 enemy sailors. English losses included two ships sunk and several hundred sailors killed and wounded.[34]

Monck's fleet was too battered to follow the Dutch home, but his work was complete enough to convince the United Provinces to seek peace. Except for one sortie to escort a convoy to the north, the Dutch navy remained in port for the rest of the war. The English closed the Channel to Dutch shipping and English squadrons harried Dutch commerce in the North Sea. During the war, the English captured 1,500 Dutch ships. Observing the English success, the Danes opened the Sound to English ships and signed a treaty of friendship with Albion giving English ships the same transit rights in the Sound as Dutch merchantmen enjoyed. Spain and France also sought the favor of the English government in their ongoing war. After extended negotiations, an Anglo–Dutch peace treaty was concluded in April 1654. The Dutch recognized English sovereignty at sea, their right of search, and their ownership of the North Sea fisheries. The English demanded no other sacrifices of the Dutch, due in large part to Cromwell's desire to end the war against a fellow-Protestant nation.[35]

Failure of the revolution

The costs of the Commonwealth's startling victories did more than anything else to decrease chances for significant domestic reforms beyond the institutional changes made in republic's first six months. By 1653, it was clear to Cromwell and other army leaders that the Rump did not intend to adhere to its commitment to dissolve itself in November 1654, as promised in November 1651. Rumpers even talked of allowing former enemies of the 'cause' to resume their places in parliament and in local governments. At this point, Cromwell and the grandees lost patience with the Rump and resumed their 'providential duty of leading God's chosen people to the promised land' by turning the parliament out by force.[36] Cromwell's coup of 20 April led to a series of political experiments, none of which adequately replaced the monarchy. In the process, the English revolutionaries failed to achieve their dreams.

Following his coup of 1653, Cromwell sought a variety of arrangements to maintain order in Ireland and Britain. None proved satisfactory because they failed to win sufficient support from the majority of Englishmen. Cromwell's need to sustain occupation forces in Scotland and Ireland, and his decision to fight a naval war against Spain beginning in 1655, prevented his government from reducing taxes, further alienating Englishmen from the Protectorate. And the militarization of Ireland and Britain prevented many of the reforms anticipated in 1649. When Cromwell died in 1658, military force again dictated political policy in London, in a period of confusion that ended with Monck's restoration of Charles II. Twenty years of warfare and suffering seemed to have been for naught.

In hindsight, the republican Commonwealth of 1649 to 1653 did not live and die in vain. It established the 'fiscal-military entity which, with its parties, ministries, and majorities, would become the "hidden republic" of England's constitutional monarchy' in the 1690s.[37] John Pym and his fellow revolutionaries laid the foundation for English liberty and for British imperial power in the world. These were no small accomplishments. War drove the processes that reshaped the institutional and political landscapes of Britain and Ireland from 1637 to 1954. This relationship of war to political change continued, as William III's and parliament's need to sustain costly and prolonged warfare from 1689 to 1697 provided the further impetus for the development of parliamentary government.

Notes

1 Abbott, ii: 462–3, Cromwell to Lenthall, 4 September 1651.

2 S. Kelsey, *Inventing a Republic* (Stanford, 1997), 2–6, 205–6.

3 Gardiner, *C & P*, ii: 69–105.

4 Hainsworth, *The Swordsmen in Power*, 22–4, 28–33; P. Hutton, *The British Republic, 1649–1660*, (New York, 1990), 7–25; C. Hill and E. Dell, eds, *The Good Old Cause* (London, 1949, 1968 edn), 19–31, 309–61; W. Waller, *Liberty and Reformation in the Puritan Revolution* (New York, 1955, 1963 edn.), xiii–xiv, 319–58.

5 Ibid., 82–6.

6 Bodl., Rawlinson MS A223, fos. 1–110 for the size of the navy from 1642 to 1651.

7 *JHC*, vi: 472.

8 PRO E351/2289, fo. 2, account of navy treasurer for 1651 (1 January to 31 December).

9 Capp, *Cromwell's Navy*, 66–8; J. Powell, 'Blake's Reduction of the Scilly Isles in 1651', *Mariner's Mirror* 17 (1931), 205–22; Hainsworth, *Swordsmen in Power*, 50–6; J. Powell, 'Blake's Reduction of Jersey in 1651', *Mariner's Mirror* 18 (1932), 64–80; J. Powell, 'Sir George Ayscue's Capture of Barbados in 1651', *Mariner's Mirror* 59 (1973), 281–90.

10 Capp, *Cromwell's Navy*, 73–5; Gardiner, *C & P*, i: 318–22.

11 Capp, *Cromwell's Navy*, 73–8.

12 Gardiner, *C & P*, i: 322–5.

13 Ibid., 325–9.

14 J. Farnell, 'The Navigation Act of 1651, the First Dutch War, and the London Merchant Community', *Economic History Review* 16 (1964), 439–54; Capp, *Cromwell's Navy*, 75–6; R. Hainsworth and C. Churches, *The Anglo-Dutch Naval Wars, 1652–1674* (Stroud, 1998), 14–16.

15 Powell, 'Ayscue's Capture of Barbados', 283; S. Gardiner, ed., *The First Dutch War* (London, 1898–1904), i: 58–61, 81–2.

16 Quote from Hainsworth and Churches, *Anglo-Dutch Naval Wars*, 17.

17 *CSPD, 1651–52*, 318, 321; *JHC*, vii: 122; Bodl., Rawlinson MS A223, fos. 118–19.

18 PRO E351/2290, navy treasurer's account for 1652.

19 Gardiner, *C & P*, ii: 184–6; *CSPD, 1651–52*, 288.

20 J. Powell, 'Blake's Capture of the French Fleet Before Calais, 4 September 1652', *Mariner's Mirror* 48 (1962), 192–201; Hainsworth and Churches, *Anglo-Dutch Naval Wars*, 29–37.

21 Gardiner, *First Dutch War*, ii: 272–80, 293–8.

22 *CSPD, 1651–52*, 384, 417; Bodl., Rawlinson MS A223, fo. 123; Rawlinson MS A226, fos. 106–200; PRO E351/2290; M. Baumber, *General-at-Sea: Robert Blake and the Seventeenth Century Revolution in Naval Warfare* (London, 1989), 137–40.

23 *FDW*, ii: 377–84; Gardiner, *C & P*, ii: 202–8.

24 J. Tanner, ed., *The Letters of Robert Blake* (London, 1937), 184–7; Gardiner, *C & P*, ii: 207–10.

25 R. Anderson, 'Denmark and the First Anglo-Dutch War', *Mariner's Mirror* 53 (1967), 55–61; R. Anderson, 'The First Dutch War in the Mediterranean', *Mariner's Mirror* 49 (1963), 241–65.

26 *A & O*, ii: 653; *JHC*, vii: 231, 241, 269; PRO E351/2291–2, treasurer's accounts for 1653–4; E351/304–5, Treasurers at War accounts, 1652–6.

27 J. Wheeler, 'Navy Finance, 1649–1660', *Historical Journal* 39 (1996), 457–66.

28   Bodl., Rawlinson MS A227, fos. 1–15; *CSPD, 1652–53*, 44, 99, 106, 140.

29   *CSPD, 1652–53*, 8, 56, 100; Hainsworth and Churches, *Anglo-Dutch Naval Wars*, 57–60.

30   Tanner, ed., *Letters of Robert Blake*, 206–10; Gardiner, *C & P*, ii: 214–19.

31   Tanner, ed., *Letters of Robert Blake*, 208–9.

32   Bodl., Rawlinson MS A227, fos. 40, 45, 52–6, 60–6, 74–7, 82–5, 90, 95–6.

33   Gardiner, *C & P*, iii: 34–9.

34   Bodl., Rawlinson MS A227, fos. 123–5; Gardiner, *C &P*, iii: 46–8.

35   Capp, *Cromwell's Navy*, 82–6; Gardiner, *C & P*, iii: 48–67; Hainsworth and Churches, *Anglo-Dutch Naval Wars*, 89–93.

36   Kelsey, *Inventing a Republic*, 3.

37   Ibid., 201–2.

Bibliography

Primary sources: printed

Abbott, W., ed., *The Writings and Speeches of Oliver Cromwell*. 4 Vols., Oxford, 1937, 1988 edn.

Calendar of State Papers, Domestic, Charles I. 25 Vols., London, 1891.

Calendar of State Papers, Interregnum. 13 Vols., London, 1891.

Calendar of State Papers, Ireland, 1633–1660. 3 Vols., London, 1901–3.

Cary, H., ed., *Memorials of the Great Civil War in England from 1642 to 1652*. London, 1842.

Clarendon, E., Earl of, *A History of the Rebellion and Civil Wars in England*. 6 Vols., Oxford, 1732 edn.

Firth, C., ed., *The Clarke Papers*. 4 Vols., London, 1891–1901.

Firth, C. and R. Rait, eds, *Acts and Ordinances of the Interregnum, 1642–1660*. 3 Vols., London, 1911.

Gardiner, S., ed., *Constitutional Documents of the Puritan Revolution, 1628–1660*. Oxford, 1889.

Gilbert, J., ed., *A Contemporary History of Affairs in Ireland, from AD 1641–1652*. 3 Vols., Dublin, 1879–80.

Journals of the House of Commons. Vols. 2–7, 1640–60.

Hogan, E., ed., *The History of the War in Ireland from 1641 to 1653*. Dublin, 1973.

Laing, D., ed., *Letters and Journals of Robert Baillie, 1637–1662*. 3 Vols., Edinburgh, 1841–2.

Tanner, J., ed., *The Letters of Robert Blake*. London, 1937.

Temple, J., *The Irish Rebellion*. London, 1646.

Terry, C., *Papers Relating to the Army of the Solemn League and Covenant, 1637–1647*. 2 Vols., Edinburgh, 1917.

The Thomason Tracts. London, 1640–60. Numerous numbers.

Tuchet, James, Earl of Castlehaven, *The Earl of Castlehaven's Review: Or his Memoirs of his Engagement and Carriage in the Irish Wars*. London, 1684.

Whitelocke, B., *Memorials of English Affairs*. London, 1682.

Primary sources: manuscripts

In the Bodleian Library, Oxford

Carte MSS 1–30, Papers of the Marquess of Ormond, 1640–54.
Carte MS 118, Proceedings of the Leinster Army, Oct. 1647.
Rawlinson MS A195, Treasurers at War Accounts, 1645–51.
Rawlinson MS A207, Navy Committee Warrant Books, 1650–3.
Rawlinson MS A208, Treasurers at War Accounts, 1653–9.
Rawlinson MS A223, Navy Commissioners' Record Books, 1643–54.
Rawlinson MS A225–7, Admiralty Committee Proceedings, 1650–3.

In the British Library, London

Additional MS 4761, Irish Establishments.
Additional MS 5500, Prize Commissioners, 1649–60.
Additional MS 17503, Lists of Naval Strength and Costs, 1642–7.
Additional MS 28854, Revenue of the Protectorate, 1654.

In the Public Record Office, London

AO1/1705/85–8, Navy Treasurer Accounts, 1639–41.
AO1/1706/89, Navy Treasurer Account, 1642.
AO1/1708/95–7, Navy Treasurer Accounts, 1653–4.
E101/612/65, Account of Navy Sick and Maimed, 1653–60.
E101/676/51, Assessment Levies, 1653–60.
E351/292–3, Uvedale's Treasurer at War Accounts, 1639–40.
E351/294, Treasurer at War, Ireland, 1640–1.
E351/295, Patrick Ruthwen's Accounts for Edinburgh Castle, 1640.
E351/296–7, Lecharte's Paymaster Accounts in the North, 1639–40.
E351/298–9, Accounts for Hamilton's Forces, 1639–40.
E351/302, Treasurers at War Accounts, 1645–51.
E351/304–7, Treasurers at War Accounts, 1652–9.
E351/440, Accounts of Sequestration Collectors, 1643–53.
E351/643–60, Customs Accounts, 1643–62.
E351/1295–1301, Excise Accounts, 1647–60.
E351/2240–334, Navy Treasurer Accounts, 1602–99.
E351/2428–47, Accounts of Surveyor of Victuals, 1628–42.
E351/2664, Ordnance Office Accounts, 1642–51.
SP25/118, Account Book of Cromwell's Irish Expedition.
SP28/1–356, Interregnum Army Accounts, 1640–60.
SP63/281, Account Book of Money Sent to Ireland, 1649–56.

In the National Archives of Ireland, Dublin

M2450–1, *The Treasury Order Books of the Lords Justices and Council,* (2 vols., Dublin), August–30 September 1642.

Secondary sources

Anderson, R., 'The Operations of the English Fleet, 1648–52', *English Historical Review*, 31 (1916), 406–28.

—— 'Denmark and the First Anglo-Dutch War', *Mariner's Mirror* 53 (1967), 55–61.

—— 'The First Dutch War in the Mediterranean', *Mariner's Mirror* 49 (1963), 241–65.

Ashley, M., *The English Civil War.* London, 1974, 1980 edn.

Ashton, R., *Counter Revolution: The Second Civil War and its Origins, 1646–8.* Yale, 1994.

Atkin, M., *Cromwell's Crowning Mercy: The Battle of Worcester, 1651.* Stroud, 1998.

Aylmer, G., *The State's Servants.* London, 1973.

Barratt, J., *Cavaliers: The Royalist Army at War, 1642–1646.* Stroud, 2000.

Bartlett, T. and K. Jeffrey, eds, *A Military History of Ireland.* Cambridge, 1996.

Baumber, M., *General-at-Sea: Robert Blake and the Seventeenth Century Revolution in Naval Warfare.* London, 1989.

Beckett, J., *The Cavalier Duke: A Life of James Butler, the First Duke of Ormond.* Belfast, 1990.

Bennett, M., *The Civil Wars in Britain and Ireland, 1638–1651.* Oxford, 1997.

Bottigheimer, K., *English Money, Irish Land.* Oxford, 1971.

Boynton, L., *The Elizabethan Militia, 1558–1638.* London, 1976.

Braddick, M., *The Nerves of State: Taxation and the Financing of the English State, 1558–1714.* Manchester, 1996.

—— *Parliamentary Taxation in Seventeenth-Century England.* Woodbridge, 1994.

Burke, J., 'The New Model Army and the Problem of Siege Warfare', *Irish Historical Review* 27 (1990), 1–29.

Capp, B., *Cromwell's Navy: The Fleet and the English Revolution, 1648–1660.* Oxford, 1989.

Carlton, C., *Going to the Wars: The Experience Of the British Civil Wars, 1638–1651.* London, 1992.

Carte, T., *The Life of James, Duke of Ormond ... with a Collection of Letters.* Oxford, 1851 edn.

Casway, J., *Owen Roe O'Neill and the Struggle for Catholic Ireland.* Philadelphia, 1984.

Clarke, A., *The Old English in Ireland, 1625–1642.* Ithaca, NY, 1966.

Corish, D., 'The Crisis in Ireland in 1648: The Nuncio and the Supreme Council: Conclusions', *Irish Theological Quarterly* 22 (July 1955), 230–57.

Corish, D., 'Rinuccini's Censure of 27 May 1648', *Irish Theological Quarterly* 18 (1951), 322–27.

Cust, R., *The Forced Loan and English Politics, 1626–28.* Oxford, 1987.

Davies, G., 'The Parliamentary Army Under the Earl of Essex, 1642–5', *English Historical Review* 49 (1934), 32–54.

Dietz, F., *English Public Finance, 1558–1641.* New York, 1932.

—— 'The Receipts and Issues of the Exchequer During the Reigns of James I and Charles I', *Smith College Studies in History* 13 (1928), 117–71.

Donagon, B., 'Halcyon Days and the Literature of War: England's Military Education Before 1642', *Past and Present* 147 (1995), 65–100.

Douglas, W., *Cromwell's Scotch Campaigns, 1650–51*. London, 1898.

Dow, F., *Cromwellian Scotland*. Edinburgh, 1979.

Duggan, L., 'The Irish Brigade with Montrose', *Irish Ecclesiastical Record* 89 (1958), 171–84, 246–58.

Dunlop, R., ed., *Ireland Under the Commonwealth*. 2 Vols., Manchester, 1913.

Edwards, P., *Dealing in Death: The Arms Trade and the British Civil Wars, 1638–1652*. Stroud, 2000.

Elkin, R., 'The Interaction between the Irish Rebellion and the English Civil War', PhD Dissertation, University of Illinois, Urbana, 1971.

Engberg, J., 'Royalist Finances During the English First Civil War, 1642–46', *Scandinavian Economic History Review* 14 (1966), 73–96.

Falls, C., *Elizabeth's Irish Wars*. Syracuse, 1950, 1997 edn.

Farnell, J., 'The Navigation Act of 1651, the First Dutch War, and the London Merchant Community', *Economic History Review* 16 (1964), 439–54.

Firth, C., *Cromwell's Army*. London, 1902, 1992 edn.

—— 'Marston Moor', *Transactions of the Royal Historical Society* 12 (1898), 18–79.

Fissel, M., *The Bishops' Wars: Charles I's Campaigns Against Scotland, 1638–1640*. Cambridge, 1994.

—— ed., *War and Government in Britain, 1598–1650*. Manchester, 1991.

Fletcher, A., *Reform in the Provinces: The Government of Stuart England*. Yale, 1986.

—— *The Outbreak of the English Civil War*. London, 1981.

Gardiner, S., *The History of England, 1603–1642*. 10 Vols., London, 1883–4.

—— *The History of the Great Civil War, 1642–1649*. 4 Vols., London, 1894.

—— ed., *The Constitutional Documents of the Puritan Revolution, 1628–1660*. Oxford, 1889.

—— *The History of the Commonwealth and Protectorate, 1649–1656*. 4 Vols., London, 1913.

—— *The First Dutch War*. 5 Vols., London, 1898–1904.

Gentles, I., *The New Model Army in England, Ireland, and Scotland, 1645–1653*. Oxford, 1992.

—— 'The Choosing of Officers for the New Model Army', *Bulletin of the Institute of Historical Research* 67 (1994), 264–85.

Glete, J., *Navies and Nations: Warships, Navies, and State Building in Europe and America*. Stockholm, 1993.

Glow, L., 'The Manipulation of Committees in the Long Parliament, 1641–1642', *Journal of British History*, v (1965), 31–52.

—— 'The Committee-Men in the Long Parliament, August 1642–December 1643', *Historical Journal* 8 (1965), 1–15.

Grainger, J., *Cromwell Against the Scots: The last Anglo-Scottish War, 1650–52*. East Linton, 1997.

Hainsworth, R., *The Swordsmen in Power: War and Politics under the English Republic, 1649–1660*. Stroud, 1997.

Hainsworth, R., and C. Churches, *The Anglo-Dutch Naval Wars, 1652–1674*. Stroud, 2000.

Haller, W., *Liberty and Reformation in the Puritan Revolution*. New York, 1963.

Hazlett, H., 'A History of the Military Forces Operating in Ireland, 1641–9', PhD Dissertation, Queen's University, Belfast, 1938.

—— 'The Recruitment and Organization of the Scottish Army in Ulster, 1642–49', in T. Moody et al., eds, *Essays in British and Irish History in Honor of James Eadie Todd*. London, 1949.

Hexter, J., *Reappraisals in History*. Chicago, 1961, 1979 edn.

—— *The Reign of King Pym*. Cambridge, MA, 1941.

Hill, C. and E. Dell, eds, *The Good Old Cause*. London, 1949, 1968 edn.

Hutton, R., *The British Republic, 1649–1660*. New York, 1990.

—— *The Royalist War Effort, 1642–1646*. London, 1982, 1999 edn.

Jones, J., 'The War in the North: The Northern Parliamentarian Army in the English Civil War, 1642–1645', PhD Dissertation, York University, Ontario, 1991.

Kearney, H., *Strafford in Ireland, 1633–41*. Cambridge, 1959, 1989 edn.

Kelsey, S., *Inventing a Republic*. Stanford, 1997.

Kennedy, P., *The Rise and Fall of British Naval Mastery*. London, 1976, 1986 edn.

Kenyon, J., *The Civil Wars of England*. New York, 1988.

—— and J. Ohlmeyer, eds, *The Civil Wars: A Military History of England, Scotland, and Ireland, 1638–1660*. Oxford, 1998.

Kerr, A., *An Ironside of Ireland: The Remarkable Career of Lieutenant General Michael Jones*. London, 1923.

Kishlansky, M., *The Rise of the New Model Army*. Cambridge, 1979.

Lenihan, P., *Confederate Catholics at War, 1641–49*. Cork, 2001.

—— ed., *Conquest and Resistance: War in Seventeenth-Century Ireland*. Leiden, 2001.

Lindley, K., 'The Impact of the 1641 Rebellion Upon England and Wales, 1641–5', *Irish Historical Studies* 18 (1972), 143–75.

—— *Popular Politics and Religion in Civil War London*. Aldershot, 1997.

Lowe, J., ed., 'Charles I and the Confederation of Kilkenny, 1643–9', *Irish Historical Studies* 14 (1964), 1–19.

—— 'The Glamorgan Mission to Ireland', *Studia Hibernica* iv (1964), 155–62.

—— ed., *The Letter-Book of the Earl of Clanricarde*. Dublin, 1983.

MacCormack, J., *Revolutionary Politics in the Long Parliament*. Cambridge, MA, 1973.

Mac Cuarta, B., ed., *Ulster, 1641*. Belfast, 1993.

Malcolm, J., 'All the King's Men: The Impact of the Crown's Irish Soldiers on the English Civil Wars', *Irish Historical Studies* 22 (1979), 239–64.

—— *Caesar's Due: Loyalty and King Charles, 1642–1646*. New Jersey, 1983.

Moody, T., ed., *New History of Ireland: Early Modern Ireland*. Oxford, 1976, 1999 edn.

Morrill, J., *The Revolt of the Provinces: Conservatives and Radicals in the English Civil War, 1630–1650*. London, 1976.

—— ed., *Oliver Cromwell and the English Revolution*. New York, 1990.

Murphy, D., *Cromwell in Ireland*. Dublin, 1897.

Nusbacher, E., 'Civil Supply in the Civil War: Supply of Victuals to the New Model Army in the Naseby Campaign, 1–14 June 1645', *English Historical Review* (2000), 145–60.

Ohlmeyer, J., *Civil War and Restoration in the Three Stuart Kingdoms: The Career of Randall MacDonnell, the Marquis of Antrim, 1609–1683*. Cambridge, 1993.

—— ed., *Ireland: From Independence to Occupation, 1641–1660*. Cambridge, 1995.

—— 'The Dunkirk of Ireland: Wexford Privateers During the 1640s', *Journal of the Wexford Historical Society* 10 (1988–9), 23–49.

—— 'Irish Privateers during the Civil War, 1642–50', *Mariner's Mirror* 76 (1990), 119–33.

—— *Awkward Neighbours*, Forthcoming, 2002.

O'Siochru, M., *Confederate Ireland, 1642–1649*. Dublin, 1999.

Parker, G. *The Military Revolution: Military Innovation and the Rise of the West*. Cambridge, 1988, 1996 edn.

Pearl, V., *London and the Outbreak of the Puritan Revolution, 1625–1643*. Oxford, 1961

Perry, N., 'The Infantry of the Confederate Army of Leinster', *Irish Sword* 15 (1983), 233–50.

Pringle, J., 'The Committee for Compounding with Delinquents, 1643–1654', PhD Dissertation, University of Illinois, 1961.

Powell, J., 'Blake's Reduction of the Scilly Isles in 1651', *Mariners Mirror* 17 (1931), 205–22.

—— 'Blake's Reduction of Jersey in 1651', *Mariners Mirror* 18 (1932), 64–80.

—— 'Sir George Ayscue's Capture of Barbados in 1651', *Mariners Mirror* 59 (1973), 281–90.

—— 'Blake's Capture of the French Fleet Before Calais, 4 September 1652', *Mariners Mirror* 48 (1962), 192–201.

Ramsey, R., *Henry Ireton*. London, 1949.

Reid, S., *Scots Armies of the 17th Century*. Belfast, 1988.

Reilly, T., *Cromwell: An Honorable Enemy. The Untold Story of the Cromwellian Invasion of Ireland*. London, 1999.

Rodger, N., *The Safeguard of the Seas: A Naval History of Britain, 1660–1649*. New York, 1998.

Roy, I. 'The Royalist Army in the First Civil War', PhD Dissertation, Oxford, 1963.

—— The Royalist Council of War, 1642–46', *Bulletin of Historical Research* 35 (1962), 150–68.

Russell, C., 'The British Problem and the English Civil War', *History* 72 (1987), 395–415.

—— *The Crisis of Parliaments*. Oxford, 1971, 1992 edn.

—— *The Fall of the British Monarchies, 1637–1642*. Oxford, 1991.

Ryder, I., *An English Army for Ireland*. Belfast, 1987.

Shagan, E., 'Constructing Discord: Ideology, Propaganda, and English Responses to the Irish Rebellion of 1641', *Journal of British Studies* 36 (1997), 4–34.

Sharpe, K., *The Personal Rule of Charles I*. Yale, 1992.

Stevenson, D., *The Scottish Revolution, 1637–44*. New York, 1973.

—— 'The King's Scottish Revenues and the Covenanters, 1625–1651', *Historical Journal* xvii (1974), 20–30.

—— 'The Financing of the Cause of the Covenanters, 1638–1651', *Scottish Historical Review* li (1972), 89–123.

—— *Scottish Covenanters and Irish Confederates.* Belfast, 1981.

Stone, L. *The Causes of the English Revolution.* New York, 1972.

Stradling, R., *The Spanish Monarchy and Irish Mercenaries: The Wild Geese in Spain, 1618–1668.* Dublin, 1994.

Underdown, D., *Revel, Riot, and Rebellion: Popular Politics and Culture in England, 1603–1660.* Oxford, 1985, 1987 edn.

Waller, W., *Liberty and Reformation in the Puritan Revolution.* New York, 1955, 1963 edn.

Wedgwood, C., *The King's Peace, 1637–1641.* New York, 1955, 1991 edn.

—— *Coffin for King Charles.* New York, 1965, 1991 edn.

—— *The King's War, 1641–1647.* New York, 1958, 1991 edn.

—— *Montrose.* New York, 1952, 1995 edn.

Wheeler, J., *The Making of a World Power.* Stroud, 1999.

—— *Cromwell in Ireland.* Dublin, 1999.

—— 'The Logistics of the Cromwellian Conquest of Scotland 1650–1651', *War and Society* 10 (May 1992), 1–18.

—— 'Navy Finance, 1649–1660', *Historical Journal* 39 (1996), 457–66.

Wilson, D., *The King and the Gentleman: Charles Stuart and Oliver Cromwell, 1599–1649.* New York, 1999.

Wilson, J., *Fairfax, General of Parliament's Forces in the English Civil War.* New York, 1985.

Worden, B., *The Rump Parliament.* Cambridge, 1974, 1977 edn.

Young, J., ed., *Celtic Dimensions of the British Civil Wars.* Edinburgh, 1997.

Young, P. and A. Burne, *The Great Civil War.* Moreton-in-Marsh, 1959, 1998 edn.

Index

4320066

CONCORDIA UNIVERSITY LIBRARIES
GEORGES P. VANIER LIBRARY LOYOLA CAMPUS